AA

TRUCKER'S ATLAS

BRITAIN

Scale 1:190,000
or 3 miles to 1 inch

10th edition October 2019

© AA Media Limited 2019

Cartography: All cartography in this atlas edited, designed and produced by the Mapping Services Department of AA Media Limited (A05706).

© Crown copyright and database rights 2019 Ordnance Survey. 100021153

Publisher's notes: Published by AA Media Limited, whose registered office is Grove House, Lutyens Close, Chineham Court, Basingstoke, Hampshire RG24 8AG. Registered number 06112600.

ISBN: 978 0 7495 8199 2

A CIP catalogue record for this book is available from The British Library.

Disclaimer: The contents of this atlas are believed to be correct at the time of the latest revision, it will not contain any subsequent amended, new or temporary information including diversions and traffic control or enforcement systems. The publishers cannot be held responsible or liable for any loss or damage occasioned to any person acting or refraining from action as a result of any use or reliance on material in this atlas, nor for any errors, omissions or changes in such material. This does not affect your statutory rights. The publishers would welcome information to correct any errors or omissions and to keep this atlas up to date. Please write to the Atlas Editor, AA Media Limited, Grove House, Lutyens Close, Chineham Court, Basingstoke, Hampshire, RG24 8AG
E-mail: roadatlasfeedback@aamediagroup.co.uk

Acknowledgements: AA Media Ltd would like to thank the following for their assistance in producing this atlas:
Network Rail (information, photographs and images), Highways England, Transport Scotland, Welsh Government, Isle of Man (Dept. of Infrastructure), local highway authorities (various). Traffic signs © Crown copyright 2019. Reproduced under the terms of the Open Government Licence. Boundary data from Transport for London Transport Data Service powered by TfL Open Data. Contains OS data © Crown copyright and database rights 2019 Ordnance Survey 100021153. Nexus (Newcastle district map).

Printer: Oriental Press, Dubai

Atlas contents

NetworkRail

LORRIES CAN'T LIMBO

Wise up
Size up

How to avoid bridge strikes

A bridge strike is an incident in which a vehicle or load collides with a bridge. More than 1,900 Network Rail bridges were struck last year - an average of more than five strikes per day. Most bridge strikes occur where roads pass under railway bridges.

A bridge strike can result in injury or loss of life to road users. A bridge strike may cause a serious incident on the railway, such as a train derailment. Bridge strikes also cause significant costs, disruption, damage and delay to the freight industry, other road users, and infrastructure maintainers and users of the railways.

Know your height, know your route, obey road traffic signs. **It's your responsibility.**

Know your height

Checking the height of a car transporter using a telescopic measuring device.

- Check the height of your vehicle
- If your vehicle is over 9 feet 10 inches (3 metres) display the height in your cab
- The height of a trailer can be shown on the trailer. Remember, if your trailer changes, to check its height and change the display in your cab

Always check the maximum height of your vehicle, its load and equipment.

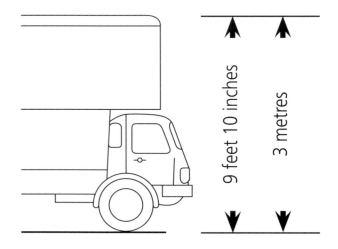

9 feet 10 inches

3 metres

The law requires you to have a notice in your cab, visible from your driving seat, displaying the height of your vehicle and its load if it is over 9 feet 10 inches (3 metres) high.

Know your route

- Use this atlas to plan your route avoiding bridges that are too low for your vehicle and load
- When planning your route check for advance notice of any possible route problems
- Stick to your route and avoid short cuts to try and save time
- If using a satnav make sure it's a specific one for a heavy goods vehicle that contains low bridge heights. Most pre-installed maps on mobile phones do not contain bridge height data
- If diverted from your planned route, **STOP** and replan your route using this atlas; a signed diversion might not be suitable for all vehicles
- Obey road traffic signs, do **NOT** ignore them
- Bridges with a safe vehicle height of more than 16 feet 3 inches (4.95 metres) are **NOT** normally signed
- If your vehicle is over 16 feet 3 inches (4.95 metres) you do **NOT** know what bridges you can go under

- Remember – if you have a long load, take special care at bridges where the road curves or dips
- Special arrangements apply for the routing of very high loads, especially with regard to clearance of overhead power cables: utilise High Load Grids (advisory routes from Highways England) and Transport Scotland's routing advisory service; check your route with local highway authorities and structure owners such as Network Rail
- Never use a hand held mobile phone whilst driving – it is against the law
- If you find a bridge headroom sign that is different from that shown in this atlas please contact:
  The Cartographic Editor, AA Media Limited, Grove House, Lutyens Close, Chineham Court, Basingstoke, Hampshire RG24 8AG
  E-mail: *roadatlasfeedback@theaa.com*

The consequences of striking bridges are potentially dangerous and expensive

You could:

- Lose your life
- Suffer injury leading to loss of earnings, overtime or reduced sick pay
- Be found guilty of causing death or injury by dangerous driving
- Have to pay repair costs and compensation for train delays recoverable by Network Rail

- Lose your job
- Be fined and have penalty points endorsed on your driving licence
- Cause your company to lose its operators licence
- Cause severe delays and distruption to the train and road network

Don't take a chance – bridge strikes can happen

THIS IS BRIDGE EGM1/043

at Linlithgow

In the event of any road vehicles striking this bridge please phone

THE RAILWAY AUTHORITY on 0141 335 3399

as quickly as possible. The safety of trains may be affected.

Don't hit and run

If you hit a railway bridge, report it, first to the Rail Authority and then to the Police using '999'. Failure to report a collision is an offence. Look for a sign mounted on or near the bridge. This will show a telephone number and the bridge identification and location details. If there is no sign report the bridge strike to the Police immediately using '999'.

Remember the three simple safety rules:

Know your height • Know your route • Obey road traffic signs

Safe vehicle height code

Always

- Check the height of your vehicle, load or equipment
- Know the height of your vehicle or load in feet and inches and metres
- Plan your route to avoid low bridges
- Watch out for low bridge warning signs
- Slow down when approaching bridges
- When passing under an arched bridge, keep between the chord lines (goal posts) on the bridge or lines marked on the road. Wait your turn. Check the road ahead is clear so that you don't have to change direction to avoid an oncoming vehicle and hit the arch.

Obey road traffic signs

Road traffic signs are provided at bridges to show the maximum permitted vehicle height when 16 feet 3 inches (4.95 metres) or less.

The maximum permitted vehicle height may be shown both in feet and inches and the equivalent metres. Alternatively separate signs may be provided to show both heights, or signs may just be in feet and inches.

Regulatory circular signs and warning triangular signs can be used depending on the type of bridge.

In some special cases additional warning signs controlled by infrared beams are used.

If your vehicle or load is higher than the height shown on a circular sign, **YOU ARE LEGALLY REQUIRED TO STOP** before the sign and find another route.

At arched bridges white lines may also be painted on the road or 'goal posts' provided on the bridge to guide you safely through the highest part of the arch. There may be two or more sets of 'goal posts' showing the different heights through an arch.

As long as your vehicle height is less than the greater height limit shown and can pass between the goal posts, drive your vehicle under the central goal post to pass safely through the bridge.

All signs are provided for your protection, do **NOT** ignore them.

Vehicles over the height shown must STOP and not proceed

Maximum safe headroom at arched bridge

Warning signs indicate maximum headroom ahead. Vehicles over the height shown should not proceed

Red circles prohibit • Red triangles warn

Abnormal loads

An 'abnormal load' is a vehicle that has any of the following:

- A weight of more than 44,000 kilograms
- An axle load of more than 10,000 kilograms for a single non-driving axle and 11,500 kilograms for a single driving axle
- A width of more than 2.9 metres
- A rigid length of more than 18.65 metres

If you're responsible for transporting an abnormal load, you need to follow regulations for notifying the authorities.

Depending on the load you're moving and your route, you may need to give advance warning to:

- The police
- Highway authorities
- Bridge and structure owners like Network Rail

Registered users can use Highways England's electronic service delivery for abnormal loads (ESDAL) to:

- Plot your route
- Notify the police, highways and bridge authorities of your abnormal load movements around the road network
- Get advance notice of any possible route problems
- Save vehicle details and routes for future use

For more details visit *www.esdal2.com*

If you are not a user of the ESDAL system then you can still make an application to move an abnormal load using a downloadable form from *www.gov.uk/esdal-and-abnormal-loads* Alternatively telephone 0300 470 3004 for information.

Remember that if you ignore a mandatory bridge sign you could face fines of £1,000 **plus** penalty points on your licence, **plus** the possibility of being disqualified.

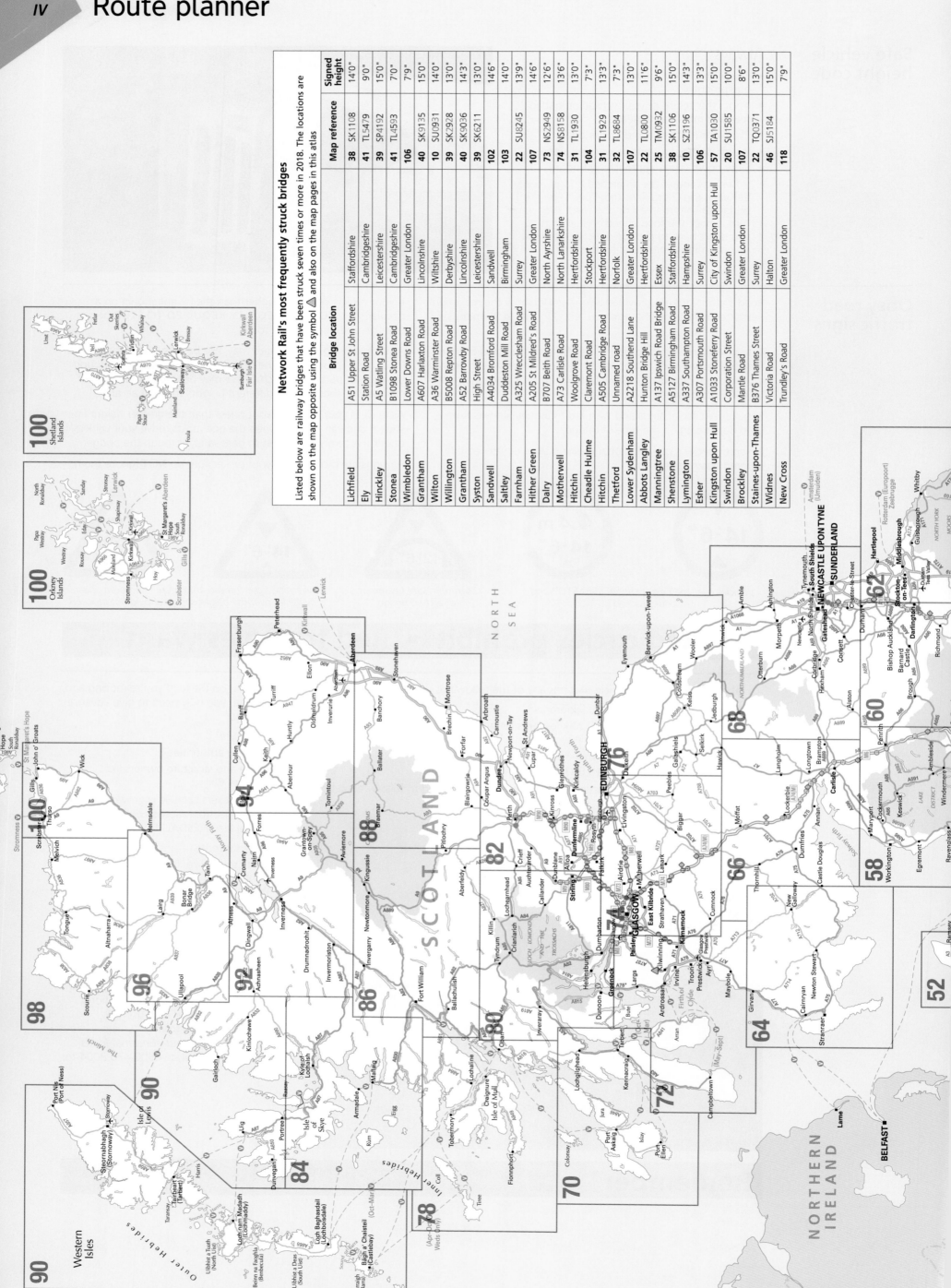

Network Rail's most frequently struck bridges

Listed below are railway bridges that have been struck seven times or more in 2018. The locations are shown on the map opposite using the symbol △ and also on the map pages in this atlas

Bridge location			Map reference		Signed height
Lichfield	A51 Upper St John Street	Staffordshire	38	SK1108	14'0"
Ely	Station Road	Cambridgeshire	41	TL5479	9'0"
Hinckley	A5 Watling Street	Leicestershire	39	SP4192	15'0"
Stonea	B1098 Stonea Road	Cambridgeshire	41	TL4593	7'0"
Wimbledon	Lower Downs Road	Greater London	106		7'9"
Grantham	A607 Harlaxton Road	Lincolnshire	40	SK9135	15'0"
Wilton	A36 Warminster Road	Wiltshire	10	SU0931	14'0"
Willington	B5008 Repton Road	Derbyshire	39	SK2928	13'0"
Grantham	A52 Barrowby Road	Lincolnshire	40	SK9036	14'3"
Syston	High Street	Leicestershire	39	SK6211	13'0"
Sandwell	A4034 Bromford Road	Sandwell	102		14'6"
Saltley	Duddeston Mill Road	Birmingham	103		14'0"
Farnham	A325 Wrecclesham Road	Surrey	22	SU8245	13'9"
Hither Green	A205 St Mildred's Road	Greater London	107		14'6"
Dalry	B707 Beith Road	North Ayrshire	73	NS2949	12'6"
Motherwell	A73 Carlisle Road	North Lanarkshire	74	NS8158	13'6"
Hitchin	Woolgrove Road	Hertfordshire	31	TL1930	13'0"
Cheadle Hulme	Claremont Road	Stockport	104		7'3"
Hitchin	A505 Cambridge Road	Hertfordshire	31	TL1929	13'3"
Thetford	Unnamed road	Norfolk	32	TL8684	7'3"
Lower Sydenham	A2218 Southend Lane	Greater London	107		13'0"
Abbots Langley	Hunton Bridge Hill	Hertfordshire	22	TL0800	11'6"
Manningtree	A137 Ipswich Road Bridge	Essex	25	TM0932	9'6"
Shenstone	A5127 Birmingham Road	Staffordshire	38	SK1106	15'0"
Lymington	A337 Southampton Road	Hampshire	10	SZ3196	14'3"
Esher	A307 Portsmouth Road	Surrey	106		13'3"
Kingston upon Hull	A1033 Stoneferry Road	City of Kingston upon Hull	57	TA1030	15'0"
Swindon	Corporation Street	Swindon	20	SU1585	10'0"
Brockley	Mantle Road	Greater London	107		8'6"
Staines-upon-Thames	B376 Thames Street	Surrey	22	TQ0371	13'0"
Widnes	Victoria Road	Halton	46	SJ5184	15'0"
New Cross	Trundley's Road	Greater London	118		7'9"

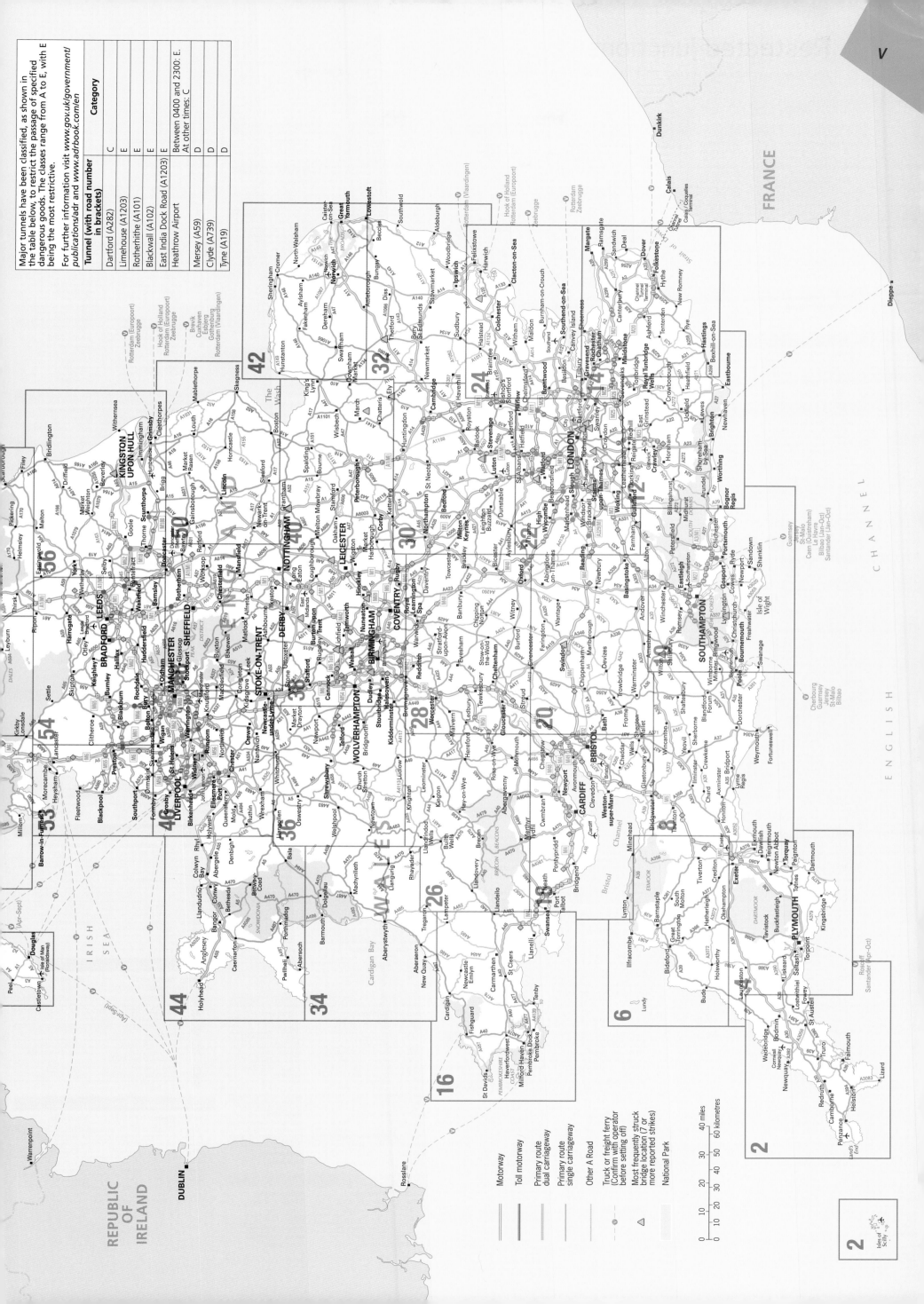

Restricted junctions

Motorway and primary route junctions which have access or exit restrictions are shown on the map pages thus:

M1 London - Leeds

Junction	Northbound	Southbound
2	Access only from A1 (northbound)	Exit only to A1 (southbound)
4	Access only from A41 (northbound)	Exit only to A41 (southbound)
6A	Access only from M25 (no link from A405)	Exit only to M25 (no link from A405)
7	Access only from A414	Exit only to A414
17	Exit only to M45	Access only from M45
19	Exit only to M6 (northbound)	Exit only to A14 (southbound)
21A	Exit only, no access	Access only, no exit
24A	Access only, no exit	Access only from A50 (eastbound)
35A	Exit only, no access	Access only, no exit
43	Exit only to M621	Access only from M621
48	Exit only to A1(M) (northbound)	Access only from A1(M) (southbound)

M2 Rochester - Faversham

Junction	Westbound	Eastbound
1	No exit to A2 (eastbound)	No access from A2 (westbound)

M3 Sunbury - Southampton

Junction	Northeastbound	Southwestbound
8	Access only from A303, no exit	Exit only to A303, no access
10	Exit only, no access	Access only, no exit
14	Access from M27 only, no exit	No access to M27 (westbound)

M4 London - South Wales

Junction	Westbound	Eastbound
1	Access only from A4 (westbound)	Exit only to A4 (eastbound)
2	Access only from A4 (westbound)	Access only from A4 (eastbound)
21	Exit only to M48	Access only from M48
23	Access only from M48	Exit only to M48
25	Exit only, no access	Access only, no exit
25A	Exit only, no access	Access only, no exit
29	Exit only to A48(M)	Access only from A48(M)
38	Exit only, no access	No restriction
39	Access only, no exit	No access or exit
42	Exit only to A483	Access only from A483

M5 Birmingham - Exeter

Junction	Northeastbound	Southwestbound
10	Access only, no exit	Exit only, no access
11A	Access only from A417 (westbound)	Exit only to A417 (eastbound)
18A	Exit only to M49	Access only from M49
18	Exit only, no access	Access only, no exit

M6 Toll Motorway

Junction	Northwestbound	Southeastbound
T1	Access only, no exit	No access or exit
T2	No access or exit	Exit only, no access
T5	Access only, no exit	Exit only to A5148 (northbound), no access
T7	Exit only, no access	Access only, no exit
T8	Exit only, no access	Access only, no exit

M6 Rugby - Carlisle

Junction	Northbound	Southbound
3A	Exit only to M6 Toll	Access only from M6 Toll
4	Exit only to M42 (southbound) & A446	Exit only to A446
4A	Access only from M42 (southbound)	Exit only to M42
5	Exit only, no access	Access only, no exit
10A	Exit only to M54	Access only from M54
11A	Access only from M6 Toll	Exit only to M6 Toll
with M56 (jct 20A)	No restriction	Access only from M56 (eastbound)
20	Exit only to M56 (westbound)	Access only from M56 (eastbound)
24	Access only, no exit	Exit only, no access
25	Exit only, no access	Access only, no exit
30	Access only from M61	Exit only to M61
31A	Exit only, no access	Access only, no exit
45	Exit only, no access	Access only, no exit

M8 Edinburgh - Bishopton

Junction	Westbound	Eastbound
6	Exit only, no access	Access only, no exit
6A	Access only, no exit	Exit only, no access
7	Access only, no exit	Exit only, no access
7A	Exit only, no access	Access only from A725 (northbound), no exit
8	No access from M73 (southbound) or from A8 (eastbound) & A89	No exit to M73 (northbound) or to A8 (westbound) & A89
9	Access only, no exit	Exit only, no access
13	Access only from M80 (southbound)	Exit only to M80 (northbound)
14	Access only, no exit	Exit only, no access
16	Exit only to A804	Access only from A879
17	Exit only to A82	No restriction
18	Access only from A82 (eastbound)	Exit only to A814
19	No access from A814 (westbound)	Exit only to A814 (westbound)
20	Exit only, no access	Access only, no exit
21	Access only, no exit	Exit only to A8
22	Exit only to M77 (southbound)	Access only from M77 (northbound)
23	Exit only to B768	Access only from B768
25	No access or exit from or to A8	No access or exit from or to A8
25A	Exit only, no access	Access only, no exit
28	Exit only, no access	Access only, no exit
28A	Exit only to A737	Access only from A737
29A	Exit only to A8	Access only, no exit

M9 Edinburgh - Dunblane

Junction	Northwestbound	Southeastbound
2	Access only, no exit	Exit only, no access
3	Exit only, no access	Access only, no exit
6	Access only, no exit	Exit only to A905
8	Exit only to M876 (southwestbound)	Access only from M876 (northeastbound)

M11 London - Cambridge

Junction	Northbound	Southbound
4	Access only from A406 (eastbound)	Exit only to A406
5	Exit only, no access	Access only, no exit
8A	Exit only, no access	No direct access, use jct 8
9	Exit only to A11	Access only from A11
13	Exit only, no access	Access only, no exit
14	Exit only, no access	Access only, no exit

M20 Swanley - Folkestone

Junction	Northwestbound	Southeastbound
2	Staggered junction; follow signs - access only	Staggered junction; follow signs - exit only
3	Exit only to M26 (westbound)	Access only from M26 (eastbound)
5	Access only from A20	For access follow signs - exit only to A20
6	No restriction	For exit follow signs
11A	Access only, no exit	Exit only, no access

M23 Hooley - Crawley

Junction	Northbound	Southbound
7	Exit only to A23 (northbound)	Access only from A23 (southbound)
10A	Access only, no exit	Exit only, no access

M25 London Orbital Motorway

Junction	Clockwise	Anticlockwise
1B	No direct access, use slip road to jct 2 Exit only	Access only, no exit
5	No exit to M26 (eastbound)	No access from M26
19	Exit only, no access	Access only, no exit
21	Access only from M1 (southbound) Exit only to M1 (northbound)	Access only from M1 (southbound) Exit only to M1 (northbound)
31	No exit (use slip road via jct 30), access only	No access (use slip road via jct 30), exit only

M26 Sevenoaks - Wrotham

Junction	Westbound	Eastbound
with M25 (jct 5)	Exit only to clockwise M25 (westbound)	Access only from anticlockwise M25 (eastbound)
with M20 (jct 3)	Access only from M20 (northwestbound)	Exit only to M20 (southeastbound)

M27 Cadnam - Portsmouth

Junction	Westbound	Eastbound
4	Staggered junction; follow signs - access only from M3 (southbound). Exit only to M3 (northbound)	Staggered junction; follow signs - access only from M3 (southbound). Exit only to M3 (northbound)
10	Exit only, no access	Access only, no exit
12	Staggered junction; follow signs - exit only to M275 (southbound)	Staggered junction; follow signs - access only from M275 (northbound)

M40 London - Birmingham

Junction	Northwestbound	Southeastbound
3	Exit only, no access	Access only, no exit
7	Exit only, no access	Access only, no exit
8	Exit only to M40/A40	Access only from M40/A40
13	Exit only, no access	Access only, no exit
14	Access only, no exit	Exit only, no access
16	Access only, no exit	Exit only, no access

M42 Bromsgrove - Measham

Junction	Northeastbound	Southwestbound
1	Access only, no exit	Exit only, no access
7	Exit only to M6 (northwestbound)	Access only from M6 (northwestbound)
7A	Exit only to M6 (southeastbound)	No access or exit
8	Access only from M6 (southeastbound)	Exit only to M6 (northwestbound)

M45 Coventry - M1

Junction	Westbound	Eastbound
Dunchurch (unnumbered)	Access only from A45	Exit only, no access
with M1 (jct 17)	Access only from M1 (northbound)	Exit only to M1 (southbound)

M48 Chepstow

Junction	Westbound	Eastbound
21	Access only from M4 (westbound)	Exit only to M4 (eastbound)
23	No exit to M4 (eastbound)	No access from M4 (westbound)

M53 Mersey Tunnel - Chester

Junction	Northbound	Southbound
11	Access only from M56 (westbound) Exit only to M56 (eastbound)	Access only from M56 (westbound) Exit only to M56 (eastbound)

M54 Telford - Birmingham

Junction	Westbound	Eastbound
with M6 (jct 10A)	Access only from M6 (northbound)	Exit only to M6 (southbound)

M56 Chester - Manchester

Junction	Westbound	Eastbound
1	Access only from M60 (westbound)	Exit only to M60 (eastbound) & A34 (northbound)
2	Exit only, no access	Access only, no exit
3	Access only, no exit	Exit only, no access
4	Exit only, no access	Access only, no exit
7	Exit only, no access	No restriction
8	Access only, no exit	No access or exit
9	No exit to M6 (southbound)	No access from M6 (northbound)
15	Exit only to M53	Access only from M53
16	No access or exit	No restriction

M57 Liverpool Outer Ring Road

Junction	Northwestbound	Southeastbound
3	Access only, no exit	Exit only, no access
5	Access only from A580 (westbound)	Exit only, no access

M58 Liverpool - Wigan

Junction	Westbound	Eastbound
1	Exit only, no access	Access only, no exit

M60 Manchester Orbital

Junction	Clockwise	Anticlockwise
2	Access only, no exit	Exit only, no access
3	No access from M56	Access only from A34 (northbound)
4	Access only from A34 (northbound). Exit only to M56	Access only from M56 (eastbound). Exit only to A34 (southbound)
5	Access and exit only from and to A5103 (northbound)	Access and exit only from and to A5103 (southbound)
7	No direct access, use slip road to jct 8. Exit only to A56	Access only from A56. No exit, use jct 8
14	Access from A580 (eastbound)	Exit only to A580 (westbound)
16	Access only, no exit	Exit only, no access
20	Exit only, no access	Access only, no exit
22	No restriction	Exit only, no access
25	Exit only, no access	No restriction
26	No restriction	Exit only, no access
27	Access only, no exit	Exit only, no access

M61 Manchester - Preston

Junction	Northwestbound	Southeastbound
3	No access or exit	Exit only, no access
with M6 (jct 30)	Exit only to M6 (northbound)	Access only from M6 (southbound)

M62 Liverpool - Kingston upon Hull

Junction	Westbound	Eastbound
23	Access only, no exit	Exit only, no access
32A	No access to A1(M) (southbound)	No restriction

M65 Preston - Colne

Junction	Northeastbound	Southwestbound
9	Exit only, no access	Access only, no exit
11	Access only, no exit	Exit only, no access

M66 Bury

Junction	Northbound	Southbound
with A56	Exit only to A56 (northbound)	Access only from A56 (southbound)
1	Exit only, no access	Access only, no exit

M67 Hyde Bypass

Junction	Westbound	Eastbound
1	Access only, no exit	Exit only, no access
2	Exit only, no access	Access only, no exit
3	Exit only, no access	No restriction

M69 Coventry - Leicester

Junction	Northbound	Southbound
2	Access only, no exit	Exit only, no access

M73 East of Glasgow

Junction	Northbound	Southbound
1	No exit to A74 & A721	No exit to A74 & A721
2	No access from or exit to A89. No access from (eastbound)	No access from or exit to A89. No exit to M8 (westbound)

M74 and A74(M) Glasgow - Gretna

Junction	Northbound	Southbound
3	Exit only, no access	Access only, no exit
3A	Access only, no exit	Exit only, no access
4	No access from A74 & A721	Access only, no exit to A74 & A721
7	Access only, no exit	Exit only, no access
9	No access or exit	Exit only, no access
10	No restriction	Access only, no exit
11	Access only, no exit	Exit only, no access
12	Exit only, no access	Access only, no exit
18	Exit only, no access	Access only, no exit

M77 Glasgow - Kilmarnock

Junction	Northbound	Southbound
with M8 (jct 22)	No exit to M8 (westbound)	No access from M8 (eastbound)
4	Access only, no exit	Exit only, no access
6	Access only, no exit	Exit only, no access
7	Access only, no exit	No restriction
8	Exit only, no access	Exit only, no access

M80 Glasgow - Stirling

Junction	Northbound	Southbound
4A	Exit only, no access	Access only, no exit
6A	Access only, no exit	Exit only, no access
8	Exit only to M876 (northeastbound)	Access only from M876 (southwestbound)

M90 Edinburgh - Perth

Junction	Northbound	Southbound
1	No exit, access only	Exit only to A90 (eastbound)
2A	Exit only to A92 (eastbound)	Access only from A92 (westbound)
7	Access only, no exit	Exit only, no access
8	Exit only, no access	Access only, no exit
10	No access from A912. No exit to A912 (southbound)	No access from A912 (northbound) No exit to A912

M180 Doncaster - Grimsby

Junction	Westbound	Eastbound
1	Access only, no exit	Exit only, no access

M606 Bradford Spur

Junction	Northbound	Southbound
2	Exit only, no access	No restriction

M621 Leeds - M1

Junction	Clockwise	Anticlockwise
2A	Access only, no exit	Exit only, no access
4	No exit or access	No restriction
5	Access only, no exit	Exit only, no access
6	Exit only, no access	Access only, no exit
with M1 (jct 43)	Exit only to M1 (southbound)	Access only from M1 (northbound)

M876 Bonnybridge - Kincardine Bridge

Junction	Northeastbound	Southwestbound
with M80 (jct 5)	Access only from M80 (northeastbound)	Exit only to M80 (southwestbound)
with M9 (jct 8)	Exit only to M9 (eastbound)	Access only from M9 (westbound)

A1(M) South Mimms - Baldock

Junction	Northbound	Southbound
2	Exit only, no access	Access only, no exit
3	No restriction	Exit only, no access
5	Access only, no exit	No access or exit

A1(M) Pontefract - Bedale

Junction	Northbound	Southbound
41	No access to M62 (eastbound)	No restriction
43	Access only from M1 (northbound)	Exit only to M1 (southbound)

A1(M) Scotch Corner - Newcastle upon Tyne

Junction	Northbound	Southbound
57	Exit only to A66(M) (eastbound)	Access only from A66(M) (westbound)
65	No access Exit only to A194(M) & A1 (northbound)	No exit Access only from A194(M) & A1 (southbound)

A3(M) Horndean - Havant

Junction	Northbound	Southbound
1	Access only from A3	Exit only to A3
4	Exit only, no access	Access only, no exit

A38(M) Birmingham, Victoria Road (Park Circus)

Junction	Northbound	Southbound
with B4132	No exit	No access

A48(M) Cardiff Spur

Junction	Westbound	Eastbound
29	Access only from M4 (westbound)	Exit only to M4 (eastbound)
29A	Exit only to A48 (westbound)	Access only from A48 (eastbound)

A57(M) Manchester, Brook Street (A34)

Junction	Westbound	Eastbound
with A34	No exit	No access

A58(M) Leeds, Park Lane and Westgate

Junction	Northbound	Southbound
with A58	No restriction	No access

A64(M) Leeds, Clay Pit Lane (A58)

Junction	Westbound	Eastbound
with A58	No exit (to Clay Pit Lane)	No access (from Clay Pit Lane)

A66(M) Darlington Spur

Junction	Westbound	Eastbound
with A1(M) (jct 57)	Exit only to A1(M) (southbound)	Access only from A1(M) (northbound)

A74(M) Gretna - Abington

Junction	Northbound	Southbound
18	Exit only, no access	No exit

A194(M) Newcastle upon Tyne

Junction	Northbound	Southbound
with A1(M) (jct 65)	Access only from A1(M) (northbound)	Exit only to A1(M) (southbound)

A12 M25 - Ipswich

Junction	Northeastbound	Southwestbound
13	Access only, no exit	No restriction
14	Exit only, no access	Access only, no exit
20A	Exit only, no access	Access only, no exit
20B	Access only, no exit	Exit only, no access
21	No restriction	Access only, no exit
23	Exit only, no access	Access only, no exit
24	Access only, no exit	Exit only, no access
27	Exit only, no access	Access only, no exit
Dedham & Stratford St Mary (unnumbered)	Exit only	Access only

A14 M1 - Felixstowe

Junction	Westbound	Eastbound
with M1/M6 (jct19)	Exit only to M6 and M1 (northbound)	Access only from M6 and M1 (southbound)
4	Exit only, no access	Access only, no exit
31	Exit only to M11 (for London)	Access only, no exit
31A	Exit only to A14 (northbound)	Access only, no exit
34	Access only, no exit	Exit only, no access
36	Exit only to A11, access only from A1303	Access only from A11
38	Access only from A11	Exit only to A11
39	Exit only, no access	Access only, no exit
61	Access only, no exit	Exit only, no access

A55 Holyhead - Chester

Junction	Westbound	Eastbound
8A	Exit only, no access	Access only, no exit
23A	Access only, no exit	Exit only, no access
24A	Exit only, no access	No access or exit
27A	No restriction	No access or exit
33A	Exit only, no access	No access or exit
33B	Exit only, no access	Access only, no exit
36A	Exit only to A5104	Access only from A5104

Motoring information

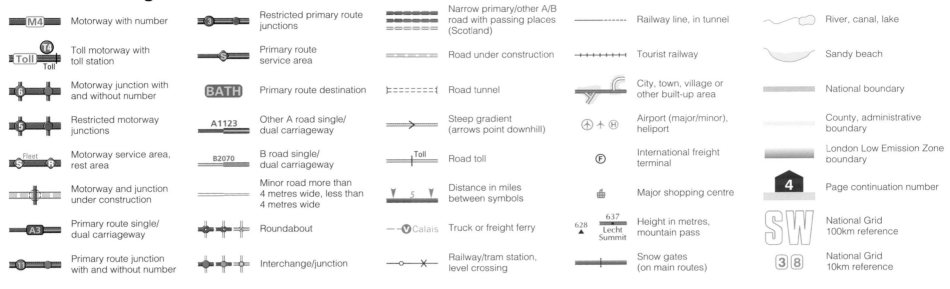

Motorway with number	Restricted primary route junctions	Narrow primary/other A/B road with passing places (Scotland)
Toll motorway with toll station	Primary route service area	Road under construction
Motorway junction with and without number	Primary route destination	Road tunnel
Restricted motorway junctions	Other A road single/dual carriageway	Steep gradient (arrows point downhill)
Motorway service area, rest area	B road single/dual carriageway	Road toll
Motorway and junction under construction	Minor road more than 4 metres wide, less than 4 metres wide	Distance in miles between symbols
Primary route single/dual carriageway	Roundabout	Truck or freight ferry
Primary route junction with and without number	Interchange/junction	Railway/tram station, level crossing

Railway line, in tunnel	River, canal, lake
Tourist railway	Sandy beach
City, town, village or other built-up area	National boundary
Airport (major/minor), heliport	County, administrative boundary
International freight terminal	London Low Emission Zone boundary
Major shopping centre	Page continuation number
Height in metres, mountain pass	National Grid 100km reference
Snow gates (on main routes)	National Grid 10km reference

District maps (see pages 101–107)

Motorway and junction	Road tunnel	Docklands Light Railway (DLR) station
M6 Toll motorway (Birmingham District)	Railway line and station	Metro station (Tyne & Wear)
Primary route single/dual carriageway	Tramway	Subway station (Glasgow)
Other A road single/dual carriageway	London Underground station	Central London Congestion Charge and Ultra Low Emission Zone
B road single/dual carriageway	London Overground station	London Low Emission Zone boundary
Other road single/dual carriageway	Rail Interchange	

Central London street map (see pages 108–119)

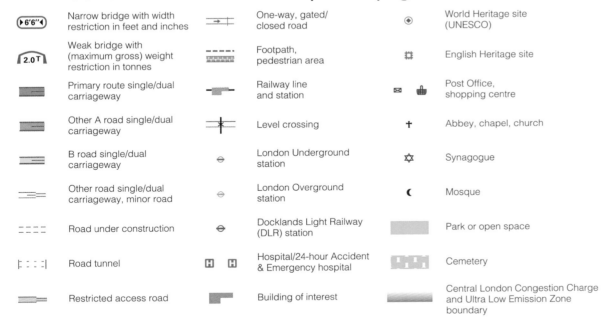

Narrow bridge with width restriction in feet and inches	One-way, gated/closed road	World Heritage site (UNESCO)
Weak bridge with (maximum gross) weight restriction in tonnes	Footpath, pedestrian area	English Heritage site
Primary route single/dual carriageway	Railway line and station	Post Office, shopping centre
Other A road single/dual carriageway	Level crossing	Abbey, chapel, church
B road single/dual carriageway	London Underground station	Synagogue
Other road single/dual carriageway, minor road	London Overground station	Mosque
Road under construction	Docklands Light Railway (DLR) station	Park or open space
Road tunnel	Hospital/24-hour Accident & Emergency hospital	Cemetery
Restricted access road	Building of interest	Central London Congestion Charge and Ultra Low Emission Zone boundary

London Low Emission Zone (LEZ)

The London Low Emission Zone (LEZ) operates 24 hours a day, every day of the year and covers most of Greater London, excluding the M25 (see pages 22-23).

Certain vehicles travelling in the zone (excluding cars and motorbikes) must meet strict emission standards to help reduce traffic pollution. If a vehicle in the zone doesn't meet the emission standards a charge must be paid each day the vehicle is within the zone.

The LEZ daily charge is £100 for larger vans, minibuses and other lighter diesel vehicles, and £200 for lorries, buses, coaches and other heavy vehicles. Charging days run from midnight to midnight.

From 26 October 2020 the LEZ standards will become stricter and the charges are changing.

For more information about the LEZ and to check if your vehicle meets the standards, visit *www.tfl.gov.uk/lez* or call 0343 222 2222.

Central London Congestion Charge Zone

The charge for driving or parking in this Central London area (see page 107) is £11.50 per vehicle per day in advance or on the day of travel. The zone operates between 7am and 6pm Monday to Friday only. There is no charge on weekends, on public holidays or between 25th Dec and 1st Jan inclusive.

For up to date information on the zone, exemptions, discounts or how to pay, telephone 0343 222 2222 or visit *www.tfl.gov.uk/congestioncharge*

Ultra Low Emission Zone (ULEZ)

All vehicles entering Central London also need to meet minimum emission standards or pay a charge. It applies to the same area covered by the Congestion Charge (see page 107) and operates every day of the year, 24 hours a day.

The charge is in addition to the Congestion Charge and LEZ charge and is £12.50 (lighter vehicles and vans up to 3.5 tonnes) or £100 (heavier vehicles).

For further information visit *www.tfl.gov.uk/ulez* or call 0343 222 2222.

London Lorry Control Scheme (LLCS)

There are additional restrictions for heavy goods vehicles over 18 tonnes maximum gross weight, when travelling at night and at weekends, on specific roads in residential areas of London. In order to travel on any of the restricted roads, permission must be obtained or a penalty charge notice will be issued. For further details visit *www.londonlorrycontrol.com*

Bridge height symbol

 Bridge location with height restriction in feet and inches. This atlas primarily shows low bridges signed at 16'6" and under on all roads selected for inclusion on the mapping.

 Bridge height only applies when travelling in direction shown: Northbound, Southbound, Eastbound, Westbound.

 Frequently struck bridge (provided by Network Rail) with height restriction in feet and inches.
Yellow symbols indicate the 32 most frequently struck bridges (as listed on page IV).

For information on road signs see page III.

OVERALL TRAVELLING HEIGHT CONVERSION
Read in feet horizontally and inches vertically, e.g. 13' 3" = 4.04 metres

Height in inches (")	Height in feet (')									
	7'	8'	9'	10'	11'	12'	13'	14'	15'	16'
9"	2.36m	2.67m	2.97m	3.28m	3.58m	3.89m	4.19m	4.50m	4.80m	5.11m
6"	2.29m	2.59m	2.90m	3.20m	3.51m	3.81m	4.11m	4.42m	4.72m	5.03m
3"	2.21m	2.51m	2.82m	3.12m	3.43m	3.73m	4.04m	4.34m	4.65m	4.95m
0"	2.13m	2.44m	2.74m	3.05m	3.35m	3.66m	3.96m	4.27m	4.57m	4.88m

See inside front cover for full table

Isles of Scilly

SV

St Helen's
White Island
BRYHER
ST MARTIN'S
Old Grimsby
38
49 St Martin's Head
Higher Town
New Lizard Point
42
Grimsby
Eastern Isles
Great Ganilly
TRESCO
Crow Bar
Samson
Crow Sound
North West Passage
A3111
ST MARY'S
Hugh Town
Deep Point
Isles of Scilly (St Mary's)
Old Town
Peninnis Head
Middle Town
St Mary's Sound
Annet
Gugh
ST AGNES
Broad Sound
Smith Sound
Horse Point
Western Rocks

| 0 | | 1 | | 2 | | 3 | | 4 miles |
| 0 | 1 | 2 | 3 | 4 | 5 | 6 kilometres |

SW

Water
Bay
Towan
Head
Newquay
Bay
Newquay
Fistral Bay
Kelsey Head
West Pentire
Pentire
Bed
Holywell Bay
Penhale Point
Holywell
Grif
Ligger Point
Tresean Treval
Cubert
St New East
Ligger or Perran Bay
Rose
Perranporth
Cligga Point
St New
B3285
Fiddlers Green
Bolingey
14'6"
Goonhavern
Trevellas Downs
12'3"
Perranzabuloe
Zela
ST AGNES HEAD
St Agnes
Mithian
Penhallow
Callestick
Goonvrea
Barkla Shop
Goonbell
B3284
8
Porthtowan
Mount Hawke
Shortlanesend
A390
Portreath
B3300
Cambrose
15'0"
Threemilestone
Ker
Illogan
11'0"
Blackwater
Chacewater
15'3"
A30
13'6"
12'0"
South Tehidy
9'0"
16'3"
Mount Ambrose
Scorrier
St Day
higher
Reskadinnick
Tuckingmill
Carn Brea
Redruth
Twelveheads
14'3"
Pla
Ph
Kehelland
Camborne
8'3"
Carn Brea
Carharrack
12'0"
Bissoe
Carnon Downs
Penponds
Carnkie
Gwennap
A393
Devoran
Connor Downs
High Gwinear
Barripper
Perranwell
Perranarworthal
A39
Phillack
Angarrack
Realwa
Carnhell Green
Four Lanes
Penhalvean
Feoc
Hayle
11'6"
Copperhouse
Lanes
St Erth Praze
Troon
Ponsanooth
14'3"
Carbis Bay
Lelant
Crowan
Stithians
Mylor Bridge
St Ives
15'0"
Canonstown
A30
13'0"
Leedstown
B3280
Carnkie
Longdowns
14'9"
St Erth
B3303
Praze-an-Beeble
Mabe Burnthouse
Penryn
R Hayle
16'3"
Crowan
Porkellis
Rame
A39
Townshend
Budock Water
Crowlas
Ludgvan
Relubbus
Godolphin Cross
Treverva
Fal
New Mill
St Hilary
Trenear
A394
14'6"
Madron
Gulval
Longrock
Marazion
Trescowe
Carleen
Prospidnick
Wendron
Seworgan
Fal
Heamoor
Goldsithney
Ashton
Sithney
Constantine
Mawnan Smith
A30
Perranuthnoe
Breage
Coverack
Porth Navas
ROSEMULLI
Chyandour
A30
14'0"
Helston
Bridges
Penzance
Praa Sands
A394
Gweek
Helford Passage
Durgan
Mawnan
Newlyn
Cudden Point
Rinsey Head
10
Mawgan
Helford
St Anthony-in-M
Paul
Trewavas Head
Manaccan
Nare Point
Sancreed
Drift
Crows-an-Wra
A30
10
Mousehole
MOUNT'S BAY
Porthleven
A3083
Garras
St Martin
Porthallo
St Buryan
Gunwalloe
Mawgan
Porthe
Man
Lamorna
White Cross
St Keverne
Sennen
Lamorna Cove
Cury
Trevescan
B3315
Poldhu Point
Trethewey
B3315
Merthen Point
GOONHILLY DOWNS
Treen
Porthcurno
Cribba Head
Mullion Cove
Mullion
Coverack
Gwennap Head
St Levan
Mullion Island
Ruan Major
Kuggar
Predannack Head
Black Head
Vellan Head
Ruan Minor
Cadgwith
Lizard Head
A3083
Church Cove
Kynance Cove
Lizard
7
Bass Point
LIZARD POINT

Wise up Size up
Prevent bridge strikes #wiseupsizeup
Wise up Sizeup

OVERALL TRAVELLING HEIGHT CONVERSION
Read in feet horizontally and inches vertically, e.g. 13′ 3″ = 4.04 metres

Height in feet (′)

Height in inches (″)	7′	8′	9′	10′	11′	12′	13′	14′	15′	16′
9″	2.36m	2.67m	2.97m	3.28m	3.58m	3.89m	4.19m	4.50m	4.80m	5.11m
6″	2.29m	2.59m	2.90m	3.20m	3.51m	3.81m	4.11m	4.42m	4.72m	5.03m
3″	2.21m	2.51m	2.82m	3.12m	3.43m	3.73m	4.04m	4.34m	4.65m	4.95m
0″	2.13m	2.44m	2.74m	3.05m	3.35m	3.66m	3.96m	4.27m	4.57m	4.88m

See inside front cover for full table

4

OVERALL TRAVELLING HEIGHT CONVERSION
Read in feet horizontally and inches vertically, e.g. 13' 3" = 4.04 metres

Height in feet (')

Height in inches (")	7'	8'	9'	10'	11'	12'	13'	14'	15'	16'
9"	2.36m	2.67m	2.97m	3.28m	3.58m	3.89m	4.19m	4.50m	4.80m	5.11m
6"	2.29m	2.59m	2.90m	3.20m	3.51m	3.81m	4.11m	4.42m	4.72m	5.03m
3"	2.21m	2.51m	2.82m	3.12m	3.43m	3.73m	4.04m	4.34m	4.65m	4.95m
0"	2.13m	2.44m	2.74m	3.05m	3.35m	3.66m	3.96m	4.27m	4.57m	4.88m

See inside front cover for full table

Port of Plymouth

Prevent bridge strikes #wiseupsizeup

Wise up Size up

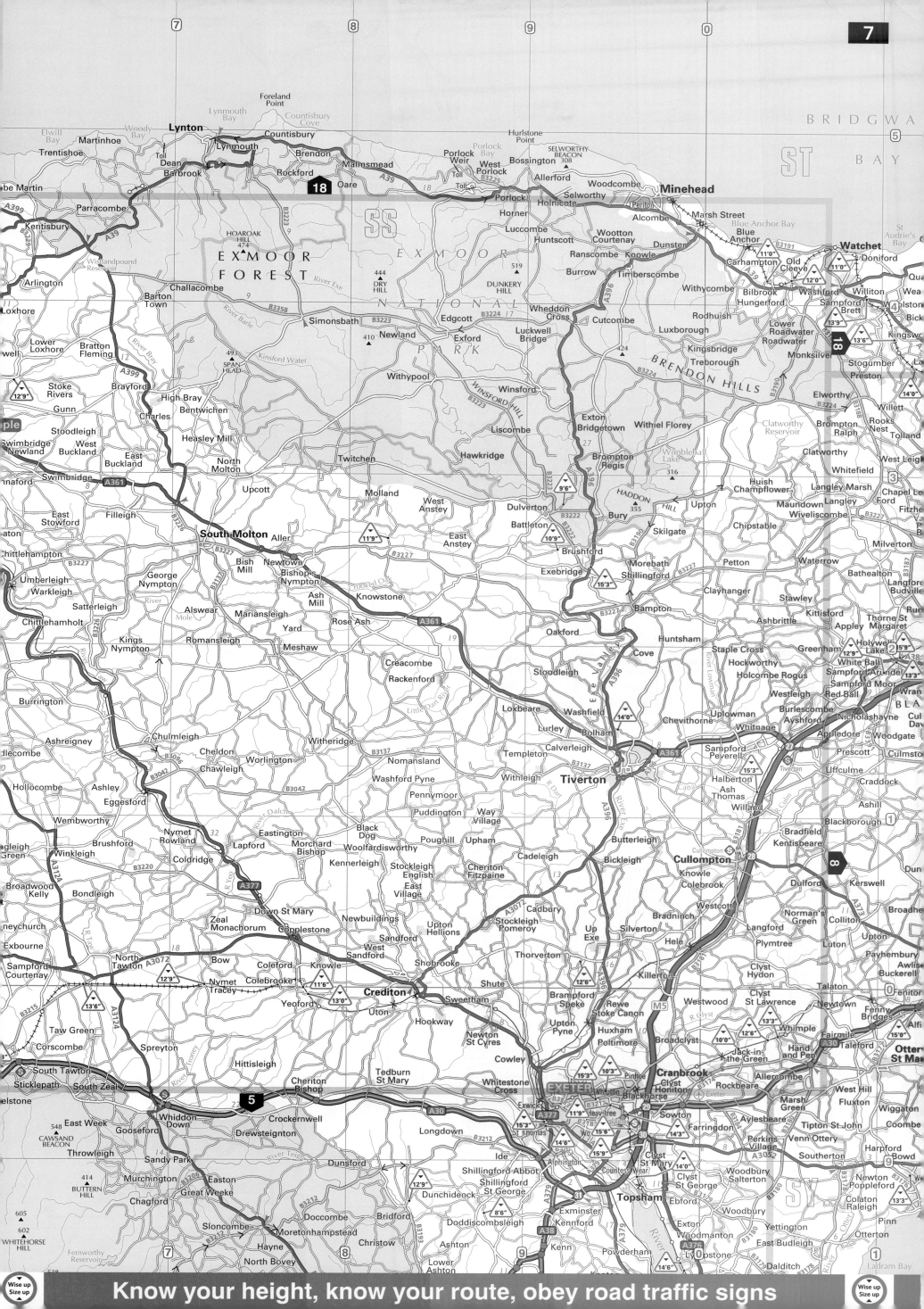

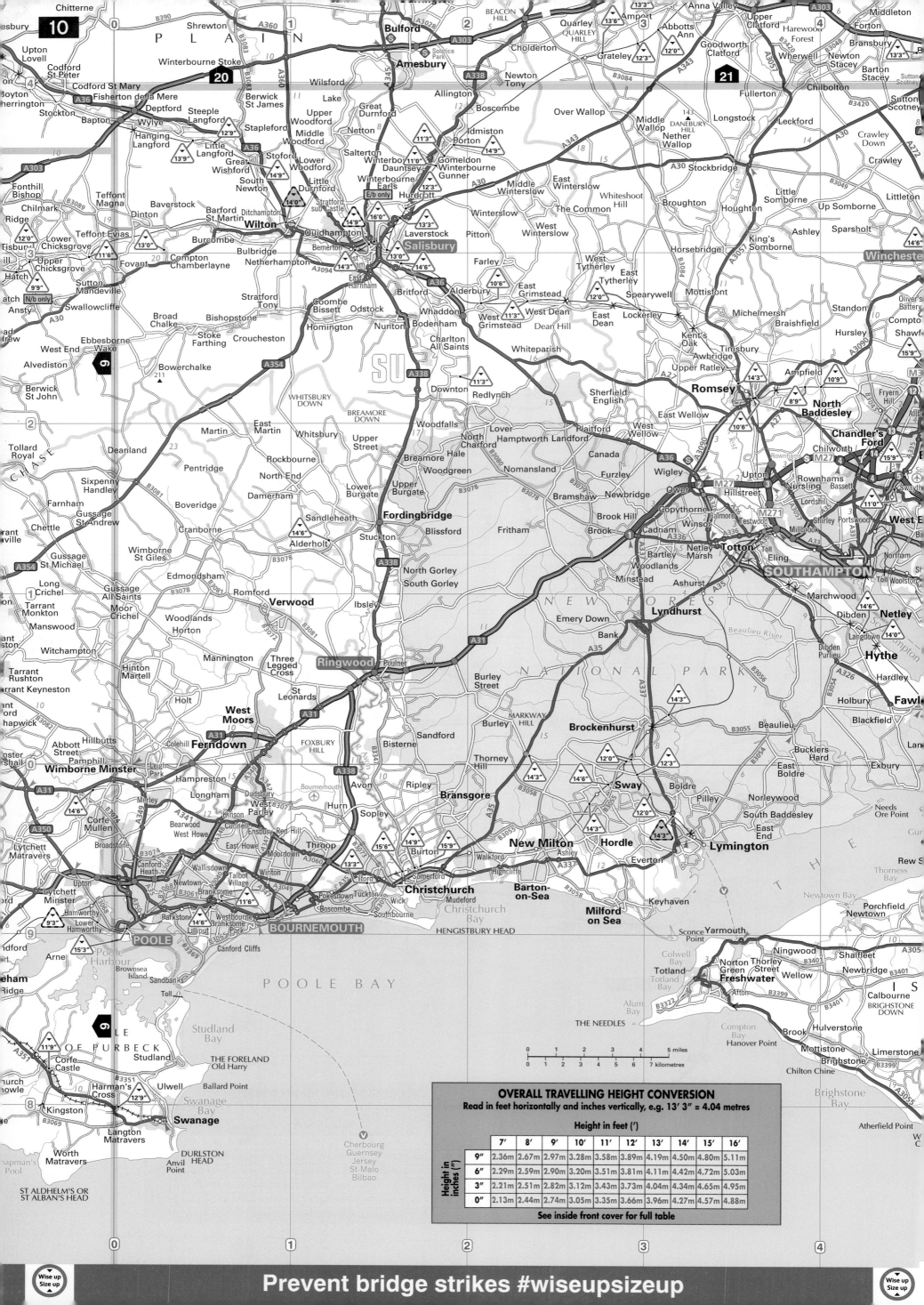

OVERALL TRAVELLING HEIGHT CONVERSION
Read in feet horizontally and inches vertically, e.g. 13' 3" = 4.04 metres

Height in feet (')

Height in inches (")	7'	8'	9'	10'	11'	12'	13'	14'	15'	16'
9"	2.36m	2.67m	2.97m	3.28m	3.58m	3.89m	4.19m	4.50m	4.80m	5.11m
6"	2.29m	2.59m	2.90m	3.20m	3.51m	3.81m	4.11m	4.42m	4.72m	5.03m
3"	2.21m	2.51m	2.82m	3.12m	3.43m	3.73m	4.04m	4.34m	4.65m	4.95m
0"	2.13m	2.44m	2.74m	3.05m	3.35m	3.66m	3.96m	4.27m	4.57m	4.88m

See inside front cover for full table

Know your height, know your route, obey road traffic signs

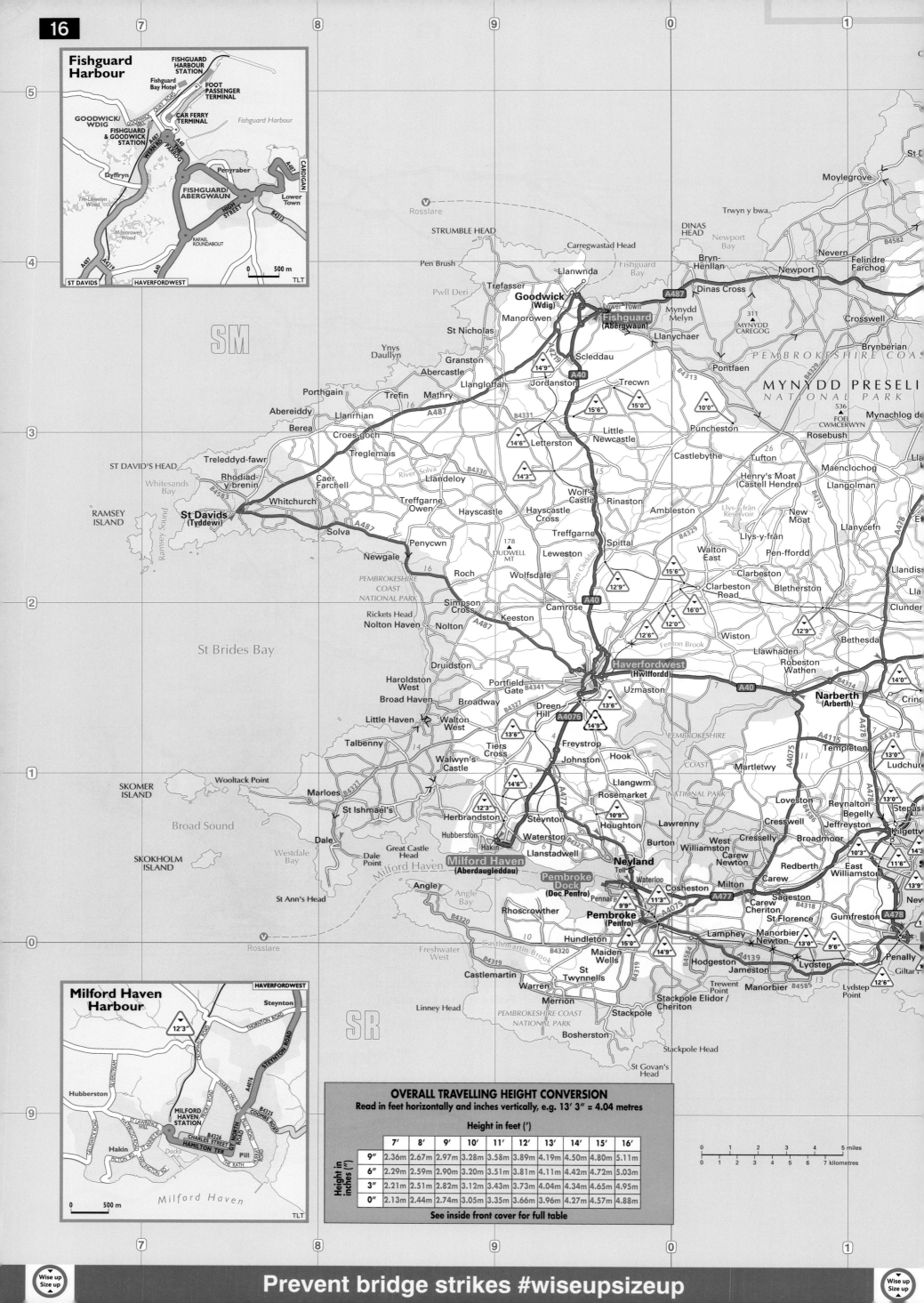

Fishguard Harbour

FISHGUARD HARBOUR STATION
FOOT PASSENGER TERMINAL
CAR FERRY TERMINAL
Fishguard Bay Hotel
GOODWICK/WDIG
FISHGUARD & GOODWICK STATION
THE PARROG
WERN RD
A40
A487
HIGH STREET
FISHGUARD/ABERGWAUN
Penyraber
Fishguard Harbour
Lower Town
CARDIGAN
B4313
Dyffryn
Tre-Llewelyn Wood
Manorowen Wood
RAFAEL ROUNDABOUT
A487
A4019
A40

ST DAVIDS | HAVERFORDWEST

0   500 m   TLT

OVERALL TRAVELLING HEIGHT CONVERSION
Read in feet horizontally and inches vertically, e.g. 13′ 3″ = 4.04 metres

Height in feet (′)

Height in inches (″)	7′	8′	9′	10′	11′	12′	13′	14′	15′	16′
9″	2.36m	2.67m	2.97m	3.28m	3.58m	3.89m	4.19m	4.50m	4.80m	5.11m
6″	2.29m	2.59m	2.90m	3.20m	3.51m	3.81m	4.11m	4.42m	4.72m	5.03m
3″	2.21m	2.51m	2.82m	3.12m	3.43m	3.73m	4.04m	4.34m	4.65m	4.95m
0″	2.13m	2.44m	2.74m	3.05m	3.35m	3.66m	3.96m	4.27m	4.57m	4.88m

See inside front cover for full table

Milford Haven Harbour

HAVERFORDWEST
Steynton
12′3″
STEYNTON ROAD
THORNTON ROAD
A4076
B4325 COOMBS ROAD
MILFORD HAVEN STATION
ST LAWRENCE HILL
CHARLES STREET
HAMILTON TER
Hubberston
Hakin
Docks
Pill
THE RATH
Milford Haven

0   500 m   TLT

---

0   1   2   3   4   5 miles
0   7 kilometres

Prevent bridge strikes #wiseupsizeup

Wise up Size up

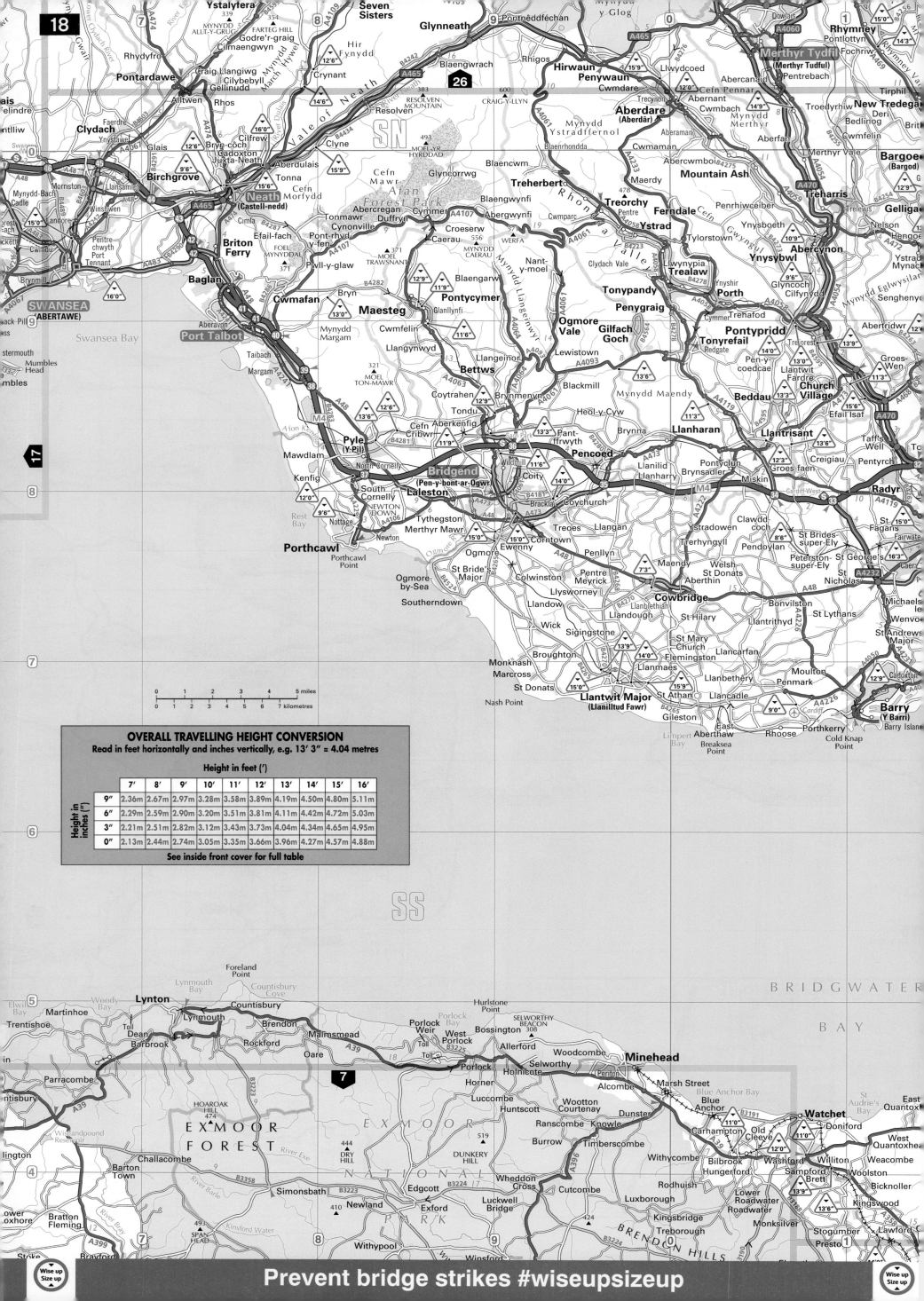

OVERALL TRAVELLING HEIGHT CONVERSION

Read in feet horizontally and inches vertically, e.g. 13' 3" = 4.04 metres

	Height in feet (')									
	7'	8'	9'	10'	11'	12'	13'	14'	15'	16'
9"	2.36m	2.67m	2.97m	3.28m	3.58m	3.89m	4.19m	4.50m	4.80m	5.11m
6"	2.29m	2.59m	2.90m	3.20m	3.51m	3.81m	4.11m	4.42m	4.72m	5.03m
3"	2.21m	2.51m	2.82m	3.12m	3.43m	3.73m	4.04m	4.34m	4.65m	4.95m
0"	2.13m	2.44m	2.74m	3.05m	3.35m	3.66m	3.96m	4.27m	4.57m	4.88m

Height in inches (")

See inside front cover for full table

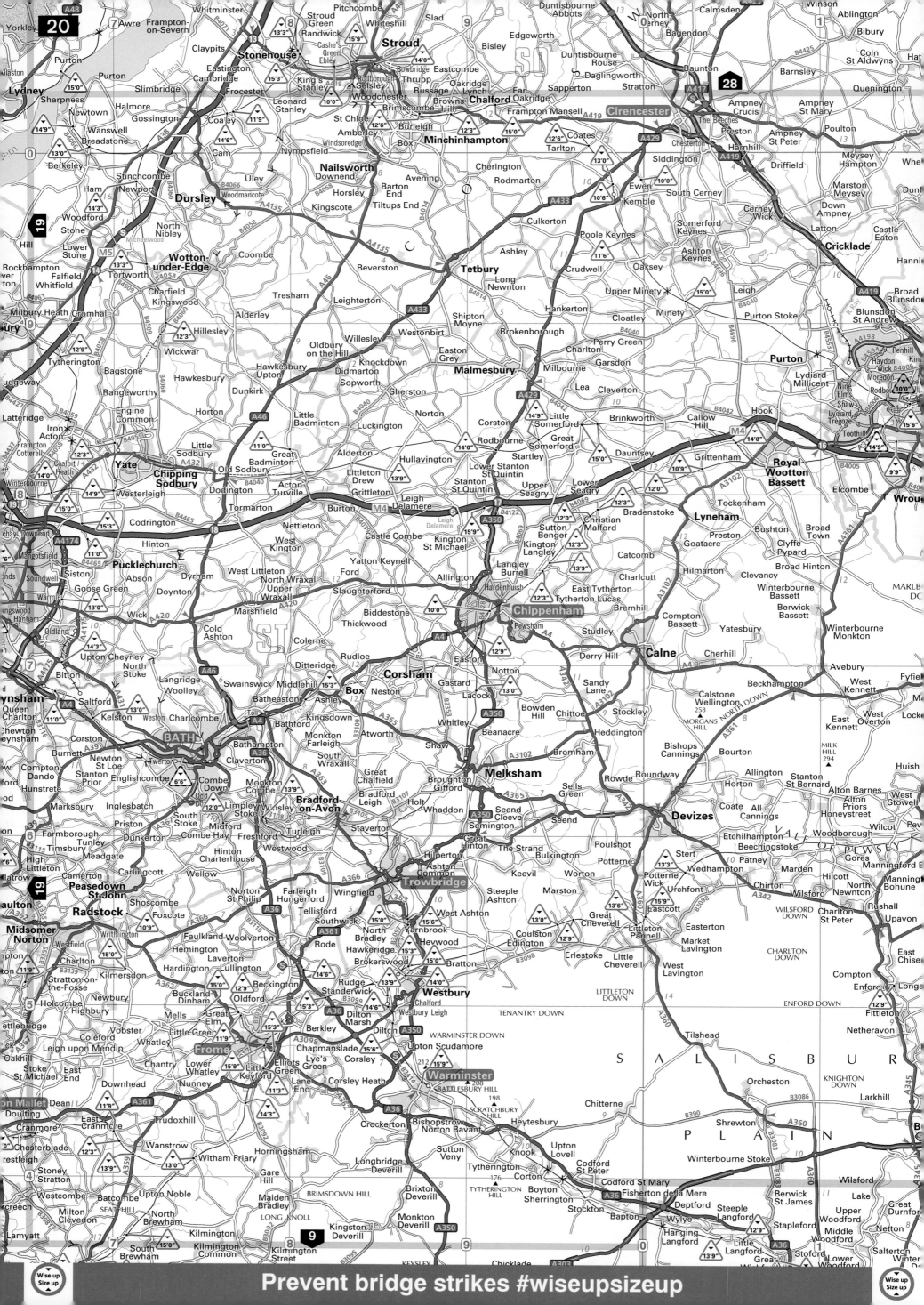

Know your height, know your route, obey road traffic signs

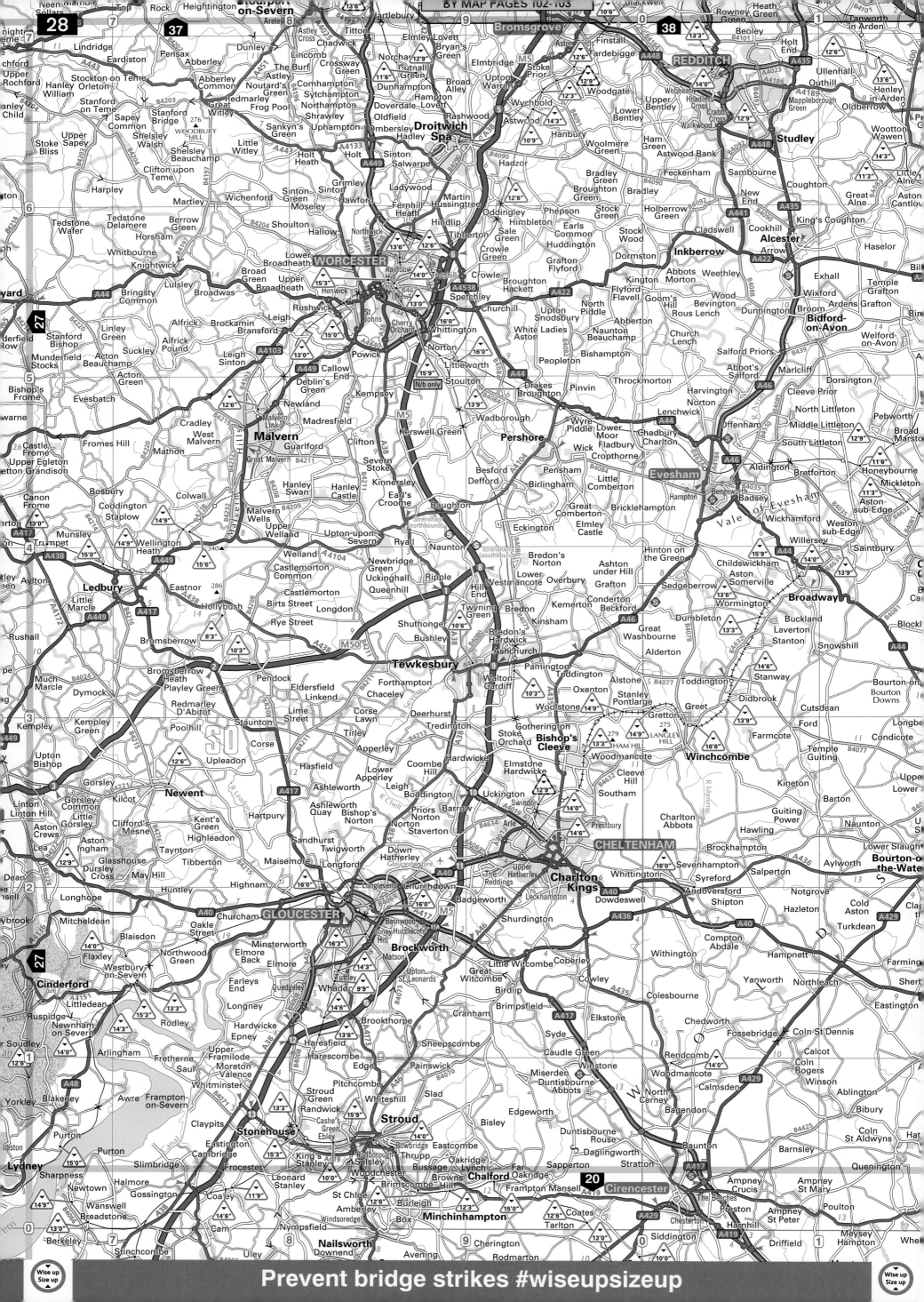

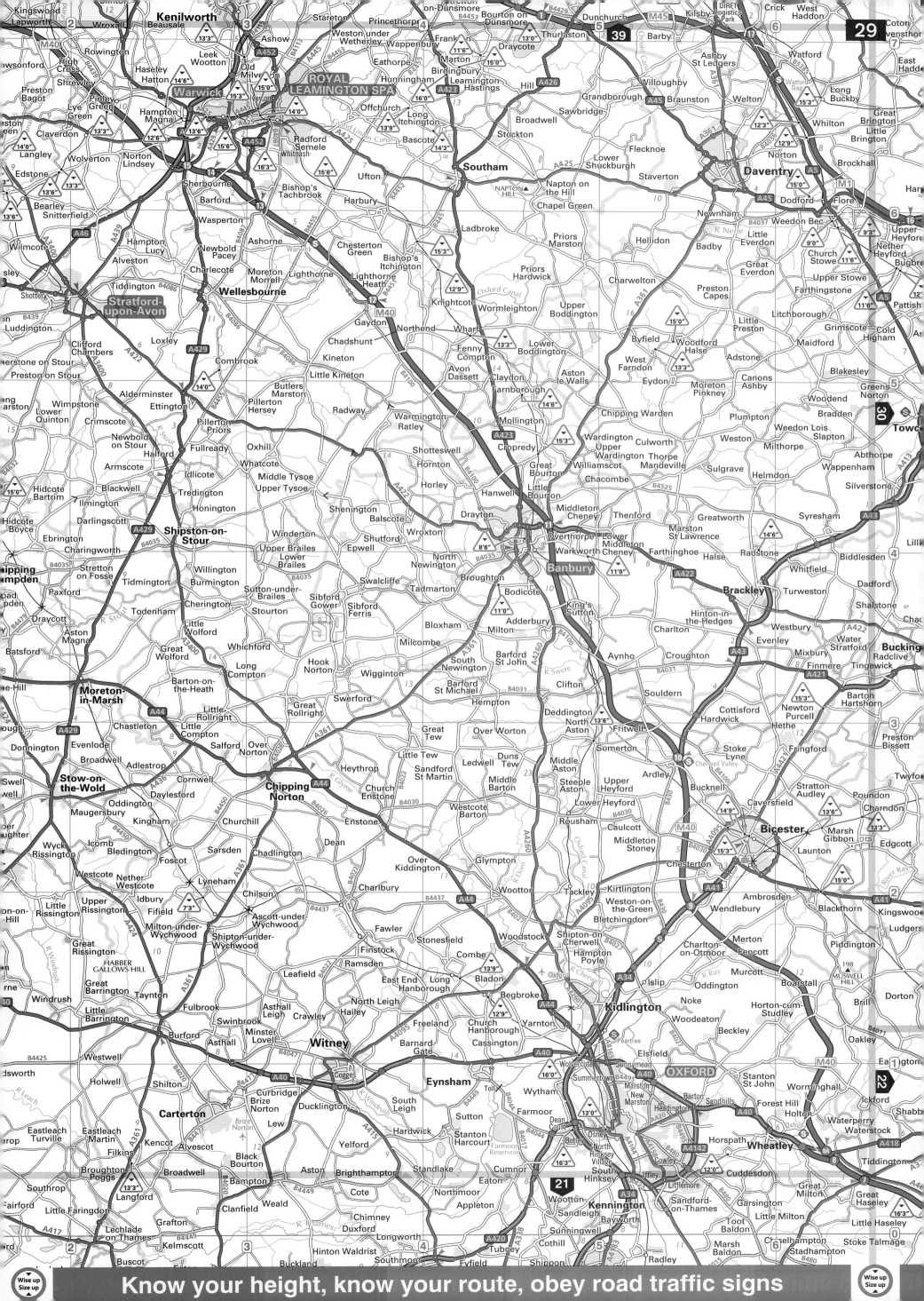

Prevent bridge strikes #wiseupsizeup

Know your height, know your route, obey road traffic signs

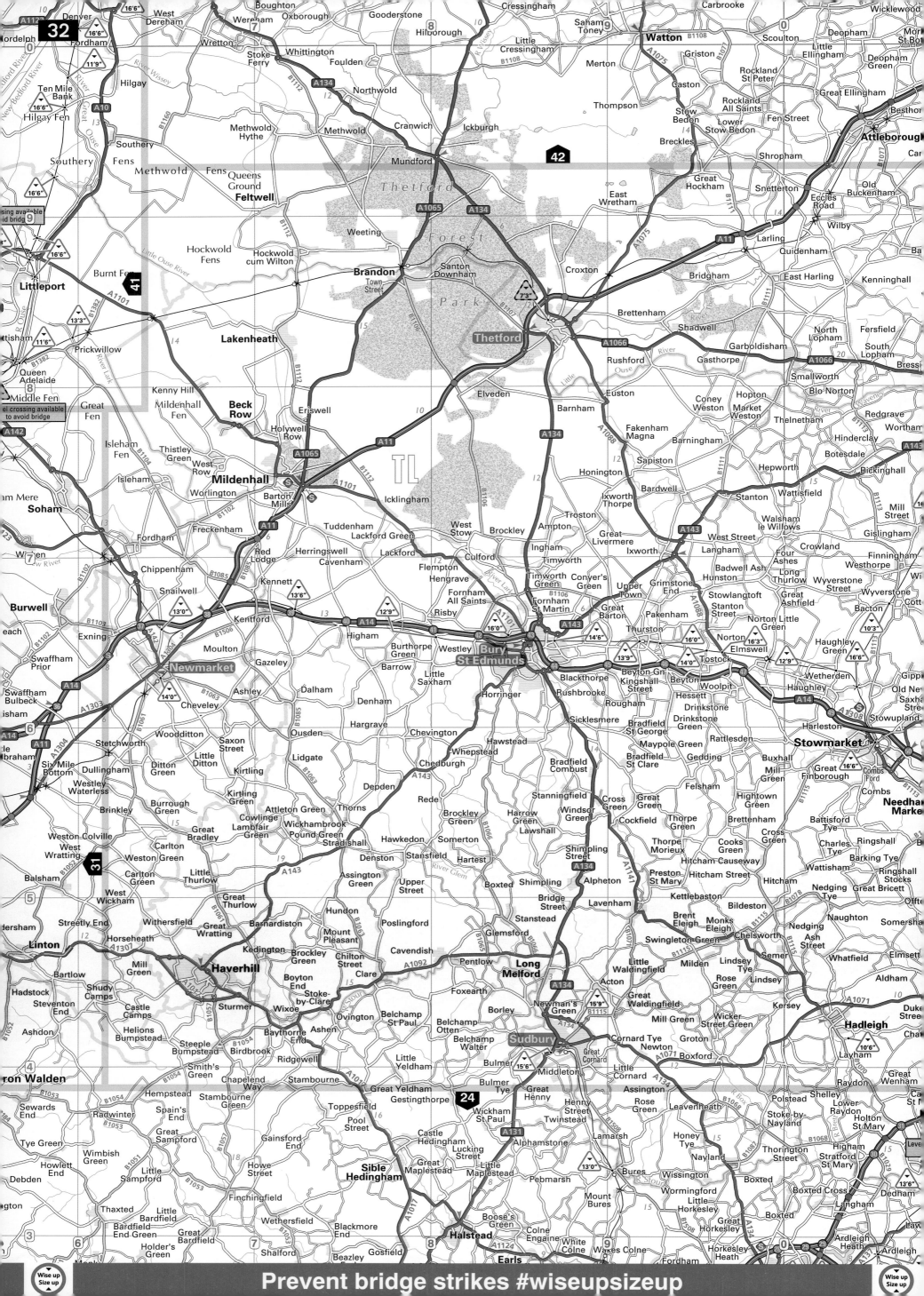

St Tudwal's Island East
St Tudwal's Island West

Aberdaron
Llanfaelrhys
Porth Neigwl or Hell's Mouth
Bwlchtocyn
Marchros
Aberdaron Bay
Porth Ysgo
Porth Ceiriad

Bardsey Sound

BARDSEY ISLAND

Dyffryn Ardudwy
Llanddwywe

Barmouth
Barmouth Bay
Fairbo

SH

Llangelynin
Rhoslefa

Aber Dysynni

Tywyn
10'0"

C A R D I G A N

B A Y

SN

Clarach Bay

Aberystwyth
12'0"

Llanfarian

Blaenplwyf

Llanddeinio

Llanrhystud
A487

Llansantffraid
Llanon
Joppa

Nebo

Aberarth
Aberaeron

New Quay
(Ceinewydd)

Cilcennin

Llanina
Llwyncelyn
A482
Bwlchlla

Maen-y-groes
Gilfachrheda
Llanarth
Cross Inn
Oakford
Trefilan
Talsarn
Nanternis
Ynys-Lochtyn
Llwyndafydd
Caerwedros
Dihewyd
Ystrad Aeron
Mydroilyn
Llangrannog
Pontgarreg
Temple Bar

17

0   1   2   3   4   5 miles
0   1   2   3   4   5   6   7 kilometres

OVERALL TRAVELLING HEIGHT CONVERSION
Read in feet horizontally and inches vertically, e.g. 13′ 3″ = 4.04 metres

Height in feet (′)

Height in inches (″)	7′	8′	9′	10′	11′	12′	13′	14′	15′	16′
9″	2.36m	2.67m	2.97m	3.28m	3.58m	3.89m	4.19m	4.50m	4.80m	5.11m
6″	2.29m	2.59m	2.90m	3.20m	3.51m	3.81m	4.11m	4.42m	4.72m	5.03m
3″	2.21m	2.51m	2.82m	3.12m	3.43m	3.73m	4.04m	4.34m	4.65m	4.95m
0″	2.13m	2.44m	2.74m	3.05m	3.35m	3.66m	3.96m	4.27m	4.57m	4.88m

See inside front cover for full table

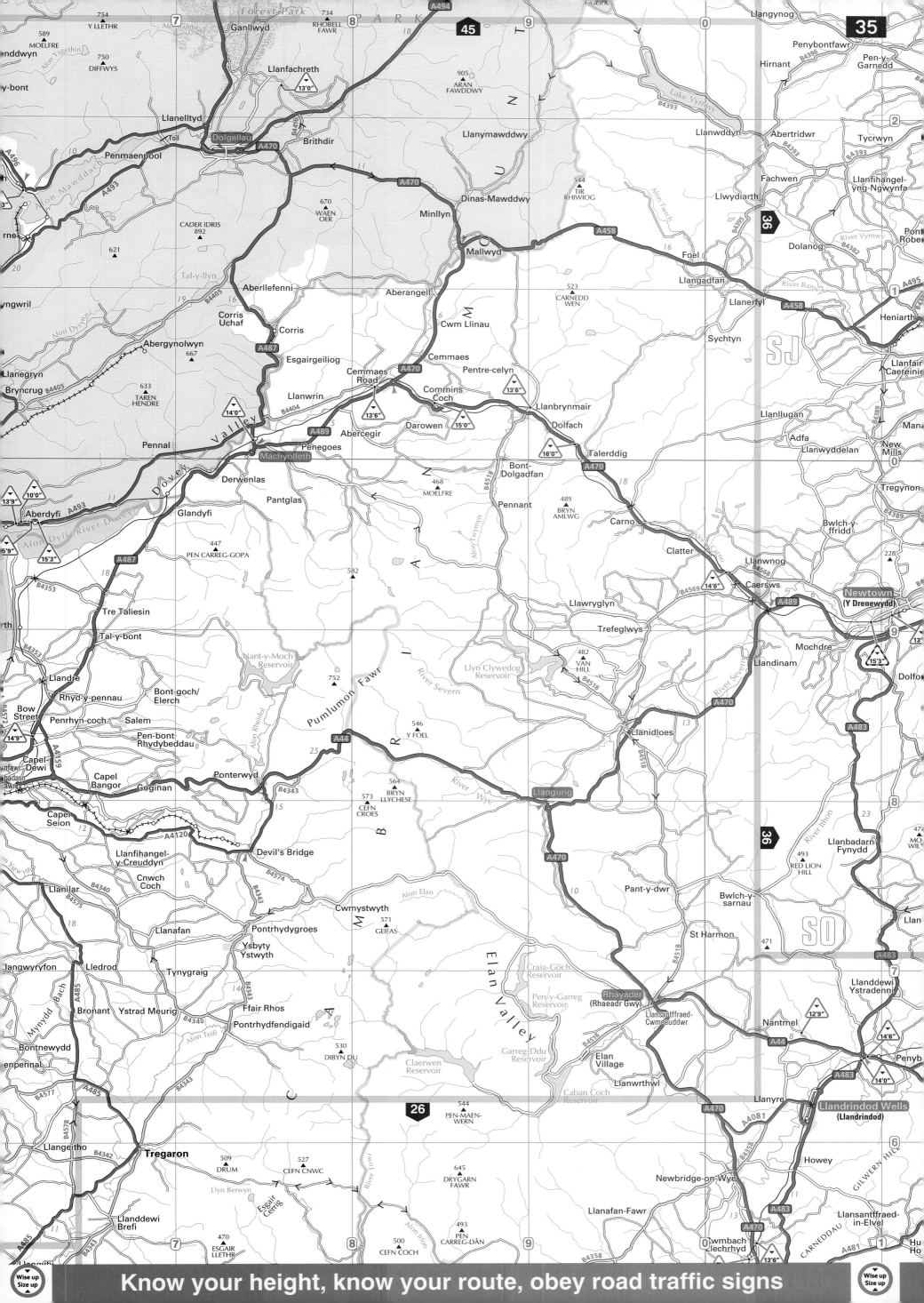

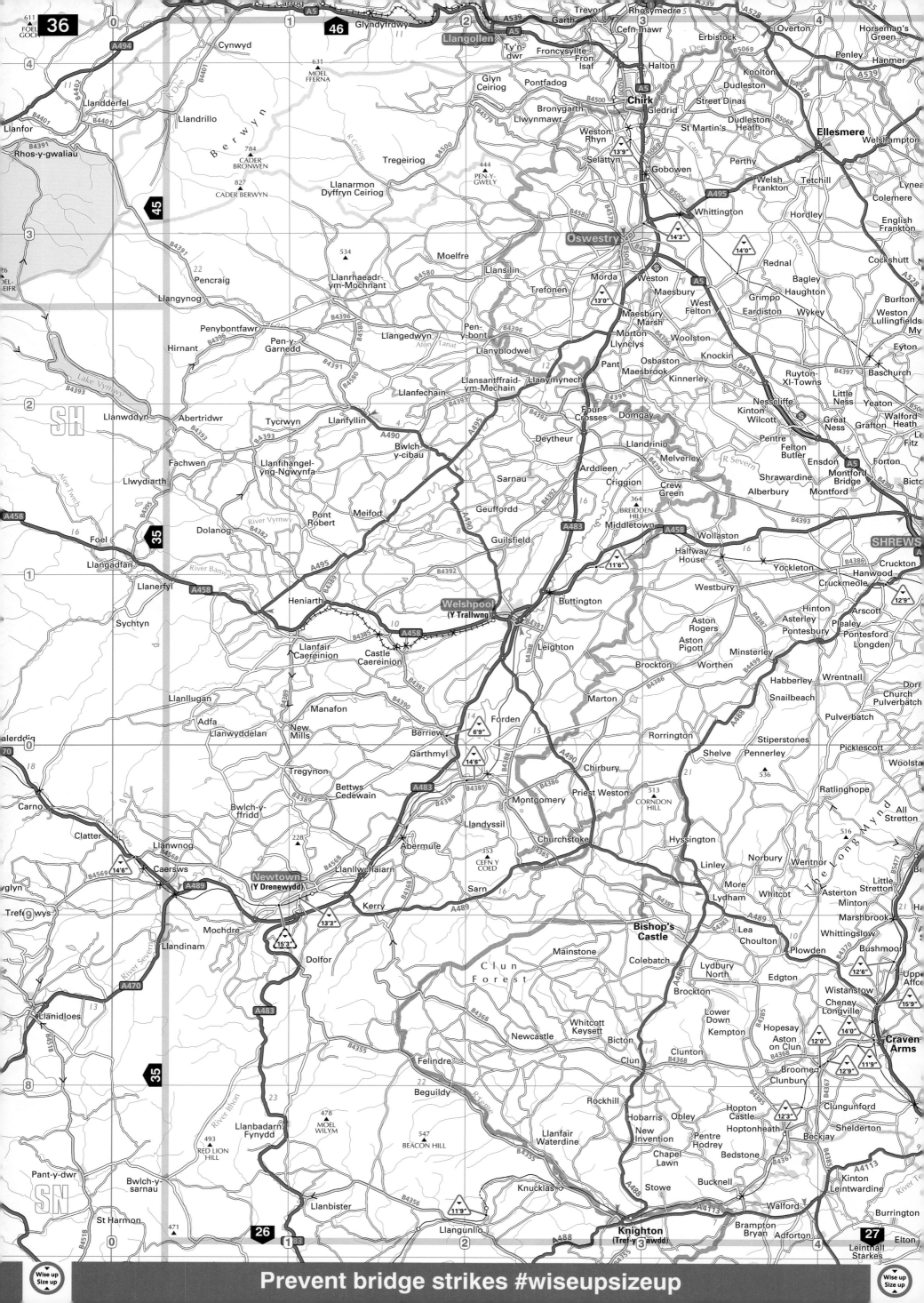

Brancaster
Bay

Holkham Bay

Blakeney Point

Cley next the Sea

Holme next
the Sea
Brancaster
Brancaster
Staithe
Burnham
Deepdale
Burnham
Overy
Staithe
Holkham
Wells-next-
the-Sea
Morston
Blakeney
Stiffkey
Cockthorpe
Wiveton
Glandford

Old
Hunstanton
Thornham
Titchwell
Burnham
Norton
Burnham Overy
Warham
Wighton
Langham
Saxlingham

Hunstanton
Ringstead
Burnham
Market
Burnham
Thorpe
Little
Walsingham
Great
Walsingham
Hindringham
Binham
Field
Dalling
Letheringsett
Sharrington

Heacham
Summerfield
North
Creake
North
Barsham
Houghton St Giles
Bale
Thornage
Brinton
Stody

Sedgeford
Docking
Stanhoe
South
Creake
West
Barsham
East
Barsham
Great
Snoring
Thursford
Barney
Melton
Constable
Swanton
Novers

Snettisham
Fring
Bircham
Newton
Syderstone
Wicken Green
Village
Sculthorpe
Little
Snoring
Croxton
Kettlestone
Fulmodeston
Hindolveston

Ingoldisthorpe
Shernborne
Great
Bircham
Bircham
Tofts
Dunton
Coxford
Shereford
Hempton
Fakenham
Stibbard
Wood
Norton
Guestwick

Dersingham
Anmer
West
Rudham
Tattersett
Tatterford
Toftrees
Little Ryburgh
Great
Ryburgh
Gateley
Twyford
Foulsham

Wolferton
Sandringham
West
Newton
Flitcham
New
Houghton
East
Rudham
East
Raynham
Colkirk
Whissonsett
Horningtoft
Bintree
Billingford
Foxley

Castle Rising
Hillington
Harpley
Helhoughton
West
Raynham
South
Raynham
Wellingham
Brisley
North
Elmham
Worthing

North
Wootton
Congham
Little
Massingham
Weasenham
St Peter
Tittleshall
Stanfield
East
Bilney
Old
Beetley
Beetley
Swanton
Morley

King's Lynn
Roydon
Grimston
Great
Massingham
Weasenham
All Saints
Rough
Mileham
Litcham
Gressenhall
Green
Gressenhall
Hoe
Elsing

West
Lynn
South
Wootton
Gaywood
Fairstead
Gayton
Ashwicken
Gayton
Thorpe
Castle
Acre
West
Lexham
East
Lexham
Beeston
Longham
Dereham
North
Tuddenham

Clenchwarton
Fair Green
East
Winch
West
Acre
Newton
Great
Dunham
Wendling
Scarning
Westfield
Yaxham
Mattishall
Mattishall
Burgh

Tilney
All Saints
Saddlebow
West
Winch
Middleton
East
Walton
West
Bilney
West
Acre
South
Acre
Little
Dunham
Great
Fransham
Little
Fransham
Clint
Green
South
Green

Wiggenhall
St Germans
North
Runcton
Setchey
Blackborough
End
Pentney
Narborough
South
Acre
Sporle
Necton
East
Bradenham
Whinburgh
Brandon
Parva

Wiggenhall
St Mary the
Virgin
Watlington
Tottenhill
Wormegay
Marham
Shouldham
Swaffham
North
Pickenham
Holme
Hale
West
Bradenham
Shipdham
Runhall
Garvestone
Thuxton
Coston

Wiggenhall
Mary Magdalen
Runcton
Holme
South
Runcton
Shouldham
Thorpe
Fincham
Barton
Bendish
Beachamwell
Cockley
Cley
South
Pickenham
Ashill
Saham
Hills
Cranworth
Reymerston

Stowbridge
Stow
Bardolph
Stradsett
Crimplesham
Boughton
Oxborough
Gooderstone
Great
Cressingham
Saham
Toney
Woodrising
Hardingham
Hingham
Southburgh
Hackford

Wimbotsham
Downham
Market
Bexwell
Wereham
Hilborough
Ovington
Carbrooke
Deopham

Denver
West
Dereham
Wretton
Whittington
Foulden
Little
Cressingham
Watton
Griston
Rockland
St Peter
Little
Ellingham
Deopham
Green

Ten Mile
Bank
Hilgay
Stoke
Ferry
Northwold
Merton
Caston
Rockland
All Saints
Fen Street
Great Ellingham

Hilgay Fen
Methwold
Hythe
Methwold
Cranwich
Ickburgh
Thompson
Stow
Bedon
Lower
Stow Bedon
Shropham

Southery
Feltwell
Weeting
Mundford
East
Wretham
Great
Hockham
Snetterton
Eccles
Road
Wilby

Southery
Fens
Methwold Fens
Queens
Ground
Hockwold
Fens
Santon
Downham
Croxton
Larling
Quidenham

Littleport
Burnt Fen
Hockwold
cum Wilton
Brandon
Town
Street
Bridgham
East Harling
Kenninghall

Brettenham
Attleborough

Holkham Bay

TF   **TL**

A149   A148   A47   A10   A1065   A1122   A134   A1101   A11   A1075   A47

OVERALL TRAVELLING HEIGHT CONVERSION

Read in feet horizontally and inches vertically, e.g. 13' 3" = 4.04 metres

		7'	8'	9'	10'	11'	12'	13'	14'	15'	16'
Height in inches (")	9"	2.36m	2.67m	2.97m	3.28m	3.58m	3.89m	4.19m	4.50m	4.80m	5.11m
	6"	2.29m	2.59m	2.90m	3.20m	3.51m	3.81m	4.11m	4.42m	4.72m	5.03m
	3"	2.21m	2.51m	2.82m	3.12m	3.43m	3.73m	4.04m	4.34m	4.65m	4.95m
	0"	2.13m	2.44m	2.74m	3.05m	3.35m	3.66m	3.96m	4.27m	4.57m	4.88m

See inside front cover for full table

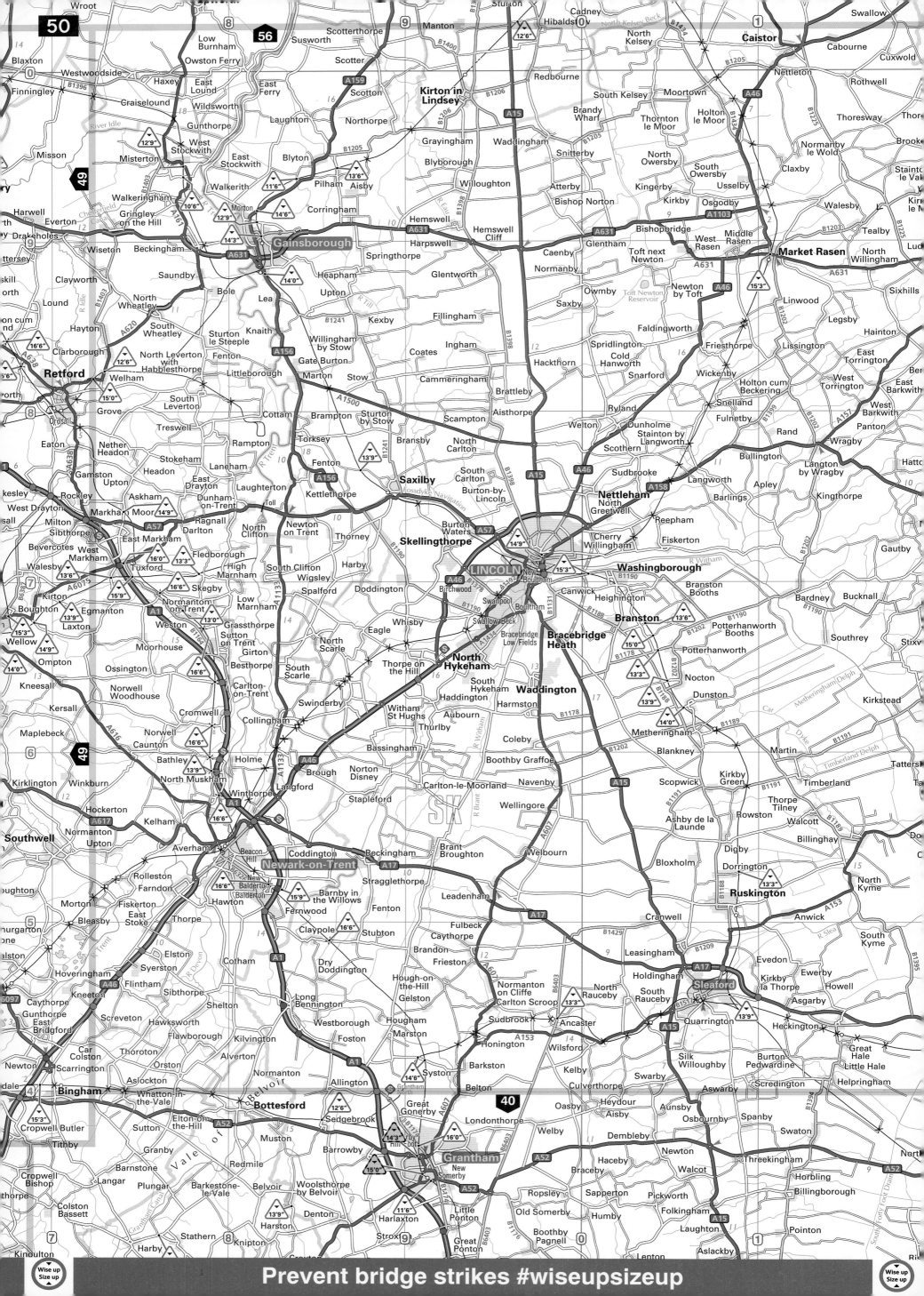

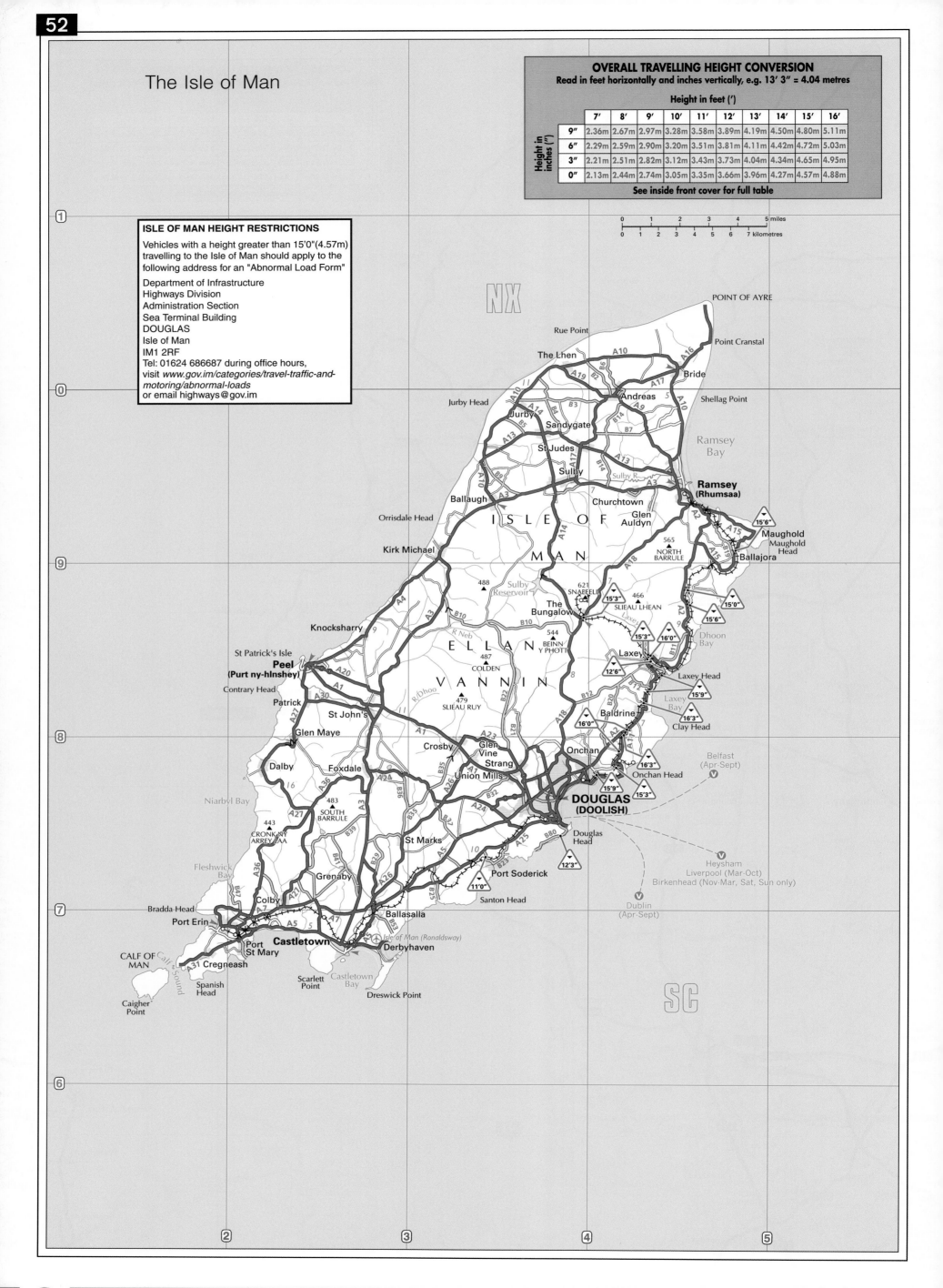

The Isle of Man

OVERALL TRAVELLING HEIGHT CONVERSION
Read in feet horizontally and inches vertically, e.g. 13' 3" = 4.04 metres

Height in feet (')

Height in inches (")	7'	8'	9'	10'	11'	12'	13'	14'	15'	16'
9"	2.36m	2.67m	2.97m	3.28m	3.58m	3.89m	4.19m	4.50m	4.80m	5.11m
6"	2.29m	2.59m	2.90m	3.20m	3.51m	3.81m	4.11m	4.42m	4.72m	5.03m
3"	2.21m	2.51m	2.82m	3.12m	3.43m	3.73m	4.04m	4.34m	4.65m	4.95m
0"	2.13m	2.44m	2.74m	3.05m	3.35m	3.66m	3.96m	4.27m	4.57m	4.88m

See inside front cover for full table

ISLE OF MAN HEIGHT RESTRICTIONS

Vehicles with a height greater than 15'0"(4.57m) travelling to the Isle of Man should apply to the following address for an "Abnormal Load Form"

Department of Infrastructure
Highways Division
Administration Section
Sea Terminal Building
DOUGLAS
Isle of Man
IM1 2RF
Tel: 01624 686687 during office hours,
visit www.gov.im/categories/travel-traffic-and-motoring/abnormal-loads
or email highways@gov.im

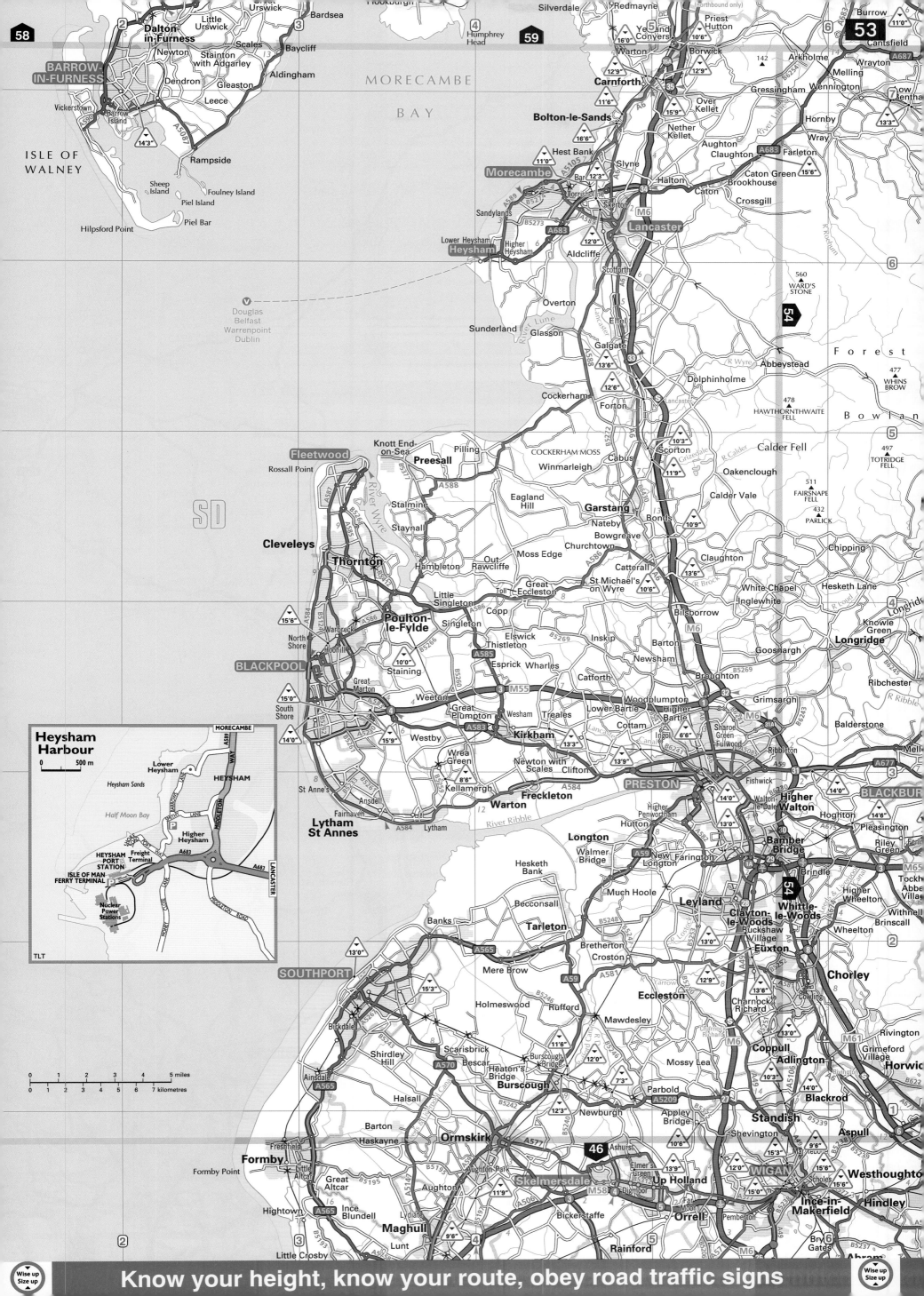

Heysham Harbour

MORECAMBE

0   500 m

Lower Heysham

HEYSHAM

Half Moon Bay

Heysham Sands

P

Higher Heysham

P   Freight Terminal

HEYSHAM PORT STATION

ISLE OF MAN FERRY TERMINAL   P

Nuclear Power Stations

TLT

ISLE OF WALNEY

BARROW-IN-FURNESS

Vickerstown

Barrow Island

Dalton-in-Furness

Little Urswick

Urswick   Bardsea

Newton   Scales   Bayliff

Stainton with Adgarley

Dendron   Gleaston   Aldingham

Leece

Rampside

Sheep Island

Foulney Island

Piel Island

Hilpsford Point   Piel Bar

MORECAMBE   BAY

Humphrey Head

Silverdale

Redmayne

Priest Hutton

Burrow

Cantsfield

Ye and Conyers   Warton   Borwick

Arkholme   Melling   Wrayton

Gressingham   Wennington

Carnforth

Over Kellet   Hornby   Wray

Bolton-le-Sands

Nether Kellet

Aughton   Claughton   Farleton

Hest Bank

Slyne   Halton   Caton Green

Morecambe   Bar   Torrisholme   Skerton   Caton   Brookhouse   Crossgill

Sandylands   Lancaster

Lower Heysham

Heysham   Higher Heysham   Aldcliffe   Scotforth

Douglas   Belfast   Warrenpoint   Dublin

WARD'S STONE   560

Overton   Ellel

Sunderland   Glasson   Galgate   Abbeystead

FOREST

WHINS BROW   477

Cockerham   Forton   Dolphinholme   HAWTHORNTHWAITE FELL   478

Bowland

Fleetwood

Knott End-on-Sea   Pilling   Scorton   Calder Fell   TOTRIDGE FELL   497

Rossall Point

Preesall   COCKERHAM MOSS   Cabus   Oakenclough   FAIRSNAPE FELL   511

Winmarleigh   Calder Vale   PARLICK   432

SD

Stalmine   Eagland Hill   Garstang   Nateby   Bonds   Chipping

Staynall   Bowgreave   Churchtown

Cleveleys   Moss Edge   Claughton   White Chapel   Hesketh Lane

Thornton   Hambleton   Out Rawcliffe   Catterall   Inglewhite

Little Singleton   Great Eccleston   St Michael's on Wyre   Bilsborrow   Knowle Green

Toll   Longridge

Poulton-le-Fylde   Copp   Barton   Goosnargh   Ribchester

North Shore   Singleton   Elswick   Thistleton   Newsham   Balderstone

Warbreck   Esprick   Wharles   Broughton

Boohill   Staining   Catforth   Woodplumpton   Grimsargh

BLACKPOOL   Weeton   Wesham   Treales   Lower Bartle   Higher Bartle

Great Marton   Great Plumpton   Cottam   Sharoe Green   Fulwood   Ingol

South Shore   Westby   Kirkham   Newton with Scales   Clifton   PRESTON   Fishwick

Wrea Green   Kellamergh   Higher Penwortham   Walton-le-Dale   Higher Walton   BLACKBURN

St Anne's   Ansdell   Freckleton   Warton   Hutton   Pleasington

Fairhaven   River Ribble   Longton   New Faringdon   Bamber Bridge   Riley Green

Lytham St Annes   Lytham   Walmer Bridge   Brindle   Higher Wheelton

St Anne's   Hesketh Bank   Longton   Much Hoole   Leyland   Whittle-le-Woods   Withnell   Abbey Village

Banks   Becconsall   Tarleton   Clayton-le-Woods   Euxton   Brinscall

SOUTHPORT   Mere Brow   Bretherton   Croston   Buckshaw Village   Wheelton   Chorley

Birkdale   Holmeswood   Rufford   Eccleston   Charnock Richard   Cowling   Rivington

Scarisbrick   Mawdesley   Mossy Lea   Coppull   Grimeford Village

Shirdley Hill   Bescar   Heaton's Bridge   Burscough   Parbold   Adlington   Horwich

Ainsdale   Halsall   Newburgh   Appley Bridge   Standish   Blackrod

Barton   Burscough Bridge   Shevington   Aspull

Formby   Haskayne   Ormskirk   Ashurst   Up Holland   WIGAN   Westhoughton

Formby Point   Great Altcar   Aughton   Elmer's Green   Ince-in-Makerfield   Hindley

Hightown   Ince Blundell   Lydiate   Skelmersdale   Bickerstaffe   Orrell   Pemberton   Bryn   Gates

Maghull   Lunt   Rainford   Abram

Little Crosby

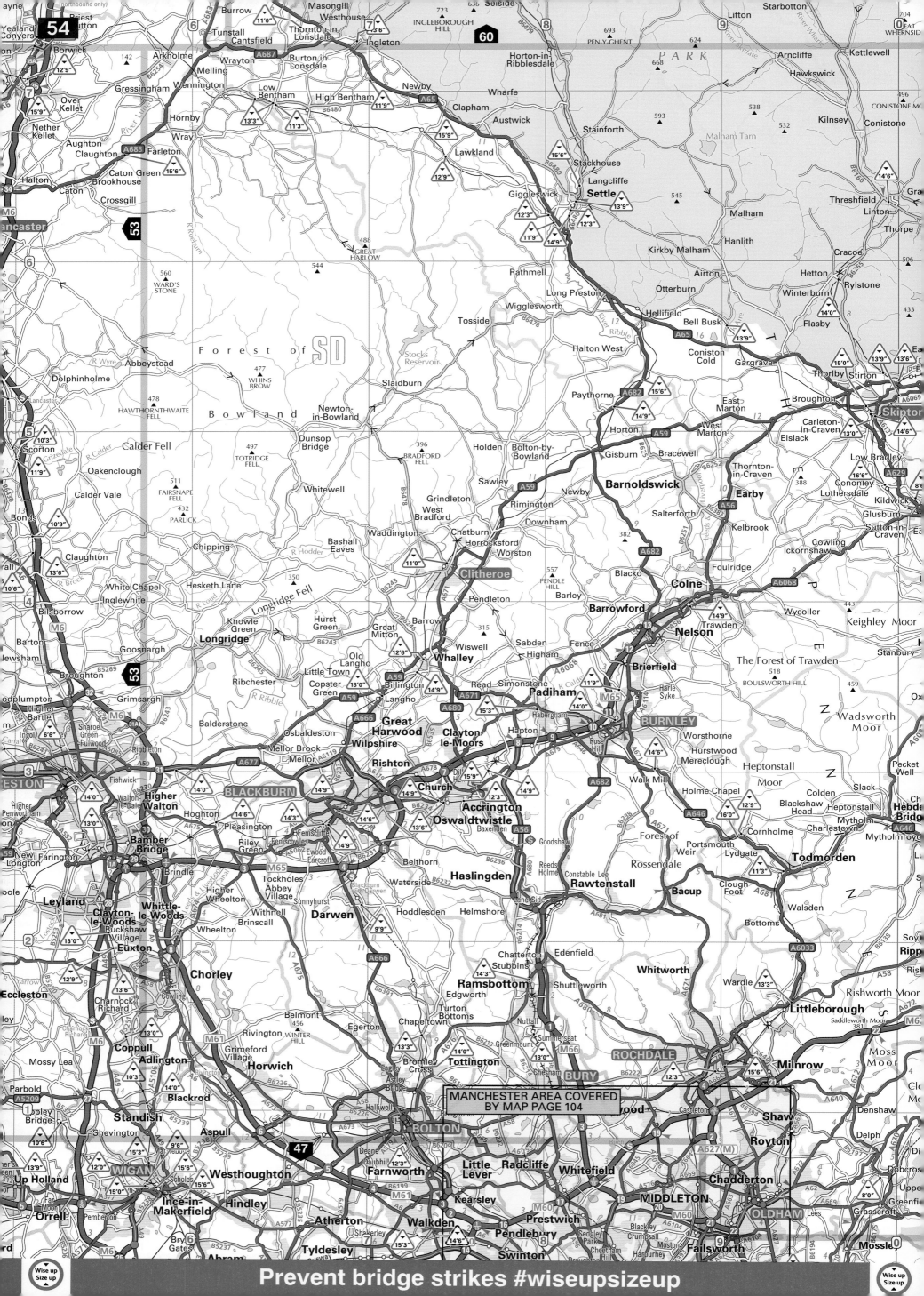

Port of Hull

0   1 km

TLT

Killingholme

0   1 km

SCUNTHORPE   TLT   GRIMSBY

Port of Immingham

0   1km

TLT   GRIMSBY

0   1   2   3   4   5 miles
0   1   2   3   4   5   6   7 kilometres

Wold Newton · Burton Fleming · Speeton · Thornwick Bay · North Landing · Buckton · Bempton · Flamborough · Selwicks Bay · FLAMBOROUGH HEAD
Thwing · Grindale · Sewerby
Rudston · Boynton · Bridlington · BRIDLINGTON BAY
Bessingby · Carnaby · Hilderthorpe
Haisthorpe · Thornholme · Burton Agnes · Harpham · Lowthorpe · Nafferton
Kilham · Ruston Parva
Great Kelk · Lissett · Gransmoor · Fraisthorpe
Wansford · Gembling · Barmston
Skerne · Brigham · Foston on the Wolds · Beeford · Ulrome · Skipsea
North Frodingham · Dunnington · Atwick
Bewholme
Brandesburton · Seaton · Hornsea · Horrnsea Mere
Leven · Catwick · Sigglesthorne · Goxhill · Rolston
Routh · Long Riston · Rise · Great Hatfield · Mappleton · Mappleton Sands
Tickton · Arnold · Great Cowden
Weel · Skirlaugh · New Ellerby · Marton · Withernwick
Woodmansey · Wawne · Old Ellerby · West Newton · Aldbrough
Thearne · Dunswell · Swine · Coniston · Flinton
Bransholme · Ganstead · Wyton · Sproatley · Humbleton · Hilston
Sutton-on-Hull · Bilton · Lelley · Owstwick
Stoneferry · Newland · Elstronwick · Burton Pidsea · Roos · Tunstall
KINGSTON UPON HULL · Marfleet · Preston · Rimswell · Owthorne
East Ella · Hedon · Burstwick · Halsham · Withernsea
Paull · Thorngumbald · Keyingham · Hollym
New Holland · Ottringham · Winestead · Holmpton
Barrow Haven · Barrow-upon-Humber · Patrington · Patrington Haven · Welwick · Weeton · Skeffling · Easington
Goxhill · East Halton · Kilnsea
Thornton Curtis · North Killingholme · South Killingholme · Immingham Dock
Wootton · Ulceby Skitter · Ulceby · Immingham
Habrough · Croxton · Kirmington · Brocklesby · Stallingborough · GRIMSBY · Cleethorpes · SPURN HEAD
Melton Ross · Keelby · Healing · Great Coates · Little Coates · Old Clee
Barnetby le Wold · Great Limber · Aylesby · Nunsthorpe · West Marsh · Humberston
Bigby · Somerby · Riby · Bradley · Laceby · Scartho · New Waltham
Searby · Owmby · Grasby · Clixby · Irby upon Humber · Waltham · Holton le Clay
Caistor · Swallow · Cabourne · Barnoldby le Beck · Brigsley · Beelsby · Ashby cum

Rotterdam (Europoort) Zeebrugge
Hook of Holland Rotterdam (Europoort) Zeebrugge
Brevik, Cuxhaven Esbjerg, Gothenburg Rotterdam (Vlaardingen)

Know your height, know your route, obey road traffic signs

Wise up Size up

67

OVERALL TRAVELLING HEIGHT CONVERSION
Read in feet horizontally and inches vertically, e.g. 13' 3" = 4.04 metres

Height in feet (')

		7'	8'	9'	10'	11'	12'	13'	14'	15'	16'
Height in inches (")	9"	2.36m	2.67m	2.97m	3.28m	3.58m	3.89m	4.19m	4.50m	4.80m	5.11m
	6"	2.29m	2.59m	2.90m	3.20m	3.51m	3.81m	4.11m	4.42m	4.72m	5.03m
	3"	2.21m	2.51m	2.82m	3.12m	3.43m	3.73m	4.04m	4.34m	4.65m	4.95m
	0"	2.13m	2.44m	2.74m	3.05m	3.35m	3.66m	3.96m	4.27m	4.57m	4.88m

See inside front cover for full table

Prevent bridge strikes #wiseupsizeup

Wise up Size up

52

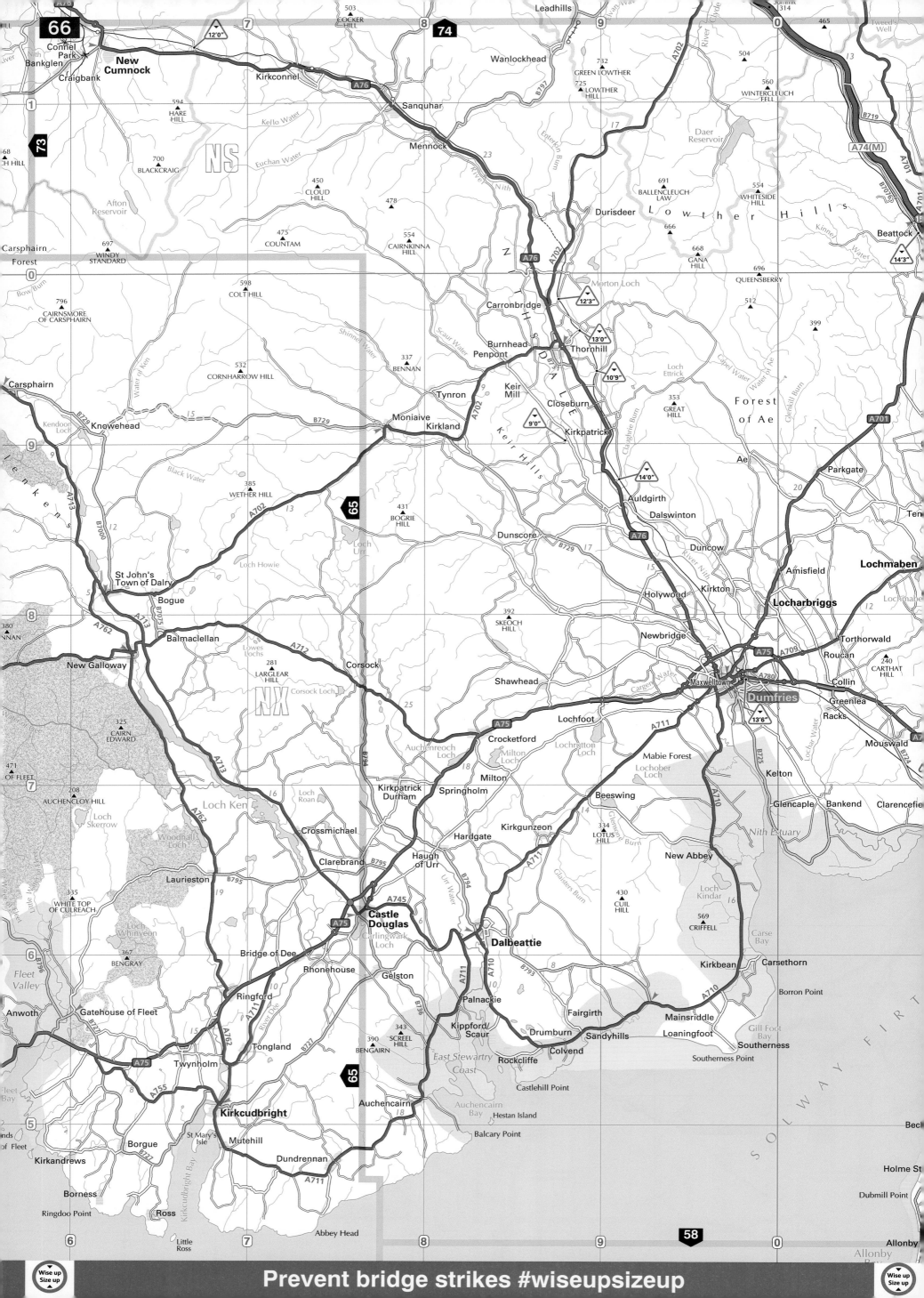

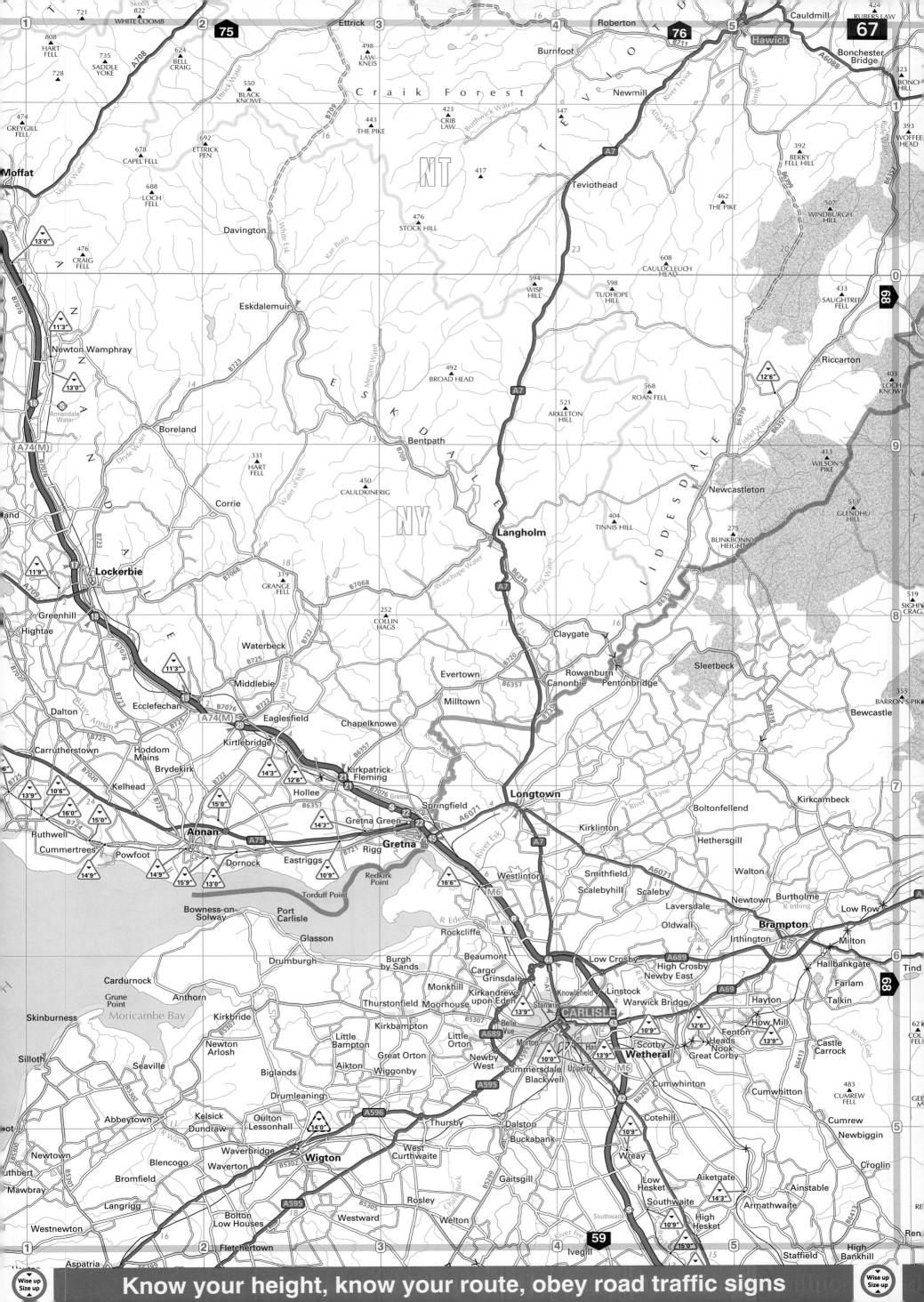

OVERALL TRAVELLING HEIGHT CONVERSION
Read in feet horizontally and inches vertically, e.g. 13' 3" = 4.04 metres

	Height in feet (')									
	7'	**8'**	**9'**	**10'**	**11'**	**12'**	**13'**	**14'**	**15'**	**16'**
9"	2.36m	2.67m	2.97m	3.28m	3.58m	3.89m	4.19m	4.50m	4.80m	5.11m
6"	2.29m	2.59m	2.90m	3.20m	3.51m	3.81m	4.11m	4.42m	4.72m	5.03m
3"	2.21m	2.51m	2.82m	3.12m	3.43m	3.73m	4.04m	4.34m	4.65m	4.95m
0"	2.13m	2.44m	2.74m	3.05m	3.35m	3.66m	3.96m	4.27m	4.57m	4.88m

Height in inches (")

See inside front cover for full table

Port of Tyne

Dangerous goods restriction: Category D

TYNE & WEAR AREA COVERED BY MAP PAGE 105

Amsterdam (IJmuiden)

Know your height, know your route, obey road traffic signs

Wise up Size up

COLONSAY

Kiloran Bay

143
CARNAN EOIN

Rubh' a' Geodha

Eilean Dubh

Colonsay - Oban

Scalasaig

B8087

B8086

B8085

Colonsay

Rubha Bàn

Dubh Eilean

ORONSAY

Eilean Ghaoideamal

Corpach Bay

JURA

Shian Bay

45
RAINBER

Loch Right Mòr

Colonsay - Port Askaig

Rubh' an t-Sàilein

Loch Tarbert

Rubha a' Mhàil

Rubha Bholsa

363
SGARBH BREAC

506
SCRINADLE

398
BEINN TARSUINN

Jura Forest

784
BEINN AN OIR

734

Paps of Jura

Loch a' Chnuic Bhric

24

J u r a

560
GLAS BHEINN

529
DUBH BHEINN

342
BRAT BHEINN

Craighouse

A846

Small Isles

Rubha na Caillich

Nave Island

Ardnave Point

Gortantaoid Point

Bunnahabhain

316
GUIR-BHEINN

NR

Tòn Mhòr

Eilean Mòr

Sanaigmore

Rubha Lamanais

Loch Gorr

Saligo Bay

Coul Point

Kilchoman

Machir Bay

Kilchiaran Bay

Bruichladdich

B8018

B8017

Gleann Mòr

Loch Gruinart

A847

B8018

Loch Finlaggan

Port Askaig

Keills

Ballygrant

8
A846

Loch Ballygrant

Loch Lossit

Bridgend

Loch Indaal

Bowmore

266
BEINNE DUBH

Sound of Islay

Am Fraoch Eilean

Brosdale Island

Rubha na Tràille

429
SGÒRR NAM FAOILEANN

471

McArthur's Head

Kilennan Burn

RHINNS OF ISLAY

15

Port Charlotte

231
BEINN TART A'MHILL

Lossit Bay

Rubha na Faing

Portnahaven

Port Wemyss

Orsay

RHINNS POINT

Laggan Point

Laggan Bay

Duich R

River Laggan

A846

B8016

ISLAY

Islay

490
BEINN BHEIGEIR

Rubha Liath

454
BEINN URARAIDH

Loch Uraraidh

Claggain Bay

Ardmore Point

346
BEINN SHOLUM

Rubha Mòr

MAOL BUIDHE
165

THE OA

MULL OF OA

Loch Kinnabus

Kilnaughton Bay

Port Ellen

A846

Texa

Laphroaig

Lagavulin

Ardbeg

3

Rubha na Gainmhich

Eilean a' Chùirn

Port Ellen - Kennacraig

Port Ellen - Kennacraig

Rubha nan Leacan

OVERALL TRAVELLING HEIGHT CONVERSION
Read in feet horizontally and inches vertically, e.g. 13' 3" = 4.04 metres

Height in feet (')

Height in inches (")	7'	8'	9'	10'	11'	12'	13'	14'	15'	16'
9"	2.36m	2.67m	2.97m	3.28m	3.58m	3.89m	4.19m	4.50m	4.80m	5.11m
6"	2.29m	2.59m	2.90m	3.20m	3.51m	3.81m	4.11m	4.42m	4.72m	5.03m
3"	2.21m	2.51m	2.82m	3.12m	3.43m	3.73m	4.04m	4.34m	4.65m	4.95m
0"	2.13m	2.44m	2.74m	3.05m	3.35m	3.66m	3.96m	4.27m	4.57m	4.88m

See inside front cover for full table

0 1 2 3 4 5 miles
0 1 2 3 4 5 6 7 kilometres

OVERALL TRAVELLING HEIGHT CONVERSION
Read in feet horizontally and inches vertically, e.g. 13' 3" = 4.04 metres

	Height in feet (')									
	7'	**8'**	**9'**	**10'**	**11'**	**12'**	**13'**	**14'**	**15'**	**16'**
9"	2.36m	2.67m	2.97m	3.28m	3.58m	3.89m	4.19m	4.50m	4.80m	5.11m
6"	2.29m	2.59m	2.90m	3.20m	3.51m	3.81m	4.11m	4.42m	4.72m	5.03m
3"	2.21m	2.51m	2.82m	3.12m	3.43m	3.73m	4.04m	4.34m	4.65m	4.95m
0"	2.13m	2.44m	2.74m	3.05m	3.35m	3.66m	3.96m	4.27m	4.57m	4.88m

Height in inches (")

See inside front cover for full table

Prevent bridge strikes #wiseupsizeup

Wise up Size up

Wise up Size up

OVERALL TRAVELLING HEIGHT CONVERSION
Read in feet horizontally and inches vertically, e.g. 13' 3" = 4.04 metres

	Height in feet (')									
	7'	8'	9'	10'	11'	12'	13'	14'	15'	16'
9"	2.36m	2.67m	2.97m	3.28m	3.58m	3.89m	4.19m	4.50m	4.80m	5.11m
6"	2.29m	2.59m	2.90m	3.20m	3.51m	3.81m	4.11m	4.42m	4.72m	5.03m
3"	2.21m	2.51m	2.82m	3.12m	3.43m	3.73m	4.04m	4.34m	4.65m	4.95m
0"	2.13m	2.44m	2.74m	3.05m	3.35m	3.66m	3.96m	4.27m	4.57m	4.88m

Height in inches (")

See inside front cover for full table

Ardnamurchan Point

Bàgh a' Chaisteil
(Castlebay)
Loch Baghasdail
(Lochboisdale)
(Oct-Mar)

Eilean Mòr

Rubha
Mòr

Rubha
Sgor-innis

Bousd

Cliad
Bay

B8072

Arnabost

B8071

Loch
Cliad

Hogh Bay

Arinagour

COLL

Coll Oban

Quinish Point

Bàgh a' Chaisteil
(Castlebay)

(Apr-Oct, Weds only)

Feall
Bay

Coll

Eilean
Ornsay

Caliach Point

Calgary

Calgary Point

Crossapol
Bay

Loch Breachacha

Rubha
Fàsachd

Gunna

Calgary Bay

342
CÀRN MÒR

Treshnish Point

Rubh' a' Chaoil

Rubha Port
Bhiosd

Balephetrish
Bay

B8068

Caoles

B8069

Rubha Dubh

Ruaig

Fladda

Lunga

Loch Tu

Loch
Bhasapoll

Hough
Bay

Ballevullin

B8068

Gott
Bay

Tiree

Scarinish

B8065

Crossapol

TIREE

Hynish Bay

Gometra

ULVA

Balemartine

B8065

B8067

Loch a
Phuill

Rinn
Thorbhais

Hynish

Balephuill Bay

TRESHNISH
ISLES

Bac Mòr or Dutchman's Cap

Bac Beag

Staffa

Little Colonsay

Inch

Loch na Keal
Isle of Mull

NL

IONA

Rubha nan Cearc

Kintra

Fionnphort

Sound of Iona

Loch na
Lathaich

CREAC

A849

Bunessan

Loch Ass

ROSS OF MULL

Soa Island

Erraid

Rubh'
Ardalanish

Torran Rocks

Kiloran Bay

143
CARNAN
EOIN

COLONSAY

0 1 2 3 4 5 miles
0 1 2 3 4 5 6 7 kilometres

OVERALL TRAVELLING HEIGHT CONVERSION
Read in feet horizontally and inches vertically, e.g. 13' 3" = 4.04 metres

Height in feet (')

Height in inches (")	7'	8'	9'	10'	11'	12'	13'	14'	15'	16'
9"	2.36m	2.67m	2.97m	3.28m	3.58m	3.89m	4.19m	4.50m	4.80m	5.11m
6"	2.29m	2.59m	2.90m	3.20m	3.51m	3.81m	4.11m	4.42m	4.72m	5.03m
3"	2.21m	2.51m	2.82m	3.12m	3.43m	3.73m	4.04m	4.34m	4.65m	4.95m
0"	2.13m	2.44m	2.74m	3.05m	3.35m	3.66m	3.96m	4.27m	4.57m	4.88m

See inside front cover for full table

Wise up
Size up

Prevent bridge strikes #wiseupsizeup

Wise up
Size up

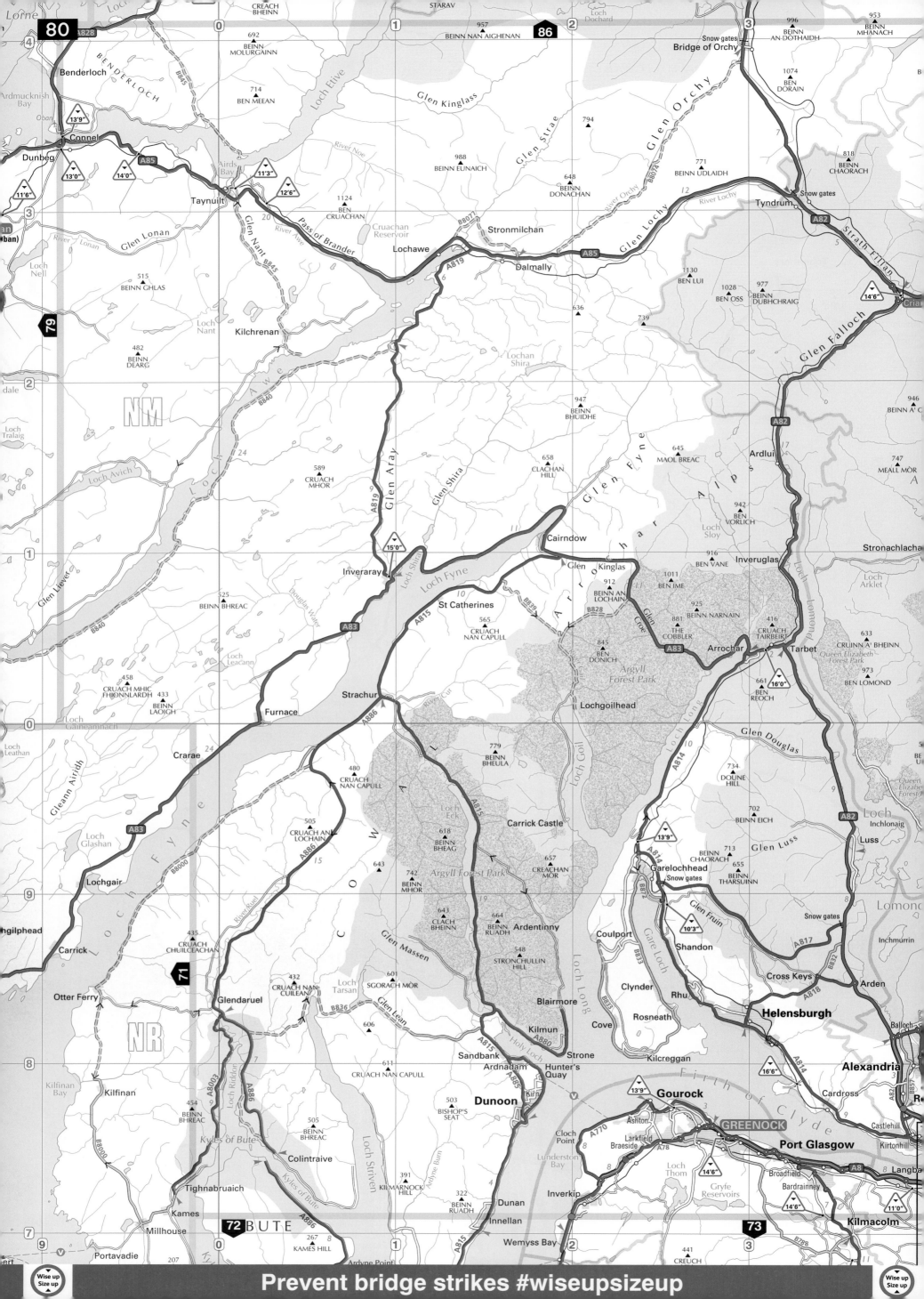

Port of Rosyth

0   500 m

DUNFERMLINE   A823(M)   PERTH
ROSYTH STATION
Rosyth
ADMIRALTY ROAD   A985
A985
Admiralty Business Park
HILTON ROAD
HM Naval Base
Rosyth Dockyard
Inverkeithing
13'9"
13'3"
Buses & taxis only
13'6"
North Queensferry
St Margaret's Hope
EDINBURGH
TLT

OVERALL TRAVELLING HEIGHT CONVERSION
Read in feet horizontally and inches vertically, e.g. 13' 3" = 4.04 metres

Height in feet (')

Height in inches (")	7'	8'	9'	10'	11'	12'	13'	14'	15'	16'
9"	2.36m	2.67m	2.97m	3.28m	3.58m	3.89m	4.19m	4.50m	4.80m	5.11m
6"	2.29m	2.59m	2.90m	3.20m	3.51m	3.81m	4.11m	4.42m	4.72m	5.03m
3"	2.21m	2.51m	2.82m	3.12m	3.43m	3.73m	4.04m	4.34m	4.65m	4.95m
0"	2.13m	2.44m	2.74m	3.05m	3.35m	3.66m	3.96m	4.27m	4.57m	4.88m

See inside front cover for full table

Rape
Hoe Point
488
HEALAVAL BHEAG
Harlosh
Harlosh Island
Colbost Point
Glen Ose
ISLE
417
BEINN NA GRÈINE
412
BEN TIANAVAIG
444
DUN CAAN
Rubha na' Lea

368
BEINN NA BOINEID
Tarner Island
Bracadale
Coillore
Loch Duagrich
A87
Tianavaig Bay
Clachan
310
BEINN NA LEAC

Loch Bracadale
Struan
Wiay
439
ROINEVAL
OF
The Braes
V
Eyre Point

Idrigill Point
Oronsay
The Braes
444
BEN LEE
Suisnish Point

Rubha nan Clach
B8009
SKYE
Sconser
396
MULLACH NA CARN

369
ARNAVAL
Carbost
Drynoch
A863
Glen Drynoch
Sligachan
773
GLAMAIG
A87
Loch Ainort
Dunan

Talisker Bay
Glen Eynort
369
BEINN BHREAC
NG
564
GLAS BHEIN MHORN
708
BEINN DEORG MHOR
732
BEINN NA CAILLICH
Broadf

Minginish
Glen Brittle Forest
965
SGURR NAN GILLEAN
The Cuillin Hills
927
BLAVEN
Torrin

447
BEINN BHREAC
974
SGURR A' GHEADAIDH
Cuillin Hills
Loch na Crèithéach

Loch Eynort
1009
SGURR ALASDAIR
Loch Coruisk
344
BEN MEABOST
Rubha Suisnish

434
AN CRUACHIN
Loch Brittle
225
CEANN NA BEINNE
894
GARS BHEINN
Elgol
Loch Eishor

Rubha an Dùnain
Soay Sound
139
BEINN BHREAC
Loch Scavaig
Strathaird Point

SOAY
Rubh' Aonghais
Tarskavaig

CUILLIN SOUND
Tarskavaig Bay

Loch Baghasdail (Lochboisdale)
V

CANNA
210
CÀRN A' GHAILL
Ardvasa

Garrisdale Point
Canna Harbour
Sanday
Kilmory Bay
Rubha Shamhnan Insir
302
MULLACH MOR
Rubha na Roinne
Aird of Sleat

Sound of Canna
A' Bhrìdeanach
570
ORVAL
Kinloch
Loch Cresort
Point of Sleat
Ard Thurinish

Oigh-sgeir
RÙM
810
ASKIVAL

Harris Bay
763
SGÙRR NAN GILLEAN
NM

The Small Isles
Rubha nam Meirleach
Sound of Rùm

Bay of Laig
299
AN CRUACHAN
Eilean Igh

Rubha an Fhasaidh
EIGG
Luinga Mhòr

393
AN SGÙRR
Rubh' Arisaig

Sound of Eigg
Eilean Chathastail
CRU DO

Eilean nan Each
MUCK

Rubha Àird Druimnich

Ockle Point
Morar, Moidart
Ardnamurchar

0 1 2 3 4 5 miles
0 1 2 3 4 5 6 7 kilometres

OVERALL TRAVELLING HEIGHT CONVERSION
Read in feet horizontally and inches vertically, e.g. 13' 3" = 4.04 metres

Height in feet (')

Height in inches (")	7'	8'	9'	10'	11'	12'	13'	14'	15'	16'
9"	2.36m	2.67m	2.97m	3.28m	3.58m	3.89m	4.19m	4.50m	4.80m	5.11m
6"	2.29m	2.59m	2.90m	3.20m	3.51m	3.81m	4.11m	4.42m	4.72m	5.03m
3"	2.21m	2.51m	2.82m	3.12m	3.43m	3.73m	4.04m	4.34m	4.65m	4.95m
0"	2.13m	2.44m	2.74m	3.05m	3.35m	3.66m	3.96m	4.27m	4.57m	4.88m

See inside front cover for full table

Wise up Size up

Prevent bridge strikes #wiseupsizeup

Wise up Size up

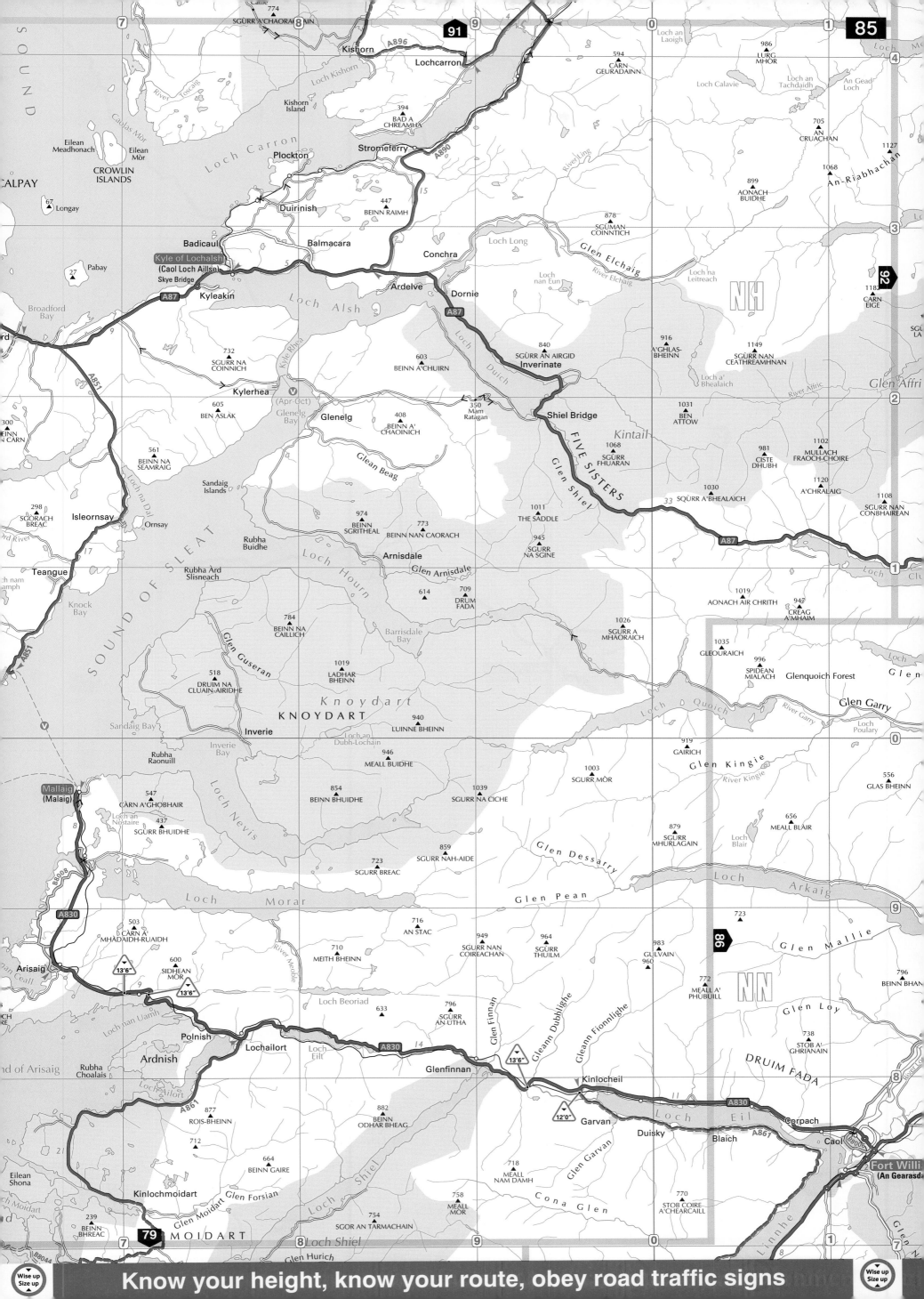

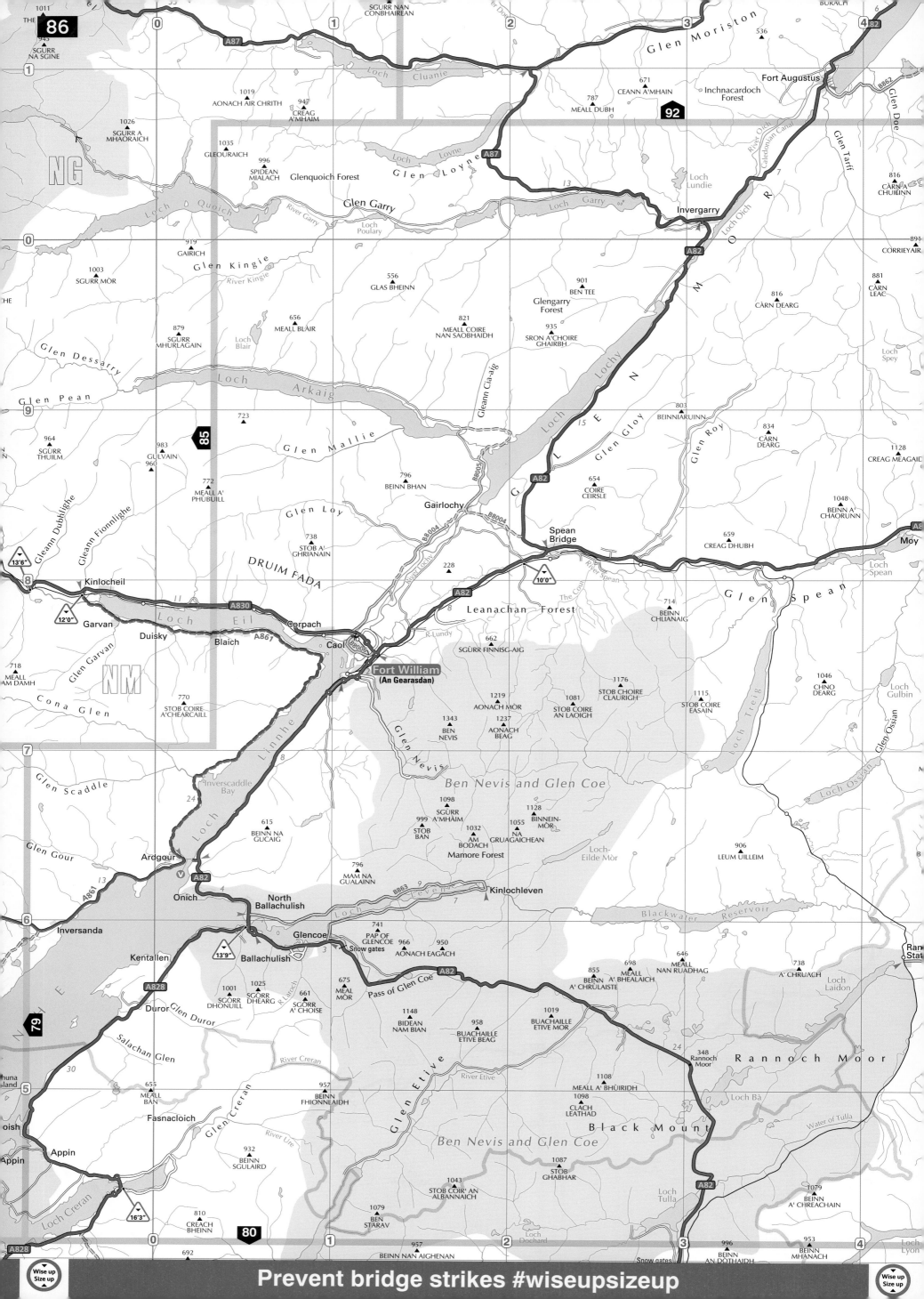

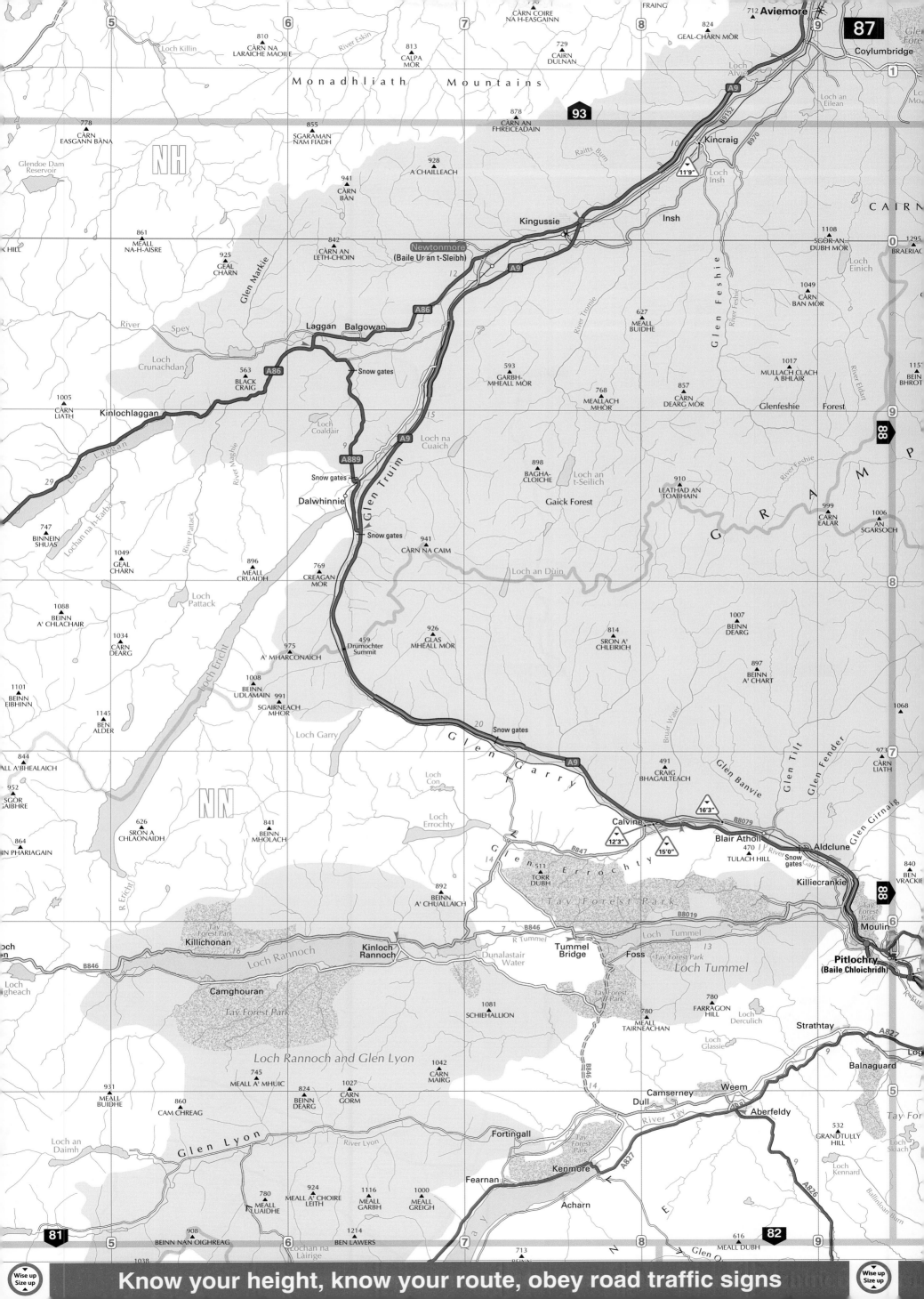

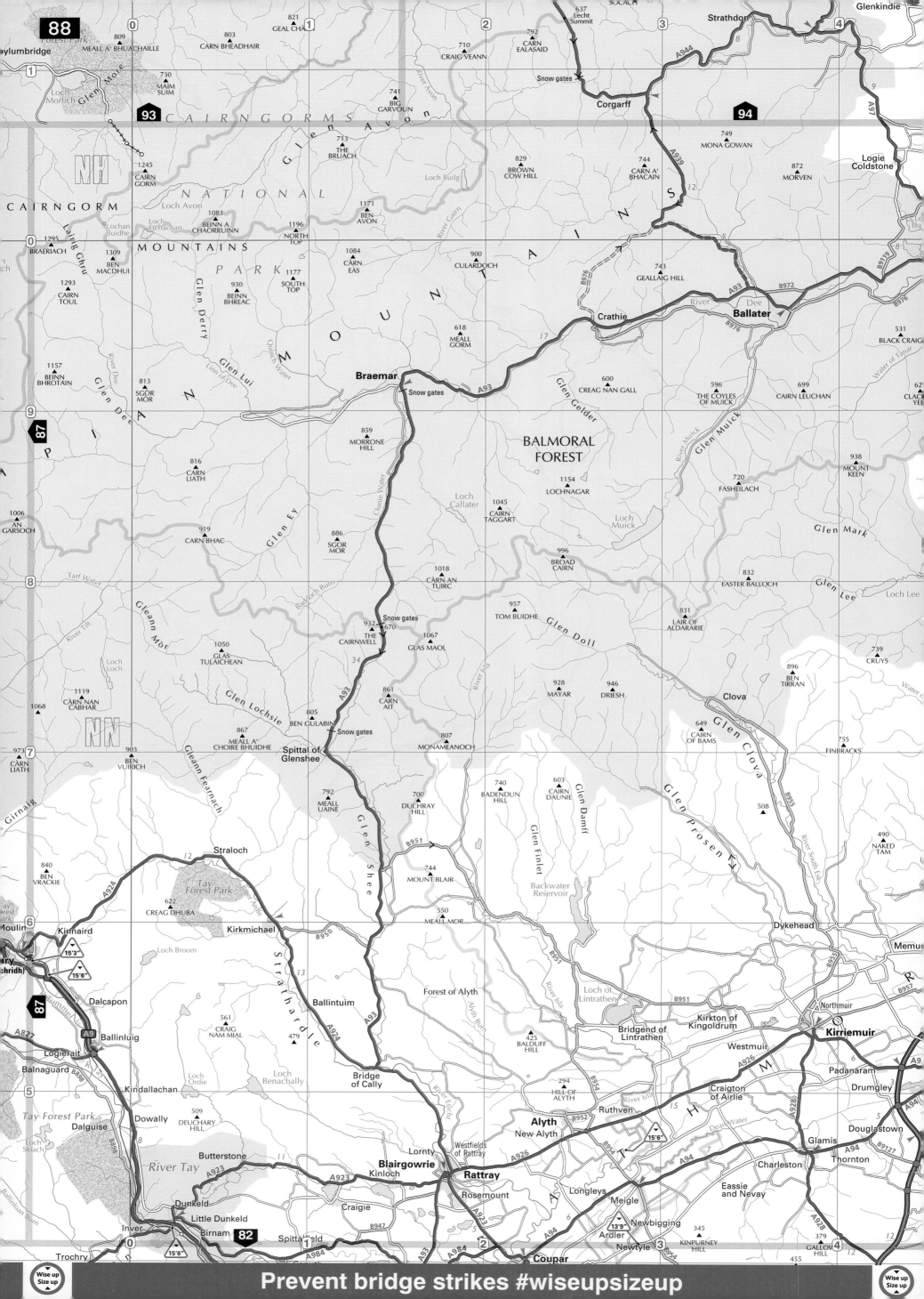

OVERALL TRAVELLING HEIGHT CONVERSION
Read in feet horizontally and inches vertically, e.g. 13' 3" = 4.04 metres

	Height in feet (')									
	7'	**8'**	**9'**	**10'**	**11'**	**12'**	**13'**	**14'**	**15'**	**16'**
9"	2.36m	2.67m	2.97m	3.28m	3.58m	3.89m	4.19m	4.50m	4.80m	5.11m
6"	2.29m	2.59m	2.90m	3.20m	3.51m	3.81m	4.11m	4.42m	4.72m	5.03m
3"	2.21m	2.51m	2.82m	3.12m	3.43m	3.73m	4.04m	4.34m	4.65m	4.95m
0"	2.13m	2.44m	2.74m	3.05m	3.35m	3.66m	3.96m	4.27m	4.57m	4.88m

Height in inches (")

See inside front cover for full table

0   1   2   3   4   5 miles
0   1   2   3   4   5   6   7 kilometres

Know your height, know your route, obey road traffic signs

Wise up Size up

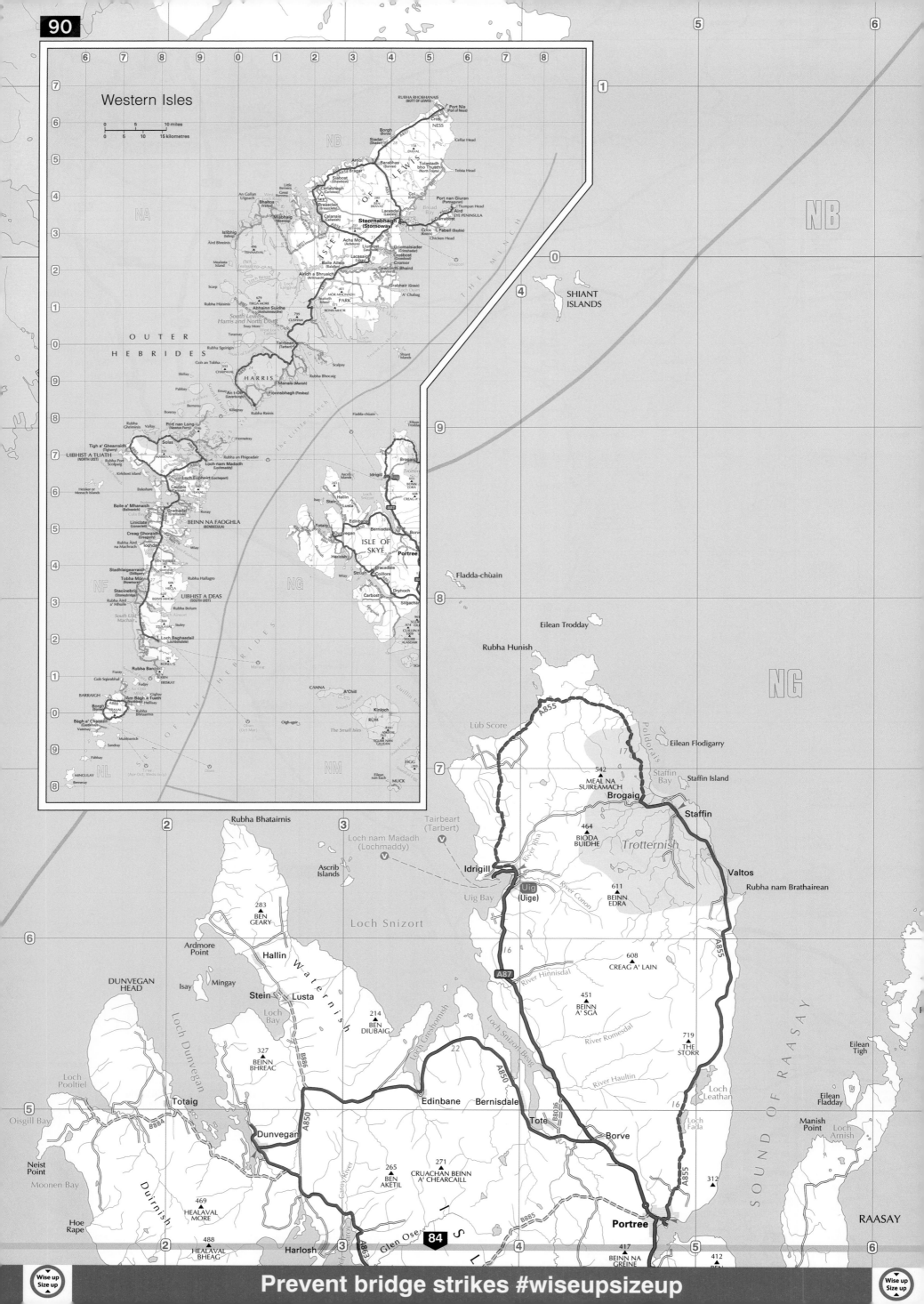

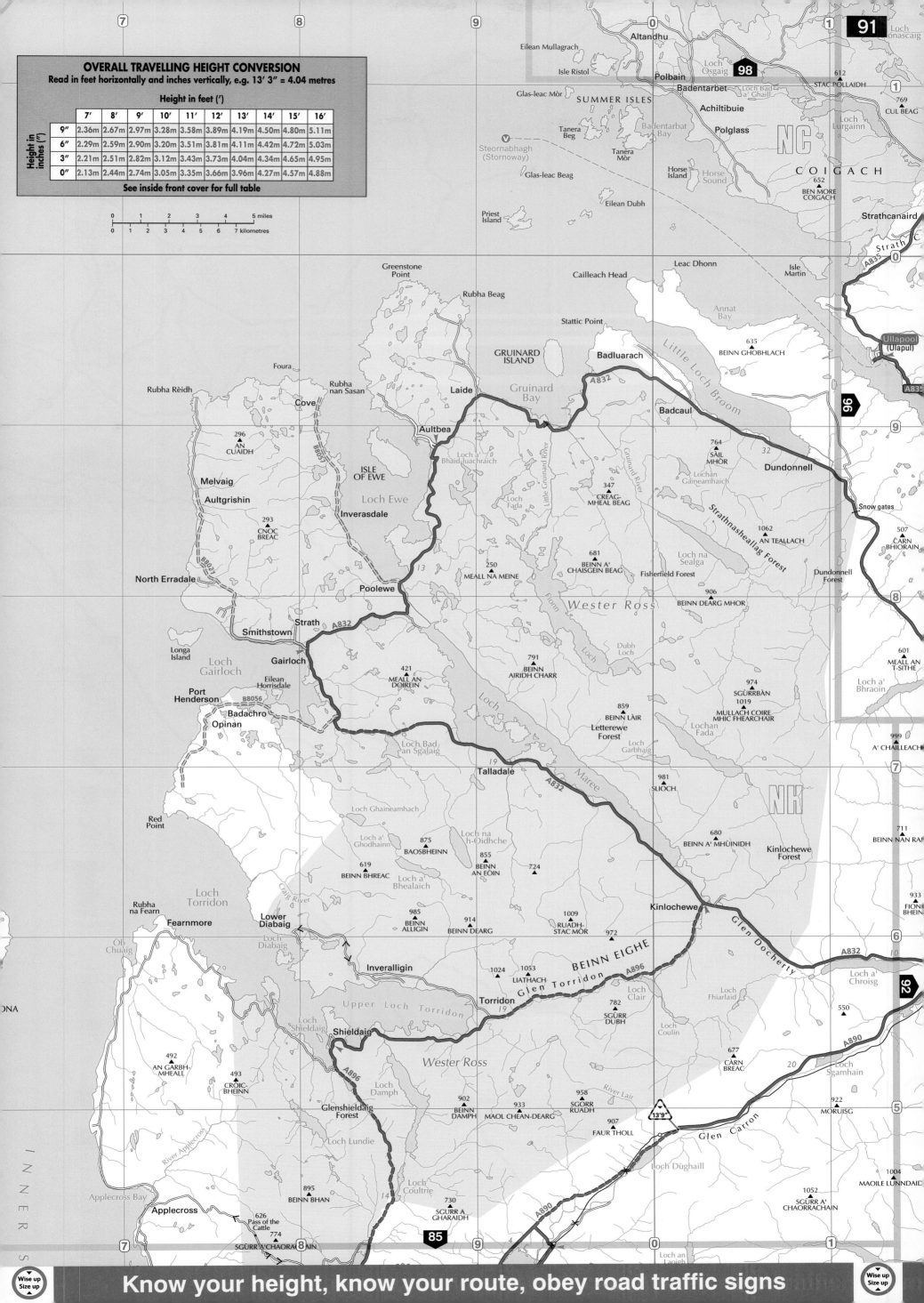

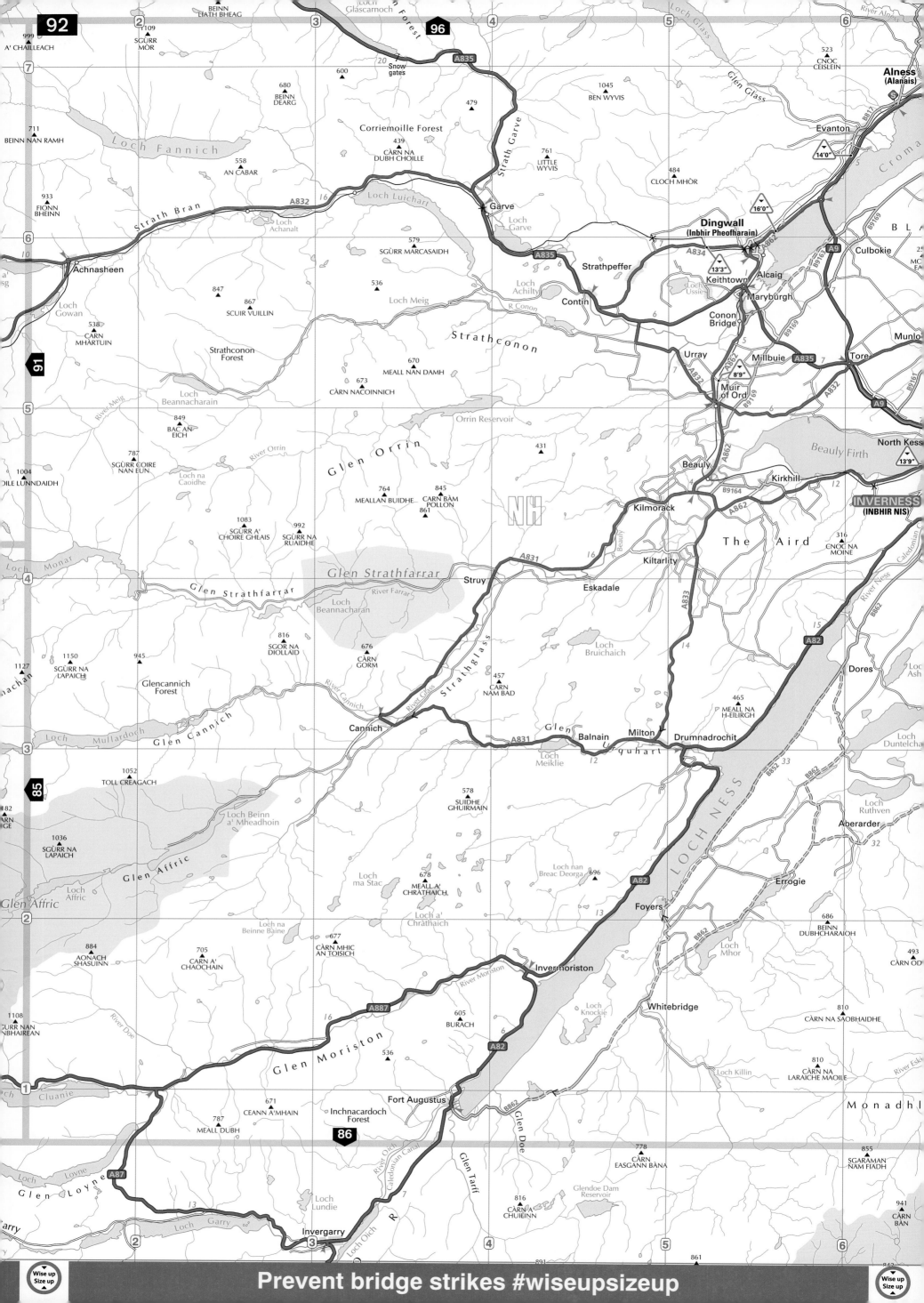

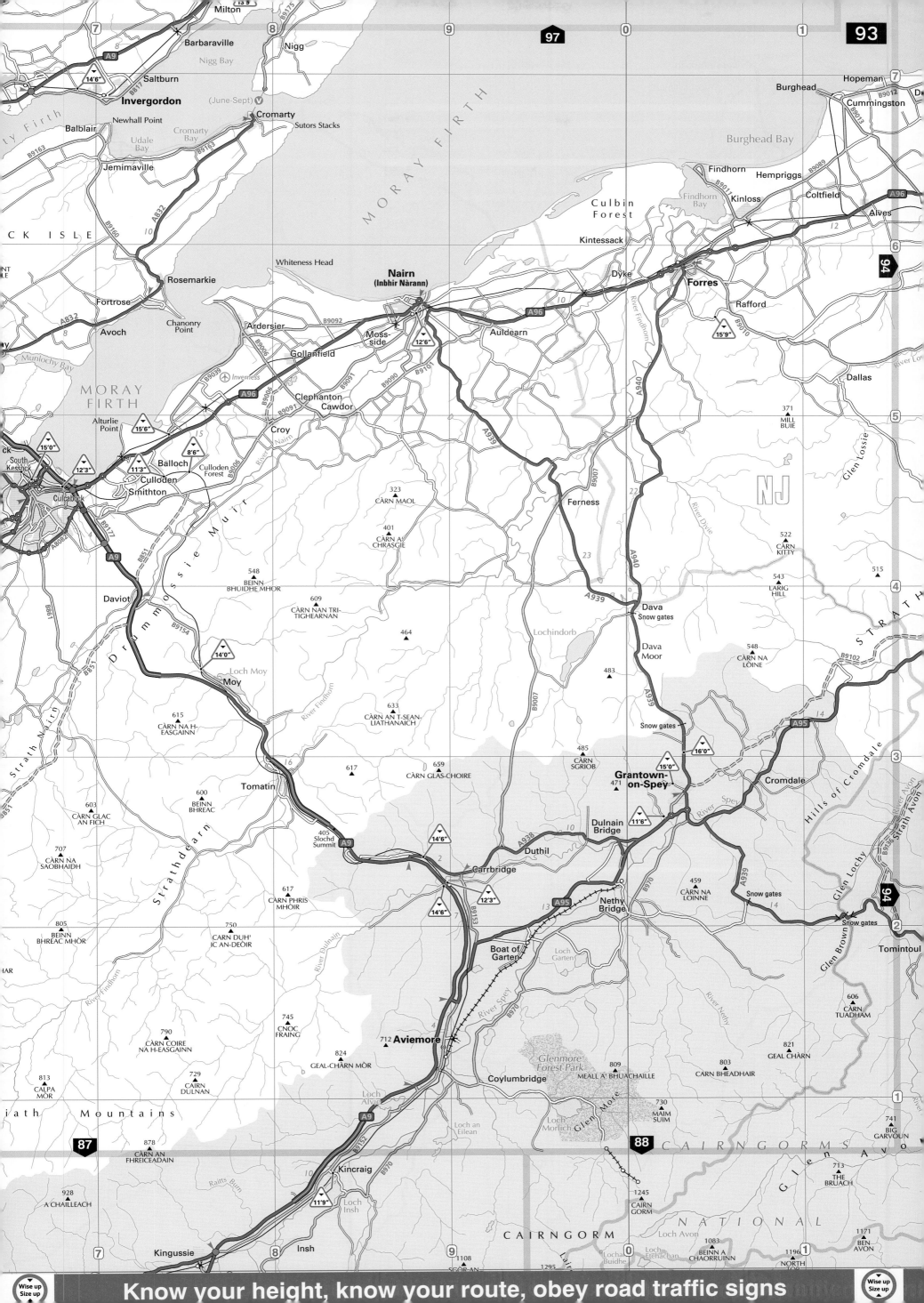

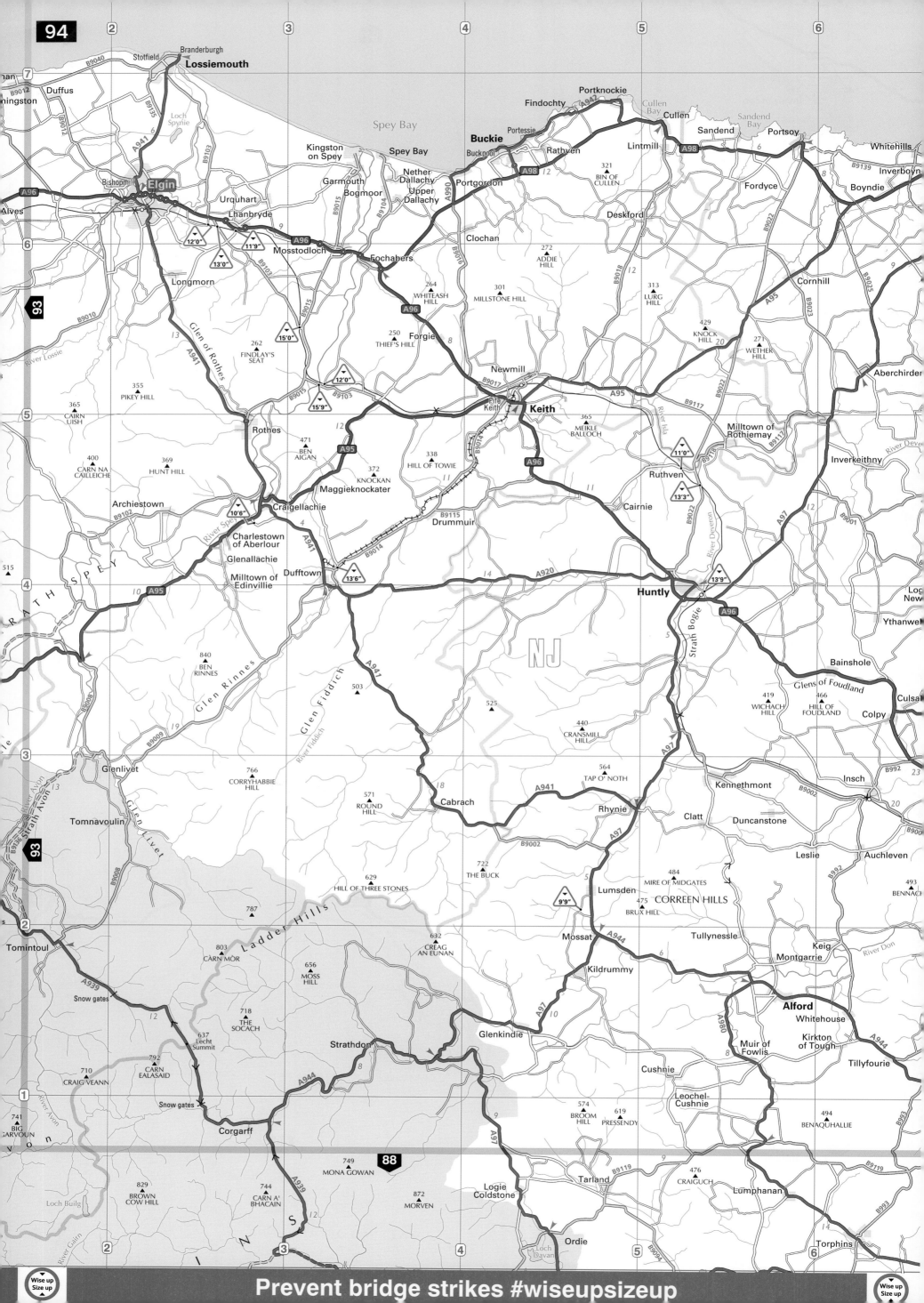

Wise up Size up

Wise up Size up

Know your height, know your route, obey road traffic signs

Wise up
Size up

Wise up
Size up

Aberdeen Harbour

0 · · · 500 m

ELGIN · PETERHEAD

ABERDEEN

ABERDEEN STATION

FERRY TERMINAL

Footdee

North Pier

Ferryhill

Torry

DUNDEE · TLT

Banff · Macduff
Boyndie Bay · Banff Bay

Kirktown of Alvah

Troup Head · Cullykhan Bay
Gardenstown · Crovie · Pennan
New Aberdour · Aberdour Bay

Rosehearty · Pittulie · Sandhaven
Peathill · Kinnaird Head
Kirktown · **Fraserburgh**
Fraserburgh Bay

Inverallochy
Whitelinks Bay
St Combs

Memsie

Rathen

Crimond · Loch of Strathbeg
Rattray Head

BRACKLAMORE HILL · 221

New Pitsligo

WAUGHTON HILL · 234
Strichen

New Leeds

St Fergus
Scotstown Head

Garmond

Cuminestown

New Deer

Maud

Fetterangus

Old Deer

Rora

Turriff

Auchterless

Fyvie · Woodhead

Methlick
R. Ythan

Gordonstown

Rothienorman

Barthol Chapel

Tarves

Kirkton of Rayne
Old Rayne

Durno

Whiteford
Oyne · Pitcaple
Chapel of Garioch

518

Daviot

Oldmeldrum

Stuartfield

Clola

Auchnagatt

Mintlaw · Longside
River Ugie
Peterhead

NK

Hatton

Bogbrae

Birness

Ellon

Kirkton of Logie Buchan
Collieston

Whinnyfold · The Skares

Buchanhaven · **Peterhead**
Invernettie
Peterhead Bay
Boddam
Buchan Ness

Cruden Bay
Bay of Cruden

North Haven

Pitmedden
Logierieve

Newburgh

Inverurie
Port Elphinstone

Kirktown of Bourtie

Udny Green
Udny Station

Cultercullen

Balmedie

Kemnay · Kintore

Monymusk

Sauchen
Lyne of Skene

Dunecht

Echt · Garlogie

HILL OF FARE · 471

Blackburn

Hatton of Fintray

Newmachar · Kingseat

Potterton

Dyce
Stoneywood
Bankhead
Middleton Denmore Park

Bridge of Don

Old Aberdeen

Westhill · Kingswells
Kirkton of Skene
Loch of Skene
BRIMMOND HILL · 265

Northfield

Kittybrewster

ABERDEEN

Peterculter
Milltimber
Milton of Murtle
Bieldside · Cults

Ruthrieston
Mannofield

Torry

Nigg Bay

Altens Haven
Cove Bay

Kirkwall
Lerwick

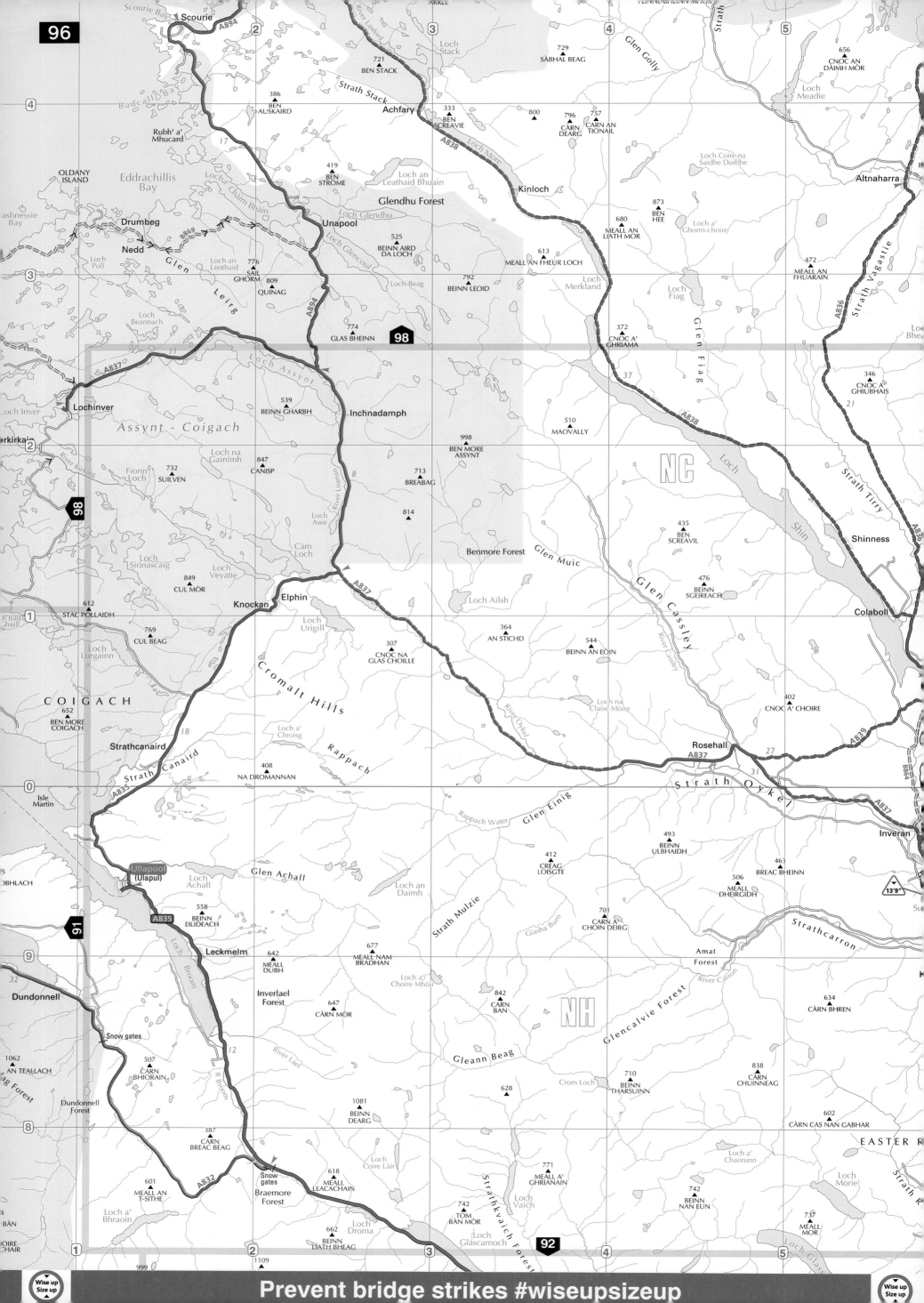

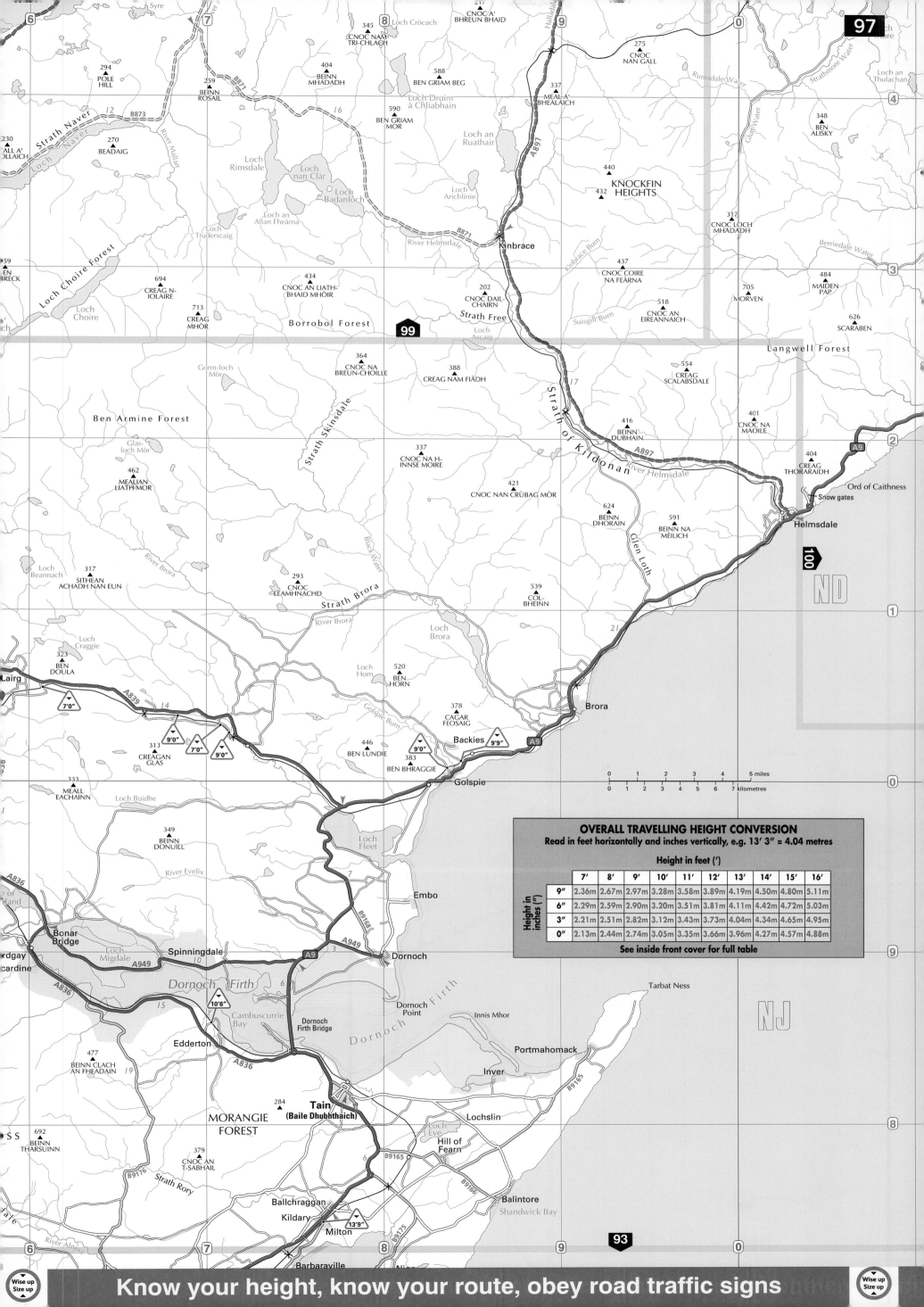

OVERALL TRAVELLING HEIGHT CONVERSION
Read in feet horizontally and inches vertically, e.g. 13' 3" = 4.04 metres

	Height in feet (')									
	7'	**8'**	**9'**	**10'**	**11'**	**12'**	**13'**	**14'**	**15'**	**16'**
9"	2.36m	2.67m	2.97m	3.28m	3.58m	3.89m	4.19m	4.50m	4.80m	5.11m
6"	2.29m	2.59m	2.90m	3.20m	3.51m	3.81m	4.11m	4.42m	4.72m	5.03m
3"	2.21m	2.51m	2.82m	3.12m	3.43m	3.73m	4.04m	4.34m	4.65m	4.95m
0"	2.13m	2.44m	2.74m	3.05m	3.35m	3.66m	3.96m	4.27m	4.57m	4.88m

(row label: Height in inches ("))

See inside front cover for full table

Know your height, know your route, obey road traffic signs

Wise up Size up

CAPE WRATH

Kearvaig Bay

Cléit Dhubh

Faraid Head

371 SGRIBHIS-BHEINN

Balnakeil Bay

Sango Bay

297 CNOC A' GHIUBHAIS

300 MAOVALLY

THE PARPH

Durness

Eilean Hoa

457 FASHVEN

Loch Àirigh na Beinne

Loch Meadaidh

Sandwood Bay

423 MEALL MEADHONACH

Sandwood Loch

485 CREAG RIABACH

Rubh' an Fhir Lèithe

468 BEINN DEARG MHÒR

464 MEALL NA MÒINE

331 GHLAS-BHEINN

NC

A838

489 MEALL NA CRÀ

230 BEN ARNABOLL

Balchreick

355 AN SOCACH

521 FARVEALL

19

773 BEINN SPIONNAIDH

Kinlochbervie

Loch Clash

B801

801 CRANSTACKIE

Strath Beag

520 AN LEAN-CHÀRN

Rubha Ruadh

Rhiconich

Loch na Claise Càrnaich

Strath Dionard

River Dionard

A838

908 FOINAVEN

HANDA ISLAND

North-west Sutherland

Loch na Tuadh

463 FEINNE-BHEINN MHÒR

Strath More

Loch Laxford

786 ARKLE

Scourie Bay

7

Scourie

A894

River Laxford

Loch Stack

729 SÀBHAL BEAG

Glen Golly

721 BEN STACK

Strath Stack

386 BEN AUSKAIRD

Badcall Bay

Achfary

333 BEN SCREAVIE

800

796 CÀRN DEARG

757 CARN AN TIONAIL

Rubh' a' Mhucard

17

A838

Loch More

Loch Coire Saidhe Dui

Point of Stoer

OLDANY ISLAND

Eddrachillis Bay

Lochan Chàirn Bhàin

419 BEN STROME

Loch an Leathaid Bhuain

Kinloch

873 BEN HEE

680 MEALL AN LIATH MÒR

Loch a' Ghorm-choire

Old Man of Stoer

Clashnessie Bay

Drumbeg

B869

Glendhu Forest

Loch Glendhu

Nedd

Glen Leirg

Loch an Leothaid

776 SAIL GHORM

Unapool

Loch Glencoul

525 BEINN AIRD DA LOCH

613 MEALL AN FHEUR LOCH

Stoer

B869

809 QUINAG

792 BEINN LEOID

Loch Merkland

Loch Fiag

Bay of Clachtoll

Loch Beannach

Loch-Beag

372 CNOC A' GHRIAMA

Glen Fiag

Achmelvich Bay

A837

774 GLAS BHEINN

96

37

Soyea Island

Loch Inver

Lochinver

539 BEINN GHARBH

Loch Assynt

Inchnadamph

A838

Inverkirkaig

Assynt - Coigach

510 MAOVALLY

Rubha Còigeach

River Kirkaig

Loch na Gainimh

847 CANISP

998 BEN MORE ASSYNT

Rubha Mòr

Eilean Mòr

Fionn Loch

732 SUILVEN

713 BREABAG

Enard Bay

River Oykel

814

435 BEN SCREAVIL

Altandhu

Loch Sìonascaig

849 CUL MÒR

Loch Veyatie

Loch Awe

Benmore Forest

Glen Muic

Rubha Mòr

Càm Loch

476 BEINN SGEIREACH

Polbain

Badentarbet

91

612 STAC POLLAIDH

Knockan

Elphin

A837

Loch Ailsh

Glen Cassley

SUMMER ISLES

Achiltibuie

Loch Lurgainn

769 CUL BEAG

Loch Urigill

364 AN STICHD

544 BEINN AN EÒIN

River Cassley

Polglass

Badentarbat Bay

Tanera

307 CNOC NA GLAS CHOILLE

Strath Oykel

Wise up Size up

Wise up Size up

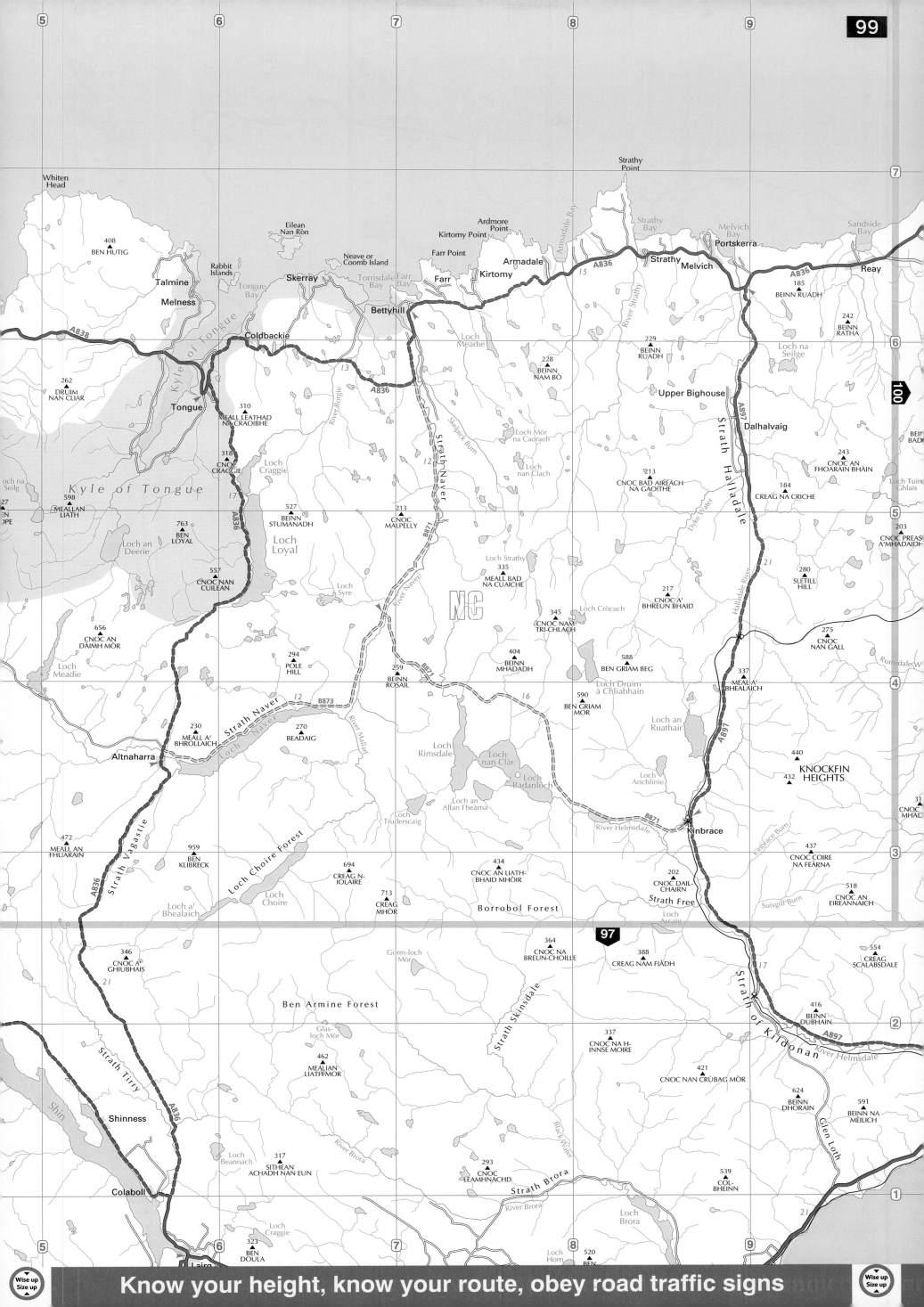

Whiten Head

408
BEN HUTIG

Talmine

Melness

Rabbit Islands

Eilean Nan Ròn

Skerray

Neave or Coomb Island

Farr Point

Ardmore Point

Kirtomy Point

Farr

Kirtomy

Armadale

A836

Strathy

Strathy Point

Strathy Bay

Melvich Bay

Portskerra

Sandside Bay

A836

Reay

185
BEINN RUADH

242
BEINN RATHA

A838

Coldbackie

Tongue Bay

Bettyhill

Torrisdale Bay

Farr Bay

A836

Loch Meadie

228
BEINN NAM BÒ

229
BEINN RUADH

River Strathy

15

A836

Melvich

Loch na Seilge

6

262
DRUIM NAN CLIAR

Tongue

310
MEALL LEATHAD NA CRAOIBHE

13

River Borgie

A836

River Strathy

Upper Bighouse

Dalhalvaig

A897

Strath Halladale

Loch Tuim

318
CNOC CRAGGIE

Loch Craggie

Loch Mòr na Caoraeh

243
CNOC AN FHOARAIN BHÀIN

Loch na Seilg

17

Kyle of Tongue

Meallan Liath

A836

Strath Naver

12

Loch nan Clach

213
CNOC BAD AIREACH NA GAOITHE

184
CREAG NA CRICHE

5

BEN HOPE

763
BEN LOYAL

527
BEINN STUMANADH

213
CNOC MALPELLY

B871

Loch Strathy

280
SLETILL HILL

203
CNOC PREAS A'MHADAIDH

Loch an Deerie

Loch Loyal

335
MEALL BAD NA CUAICHE

NC

217
CNOC A' BHREUN BHAID

21

557
CNOC NAN CUILEAN

Loch Syre

River Naver

345
CNOC NAM TRI-CHLACH

Loch Cròcach

275
CNOC NAN GALL

656
CNOC AN DÀIMH MÒR

404
BEINN MHADADH

588
BEN GRIAM BEG

Loch Druim à Chliabhain

337
MEALL A' BHEALAICH

Rumsdale W

4

Loch Meadie

294
POLE HILL

259
BEINN ROSAIL

B871

16

590
BEN GRIAM MOR

Loch an Ruathair

230
MEALL A' BHROLLAICH

B873

12

270
BEADAIG

Strath Naver

Loch Naver

River Mallait

Loch Rimsdale

Loch nan Clàr

Loch Arichlinie

440

432

KNOCKFIN HEIGHTS

Altnaharra

Loch Badanloch

Loch an Altan Fheàrna

A897

Strath Vagastie

A836

Loch Truderscaig

River Helmsdale

B871

Kinbrace

Kinbrace Burn

437
CNOC COIRE NA FEARNA

31
CNOC MHAD

3

472
MEALL AN FHUARAIN

959
BEN KLIBRECK

Loch Choire Forest

694
CREAG N-IOLAIRE

434
CNOC AN LIATH-BHAID MHÒIR

202
CNOC DAIL-CHAIRN

Strath Free

518
CNOC AN EIREANNAICH

346
CNOC A' GHIUBHAIS

Loch a' Bhealaich

Loch Choire

713
CREAG MHÒR

Borrobol Forest

Loch Ascaig

97

554
CREAG SCALABSDALE

21

Gorm-loch Mòr

364
CNOC NA BREUN-CHOILLE

388
CREAG NAM FIÀDH

17

Strath of Kildonan

416
BEINN DUBHAIN

A897

Ben Armine Forest

Strath Skinsdale

337
CNOC NA H-INNSE MOIRE

River Helmsdale

Strath Tirry

A836

Glas-loch Mòr

462
MEALAN LIATH MÒR

421
CNOC NAN CRÙBAG MÒR

Glen Loth

Shin

Shinness

River Brora

624
BEINN DHORAIN

591
BEINN NA MÈILICH

Loch Beannach

317
SITHEAN ACHADH NAN EUN

293
CNOC LEAMHNACHD

Black Water

539
COL-BHEINN

Colaboll

323
BEN DOULA

Loch Craggie

Strath Brora

River Brora

Loch Brora

Loch Horn

520
BEN

1

21

Lairg

5   6   7   8   9

Know your height, know your route, obey road traffic signs

Wise up Size up

Wise up Size up

London Emission Zones apply - for details visit www.tfl.gov.uk/driving

STRATFORD

University of East London (Stratford Campus)

WEST HAM

QUEEN ELIZABETH OLYMPIC PARK

East Wick

Sweetwater (under construction)

London Stadium (West Ham United FC)

POPLAR

Bromley

Index to place names

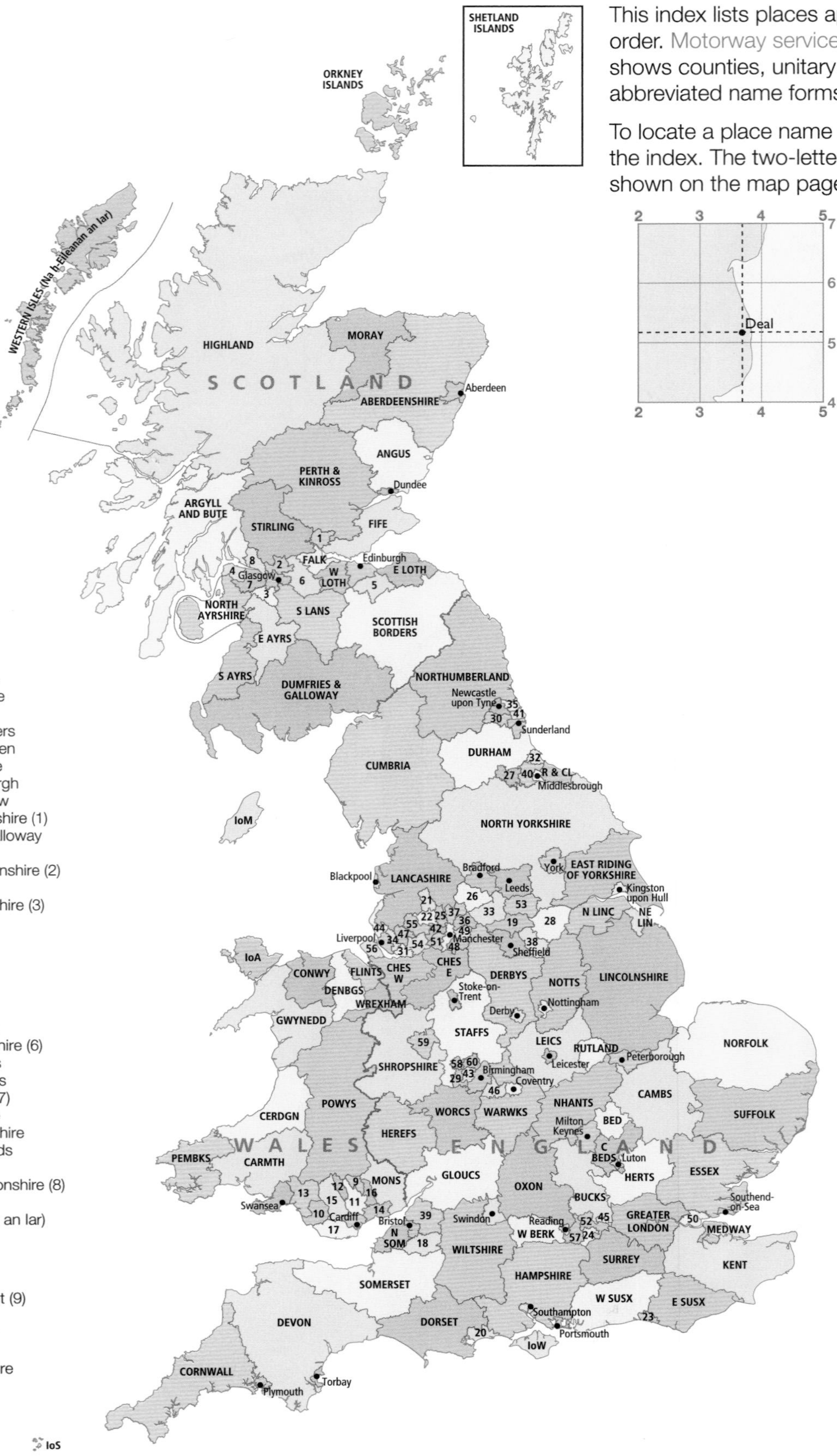

This index lists places appearing in the main map section of the atlas in alphabetical order. Motorway service areas are indexed in blue and airports in blue *italic*. The map shows counties, unitary authorities and administrative areas, together with a list of the abbreviated name forms used in the index.

To locate a place name in the atlas turn to the map page indicated in bold type in the index. The two-letter prefix denotes the 100km square of the National Grid, also shown on the map pages, and the four figure reference gives a more precise location.

Example:

Deal Kent **15** TR3752

Turn to page 15

Find 3 along the bottom or top of the page

Move a further 7 tenths of the square to the right (easting)

Find 5 up the side of the page

Move a further 2 tenths up (northing)

Deal will be found where the easting and northing intersect

Scotland

Abers	Aberdeenshire
Ag & B	Argyll and Bute
Angus	Angus
Border	Scottish Borders
C Aber	City of Aberdeen
C Dund	City of Dundee
C Edin	City of Edinburgh
C Glas	City of Glasgow
Clacks	Clackmannanshire (1)
D & G	Dumfries & Galloway
E Ayrs	East Ayrshire
E Duns	East Dunbartonshire (2)
E Loth	East Lothian
E Rens	East Renfrewshire (3)
Falk	Falkirk
Fife	Fife
Highld	Highland
Inver	Inverclyde (4)
Mdloth	Midlothian (5)
Moray	Moray
N Ayrs	North Ayrshire
N Lans	North Lanarkshire (6)
Ork	Orkney Islands
P & K	Perth & Kinross
Rens	Renfrewshire (7)
S Ayrs	South Ayrshire
S Lans	South Lanarkshire
Shet	Shetland Islands
Stirlg	Stirling
W Duns	West Dunbartonshire (8)
W Isls	Western Isles (Na h-Eileanan an Iar)
W Loth	West Lothian

Wales

Blae G	Blaenau Gwent (9)
Brdgnd	Bridgend (10)
Caerph	Caerphilly (11)
Cardif	Cardiff
Carmth	Carmarthenshire
Cerdgn	Ceredigion
Conwy	Conwy
Denbgs	Denbighshire
Flints	Flintshire
Gwynd	Gwynedd
IoA	Isle of Anglesey
Mons	Monmouthshire
Myr Td	Merthyr Tydfil (12)
Neath	Neath Port Talbot (13)
Newpt	Newport (14)
Pembks	Pembrokeshire
Powys	Powys
Rhondd	Rhondda Cynon Taf (15)
Swans	Swansea
Torfn	Torfaen (16)
V Glam	Vale of Glamorgan (17)
Wrexhm	Wrexham

Isle of Man

IoM	Isle of Man

England

BaNES	Bath & N E Somerset (18)
Barns	Barnsley (19)
BCP	Bournemouth, Christchurch and Poole (20)
Bed	Bedford
Birm	Birmingham
Bl w D	Blackburn with Darwen (21)
Bolton	Bolton (22)
Bpool	Blackpool
Br & H	Brighton & Hove (23)
Br For	Bracknell Forest (24)
Bristl	City of Bristol
Bucks	Buckinghamshire
Bury	Bury (25)
C Beds	Central Bedfordshire
C Brad	City of Bradford
C Derb	City of Derby
C KuH	City of Kingston upon Hull
C Leic	City of Leicester
C Nott	City of Nottingham
C Pete	City of Peterborough
C Plym	City of Plymouth
C Port	City of Portsmouth
C Sotn	City of Southampton
C Stke	City of Stoke-on-Trent
C York	City of York
Calder	Calderdale (26)
Cambs	Cambridgeshire
Ches E	Cheshire East
Ches W	Cheshire West and Chester
Cnwll	Cornwall
Covtry	Coventry
Cumb	Cumbria
Darltn	Darlington (27)
Derbys	Derbyshire
Devon	Devon
Donc	Doncaster (28)
Dorset	Dorset
Dudley	Dudley (29)
Dur	Durham
E R Yk	East Riding of Yorkshire
E Susx	East Sussex
Essex	Essex
Gatesd	Gateshead (30)
Gloucs	Gloucestershire
Gt Lon	Greater London
Halton	Halton (31)
Hants	Hampshire
Hartpl	Hartlepool (32)
Herefs	Herefordshire
Herts	Hertfordshire
IoS	Isles of Scilly
IoW	Isle of Wight
Kent	Kent
Kirk	Kirklees (33)
Knows	Knowsley (34)
Lancs	Lancashire
Leeds	Leeds
Leics	Leicestershire
Lincs	Lincolnshire
Lpool	Liverpool
Luton	Luton
M Keyn	Milton Keynes
Manch	Manchester
Medway	Medway
Middsb	Middlesbrough
N Linc	North Lincolnshire
N Som	North Somerset
N Tyne	North Tyneside (35)
N u Ty	Newcastle upon Tyne
N York	North Yorkshire
NE Lin	North East Lincolnshire
Nhants	Northamptonshire
Norfk	Norfolk
Notts	Nottinghamshire
Nthumb	Northumberland
Oldham	Oldham (36)
Oxon	Oxfordshire
R & Cl	Redcar & Cleveland
Readg	Reading
Rochdl	Rochdale (37)
Rothm	Rotherham (38)
Rutlnd	Rutland
S Glos	South Gloucestershire (39)
S on T	Stockton-on-Tees (40)
S Tyne	South Tyneside (41)
Salfd	Salford (42)
Sandw	Sandwell (43)
Sefton	Sefton (44)
Sheff	Sheffield
Shrops	Shropshire
Slough	Slough (45)
Solhll	Solihull (46)
Somset	Somerset
St Hel	St Helens (47)
Staffs	Staffordshire
Sthend	Southend-on-Sea
Stockp	Stockport (48)
Suffk	Suffolk
Sundld	Sunderland
Surrey	Surrey
Swindn	Swindon
Tamesd	Tameside (49)
Thurr	Thurrock (50)
Torbay	Torbay
Traffd	Trafford (51)
W & M	Windsor & Maidenhead (52)
W Berk	West Berkshire
W Susx	West Sussex
Wakefd	Wakefield (53)
Warrtn	Warrington (54)
Warwks	Warwickshire
Wigan	Wigan (55)
Wilts	Wiltshire
Wirral	Wirral (56)
Wokham	Wokingham (57)
Wolves	Wolverhampton (58)
Worcs	Worcestershire
Wrekin	Telford & Wrekin (59)
Wsall	Walsall (60)

A

Abbas Combe Somset 9 ST7022
Abberley Worcs 28 SO7567
Abberley Common Worcs 28 SO7467
Abberton Essex 25 TM0019
Abberton Worcs 28 SO9953
Abbess Roding Essex 24 TL5711
Abbeydale Sheff 49 SK3281
Abbey Dore Herefs 27 SO3830
Abbey Green Staffs 48 SJ9757
Abbey St Bathans Border 76 NT7661
Abbeystead Lancs 53 SD5654
Abbeytown Cumb 67 NY1750
Abbey Village Lancs 54 SD6422
Abbey Wood Gt Lon 23 TQ4779
Abbots Bickington Devon 6 SS3813
Abbots Bromley Staffs 38 SK0724
Abbotsbury Dorset 9 SY5785
Abbotsham Devon 6 SS4226
Abbotskerswell Devon 5 SX8568
Abbots Langley Herts 22 TL0901
Abbots Leigh N Som 19 ST5474
Abbotsley Cambs 31 TL2256
Abbots Morton Worcs 28 SP0255
Abbots Ripton Cambs 31 TL2377
Abbot's Salford Warwks 28 SP0650
Abbots Worthy Hants 11 SU4932
Abbotts Ann Hants 21 SU3243
Abbott Street Dorset 9 ST9800
Abdon Shrops 37 SO5786
Aberaeron Cerdgn 34 SN4562
Aberaman Rhondd 18 SO0100
Aberangell Gwynd 35 SH8410
Aberarder Highld 92 NH6225
Aberargie P & K 82 NO1615
Aberarth Cerdgn 34 SN4763
Aberavon Neath 18 SS7489
Abercanaid Myr Td 26 SO0503
Abercarn Caerph 19 ST2194
Abercastle Pembks 16 SM8533
Abercegir Powys 35 SH8001
Aberchirder Abers 94 NJ6252
Abercraf Powys 26 SN8212
Abercregan Neath 18 SS8496
Abercwmboi Rhondd 18 ST0299
Abercych Pembks 17 SN2441
Abercynon Rhondd 18 ST0794
Aberdare Rhondd 18 SO0002
Aberdaron Gwynd 44 SH1726
Aberdeen C Aber 89 NJ9306
Aberdeen Airport C Aber 95 NJ8712
Aberdour Fife 82 NT1985
Aberdulais Neath 18 SS7799
Aberdyfi Gwynd 35 SN6196
Aberedw Powys 26 SO0847
Abereiddy Pembks 16 SM7931
Abererch Gwynd 44 SH3936
Aberfan Myr Td 18 SO0700
Aberfeldy P & K 87 NN8549
Aberffraw IoA 44 SH3569
Aberford Leeds 55 SE4337
Aberfoyle Stirlg 81 NN5200
Abergavenny Mons 27 SO2914
Abergele Conwy 45 SH9477
Abergorlech Carmth 17 SN5833
Abergwesyn Powys 26 SN8552
Abergwili Carmth 17 SN4320
Abergwynfi Neath 18 SS8995
Abergwyngregyn Gwynd 45 SH6572
Abergynolwyn Gwynd 35 SH6806
Aberkenfig Brdgnd 18 SS8984
Aberlady E Loth 83 NT4679
Aberlemno Angus 89 NO5255
Aberllefenni Gwynd 35 SH7609
Aberllynfi Powys 27 SO1737
Aberlour, Charlestown of Moray 94 NJ2642
Abermule Powys 36 SO1694
Abernant Carmth 17 SN3323
Abernant Rhondd 18 SO0003
Abernethy P & K 82 NO1816
Abernyte P & K 83 NO2531
Aberporth Cerdgn 17 SN2651
Abersoch Gwynd 44 SH3127
Abersychan Torfn 27 SO2603
Aberthin V Glam 18 ST0074
Abertillery Blae G 27 SO2104
Abertridwr Caerph 18 ST1289
Abertridwr Powys 36 SJ0319
Aberuthven P & K 82 NN9615
Aberystwyth Cerdgn 34 SN5881
Abingdon-on-Thames Oxon 21 SU4997
Abinger Common Surrey 12 TQ1145
Abinger Hammer Surrey 12 TQ0947
Abington Nhants 30 SP7861
Abington S Lans 75 NS9322
Abington Pigotts Cambs 31 TL3044
Abington Services S Lans 75 NS9324
Abingworth W Susx 12 TQ1016
Ab Kettleby Leics 40 SK7223
Ablington Gloucs 28 SP1007
Abney Derbys 48 SK1980
Aboyne Abers 89 NO5298
Abhainn Suidhe W Isls 90 NB0408
Abram Wigan 47 SD6001
Abridge Essex 23 TQ4696
Abronhill N Lans 74 NS7876
Abson S Glos 20 ST7074
Abthorpe Nhants 29 SP6446
Aby Lincs 51 TF4078
Acaster Malbis C York 56 SE5845
Acaster Selby N York 56 SE5741
Accrington Lancs 54 SD7628
Acha Mor W Isls 90 NB3029
Acharacle Highld 79 NM6767
Acharn Highld 79 NM7050
Acharn P & K 87 NN7543
Achfary Highld 98 NC2939
Achiltibuie Highld 91 NC0208
Achmore W Isls 90 NB3029
Achnacroish Ag & B 79 NM8541
Achnamara Ag & B 71 NR7887
Achnasheen Highld 92 NH1658
Achosnich Highld 79 NM4467
Achurch Nhants 40 TL0283
Acklam Middsb 62 NZ4817
Acklam N York 56 SE7861
Ackleton Shrops 37 SO7698
Acklington Nthumb 69 NU2301
Ackton Wakefd 55 SE4121
Ackworth Moor Top Wakefd 55 SE4316
Acle Norfk 43 TG4010
Acock's Green Birm 38 SP1283
Acol Kent 15 TR3067
Acomb C York 56 SE5651
Acomb Nthumb 68 NY9366
Aconbury Herefs 27 SO5133
Acton Ches E 47 SJ6352
Acton Gt Lon 23 TQ2080
Acton Staffs 38 SJ8241
Acton Suffk 32 TL8945
Acton Wrexhm 46 SJ3451
Acton Beauchamp Herefs 28 SO6850
Acton Bridge Ches W 47 SJ5975
Acton Burnell Shrops 37 SJ5302
Acton Green Herefs 28 SO6950
Acton Round Shrops 37 SO6395
Acton Scott Shrops 36 SO4589
Acton Trussell Staffs 38 SJ9318
Acton Turville S Glos 20 ST8080
Adbaston Staffs 37 SJ7627
Adber Dorset 9 ST5920
Adbolton Notts 49 SK5938
Adderbury Oxon 29 SP4735
Adderley Shrops 37 SJ6640
Addiewell W Loth 75 NS9962
Addingham C Brad 55 SE0749
Addington Bucks 30 SP7428
Addington Gt Lon 23 TQ3664
Addington Kent 14 TQ6559
Addiscombe Gt Lon 23 TQ3366
Addlestone Surrey 22 TQ0564
Addlethorpe Lincs 51 TF5468
Adeyfield Herts 22 TL0708
Adfa Powys 36 SJ0601
Adforton Herefs 36 SO4071
Adisham Kent 15 TR2253
Adlestrop Gloucs 29 SP2426
Adlingfleet E R Yk 56 SE8421
Adlington Lancs 54 SD6013
Admaston Staffs 38 SK0423
Admaston Wrekin 37 SJ6313
Adpar Cerdgn 17 SN3041
Adsborough Somset 8 ST2729
Adscombe Somset 19 ST1837
Adstock Bucks 30 SP7329
Adstone Nhants 29 SP5951
Adversane W Susx 12 TQ0723
Adwick le Street Donc 56 SE5308
Adwick upon Dearne Donc 49 SE4701
Ae D & G 66 NX9889
Affpuddle Dorset 9 SY8093
Afon-wen Flints 46 SJ1371
Afton IoW 10 SZ3486
Agglethorpe N York 61 SE0885
Aigburth Lpool 46 SJ3886
Aike E R Yk 57 TA0446
Aiketgate Cumb 67 NY4846
Aikton Cumb 67 NY2753
Ailsworth C Pete 40 TL1198
Ainderby Quernhow N York 62 SE3480
Ainderby Steeple N York 62 SE3392
Aingers Green Essex 25 TM1120
Ainsdale Sefton 53 SD3112
Ainstable Cumb 67 NY5246
Ainsworth Bury 54 SD7610
Ainthorpe N York 63 NZ7007
Aintree Sefton 46 SJ3898
Aird D & G 64 NX0960
Aird W Isls 90 NB5635
Aird of Sleat Highld 84 NG5900
Airdrie N Lans 74 NS7565
Airidh a bhruaich W Isls 90 NB2417
Airmyn E R Yk 56 SE7224
Airntully P & K 82 NO0935
Airth Falk 82 NS9087
Airton N York 54 SD9059
Aisby Lincs 40 TF0138
Aisby Lincs 50 SK8692
Aish Devon 5 SX6960
Aish Devon 5 SX8458
Aisholt Somset 8 ST1935
Aiskew N York 61 SE2788
Aislaby N York 63 NZ8608
Aislaby N York 63 SE7785
Aislaby S on T 62 NZ4012
Aisthorpe Lincs 50 SK9480
Akeld Nthumb 77 NT9529
Akeley Bucks 30 SP7037
Albaston Cnwll 4 SX4270
Alberbury Shrops 36 SJ3614
Albourne W Susx 12 TQ2516
Albrighton Shrops 37 SJ4918
Albrighton Shrops 37 SJ8004
Alburgh Norfk 33 TM2687
Albury Herts 31 TL4324
Albury Surrey 12 TQ0447
Albury Heath Surrey 12 TQ0646
Alcaig Highld 92 NH5657
Alcaston Shrops 36 SO4587
Alcester Warwks 28 SP0857
Alcester Lane End Birm 38 SP0780
Alciston E Susx 13 TQ5005
Alcombe Somset 7 SS9745
Alconbury Cambs 31 TL1875
Alconbury Weston Cambs 31 TL1777
Aldborough N York 55 SE4066
Aldborough Norfk 43 TG1834
Aldbourne Wilts 21 SU2676
Aldbrough E R Yk 57 TA2438
Aldbrough St John N York 61 NZ2011
Aldbury Herts 30 SP9612
Aldcliffe Lancs 53 SD4660
Aldclune P & K 87 NN8964
Aldeburgh Suffk 33 TM4656
Aldeby Norfk 43 TM4493
Aldenham Herts 22 TQ1498
Alderbury Wilts 10 SU1827
Alderford Norfk 43 TG1218
Alderholt Dorset 10 SU1212
Alderley Gloucs 20 ST7690
Alderley Edge Ches E 47 SJ8478
Aldermans Green Covtry 39 SP3683
Aldermaston W Berk 21 SU5965
Alderminster Warwks 29 SP2348
Aldershot Hants 22 SU8650
Alderton Gloucs 28 SP0033
Alderton Nhants 30 SP7446
Alderton Suffk 33 TM3441
Alderton Wilts 20 ST8482
Aldfield N York 55 SE2669
Aldford Ches W 46 SJ4159
Aldgate Rutlnd 40 SK9804
Aldham Essex 24 TL9126
Aldham Suffk 32 TM0445
Aldingbourne W Susx 12 SU9205
Aldingham Cumb 53 SD2870
Aldington Kent 15 TR0736
Aldington Worcs 28 SP0644
Aldington Corner Kent 15 TR0636
Aldreth Cambs 31 TL4473
Aldridge Wsall 38 SK0500
Aldringham Suffk 33 TM4461
Aldsworth Gloucs 28 SP1509
Aldwark Derbys 48 SK2257
Aldwark N York 55 SE4663
Aldwick W Susx 12 SZ9198
Aldwincle Nhants 40 TL0081
Aldworth W Berk 21 SU5579
Alexandria W Duns 80 NS3979
Aley Somset 19 ST1838
Alfington Devon 8 SY1197
Alfold Surrey 12 TQ0333
Alfold Crossways Surrey 12 TQ0335
Alford Abers 94 NJ5715
Alford Lincs 51 TF4575
Alford Somset 9 ST6032
Alfreton Derbys 49 SK4155
Alfrick Worcs 28 SO7453
Alfrick Pound Worcs 28 SO7452
Alfriston E Susx 13 TQ5103
Algarkirk Lincs 41 TF2935
Alhampton Somset 9 ST6234
Alkborough N Linc 56 SE8821
Alkham Kent 15 TR2542
Alkmonton Derbys 48 SK1838
Allaleigh Devon 5 SX8053
Allanbank N Lans 74 NS8458
Allanton Border 77 NT8654
Allanton N Lans 74 NS8457
Allaston Gloucs 27 SO6304
Allbrook Hants 10 SU4521
All Cannings Wilts 20 SU0661
Allendale Nthumb 68 NY8355
Allen End Warwks 38 SP1696
Allenheads Nthumb 68 NY8645
Allen's Green Herts 31 TL4516
Allensmore Herefs 27 SO4635
Allenton C Derb 39 SK3732
Aller Devon 7 SS7625
Aller Somset 8 ST4029
Allerby Cumb 58 NY0839
Allercombe Devon 7 SY0494
Allerford Somset 18 SS9046
Allerston N York 63 SE8782
Allerthorpe E R Yk 56 SE7847
Allerton C Brad 55 SE1234
Allerton Lpool 46 SJ3987
Allerton Bywater Leeds 55 SE4227
Allerton Mauleverer N York 55 SE4157
Allesley Covtry 39 SP3080
Allestree C Derb 49 SK3439
Allexton Leics 40 SK8100
Allgreave Ches E 48 SJ9767
Allhallows Medway 24 TQ8377
Allington Dorset 8 SY4693
Allington Lincs 50 SK8540
Allington Wilts 10 SU2039
Allington Wilts 20 ST8975
Allington Wilts 20 SU0663
Allithwaite Cumb 59 SD3876
Alloa Clacks 82 NS8892
Allonby Cumb 58 NY0842
Alloway S Ayrs 73 NS3318
Allowenshay Somset 8 ST3913
All Stretton Shrops 36 SO4595
Alltwalis Carmth 17 SN4431
Alltwen Neath 18 SN7303
Alltyblaca Cerdgn 17 SN5245
Allweston Dorset 9 ST6614
Almeley Herefs 27 SO3351
Almington Staffs 37 SJ7034
Almondbank P & K 82 NO0626
Almondbury Kirk 55 SE1614
Almondsbury S Glos 19 ST6084
Alne N York 55 SE4965
Alness Highld 93 NH6569
Alnham Nthumb 68 NT9810

Alnmouth – Berden 121

Alnmouth Nthumb 69 NU2410
Alnwick Nthumb 69 NU1813
Alperton Gt Lon 23 TQ1883
Alphamstone Essex 24 TL8735
Alpheton Suffk 32 TL8750
Alphington Devon 5 SX9190
Alport Derbys 48 SK2264
Alpraham Ches E 47 SJ5859
Alresford Essex 25 TM0621
Alrewas Staffs 38 SK1614
Alsager Ches E 47 SJ7955
Alsop en le Dale Derbys 48 SK1554
Alston Cumb 68 NY7146
Alston Devon 8 ST3002
Alstone Gloucs 28 SO9832
Alstonefield Staffs 48 SK1355
Alston Sutton Somset 19 ST4151
Alswear Devon 7 SS7222
Altandhu Highld 98 NB9812
Altarnun Cnwll 4 SX2281
Althorne Essex 24 TQ9198
Althorpe N Linc 56 SE8309
Altnaharra Highld 99 NC5635
Altofts Wakefd 55 SE3823
Alton Derbys 49 SK3664
Alton Hants 11 SU7139
Alton Staffs 48 SK0741
Alton Barnes Wilts 20 SU1062
Alton Pancras Dorset 9 ST7002
Alton Priors Wilts 20 SU1162
Altrincham Traffd 47 SJ7687
Alva Clacks 82 NS8897
Alvanley Ches W 46 SJ4974
Alvaston C Derb 39 SK3833
Alvechurch Worcs 38 SP0272
Alvecote Warwks 39 SK2404
Alvediston Wilts 9 ST9723
Alveley Shrops 37 SO7584
Alverdiscott Devon 6 SS5225
Alverstoke Hants 11 SZ6098
Alverstone IoW 11 SZ5785
Alverthorpe Wakefd 55 SE3121
Alverton Notts 50 SK7942
Alves Moray 93 NJ1362
Alvescot Oxon 29 SP2704
Alveston S Glos 19 ST6388
Alveston Warwks 29 SP2356
Alvingham Lincs 51 TF3691
Alvington Gloucs 19 SO6000
Alwalton C Pete 40 TL1396
Alwinton Nthumb 68 NT9106
Alwoodley Leeds 55 SE2840
Alyth P & K 88 NO2448
Am Bàgh a Tuath W Isls 90 NF7003
Ambergate Derbys 49 SK3451
Amberley Gloucs 20 SO8501
Amberley W Susx 12 TQ0213
Amble Nthumb 69 NU2604
Amblecote Dudley 38 SO8985
Ambler Thorn C Brad 55 SE0929
Ambleside Cumb 59 NY3704
Ambleston Pembks 16 SN0025
Ambrosden Oxon 29 SP6019
Amcotts N Linc 56 SE8514
Amersham Bucks 22 SU9597
Amersham Common Bucks 22 SU9697
Amersham Old Town Bucks 22 SU9597
Amersham on the Hill Bucks 22 SU9798
Amesbury Wilts 20 SU1541
Amhuinnsuidhe W Isls 90 NB0408
Amington Staffs 39 SK2304
Amisfield D & G 66 NY0082
Amlwch IoA 44 SH4492
Ammanford Carmth 17 SN6212
Amotherby N York 63 SE7473
Ampfield Hants 10 SU4023
Ampleforth N York 62 SE5878
Ampney Crucis Gloucs 20 SP0601
Ampney St Mary Gloucs 20 SP0802
Ampney St Peter Gloucs 20 SP0801
Amport Hants 21 SU3044
Ampthill C Beds 30 TL0337
Ampton Suffk 32 TL8671
Amroth Pembks 17 SN1608
Amulree P & K 82 NN8936
Amwell Herts 31 TL1613
Ancaster Lincs 50 SK9843
Ancells Farm Hants 22 SU8155
Ancroft Nthumb 77 NT9945
Ancrum Border 76 NT6224
Ancton W Susx 12 SU9800
Anderby Lincs 51 TF5275
Andover Hants 21 SU3645
Andoversford Gloucs 28 SP0219
Andreas IoM 52 SC4199
Anerley Gt Lon 23 TQ3369
Anfield Lpool 46 SJ3692
Angarrack Cnwll 2 SW5838
Angelbank Shrops 37 SO5776
Angle Pembks 16 SM8603
Angmering W Susx 12 TQ0604
Angram N York 55 SE5248
Anlaby E R Yk 57 TA0328
Anmer Norfk 42 TF7429
Anmore Hants 11 SU6611
Annan D & G 67 NY1966
Annandale Water Services D & G 67 NY1092
Anna Valley Hants 21 SU3543
Annbank S Ayrs 73 NS4023
Annfield Plain Dur 69 NZ1651
Anniesland C Glas 74 NS5368
Ansdell Lancs 53 SD3428
Ansford Somset 9 ST6433
Ansley Warwks 39 SP3091
Anslow Staffs 39 SK2125
Anslow Gate Staffs 39 SK1924
Anstey Herts 31 TL4033
Anstey Leics 39 SK5508
Anstruther Fife 83 NO5703
Ansty W Susx 12 TQ2923
Ansty Warwks 39 SP4083
Ansty Wilts 9 ST9526
Anthorn Cumb 67 NY1958
Antingham Norfk 43 TG2533
An t-Ob W Isls 90 NG0286
Anton's Gowt Lincs 51 TF3047
Antony Cnwll 4 SX4054
Antrobus Ches W 47 SJ6479
Anwick Lincs 50 TF1150
Anwoth D & G 65 NX5856
Aperfield Gt Lon 23 TQ4158
Apethorpe Nhants 40 TL0295
Apley Lincs 50 TF1075
Apperknowle Derbys 49 SK3878
Apperley Gloucs 28 SO8628
Appin Ag & B 86 NM9346
Appleby N Linc 56 SE9514
Appleby-in-Westmorland Cumb 60 NY6820
Appleby Magna Leics 39 SK3109
Appleby Parva Leics 39 SK3008
Applecross Highld 91 NG7144
Appledore Devon 6 SS4630
Appledore Devon 7 ST0614
Appledore Kent 15 TQ9529
Appleford Oxon 21 SU5293
Appleshaw Hants 21 SU3048
Appleton Halton 46 SJ5186
Appleton Oxon 21 SP4401
Appleton Warrtn 47 SJ6184
Appleton-le-Moors N York 63 SE7387
Appleton-le-Street N York 63 SE7373
Appleton Roebuck N York 56 SE5542
Appleton Thorn Warrtn 47 SJ6383
Appleton Wiske N York 62 NZ3804
Appletreewick N York 55 SE0560
Appley Somset 8 ST0721
Appley Bridge Lancs 53 SD5209
Apse Heath IoW 11 SZ5683
Apsley End C Beds 30 TL1232
Apuldram W Susx 11 SU8403
Arbirlot Angus 83 NO6040
Arborfield Wokham 22 SU7567
Arborfield Cross Wokham 22 SU7666
Arbourthorne Sheff 49 SK3785
Arbroath Angus 89 NO6441
Arbuthnott Abers 89 NO7975
Archddu Carmth 17 SN4401
Archdeacon Newton Darltn 61 NZ2517
Archiestown Moray 94 NJ2244
Arclid Ches E 47 SJ7861
Ardbeg Ag & B 70 NR4146
Arddleen Powys 36 SJ2616
Ardeley Herts 31 TL3027
Ardelve Highld 85 NG8627
Arden Ag & B 80 NS3684
Ardens Grafton Warwks 28 SP1154
Ardentinny Ag & B 80 NS1887
Ardersier Highld 93 NH7854
Ardgay Highld 97 NH5990
Ardgour Highld 86 NN0163
Ardingly W Susx 12 TQ3429
Ardington Oxon 21 SU4388
Ardleigh Essex 25 TM0529
Ardleigh Heath Essex 25 TM0430
Ardler P & K 88 NO2642
Ardley Oxon 29 SP5427
Ardlui Ag & B 80 NN3115
Ardlussa Ag & B 71 NR6487
Ardminish Ag & B 72 NR6448
Ardnadam Ag & B 80 NS1780
Ardrishaig Ag & B 71 NR8585
Ardrossan N Ayrs 73 NS2342
Ardsley East Leeds 55 SE3025
Ardvasar Highld 85 NG6303
Ardwell D & G 64 NX1045
Ardwick Manch 47 SJ8597
Areley Kings Worcs 37 SO7970
Arford Hants 11 SU8236
Argoed Caerph 19 ST1799
Aribruach W Isls 90 NB2417
Arinagour Ag & B 78 NM2257
Arisaig Highld 85 NM6586
Arkendale N York 55 SE3861
Arkesden Essex 31 TL4834
Arkholme Lancs 54 SD5871
Arkley Gt Lon 23 TQ2295
Arksey Donc 56 SE5807
Arkwright Town Derbys 49 SK4271
Arle Gloucs 28 SO9223
Arlecdon Cumb 58 NY0418
Arlesey C Beds 31 TL1936
Arleston Wrekin 37 SJ6610
Arley Ches E 47 SJ6680
Arley Warwks 39 SP2890
Arlingham Gloucs 28 SO7010
Arlington Devon 7 SS6140
Arlington E Susx 13 TQ5407
Armadale Highld 99 NC7864
Armadale W Loth 75 NS9368
Armathwaite Cumb 67 NY5046
Arminghall Norfk 43 TG2504
Armitage Staffs 38 SK0715
Armley Leeds 55 SE2833
Armscote Warwks 29 SP2444
Armthorpe Donc 56 SE6204
Arnabost Ag & B 78 NM2060
Arncliffe N York 54 SD9371
Arncroach Fife 83 NO5105
Arne Dorset 9 SY9788
Arnesby Leics 39 SP6192
Arngask P & K 82 NO1410
Arnisdale Highld 85 NG8410
Arnol W Isls 90 NB3148
Arnold E R Yk 57 TA1241
Arnold Notts 49 SK5845
Arnprior Stirlg 81 NS6194
Arnside Cumb 59 SD4578
Aros Ag & B 79 NM5645
Arrad Foot Cumb 58 SD3080
Arram E R Yk 57 TA0344
Arrathorne N York 61 SE2093
Arreton IoW 11 SZ5386
Arrington Cambs 31 TL3250
Arrochar Ag & B 80 NN2904
Arrow Warwks 28 SP0856
Arscott Shrops 36 SJ4307
Arthington Leeds 55 SE2644
Arthingworth Nhants 40 SP7581
Arundel W Susx 12 TQ0106
Asby Cumb 58 NY0620
Ascog Ag & B 73 NS1062
Ascot W & M 22 SU9268
Ascott-under-Wychwood Oxon 29 SP3018
Asenby N York 62 SE3975
Asfordby Leics 40 SK7019
Asfordby Hill Leics 40 SK7219
Asgarby Lincs 50 TF1145
Ash Kent 14 TQ6064
Ash Kent 15 TR2858
Ash Somset 8 ST4720
Ash Surrey 22 SU9051
Ashampstead W Berk 21 SU5676
Ashbocking Suffk 33 TM1854
Ashbourne Derbys 48 SK1746
Ashbrittle Somset 7 ST0521
Ashburton Devon 5 SX7570
Ashbury Devon 6 SX5098
Ashbury Oxon 21 SU2685
Ashby N Linc 56 SE8908
Ashby by Partney Lincs 51 TF4266
Ashby cum Fenby NE Lin 51 TA2500
Ashby de la Launde Lincs 50 TF0555
Ashby-de-la-Zouch Leics 39 SK3516
Ashby Folville Leics 40 SK7012
Ashby Magna Leics 39 SP5690
Ashby Parva Leics 39 SP5288
Ashby Puerorum Lincs 51 TF3271
Ashby St Ledgers Nhants 29 SP5768
Ashby St Mary Norfk 43 TG3202
Ashchurch Gloucs 28 SO9233
Ashcombe Devon 5 SX9179
Ashcombe N Som 19 ST3361
Ashcott Somset 19 ST4336
Ashdon Essex 31 TL5842
Ashe Hants 21 SU5350
Asheldham Essex 25 TL9701
Ashen Essex 32 TL7442
Ashendon Bucks 30 SP7014
Asheridge Bucks 22 SP9304
Ashfield cum Thorpe Suffk 33 TM2062
Ashfield Green Suffk 33 TM2573
Ashford Devon 5 SX6948
Ashford Devon 6 SS5335
Ashford Kent 15 TR0142
Ashford Surrey 22 TQ0771
Ashford Bowdler Shrops 27 SO5170
Ashford Carbonell Shrops 27 SO5270
Ashford Hill Hants 21 SU5562
Ashford in the Water Derbys 48 SK1969
Ash Green Surrey 22 SU9049
Ash Green Warwks 39 SP3384
Ashill Devon 8 ST0811
Ashill Norfk 42 TF8804
Ashill Somset 8 ST3217
Ashingdon Essex 24 TQ8693
Ashington Nthumb 69 NZ2687
Ashington Somset 9 ST5621
Ashington W Susx 12 TQ1315
Ashkirk Border 76 NT4722
Ashleworth Gloucs 28 SO8125
Ashleworth Quay Gloucs 28 SO8125
Ashley Cambs 32 TL6961
Ashley Ches E 47 SJ7784
Ashley Devon 7 SS6511
Ashley Gloucs 20 ST9394
Ashley Hants 10 SU3831
Ashley Hants 10 SZ2595
Ashley Kent 15 TR3048
Ashley Nhants 40 SP7990
Ashley Staffs 37 SJ7636
Ashley Wilts 20 ST8268
Ashley Green Bucks 22 SP9705
Ash Magna Shrops 37 SJ5739
Ashmansworth Hants 21 SU4157
Ashmansworthy Devon 6 SS3418
Ash Mill Devon 7 SS7823
Ashmore Dorset 9 ST9117
Ashmore Green W Berk 21 SU5069
Ashorne Warwks 29 SP3057
Ashover Derbys 49 SK3463
Ashow Warwks 29 SP3170
Ashperton Herefs 27 SO6441
Ashprington Devon 5 SX8157
Ash Priors Somset 8 ST1529
Ashreigney Devon 7 SS6313
Ash Street Suffk 32 TM0146
Ashtead Surrey 23 TQ1857
Ash Thomas Devon 7 ST0010
Ashton Ches W 46 SJ5069
Ashton Cnwll 2 SW6028
Ashton Devon 5 SX8584
Ashton Herefs 27 SO5164
Ashton Inver 80 NS2377
Ashton Nhants 30 SP7649
Ashton Nhants 40 TL0588
Ashton Common Wilts 20 ST8958
Ashton-in-Makerfield Wigan 47 SJ5798
Ashton Keynes Wilts 20 SU0494
Ashton under Hill Worcs 28 SO9937
Ashton-under-Lyne Tamesd 48 SJ9399
Ashton Vale Bristl 19 ST5670
Ashurst Hants 10 SU3310
Ashurst Kent 13 TQ5138
Ashurst Lancs 46 SD4807
Ashurst W Susx 12 TQ1715
Ashurstwood W Susx 13 TQ4136
Ash Vale Surrey 22 SU8951
Ashwater Devon 6 SX3895
Ashwell Herts 31 TL2639
Ashwell Rutlnd 40 SK8613
Ashwell End Herts 31 TL2540
Ashwellthorpe Norfk 43 TM1497
Ashwick Somset 19 ST6348
Ashwicken Norfk 42 TF7018
Askam in Furness Cumb 58 SD2177
Askern Donc 56 SE5613
Askerswell Dorset 8 SY5292
Askett Bucks 22 SP8105
Askham Cumb 59 NY5123
Askham Notts 50 SK7374
Askham Bryan C York 56 SE5548
Askham Richard C York 56 SE5347
Askrigg N York 61 SD9491
Askwith N York 55 SE1648
Aslackby Lincs 40 TF0830
Aslacton Norfk 33 TM1590
Aslockton Notts 40 SK7440
Aspatria Cumb 58 NY1441
Aspenden Herts 31 TL3528
Aspley Guise C Beds 30 SP9335
Aspley Heath C Beds 30 SP9334
Aspull Wigan 47 SD6108
Asselby E R Yk 56 SE7127
Assington Suffk 25 TL9338
Assington Green Suffk 32 TL7751
Astbury Ches E 47 SJ8461
Astcote Nhants 30 SP6753
Asterby Lincs 51 TF2679
Asterley Shrops 36 SJ3707
Asterton Shrops 36 SO3991
Asthall Oxon 29 SP2811
Asthall Leigh Oxon 29 SP3013
Astley Shrops 37 SJ5218
Astley Warwks 39 SP3189
Astley Wigan 47 SD7000
Astley Worcs 28 SO7867
Astley Abbots Shrops 37 SO7096
Astley Bridge Bolton 54 SD7111
Astley Cross Worcs 28 SO8069
Aston Birm 38 SP0888
Aston Ches E 47 SJ6146
Aston Ches W 47 SJ5578
Aston Derbys 48 SK1783
Aston Flints 46 SJ3067
Aston Herts 31 TL2722
Aston Oxon 21 SP3403
Aston Rothm 49 SK4685
Aston Shrops 37 SJ5328
Aston Shrops 37 SO8093
Aston Staffs 37 SJ7541
Aston Staffs 38 SJ8923
Aston Wokham 22 SU7884
Aston Wrekin 37 SJ6109
Aston Abbotts Bucks 30 SP8420
Aston Botterell Shrops 37 SO6384
Aston-by-Stone Staffs 38 SJ9130
Aston Cantlow Warwks 28 SP1360
Aston Clinton Bucks 30 SP8812
Aston Crews Herefs 28 SO6723
Aston End Herts 31 TL2724
Aston Fields Worcs 28 SO9669
Aston Flamville Leics 39 SP4692
Aston Ingham Herefs 28 SO6823
Aston le Walls Nhants 29 SP4950
Aston Magna Gloucs 29 SP1935
Aston Munslow Shrops 37 SO5186
Aston on Clun Shrops 36 SO3981
Aston Pigott Shrops 36 SJ3305
Aston Rogers Shrops 36 SJ3406
Aston Rowant Oxon 22 SU7299
Aston Somerville Worcs 28 SP0438
Aston-sub-Edge Gloucs 28 SP1441
Aston Tirrold Oxon 21 SU5586
Aston-upon-Trent Derbys 39 SK4129
Aston Upthorpe Oxon 21 SU5586
Astwick C Beds 31 TL2138
Astwood M Keyn 30 SP9547
Astwood Worcs 28 SO9365
Astwood Bank Worcs 28 SP0462
Aswarby Lincs 40 TF0639
Aswardby Lincs 51 TF3770
Atcham Shrops 37 SJ5409
Athelhampton Dorset 9 SY7694
Athelington Suffk 33 TM2171
Athelney Somset 8 ST3428
Athelstaneford E Loth 76 NT5377
Atherington Devon 6 SS5922
Atherstone Warwks 39 SP3097
Atherstone on Stour Warwks 29 SP2051
Atherton Wigan 47 SD6703
Atlow Derbys 48 SK2248
Atterby Lincs 50 SK9792
Attercliffe Sheff 49 SK3788
Atterton Leics 39 SP3598
Attleborough Norfk 42 TM0495
Attleborough Warwks 39 SP3790
Attlebridge Norfk 43 TG1216
Attleton Green Suffk 32 TL7454
Atwick E R Yk 57 TA1850
Atworth Wilts 20 ST8565
Aubourn Lincs 50 SK9262
Auchenblae Abers 89 NO7279
Auchenbowie Stirlg 81 NS7987
Auchencairn D & G 66 NX7951
Auchencrow Border 77 NT8560
Auchendinny Mdloth 75 NT2561
Auchengray S Lans 75 NS9954
Auchenmalg D & G 64 NX2352
Auchinleck E Ayrs 74 NS5521
Auchinloch N Lans 74 NS6570
Auchinstarry N Lans 74 NS7176
Auchleven Abers 94 NJ6224
Auchlochan S Lans 74 NS8037
Auchmillan E Ayrs 74 NS5129
Auchmithie Angus 89 NO6743
Auchnagatt Abers 95 NJ9341
Auchterarder P & K 82 NN9412
Auchterderran Fife 82 NT2195
Auchterhouse Angus 83 NO3337
Auchterless Abers 95 NJ7141
Auchtermuchty Fife 83 NO2311
Auchtertool Fife 82 NT2190
Auckley Donc 49 SE6400
Audenshaw Tamesd 48 SJ9197
Audlem Ches E 47 SJ6543
Audley Staffs 47 SJ7950
Audley End Essex 31 TL5337
Audnam Dudley 38 SO8986
Aughton E R Yk 56 SE7038
Aughton Lancs 46 SD3905
Aughton Lancs 53 SD5567
Aughton Rothm 49 SK4586
Aughton Wilts 21 SU2356
Aughton Park Lancs 46 SD4006
Auldearn Highld 93 NH9255
Aulden Herefs 27 SO4654
Auldgirth D & G 66 NX9186
Aultbea Highld 91 NG8789
Aultgrishin Highld 91 NG7485
Ault Hucknall Derbys 49 SK4665
Aunsby Lincs 40 TF0438
Aust S Glos 19 ST5788
Austerfield Donc 49 SK6594
Austrey Warwks 39 SK2906
Austwick N York 54 SD7668
Authorpe Lincs 51 TF3980
Avebury Wilts 20 SU1069
Aveley Thurr 24 TQ5680
Avening Gloucs 20 ST8898
Averham Notts 50 SK7654
Aveton Gifford Devon 5 SX6947
Aviemore Highld 93 NH8913
Avington W Berk 21 SU3767
Avoch Highld 93 NH7055
Avon Hants 10 SZ1498
Avonbridge Falk 75 NS9172
Avon Dassett Warwks 29 SP4150
Avonmouth Bristl 19 ST5178
Avonwick Devon 5 SX7158
Awbridge Hants 10 SU3224
Awliscombe Devon 8 ST1301
Awre Gloucs 28 SO7008
Awsworth Notts 49 SK4844
Axbridge Somset 19 ST4354
Axford Hants 21 SU6043
Axford Wilts 21 SU2370
Axminster Devon 8 SY2998
Axmouth Devon 8 SY2591
Aycliffe Dur 61 NZ2822
Aydon Nthumb 68 NZ0065
Aylburton Gloucs 19 SO6101
Aylesbeare Devon 5 SY0392
Aylesbury Bucks 30 SP8213
Aylesby NE Lin 57 TA2007
Aylesford Kent 14 TQ7359
Aylesham Kent 15 TR2452
Aylestone C Leic 39 SK5700
Aylestone Park C Leic 39 SK5800
Aylmerton Norfk 43 TG1839
Aylsham Norfk 43 TG1926
Aylton Herefs 28 SO6537
Aylworth Gloucs 28 SP1021
Aymestrey Herefs 27 SO4265
Aynho Nhants 29 SP5133
Ayot St Lawrence Herts 31 TL1916
Ayr S Ayrs 73 NS3321
Aysgarth N York 61 SE0088
Ayshford Devon 7 ST0415
Ayside Cumb 59 SD3983
Ayston Rutlnd 40 SK8600
Ayton Border 77 NT9260
Azerley N York 61 SE2574

B

Babbacombe Torbay 5 SX9265
Babbs Green Herts 31 TL3916
Babcary Somset 9 ST5628
Babraham Cambs 31 TL5150
Babworth Notts 49 SK6880
Backaland Ork 100 HY5630
Backford Ches W 46 SJ3971
Backies Highld 97 NC8302
Backwell N Som 19 ST4968
Baconsthorpe Norfk 43 TG1236
Bacton Herefs 27 SO3732
Bacton Norfk 43 TG3433
Bacton Suffk 32 TM0567
Bacup Lancs 54 SD8622
Badachro Highld 91 NG7873
Badbury Swindn 21 SU1980
Badby Nhants 29 SP5658
Badcaul Highld 91 NH0291
Baddeley Edge C Stke 48 SJ9150
Baddeley Green C Stke 48 SJ9051
Baddesley Clinton Warwks 39 SP2072
Baddesley Ensor Warwks 39 SP2798
Badger Shrops 37 SO7699
Badgeworth Gloucs 28 SO9019
Badgworth Somset 19 ST3952
Badicaul Highld 85 NG7529
Badingham Suffk 33 TM3068
Badlesmere Kent 15 TR0153
Badluarach Highld 91 NG9994
Badsey Worcs 28 SP0743
Badshot Lea Surrey 22 SU8648
Badsworth Wakefd 55 SE4614
Badwell Ash Suffk 32 TL9868
Bagber Dorset 9 ST7513
Bagby N York 62 SE4680
Bag Enderby Lincs 51 TF3571
Bagendon Gloucs 28 SP0106
Bàgh a' Chaisteil W Isls 90 NL6698
Bagillt Flints 46 SJ2175
Baginton Warwks 39 SP3474
Baglan Neath 18 SS7492
Bagley Shrops 36 SJ4027
Bagley Somset 19 ST4645
Bagnall Staffs 48 SJ9250
Bagshot Surrey 22 SU9063
Bagstone S Glos 20 ST6987
Bagworth Leics 39 SK4408
Bagwy Llydiart Herefs 27 SO4426
Baildon C Brad 55 SE1539
Baildon Green C Brad 55 SE1439
Baile Ailein W Isls 90 NB2920
Baile a' Mhanaich W Isls 90 NF7755
Baillieston C Glas 74 NS6764
Bainbridge N York 61 SD9390
Bainshole Abers 94 NJ6035
Bainton C Pete 40 TF0906
Bainton E R Yk 56 SE9652
Bakewell Derbys 48 SK2168
Bala Gwynd 45 SH9235
Balallan W Isls 90 NB2920
Balbeggie P & K 82 NO1629
Balblair Highld 93 NH7066
Balby Donc 49 SE5600
Balchreick Highld 98 NC1960
Balcombe W Susx 12 TQ3130
Baldersby N York 62 SE3578
Baldersby St James N York 62 SE3676
Balderstone Lancs 54 SD6332
Balderton Notts 50 SK8151
Baldinnie Fife 83 NO4211
Baldock Herts 31 TL2434
Baldock Services Herts 31 TL2336
Baldovie C Dund 83 NO4533
Baldrine IoM 52 SC4281
Baldslow E Susx 14 TQ8013
Bale Norfk 42 TG0136
Baledgarno P & K 83 NO2730
Balemartine Ag & B 78 NL9841
Balerno C Edin 75 NT1666
Balfield Angus 89 NO5468
Balfour Ork 100 HY4716
Balfron Stirlg 81 NS5489
Balgonar Fife 82 NT0293
Balgowan Highld 87 NN6494
Balgracie D & G 64 NW9860
Balham Gt Lon 23 TQ2873
Balintore Highld 97 NH8675
Balivanich W Isls 90 NF7755
Balkholme E R Yk 56 SE7828
Ballachulish Highld 86 NN0858
Ballajora IoM 52 SC4890
Ballantrae S Ayrs 64 NX0882
Ballasalla IoM 52 SC2870
Ballater Abers 88 NO3695
Ballaugh IoM 52 SC3493
Ballchraggan Highld 97 NH7675
Ballevullin Ag & B 78 NL9546
Ball Green C Stke 48 SJ8952
Ball Hill Hants 21 SU4163
Ballidon Derbys 48 SK2054
Ballindean P & K 83 NO2529
Ballinger Common Bucks 22 SP9103
Ballingham Herefs 27 SO5731
Ballingry Fife 82 NT1797
Ballinluig P & K 88 NN9752
Ballintuim P & K 88 NO1055
Balloch Highld 93 NH7247
Balloch N Lans 74 NS7374
Balloch W Duns 80 NS3982
Balls Cross W Susx 12 SU9826
Balls Green E Susx 13 TQ4936
Ballygrant Ag & B 70 NR3966
Balmacara Highld 85 NG8028
Balmaclellan D & G 65 NX6579
Balmaha Stirlg 81 NS4290
Balmalcolm Fife 83 NO3208
Balmedie Abers 95 NJ9618
Balmerino Fife 83 NO3524
Balmore E Duns 74 NS5973
Balmullo Fife 83 NO4220
Balnaguard P & K 88 NN9451
Balnain Highld 92 NH4430
Balne N York 56 SE5918
Balquhidder Stirlg 81 NN5320
Balsall Common Solhll 39 SP2376
Balsall Heath Birm 38 SP0784
Balscote Oxon 29 SP3942
Balsham Cambs 31 TL5850
Baltasound Shet 100 HP6208
Baltonsborough Somset 9 ST5434
Balvicar Ag & B 79 NM7616
Bamber Bridge Lancs 53 SD5625
Bamber's Green Essex 24 TL5722
Bamburgh Nthumb 77 NU1734
Bamford Derbys 48 SK2083
Bampton Cumb 59 NY5118
Bampton Devon 7 SS9522
Bampton Oxon 21 SP3103
Bampton Grange Cumb 59 NY5218
Banbury Oxon 29 SP4540
Bancffosfelen Carmth 17 SN4811
Banchory Abers 89 NO6995
Bancycapel Carmth 17 SN4214
Bancyfelin Carmth 17 SN3218
Banff Abers 95 NJ6863
Bangor Gwynd 44 SH5772
Bangor-on-Dee Wrexhm 46 SJ3845
Bangors Cnwll 6 SX2099
Banham Norfk 32 TM0687
Bank Hants 10 SU2807
Bankend D & G 66 NY0268
Bankfoot P & K 82 NO0635
Bankglen E Ayrs 66 NS5912
Bankhead C Aber 95 NJ9009
Banknock Falk 81 NS7779
Banks Lancs 53 SD3820
Banningham Norfk 43 TG2129
Bannister Green Essex 24 TL6920
Bannockburn Stirlg 82 NS8190
Banstead Surrey 23 TQ2559
Bantham Devon 5 SX6643
Banton N Lans 81 NS7479
Banwell N Som 19 ST3959
Bapchild Kent 14 TQ9263
Bapton Wilts 20 ST9938
Barabhas W Isls 90 NB3649
Barbaraville Highld 93 NH7472
Barbon Cumb 60 SD6282
Barbrook Devon 18 SS7147
Barby Nhants 29 SP5470
Barcombe E Susx 13 TQ4114
Barcombe Cross E Susx 13 TQ4115
Barden Park Kent 13 TQ5746
Bardfield End Green Essex 24 TL6231
Bardfield Saling Essex 24 TL6826
Bardney Lincs 50 TF1269
Bardon Leics 39 SK4412
Bardon Mill Nthumb 68 NY7764
Bardowie E Duns 74 NS5873
Bardrainney Inver 80 NS3373
Bardsea Cumb 58 SD3074
Bardsey Leeds 55 SE3643
Bardwell Suffk 32 TL9473
Bare Lancs 53 SD4564
Barford Norfk 43 TG1107
Barford Warwks 29 SP2760
Barford St John Oxon 29 SP4433
Barford St Martin Wilts 10 SU0531
Barford St Michael Oxon 29 SP4332
Barfrestone Kent 15 TR2650
Bargeddie N Lans 74 NS6964
Bargoed Caerph 19 ST1599
Barham Cambs 30 TL1375
Barham Kent 15 TR2050
Barham Suffk 33 TM1451
Bar Hill Cambs 31 TL3763
Barholm Lincs 40 TF0810
Barkby Leics 39 SK6309
Barkby Thorpe Leics 39 SK6309
Barkestone-le-Vale Leics 40 SK7734
Barkham Wokham 22 SU7766
Barking Gt Lon 23 TQ4484
Barking Suffk 32 TM0753
Barkingside Gt Lon 23 TQ4489
Barking Tye Suffk 32 TM0652
Barkisland Calder 55 SE0519
Barkla Shop Cnwll 2 SW7350
Barkston Lincs 50 SK9341
Barkston Ash N York 55 SE4936
Barkway Herts 31 TL3835
Barlanark C Glas 74 NS6664
Barlaston Staffs 48 SJ8938
Barlavington W Susx 12 SU9616
Barlborough Derbys 49 SK4777
Barlby N York 56 SE6333
Barlestone Leics 39 SK4205
Barley Herts 31 TL4038
Barley Lancs 54 SD8240
Barleythorpe Rutlnd 40 SK8409
Barling Essex 25 TQ9389
Barlings Lincs 50 TF0774
Barlow Derbys 49 SK3474
Barlow Gatesd 69 NZ1561
Barlow N York 56 SE6428
Barmby Moor E R Yk 56 SE7748
Barmby on the Marsh E R Yk 56 SE6928
Barmouth Gwynd 35 SH6116
Barmpton Darltn 62 NZ3118
Barmston E R Yk 57 TA1659
Barnack C Pete 40 TF0705
Barnard Castle Dur 61 NZ0516
Barnard Gate Oxon 29 SP4010
Barnardiston Suffk 32 TL7148
Barnburgh Donc 55 SE4803
Barnby Suffk 33 TM4789
Barnby Dun Donc 56 SE6109
Barnby in the Willows Notts 50 SK8552
Barnby Moor Notts 49 SK6684
Barnes Gt Lon 23 TQ2276
Barnes Street Kent 13 TQ6447
Barnet Gt Lon 23 TQ2496
Barnetby le Wold N Linc 57 TA0509
Barney Norfk 42 TF9932
Barnham Suffk 32 TL8779
Barnham W Susx 12 SU9503
Barnham Broom Norfk 43 TG0807
Barnhill C Dund 83 NO4731
Barningham Dur 61 NZ0810
Barningham Suffk 32 TL9676
Barnoldby le Beck NE Lin 57 TA2303
Barnoldswick Lancs 54 SD8746
Barns Green W Susx 12 TQ1226
Barnsley Barns 55 SE3406
Barnsley Gloucs 28 SP0704
Barnstaple Devon 6 SS5633
Barnston Essex 24 TL6419
Barnston Wirral 46 SJ2783
Barnstone Notts 40 SK7335
Barnt Green Worcs 38 SP0173
Barnton C Edin 75 NT1874
Barnton Ches W 47 SJ6375
Barnwell All Saints Nhants 40 TL0484
Barnwell St Andrew Nhants 40 TL0584
Barnwood Gloucs 28 SO8518
Barr S Ayrs 64 NX2794
Barra Airport W Isls 90 NF7005
Barrasford Nthumb 68 NY9173
Barrhead E Rens 74 NS4958
Barrhill S Ayrs 64 NX2382
Barrington Cambs 31 TL3849
Barrington Somset 8 ST3818
Barripper Cnwll 2 SW6338
Barrmill N Ayrs 73 NS3651
Barrow Gloucs 28 SO8824
Barrow Lancs 54 SD7338
Barrow Rutlnd 40 SK8815
Barrow Somset 9 ST7231
Barrow Suffk 32 TL7663
Barrowby Lincs 40 SK8736
Barrowden Rutlnd 40 SK9400
Barrowford Lancs 54 SD8539
Barrow Gurney N Som 19 ST5268
Barrow Haven N Linc 57 TA0622
Barrow-in-Furness Cumb 53 SD2068
Barrow Island Cumb 53 SD1968
Barrow-upon-Humber N Linc 57 TA0620
Barrow upon Soar Leics 39 SK5717
Barrow upon Trent Derbys 39 SK3528
Barry Angus 83 NO5334
Barry V Glam 18 ST1268
Barry Island V Glam 18 ST1166
Barsby Leics 40 SK6911
Barsham Suffk 33 TM3989
Barston Solhll 39 SP2078
Bartestree Herefs 27 SO5640
Barthol Chapel Abers 95 NJ8133
Bartholomew Green Essex 24 TL7221
Barthomley Ches E 47 SJ7652
Bartley Hants 10 SU3012
Bartley Green Birm 38 SP0081
Bartlow Cambs 31 TL5845
Barton Cambs 31 TL4055
Barton Ches W 46 SJ4454
Barton Gloucs 28 SP0925
Barton Lancs 53 SD3509
Barton Lancs 53 SD5137
Barton N York 61 NZ2208
Barton Oxon 29 SP5507
Barton Torbay 5 SX9167
Barton Bendish Norfk 42 TF7105
Barton End Gloucs 20 ST8498
Barton Hartshorn Bucks 29 SP6430
Barton in Fabis Notts 39 SK5232
Barton in the Beans Leics 39 SK3906
Barton-le-Clay C Beds 30 TL0830
Barton-le-Street N York 63 SE7274
Barton-le-Willows N York 56 SE7163
Barton Mills Suffk 32 TL7173
Barton-on-Sea Hants 10 SZ2393
Barton-on-the-Heath Warwks 29 SP2532
Barton Park Services N York 61 NZ2107
Barton St David Somset 9 ST5432
Barton Seagrave Nhants 30 SP8877
Barton Stacey Hants 21 SU4341
Barton Town Devon 7 SS6840
Barton Turf Norfk 43 TG3522
Barton-under-Needwood Staffs 39 SK1818
Barton-upon-Humber N Linc 56 TA0221
Barton Waterside N Linc 56 TA0222
Barvas W Isls 90 NB3649
Barway Cambs 31 TL5575
Barwell Leics 39 SP4496
Barwick Devon 6 SS5907
Barwick Somset 9 ST5513
Barwick in Elmet Leeds 55 SE3937
Baschurch Shrops 36 SJ4221
Bascote Warwks 29 SP4063
Bashall Eaves Lancs 54 SD6943
Basildon Essex 24 TQ7189
Basingstoke Hants 21 SU6352
Baslow Derbys 49 SK2572
Bason Bridge Somset 19 ST3446
Bassaleg Newpt 19 ST2786
Bassenthwaite Cumb 58 NY2332
Bassett C Sotn 10 SU4116
Bassingbourn-cum-Kneesworth Cambs 31 TL3344
Bassingham Lincs 50 SK9060
Bassingthorpe Lincs 40 SK9628
Bassus Green Herts 31 TL3025
Baston Lincs 40 TF1113
Bastwick Norfk 43 TG4217
Batchworth Herts 22 TQ0694
Batcombe Dorset 9 ST6103
Batcombe Somset 20 ST6938
Batford Herts 30 TL1415
Bath BaNES 20 ST7464
Bathampton BaNES 20 ST7766
Bathealton Somset 8 ST0823
Batheaston BaNES 20 ST7767
Bathford BaNES 20 ST7866
Bathgate W Loth 75 NS9768
Bathley Notts 50 SK7759
Bathpool Cnwll 4 SX2874
Bathpool Somset 8 ST2526
Bath Side Essex 25 TM2532
Bathway Somset 19 ST5952
Batley Kirk 55 SE2223
Batsford Gloucs 29 SP1833
Battersby N York 62 NZ5907
Battersea Gt Lon 23 TQ2776
Battisford Tye Suffk 32 TM0354
Battle E Susx 14 TQ7515
Battle Powys 26 SO0130
Battlesbridge Essex 24 TQ7894
Battleton Somset 7 SS9127
Baughton Worcs 28 SO8841
Baughurst Hants 21 SU5860
Baulking Oxon 21 SU3191
Baumber Lincs 51 TF2274
Baunton Gloucs 28 SP0104
Baverstock Wilts 10 SU0332
Bawburgh Norfk 43 TG1508
Bawdeswell Norfk 42 TG0420
Bawdrip Somset 19 ST3439
Bawdsey Suffk 33 TM3440
Bawtry Donc 49 SK6493
Baxenden Lancs 54 SD7726
Baxterley Warwks 39 SP2896
Bayble W Isls 90 NB5231
Baybridge Hants 11 SU5223
Baycliff Cumb 53 SD2872
Baydon Wilts 21 SU2878
Bayford Herts 23 TL3108
Bayford Somset 9 ST7229
Baylham Suffk 33 TM1051
Baysham Herefs 27 SO5727
Bayston Hill Shrops 37 SJ4808
Baythorne End Essex 32 TL7242
Bayton Worcs 37 SO6973
Bayworth Oxon 21 SP4901
Beachampton Bucks 30 SP7736
Beachamwell Norfk 42 TF7505
Beacon Devon 8 ST1805
Beacon End Essex 25 TL9524
Beacon Hill Notts 50 SK8153
Beacon Hill Surrey 11 SU8736
Beacon's Bottom Bucks 22 SU7895
Beaconsfield Bucks 22 SU9490
Beaconsfield Services Bucks 22 SU9588
Beadlam N York 62 SE6584
Beadlow C Beds 30 TL1038
Beadnell Nthumb 77 NU2229
Beaford Devon 6 SS5515
Beal N York 56 SE5325
Beal Nthumb 77 NU0642
Bealsmill Cnwll 4 SX3576
Beaminster Dorset 8 ST4701
Beamish Dur 69 NZ2253
Beamsley N York 55 SE0752
Beanacre Wilts 20 ST9066
Beanley Nthumb 77 NU0818
Beardon Devon 4 SX5184
Beare Green Surrey 12 TQ1742
Bearley Warwks 29 SP1860
Bearpark Dur 69 NZ2343
Bearsden E Duns 74 NS5372
Bearsted Kent 14 TQ8055
Bearstone Shrops 37 SJ7239
Bearwood BCP 10 SZ0496
Bearwood Birm 38 SP0286
Bearwood Herefs 27 SO3856
Beattock D & G 66 NT0702
Beauchamp Roding Essex 24 TL5809
Beauchief Sheff 49 SK3381
Beaufort Blae G 27 SO1611
Beaulieu Hants 10 SU3802
Beauly Highld 92 NH5246
Beaumaris IoA 45 SH6076
Beaumont Cumb 67 NY3459
Beaumont Essex 25 TM1624
Beaumont Leys C Leic 39 SK5608
Beausale Warwks 29 SP2470
Beauworth Hants 11 SU5726
Beaworthy Devon 6 SX4699
Beazley End Essex 24 TL7429
Bebington Wirral 46 SJ3383
Beccles Suffk 33 TM4289
Becconsall Lancs 53 SD4523
Beckbury Shrops 37 SJ7601
Beckenham Gt Lon 23 TQ3769
Beckermet Cumb 58 NY0106
Beckfoot Cumb 67 NY0949
Beckford Worcs 28 SO9736
Beckhampton Wilts 20 SU0868
Beckingham Lincs 50 SK8753
Beckingham Notts 50 SK7789
Beckington Somset 20 ST8051
Beckjay Shrops 36 SO3977
Beckley E Susx 14 TQ8523
Beckley Oxon 29 SP5611
Beck Row Suffk 32 TL6977
Beck Side Cumb 58 SD2382
Beckton Gt Lon 23 TQ4381
Beckwithshaw N York 55 SE2653
Becontree Gt Lon 23 TQ4786
Bedale N York 61 SE2688
Bedchester Dorset 9 ST8517
Beddau Rhondd 18 ST0585
Beddgelert Gwynd 44 SH5948
Beddingham E Susx 13 TQ4407
Beddington Gt Lon 23 TQ3065
Beddington Corner Gt Lon 23 TQ2866
Bedfield Suffk 33 TM2166
Bedford Bed 30 TL0449
Bedgrove Bucks 30 SP8412
Bedhampton Hants 11 SU7006
Bedingfield Suffk 33 TM1868
Bedlam N York 55 SE2661
Bedlington Nthumb 69 NZ2681
Bedlinog Myr Td 18 SO0901
Bedminster Bristl 19 ST5771
Bedminster Down Bristl 19 ST5770
Bedmond Herts 22 TL0903
Bednall Staffs 38 SJ9517
Bedrule Border 76 NT6017
Bedstone Shrops 36 SO3676
Bedwas Caerph 19 ST1789
Bedwellty Caerph 19 SO1600
Bedworth Warwks 39 SP3687
Beeby Leics 39 SK6608
Beech Hants 11 SU6938
Beech Staffs 38 SJ8538
Beech Hill W Berk 22 SU6964
Beechingstoke Wilts 20 SU0859
Beedon W Berk 21 SU4878
Beeford E R Yk 57 TA1253
Beeley Derbys 49 SK2667
Beelsby NE Lin 51 TA2001
Beenham W Berk 21 SU5868
Beer Devon 8 SY2289
Beer Somset 8 ST4031
Beercrocombe Somset 8 ST3220
Beer Hackett Dorset 9 ST5911
Beesands Devon 5 SX8140
Beesby Lincs 51 TF4680
Beeson Devon 5 SX8140
Beeston C Beds 31 TL1648
Beeston Ches W 47 SJ5358
Beeston Leeds 55 SE2830
Beeston Norfk 42 TF9015
Beeston Notts 39 SK5236
Beeston Regis Norfk 43 TG1642
Beeswing D & G 66 NX8969
Beetham Cumb 59 SD4979
Beetham Somset 8 ST2712
Beetley Norfk 42 TF9717
Begbroke Oxon 29 SP4614
Begelly Pembks 16 SN1107
Beguildy Powys 36 SO1979
Beighton Norfk 43 TG3808
Beighton Sheff 49 SK4483
Beith N Ayrs 73 NS3553
Bekesbourne Kent 15 TR1955
Belaugh Norfk 43 TG2818
Belbroughton Worcs 38 SO9277
Belchalwell Dorset 9 ST7909
Belchamp Otten Essex 32 TL8041
Belchamp St Paul Essex 32 TL7942
Belchamp Walter Essex 32 TL8240
Belchford Lincs 51 TF2975
Belford Nthumb 77 NU1034
Belgrave C Leic 39 SK5906
Belhaven E Loth 83 NT6678
Bell Busk N York 54 SD9056
Belleau Lincs 51 TF4078
Bell End Worcs 38 SO9477
Bellerby N York 61 SE1192
Belle Vue Cumb 67 NY3756
Belle Vue Wakefd 55 SE3419
Bellingdon Bucks 22 SP9405
Bellingham Nthumb 68 NY8383
Bellochantuy Ag & B 72 NR6632
Bell o' th' Hill Ches W 46 SJ5245
Bellshill N Lans 74 NS7360
Bellside N Lans 74 NS8058
Bellsquarry W Loth 75 NT0565
Bells Yew Green E Susx 13 TQ6135
Belluton BaNES 19 ST6164
Belmont Bl w D 54 SD6715
Belmont Gt Lon 23 TQ2562
Belmont S Ayrs 73 NS3419
Belper Derbys 49 SK3447
Belsay Nthumb 68 NZ0978
Belses Border 76 NT5725
Belsford Devon 5 SX7659
Belsize Herts 22 TL0300
Belstead Suffk 33 TM1241
Belstone Devon 5 SX6293
Belthorn Bl w D 54 SD7124
Beltinge Kent 15 TR1967
Beltingham Nthumb 68 NY7863
Beltoft N Linc 56 SE8006
Belton Leics 39 SK4420
Belton Lincs 40 SK9339
Belton N Linc 56 SE7806
Belton Norfk 43 TG4802
Belton in Rutland Rutlnd 40 SK8101
Belvedere Gt Lon 23 TQ4978
Belvoir Leics 40 SK8133
Bembridge IoW 11 SZ6488
Bemerton Wilts 10 SU1230
Bempton E R Yk 57 TA1972
Benacre Suffk 33 TM5184
Benbecula Airport W Isls 90 NF7855
Benderloch Ag & B 79 NM9038
Benenden Kent 14 TQ8033
Benfieldside Dur 68 NZ0952
Bengeo Herts 31 TL3214
Bengeworth Worcs 28 SP0443
Benhall Green Suffk 33 TM3861
Benhall Street Suffk 33 TM3561
Beningbrough N York 56 SE5257
Benington Herts 31 TL2923
Benington Lincs 51 TF3946
Benllech IoA 44 SH5182
Benniworth Lincs 51 TF2081
Benover Kent 14 TQ7048
Ben Rhydding C Brad 55 SE1347
Benson Oxon 21 SU6291
Bentley Donc 56 SE5605
Bentley E R Yk 56 TA0136
Bentley Hants 22 SU7844
Bentley Suffk 25 TM1136
Bentley Warwks 39 SP2895
Bentpath D & G 67 NY3190
Bentwichen Devon 7 SS7333
Bentworth Hants 11 SU6640
Benvie Angus 83 NO3231
Benville Dorset 8 ST5303
Benwick Cambs 41 TL3490
Beoley Worcs 28 SP0669
Bepton W Susx 11 SU8618
Berden Essex 31 TL4629

122 Berea – Brockton

Berea Pembks 16 SM7930
Bere Alston Devon 4 SX4466
Bere Ferrers Devon 4 SX4563
Bere Regis Dorset 9 SY8494
Bergh Apton Norfk 43 TG3001
Berinsfield Oxon 21 SU5795
Berkeley Gloucs 20 ST6899
Berkhamsted Herts 22 SP9907
Berkley Somset 20 ST8049
Berkswell Solhll 39 SP2479
Bermondsey Gt Lon 23 TQ3479
Bernisdale Highld 90 NG4050
Berrick Prior Oxon 21 SU6294
Berrick Salome Oxon 21 SU6293
Berriedale Highld 100 ND1222
Berrier Cumb 59 NY3929
Berriew Powys 36 SJ1801
Berrington Shrops 37 SJ5206
Berrington Worcs 27 SO5767
Berrington Green Worcs 27 SO5766
Berrow Somset 19 ST2951
Berrow Green Worcs 28 SO7458
Berryfields Bucks 30 SP7915
Berrynarbor Devon 6 SS5646
Berry Pomeroy Devon 5 SX8261
Bersham Wrexhm 46 SJ3049
Bersted W Susx 12 SU9200
Berwick E Susx 13 TQ5105
Berwick Bassett Wilts 20 SU0973
Berwick Hill Nthumb 69 NZ1775
Berwick St James Wilts 10 SU0739
Berwick St John Wilts 9 ST9422
Berwick St Leonard Wilts 9 ST9233
Berwick-upon-Tweed Nthumb 77 NT9953
Bescar Lancs 53 SD3913
Besford Worcs 28 SO9144
Bessacarr Donc 49 SE6100
Bessingby E R Yk 57 TA1565
Bessingham Norfk 43 TG1636
Besthorpe Norfk 42 TM0595
Besthorpe Notts 50 SK8264
Bestwood Village Notts 49 SK5547
Beswick E R Yk 56 TA0147
Betchworth Surrey 12 TQ2150
Bethel Gwynd 44 SH5265
Bethel IoA 44 SH3970
Bethersden Kent 14 TQ9240
Bethesda Gwynd 45 SH6266
Bethesda Pembks 16 SN0918
Bethlehem Carmth 26 SN6825
Bethnal Green Gt Lon 23 TQ3482
Betley Staffs 47 SJ7548
Betsham Kent 14 TQ6071
Betteshanger Kent 15 TR3152
Bettiscombe Dorset 8 ST3900
Bettisfield Wrexhm 37 SJ4635
Bettws Brdgnd 18 SS9086
Bettws Newpt 19 ST2890
Bettws Cedewain Powys 36 SO1296
Bettws Ifan Cerdgn 17 SN3047
Bettws-Newydd Mons 27 SO3606
Bettyhill Highld 99 NC7061
Betws Bledrws Cerdgn 17 SN5952
Betws Gwerfil Goch Denbgs 45 SJ0346
Betws-y-Coed Conwy 45 SH7956
Betws-yn-Rhos Conwy 45 SH9073
Beulah Cerdgn 17 SN2846
Beulah Powys 26 SN9251
Bevercotes Notts 49 SK6972
Beverley E R Yk 57 TA0339
Beverston Gloucs 20 ST8694
Bewcastle Cumb 67 NY5674
Bewdley Worcs 37 SO7875
Bewerley N York 55 SE1565
Bewholme E R Yk 57 TA1649
Bexhill-on-Sea E Susx 14 TQ7407
Bexley Gt Lon 23 TQ4973
Bexleyheath Gt Lon 23 TQ4875
Bexwell Norfk 41 TF6303
Beyton Suffk 32 TL9363
Beyton Green Suffk 32 TL9363
Bhaltos W Isls 90 NB0936
Bibury Gloucs 28 SP1106
Bicester Oxon 29 SP5823
Bickenhill Solhll 39 SP1882
Bicker Lincs 41 TF2237
Bickerstaffe Lancs 46 SD4404
Bickerton N York 55 SE4550
Bickford Staffs 38 SJ8814
Bickington Devon 5 SX8072
Bickington Devon 6 SS5332
Bickleigh Devon 4 SX5262
Bickleigh Devon 7 SS9407
Bickley Ches W 47 SJ5348
Bickley Gt Lon 23 TQ4268
Bickley N York 63 SE9191
Bicknacre Essex 24 TL7802
Bicknoller Somset 18 ST1139
Bicknor Kent 14 TQ8658
Bicton Shrops 36 SJ4415
Bicton Shrops 36 SO2983
Bidborough Kent 13 TQ5643
Biddenden Kent 14 TQ8538
Biddenham Bed 30 TL0250
Biddestone Wilts 20 ST8673
Biddisham Somset 19 ST3853
Biddlesden Bucks 29 SP6340
Biddulph Staffs 47 SJ8858
Biddulph Moor Staffs 48 SJ9058
Bideford Devon 6 SS4526
Bidford-on-Avon Warwks 28 SP1052
Bielby E R Yk 56 SE7843
Bieldside C Aber 89 NJ8702
Bierley IoW 11 SZ5078
Bierton Bucks 30 SP8415
Bigbury Devon 5 SX6646
Bigbury-on-Sea Devon 5 SX6544
Bigby Lincs 57 TA0507
Biggar S Lans 75 NT0437
Biggin Derbys 48 SK1559
Biggin Hill Gt Lon 23 TQ4159
Biggleswade C Beds 31 TL1944
Bighton Hants 11 SU6134
Biglands Cumb 67 NY2553
Bignor W Susx 12 SU9814
Bigrigg Cumb 58 NY0013
Bigton Shet 100 HU3820
Bilborough C Nott 49 SK5241
Bilbrook Somset 7 ST0341
Bilbrough N York 56 SE5346
Bilbster Highld 100 ND2853
Bildershaw Dur 61 NZ2024
Bildeston Suffk 32 TL9949
Billericay Essex 24 TQ6794
Billesdon Leics 40 SK7202
Billesley Warwks 28 SP1456
Billingborough Lincs 40 TF1133
Billinge St Hel 46 SD5200
Billingford Norfk 33 TM1678
Billingford Norfk 42 TG0120
Billingham S on T 62 NZ4624
Billinghay Lincs 50 TF1554
Billingley Barns 55 SE4304
Billingshurst W Susx 12 TQ0825
Billingsley Shrops 37 SO7184
Billington C Beds 30 SP9422
Billington Lancs 54 SD7235
Billockby Norfk 43 TG4313
Billy Row Dur 61 NZ1637
Bilsborrow Lancs 53 SD5139
Bilsby Lincs 51 TF4776
Bilsham W Susx 12 SU9702
Bilsington Kent 15 TR0434
Bilsthorpe Notts 49 SK6460
Bilston Wolves 38 SO9596
Bilstone Leics 39 SK3605
Bilton E R Yk 57 TA1632
Bilton N York 55 SE3157
Bilton Warwks 39 SP4873
Bilton-in-Ainsty N York 55 SE4749
Binbrook Lincs 51 TF2093
Bincombe Dorset 9 SY6884
Binegar Somset 19 ST6149
Binfield Br For 22 SU8471
Binfield Heath Oxon 22 SU7477
Bingfield Nthumb 68 NY9772
Bingham Notts 40 SK7039
Bingley C Brad 55 SE1039
Binham Norfk 42 TF9839
Binley Covtry 39 SP3778
Binley Hants 21 SU4253
Binley Woods Warwks 39 SP3977
Binnegar Dorset 9 SY8887
Binscombe Surrey 12 SU9645
Binstead IoW 11 SZ5892
Binsted Hants 11 SU7740
Binsted W Susx 12 SU9806
Binton Warwks 28 SP1454
Bintree Norfk 42 TG0123
Birch Essex 25 TL9419
Bircham Newton Norfk 42 TF7633
Bircham Tofts Norfk 42 TF7732
Birchanger Essex 31 TL5122
Birchanger Green Services Essex 31 TL5121
Birch Cross Staffs 38 SK1230
Bircher Herefs 27 SO4765
Birchfield Birm 38 SP0790
Birch Green Essex 25 TL9418
Birchgrove Cardif 19 ST1679
Birchgrove Swans 18 SS7098
Birchgrove W Susx 13 TQ4029
Birchington Kent 15 TR3069
Birchley Heath Warwks 39 SP2894
Birchover Derbys 48 SK2362
Birch Services Rochdl 47 SD8407
Birch Vale Derbys 48 SK0286
Birchwood Lincs 50 SK9369
Birch Wood Somset 8 ST2414
Birchwood Warrtn 47 SJ6591
Bircotes Notts 49 SK6391
Birdbrook Essex 32 TL7041
Birdforth N York 62 SE4875
Birdham W Susx 11 SU8200
Birdingbury Warwks 29 SP4368
Birdlip Gloucs 28 SO9214
Birdsall N York 56 SE8165
Birds Edge Kirk 55 SE2007
Birds Green Essex 24 TL5808
Birdsgreen Shrops 37 SO7785
Birdsmoorgate Dorset 8 ST3900
Birdwell Barns 49 SE3401
Birgham Border 76 NT7939
Birkby N York 62 NZ3202
Birkdale Sefton 53 SD3214
Birkenhead Wirral 46 SJ3288
Birkenhead (Queensway) Tunnel Lpool 46 SJ3389
Birkenshaw Kirk 55 SE2028
Birkhill Angus 83 NO3534
Birkin N York 56 SE5326
Birley Herefs 27 SO4553
Birley Carr Sheff 49 SK3392
Birling Kent 14 TQ6860
Birlingham Worcs 28 SO9343
Birmingham Birm 38 SP0786
Birmingham Airport Solhll 39 SP1883
Birnam P & K 88 NO0341
Birness Abers 95 NJ9933
Birstall Kirk 55 SE2225
Birstall Leics 39 SK5909
Birstwith N York 55 SE2359
Birtley Gatesd 69 NZ2756
Birtley Herefs 27 SO3669
Birtley Nthumb 68 NY8778
Birts Street Worcs 28 SO7836
Bisbrooke Rutlnd 40 SP8899
Biscathorpe Lincs 51 TF2284
Bisham W & M 22 SU8485
Bishampton Worcs 28 SO9951
Bish Mill Devon 7 SS7425
Bishop Auckland Dur 61 NZ2028
Bishopbridge Lincs 50 TF0391
Bishopbriggs E Duns 74 NS6070
Bishop Burton E R Yk 56 SE9839
Bishop Middleham Dur 62 NZ3231
Bishopmill Moray 94 NJ2163
Bishop Monkton N York 55 SE3266
Bishop Norton Lincs 50 SK9892
Bishopsbourne Kent 15 TR1852
Bishops Cannings Wilts 20 SU0364
Bishop's Castle Shrops 36 SO3288
Bishop's Caundle Dorset 9 ST6913
Bishop's Cleeve Gloucs 28 SO9627
Bishop's Frome Herefs 28 SO6648
Bishop's Green Essex 24 TL6217
Bishop's Hull Somset 8 ST2024
Bishop's Itchington Warwks 29 SP3857
Bishops Lydeard Somset 8 ST1729
Bishop's Norton Gloucs 28 SO8424
Bishop's Nympton Devon 7 SS7523
Bishop's Offley Staffs 37 SJ7729
Bishop's Stortford Herts 31 TL4821
Bishop's Sutton Hants 11 SU6032
Bishop's Tachbrook Warwks 29 SP3161
Bishop's Tawton Devon 6 SS5729
Bishopsteignton Devon 5 SX9073
Bishopstoke Hants 11 SU4619
Bishopston Swans 17 SS5789
Bishopstone Bucks 22 SP8010
Bishopstone E Susx 13 TQ4701
Bishopstone Herefs 27 SO4143
Bishopstone Kent 15 TR2068
Bishopstone Swindn 21 SU2483
Bishopstone Wilts 10 SU0625
Bishopstrow Wilts 20 ST8943
Bishop Sutton BaNES 19 ST5859
Bishop's Waltham Hants 11 SU5517
Bishopswood Somset 8 ST2612
Bishop's Wood Staffs 38 SJ8309
Bishopsworth Bristl 19 ST5768
Bishop Thornton N York 55 SE2563
Bishopthorpe C York 56 SE5947
Bishopton Darltn 62 NZ3621
Bishopton Rens 81 NS4371
Bishop Wilton E R Yk 56 SE7955
Bishton Newpt 19 ST3887
Bishton Staffs 38 SK0220
Bisley Gloucs 28 SO9005
Bisley Surrey 22 SU9559
Bissoe Cnwll 2 SW7741
Bisterne Hants 10 SU1401
Bitchfield Lincs 40 SK9828
Bittadon Devon 6 SS5441
Bittaford Devon 5 SX6656
Bitterley Shrops 37 SO5677
Bitterne C Sotn 10 SU4513
Bitteswell Leics 39 SP5385
Bitton S Glos 20 ST6869
Bix Oxon 22 SU7284
Bixter Shet 100 HU3352
Blaby Leics 39 SP5697
Blackawton Devon 5 SX8050
Blackborough Devon 8 ST0909
Blackborough End Norfk 42 TF6615
Black Bourton Oxon 29 SP2804
Blackboys E Susx 13 TQ5220
Blackbrook Derbys 49 SK3347
Blackbrook St Hel 47 SJ5396
Blackbrook Staffs 37 SJ7638
Blackburn Abers 95 NJ8212
Blackburn Bl w D 54 SD6827
Blackburn W Loth 75 NS9865
Blackburn with Darwen Services Bl w D 54 SD6823
Black Dog Devon 7 SS8009
Blackdown Dorset 8 ST3903
Blacker Hill Barns 49 SE3602
Blackfen Gt Lon 23 TQ4674
Blackfield Hants 10 SU4402
Blackford P & K 82 NN8908
Blackford Somset 9 ST6526
Blackford Somset 19 ST4147
Blackfordby Leics 39 SK3217
Blackhall Colliery Dur 62 NZ4539
Blackhall Mill Gatesd 69 NZ1156
Blackheath Gt Lon 23 TQ3876
Blackheath Sandw 38 SO9786
Blackheath Suffk 33 TM4274
Blackheath Surrey 12 TQ0346
Blackhill Dur 68 NZ0851
Blackhorse Devon 5 SX9893
Blackley Manch 47 SD8502
Blackmarstone Herefs 27 SO5038
Blackmill Brdgnd 18 SS9386
Blackmoor Hants 11 SU7733
Blackmoor N Som 19 ST4661
Blackmoorfoot Kirk 55 SE0913
Blackmore Essex 24 TL6001
Blackmore End Essex 24 TL7430
Blackness Falk 82 NT0579
Blacknest Hants 11 SU7941
Black Notley Essex 24 TL7620
Blacko Lancs 54 SD8541
Black Pill Swans 17 SS6190
Blackpool Bpool 53 SD3036
Blackpool Devon 5 SX8547
Blackridge W Loth 74 NS8967
Blackrod Bolton 54 SD6110
Blackshaw Head Calder 54 SD9527
Blackstone W Susx 12 TQ2316
Black Street Suffk 33 TM5186
Blackthorn Oxon 29 SP6219
Blackthorpe Suffk 32 TL9063
Blacktoft E R Yk 56 SE8324
Black Torrington Devon 6 SS4605
Blackwall Derbys 49 SK2549
Blackwall Tunnel Gt Lon 23 TQ3880
Blackwater Cnwll 2 SW7346
Blackwater Hants 22 SU8459
Blackwater IoW 11 SZ5086
Blackwater Somset 8 ST2615
Blackwaterfoot N Ayrs 72 NR9028
Blackwell Cumb 67 NY4053
Blackwell Derbys 48 SK1272
Blackwell Derbys 49 SK4458
Blackwell Warwks 29 SP2443
Blackwell Worcs 38 SO9972
Blackwood Caerph 19 ST1797
Blackwood S Lans 74 NS7844
Blacon Ches W 46 SJ3868
Bladnoch D & G 64 NX4254
Bladon Oxon 29 SP4514
Blaenannerch Cerdgn 17 SN2448
Blaenau Ffestiniog Gwynd 45 SH7045
Blaenavon Torfn 27 SO2508
Blaencwm Rhondd 18 SS9298
Blaenffos Pembks 17 SN1937
Blaengarw Brdgnd 18 SS9092
Blaengwrach Neath 26 SN8605
Blaengwynfi Neath 18 SS8996
Blaenpennal Cerdgn 35 SN6264
Blaenplwyf Cerdgn 34 SN5775
Blaenporth Cerdgn 17 SN2648
Blaenrhondda Rhondd 18 SS9299
Blaenwaun Carmth 17 SN2327
Blaen-y-coed Carmth 17 SN3427
Blagdon N Som 19 ST5059
Blagdon Somset 8 ST2118
Blagdon Torbay 5 SX8561
Blagdon Hill Somset 8 ST2117
Blaich Highld 85 NN0376
Blaina Blae G 27 SO2008
Blair Atholl P & K 87 NN8665
Blairgowrie P & K 88 NO1745
Blairingone P & K 82 NS9896
Blairlogie Stirlg 82 NS8396
Blairmore Ag & B 80 NS1983
Blaisdon Gloucs 28 SO7017
Blakebrook Worcs 38 SO8276
Blakedown Worcs 38 SO8878
Blake End Essex 24 TL7023
Blakemere Ches W 47 SJ5571
Blakemere Herefs 27 SO3641
Blakenall Heath Wsall 38 SK0002
Blakeney Gloucs 28 SO6707
Blakeney Norfk 42 TG0243
Blakenhall Ches E 47 SJ7247
Blakenhall Wolves 38 SO9197
Blakesley Nhants 29 SP6250
Blanchland Nthumb 68 NY9650
Blandford Forum Dorset 9 ST8806
Blandford St Mary Dorset 9 ST8805
Blanefield Stirlg 81 NS5479
Blankney Lincs 50 TF0660
Blantyre S Lans 74 NS6957
Blaston Leics 40 SP8095
Blatherwycke Nhants 40 SP9795
Blawith Cumb 58 SD2888
Blaxhall Suffk 33 TM3656
Blaxton Donc 49 SE6700
Blaydon Gatesd 69 NZ1863
Bleadney Somset 19 ST4845
Bleadon N Som 19 ST3456
Blean Kent 15 TR1260
Bleasby Notts 49 SK7149
Blebocraigs Fife 83 NO4315
Bleddfa Powys 27 SO2068
Bledington Gloucs 29 SP2422
Bledlow Bucks 22 SP7702
Bledlow Ridge Bucks 22 SU7997
Blencarn Cumb 60 NY6331
Blencogo Cumb 67 NY1947
Blendworth Hants 11 SU7113
Blennerhasset Cumb 58 NY1741
Bletchingdon Oxon 29 SP5018
Bletchingley Surrey 12 TQ3250
Bletchley M Keyn 30 SP8633
Bletchley Shrops 37 SJ6233
Bletherston Pembks 16 SN0721
Bletsoe Bed 30 TL0258
Blewbury Oxon 21 SU5385
Blickling Norfk 43 TG1728
Blidworth Notts 49 SK5956
Blidworth Bottoms Notts 49 SK5854
Blindcrake Cumb 58 NY1434
Blindley Heath Surrey 12 TQ3645
Blisland Cnwll 3 SX1073
Blissford Hants 10 SU1713
Bliss Gate Worcs 37 SO7472
Blisworth Nhants 30 SP7253
Blithbury Staffs 38 SK0819
Blockley Gloucs 29 SP1634
Blofield Norfk 43 TG3309
Blofield Heath Norfk 43 TG3311
Blo Norton Norfk 32 TM0179
Blore Staffs 48 SK1349
Bloxham Oxon 29 SP4336
Bloxholm Lincs 50 TF0653
Bloxwich Wsall 38 SJ9902
Bloxworth Dorset 9 SY8894
Blubberhouses N York 55 SE1655
Blue Anchor Somset 7 ST0243
Blue Bell Hill Kent 14 TQ7462
Blundellsands Sefton 46 SJ3099
Blundeston Suffk 43 TM5297
Blunham C Beds 31 TL1551
Blunsdon St Andrew Swindn 20 SU1389
Bluntington Worcs 38 SO9074
Bluntisham Cambs 31 TL3674
Blurton C Stke 48 SJ8941
Blyborough Lincs 50 SK9394
Blyford Suffk 33 TM4276
Blymhill Staffs 37 SJ8112
Blyth Notts 49 SK6287
Blyth Nthumb 69 NZ3181
Blyth Bridge Border 75 NT1345
Blythburgh Suffk 33 TM4475
Blythe Bridge Staffs 48 SJ9541
Blyth Services Notts 49 SK6288
Blyton Lincs 50 SK8594
Boarhills Fife 83 NO5613
Boarhunt Hants 11 SU6008
Boarstall Bucks 29 SP6214
Boat of Garten Highld 93 NH9319
Bobbing Kent 14 TQ8865
Bobbington Staffs 37 SO8090
Bocking Essex 24 TL7623
Bocking Churchstreet Essex 24 TL7525
Boddam Abers 95 NK1342
Boddington Gloucs 28 SO8925
Bodedern IoA 44 SH3380
Bodelwyddan Denbgs 45 SJ0075
Bodenham Herefs 27 SO5350
Bodenham Wilts 10 SU1626
Bodenham Moor Herefs 27 SO5450
Bodewryd IoA 44 SH4090
Bodfari Denbgs 46 SJ0970
Bodffordd IoA 44 SH4277
Bodham Norfk 43 TG1240
Bodiam E Susx 14 TQ7825
Bodicote Oxon 29 SP4538
Bodinnick Cnwll 3 SX1352
Bodle Street Green E Susx 13 TQ6514
Bodmin Cnwll 3 SX0667
Bodsham Kent 15 TR1045
Boduan Gwynd 44 SH3237
Bodwen Cnwll 3 SX0360
Bogbrae Abers 95 NK0335
Boggs Holdings E Loth 76 NT4470
Bogmoor Moray 94 NJ3563
Bognor Regis W Susx 12 SZ9399
Bogue D & G 65 NX6481
Bohortha Cnwll 3 SW8532
Bolam Dur 61 NZ1922
Bolberry Devon 5 SX6939
Boldmere Birm 38 SP1194
Boldre Hants 10 SZ3198
Boldron Dur 61 NZ0314
Bole Notts 50 SK7987
Bolehill Derbys 49 SK2955
Bolham Devon 7 SS9515
Bolham Water Devon 8 ST1612
Bolingey Cnwll 2 SW7653
Bollington Ches E 48 SJ9377
Bolney W Susx 12 TQ2622
Bolnhurst Bed 30 TL0859
Bolnore W Susx 12 TQ3223
Bolsover Derbys 49 SK4770
Bolsterstone Sheff 49 SK2696
Boltby N York 62 SE4886
Bolton Bolton 54 SD7108
Bolton Cumb 60 NY6323
Bolton E Loth 76 NT5070
Bolton E R Yk 56 SE7752
Bolton Nthumb 69 NU1013
Bolton Abbey N York 55 SE0754
Bolton-by-Bowland Lancs 54 SD7849
Boltonfellend Cumb 67 NY4768
Boltongate Cumb 58 NY2340
Bolton-le-Sands Lancs 53 SD4867
Bolton Low Houses Cumb 67 NY2344
Bolton-on-Swale N York 61 SE2599
Bolton Percy N York 56 SE5341
Bolton upon Dearne Barns 49 SE4502
Bolventor Cnwll 3 SX1876
Bomere Heath Shrops 37 SJ4719
Bonar Bridge Highld 97 NH6191
Bonby N Linc 56 TA0015
Boncath Pembks 17 SN2038
Bonchester Bridge Border 67 NT5812
Bondleigh Devon 7 SS6505
Bonds Lancs 53 SD4944
Bo'ness Falk 82 NT0081
Boney Hay Staffs 38 SK0410
Bonhill W Duns 80 NS3979
Boningale Shrops 38 SJ8202
Bonkle N Lans 74 NS8457
Bonnington Kent 15 TR0535
Bonnybank Fife 83 NO3503
Bonnyrigg Mdloth 75 NT3065
Bonnyton Angus 83 NO3338
Bonsall Derbys 49 SK2758
Bont-Dolgadfan Powys 35 SH8800
Bont-goch Cerdgn 35 SN6886
Bontnewydd Cerdgn 35 SN6165
Bontnewydd Gwynd 44 SH4859
Bontuchel Denbgs 46 SJ0857
Bonvilston V Glam 18 ST0673
Boode Devon 6 SS5037
Booker Bucks 22 SU8391
Boosbeck R & Cl 62 NZ6617
Boose's Green Essex 24 TL8431
Boot Cumb 58 NY1700
Booth Calder 55 SE0427
Boothby Graffoe Lincs 50 SK9859
Boothby Pagnell Lincs 40 SK9730
Boothferry E R Yk 56 SE7326
Boothstown Salfd 47 SD7200
Boothville Nhants 30 SP7864
Bootle Cumb 58 SD1088
Bootle Sefton 46 SJ3495
Boraston Shrops 27 SO6169
Borden Kent 14 TQ8862
Boreham Essex 24 TL7609
Boreham Street E Susx 14 TQ6611
Borehamwood Herts 23 TQ1996
Boreland D & G 67 NY1691
Borgh W Isls 90 NB4055
Borgh W Isls 90 NF6501
Borgue D & G 65 NX6248
Borley Essex 32 TL8443
Borness D & G 65 NX6145
Boroughbridge N York 55 SE3966
Borough Green Kent 14 TQ6157
Borrowash Derbys 39 SK4134
Borrowby N York 62 SE4289
Borrowstoun Falk 82 NS9980
Borstal Medway 14 TQ7366
Borth Cerdgn 35 SN6090
Borth-y-Gest Gwynd 44 SH5637
Borve Highld 90 NG4448
Borve W Isls 90 NB4055
Borve W Isls 90 NF6501
Borwick Lancs 59 SD5272
Bosbury Herefs 28 SO6943
Boscastle Cnwll 4 SX0990
Boscombe BCP 10 SZ1191
Boscombe Wilts 10 SU2038
Bosham W Susx 11 SU8003
Bosherston Pembks 16 SR9694
Bosley Ches E 48 SJ9165
Bossall N York 56 SE7160
Bossiney Cnwll 4 SX0688
Bossingham Kent 15 TR1548
Bossington Somset 18 SS8947
Bostock Green Ches W 47 SJ6769
Boston Lincs 51 TF3243
Boston Spa Leeds 55 SE4245
Boswinger Cnwll 3 SW9841
Botallack Cnwll 2 SW3732
Botany Bay Gt Lon 23 TQ2999
Botesdale Suffk 32 TM0475
Bothal Nthumb 69 NZ2386
Bothamsall Notts 49 SK6773
Bothel Cumb 58 NY1738
Bothenhampton Dorset 8 SY4791
Bothwell S Lans 74 NS7058
Bothwell Services S Lans 74 NS7059
Botley Bucks 22 SP9802
Botley Hants 11 SU5113
Botley Oxon 29 SP4806
Botolph Claydon Bucks 30 SP7324
Botolphs W Susx 12 TQ1909
Bottesford Leics 40 SK8038
Bottesford N Linc 56 SE8906
Bottisham Cambs 31 TL5460
Bottomcraig Fife 83 NO3724
Bottoms Calder 54 SD9321
Botusfleming Cnwll 4 SX4061
Botwnnog Gwynd 44 SH2631
Bough Beech Kent 13 TQ4847
Boughrood Powys 26 SO1239
Boughton Nhants 30 SP7565
Boughton Norfk 42 TF6902
Boughton Notts 49 SK6768
Boughton Aluph Kent 15 TR0246
Boughton Green Kent 14 TQ7650
Boughton Monchelsea Kent 14 TQ7650
Boughton Street Kent 15 TR0559
Bouldon Shrops 37 SO5485
Boulmer Nthumb 69 NU2614
Boultham Lincs 50 SK9669
Bourn Cambs 31 TL3256
Bournbrook Birm 38 SP0483
Bourne Lincs 40 TF0920
Bournebridge Essex 23 TQ5094
Bourne End Bucks 22 SU8987
Bourne End C Beds 30 SP9644
Bourne End Herts 22 TL0206
Bournemouth BCP 10 SZ0890
Bournemouth Airport BCP 10 SZ1198
Bournes Green Sthend 24 TQ9186
Bournheath Worcs 38 SO9574
Bournmoor Dur 69 NZ3051
Bournville Birm 38 SP0481
Bourton Dorset 9 ST7630
Bourton Oxon 21 SU2386
Bourton Shrops 37 SO5996
Bourton Wilts 20 SU0464
Bourton on Dunsmore Warwks 29 SP4370
Bourton-on-the-Hill Gloucs 29 SP1732
Bourton-on-the-Water Gloucs 29 SP1721
Bousd Ag & B 78 NM2563
Bouth Cumb 59 SD3285
Bouthwaite N York 55 SE1271
Boveridge Dorset 10 SU0514
Bovey Tracey Devon 5 SX8178
Bovingdon Herts 22 TL0103
Bow Devon 7 SS7201
Bow Gt Lon 23 TQ3683
Bow Ork 100 ND3692
Bow Brickhill M Keyn 30 SP9034
Bowbridge Gloucs 28 SO8505
Bowburn Dur 61 NZ3037
Bowcombe IoW 11 SZ4786
Bowd Devon 8 SY1090
Bowden Border 76 NT5530
Bowden Hill Wilts 20 ST9367
Bowdon Traffd 47 SJ7686
Bower Highld 100 ND2362
Bowerchalke Wilts 10 SU0223
Bowers Staffs 37 SJ8135
Bowers Gifford Essex 24 TQ7588
Bowershall Fife 82 NT0991
Bower's Row Leeds 55 SE4028
Bowes Dur 61 NY9913
Bowgreave Lancs 53 SD4943
Bowley Herefs 27 SO5452
Bowlhead Green Surrey 12 SU9138
Bowling C Brad 55 SE1731
Bowling W Duns 81 NS4373
Bowmanstead Cumb 58 SD2996
Bowmore Ag & B 70 NR3159
Bowness-on-Solway Cumb 67 NY2262
Bowness-on-Windermere Cumb 59 SD4097
Bowriefauld Angus 89 NO5147
Bowsden Nthumb 77 NT9941
Bow Street Cerdgn 35 SN6285
Bowthorpe Norfk 43 TG1709
Box Gloucs 20 SO8600
Box Wilts 20 ST8268
Boxford Suffk 32 TL9640
Boxford W Berk 21 SU4271
Boxgrove W Susx 11 SU9007
Boxley Kent 14 TQ7758
Boxmoor Herts 22 TL0406
Boxted Essex 25 TL9933
Boxted Essex 25 TM0031
Boxted Suffk 32 TL8251
Boxted Cross Essex 25 TM0032
Boxworth Cambs 31 TL3464
Boyden Gate Kent 15 TR2265
Boylestone Derbys 39 SK1835
Boyndie Abers 94 NJ6463
Boynton E R Yk 57 TA1367
Boyton Cnwll 4 SX3292
Boyton Suffk 33 TM3747
Boyton Wilts 20 ST9539
Boyton Cross Essex 24 TL6409
Boyton End Suffk 32 TL7244
Bozeat Nhants 30 SP9058
Brabourne Kent 15 TR1041
Brabourne Lees Kent 15 TR0840
Bracadale Highld 84 NG3538
Braceborough Lincs 40 TF0713
Bracebridge Heath Lincs 50 SK9867
Bracebridge Low Fields Lincs 50 SK9666
Braceby Lincs 40 TF0135
Bracewell Lancs 54 SD8648
Brackenfield Derbys 49 SK3759
Brackla Brdgnd 18 SS9279
Bracklesham W Susx 11 SZ8096
Brackley Nhants 29 SP5837
Bracknell Br For 22 SU8769
Braco P & K 82 NN8309
Bracon Ash Norfk 43 TM1899
Bradbourne Derbys 48 SK2052
Bradbury Dur 62 NZ3128
Bradden Nhants 29 SP6448
Bradeley C Stke 47 SJ8851
Bradenham Bucks 22 SU8297
Bradenstoke Wilts 20 SU0079
Bradfield Devon 7 ST0509
Bradfield Essex 25 TM1430
Bradfield Norfk 43 TG2733
Bradfield Sheff 49 SK2692
Bradfield W Berk 21 SU6072
Bradfield Combust Suffk 32 TL8957
Bradfield Green Ches E 47 SJ6859
Bradfield Heath Essex 25 TM1430
Bradfield St Clare Suffk 32 TL9057
Bradfield St George Suffk 32 TL9059
Bradford C Brad 55 SE1632
Bradford Devon 6 SS4207
Bradford Abbas Dorset 9 ST5813
Bradford Leigh Wilts 20 ST8362
Bradford-on-Avon Wilts 20 ST8261
Bradford-on-Tone Somset 8 ST1722
Bradford Peverell Dorset 9 SY6593
Bradiford Devon 6 SS5534
Brading IoW 11 SZ6087
Bradley Derbys 48 SK2246
Bradley Hants 21 SU6341
Bradley NE Lin 57 TA2406
Bradley Staffs 38 SJ8717
Bradley Wolves 38 SO9595
Bradley Worcs 28 SO9860
Bradley Green Worcs 28 SO9862
Bradley in the Moors Staffs 48 SK0541
Bradley Stoke S Glos 19 ST6181
Bradmore Notts 39 SK5830
Bradninch Devon 7 SS9904
Bradnop Staffs 48 SK0155
Bradpole Dorset 8 SY4894
Bradshaw Calder 55 SE0729
Bradstone Devon 4 SX3880
Bradwall Green Ches E 47 SJ7563
Bradwell Derbys 48 SK1781
Bradwell Essex 24 TL8022
Bradwell M Keyn 30 SP8340
Bradwell Norfk 43 TG5003
Bradwell-on-Sea Essex 25 TM0006
Bradwell Waterside Essex 25 TL9907
Bradworthy Devon 6 SS3214
Brae Shet 100 HU3568
Braehead S Lans 75 NS9550
Braemar Abers 88 NO1591
Braeside Inver 80 NS2374
Braeswick Ork 100 HY6137
Brafferton Darltn 61 NZ2921
Brafferton N York 55 SE4370
Brafield-on-the-Green Nhants 30 SP8258
Bragar W Isls 90 NB2947
Bragbury End Herts 31 TL2621
Braidwood S Lans 74 NS8448
Brailsford Derbys 49 SK2541
Braintree Essex 24 TL7523
Braiseworth Suffk 33 TM1371
Braishfield Hants 10 SU3725
Braithwaite Cumb 58 NY2323
Braithwell Donc 49 SK5394
Bramber W Susx 12 TQ1810
Bramcote Warwks 39 SP4088
Bramdean Hants 11 SU6128
Bramerton Norfk 43 TG2904
Bramfield Herts 31 TL2915
Bramfield Suffk 33 TM3973
Bramford Suffk 33 TM1246
Bramhall Stockp 48 SJ8984
Bramham Leeds 55 SE4242
Bramhope Leeds 55 SE2543
Bramley Hants 21 SU6559
Bramley Leeds 55 SE2435
Bramley Rothm 49 SK4892
Bramley Surrey 12 TQ0044
Bramling Kent 15 TR2256
Brampford Speke Devon 7 SX9298
Brampton Cambs 31 TL2170
Brampton Cumb 60 NY6723
Brampton Cumb 67 NY5361
Brampton Lincs 50 SK8479
Brampton Norfk 43 TG2223
Brampton Rothm 49 SE4101
Brampton Suffk 33 TM4381
Brampton Abbotts Herefs 27 SO6026
Brampton Ash Nhants 40 SP7987
Brampton Bryan Herefs 36 SO3772
Brampton-en-le-Morthen Rothm 49 SK4887
Bramshall Staffs 38 SK0532
Bramshaw Hants 10 SU2615
Bramshott Hants 11 SU8432
Bramwell Somset 8 ST4329
Brancaster Norfk 42 TF7743
Brancaster Staithe Norfk 42 TF7944
Brancepeth Dur 61 NZ2237
Branderburgh Moray 94 NJ2371
Brandesburton E R Yk 57 TA1147
Brandeston Suffk 33 TM2460
Brandiston Norfk 43 TG1421
Brandon Dur 61 NZ2340
Brandon Lincs 50 SK9048
Brandon Suffk 32 TL7886
Brandon Warwks 39 SP4176
Brandon Parva Norfk 42 TG0708
Brandsby N York 56 SE5872
Brandy Wharf Lincs 50 TF0196
Bran End Essex 24 TL6525
Branksome BCP 10 SZ0492
Branksome Park BCP 10 SZ0590
Bransbury Hants 21 SU4242
Bransby Lincs 50 SK8978
Branscombe Devon 8 SY1988
Bransford Worcs 28 SO7952
Bransgore Hants 10 SZ1897
Bransholme C KuH 57 TA1033
Bransley Shrops 37 SO6575
Branston Leics 40 SK8129
Branston Lincs 50 TF0166
Branston Staffs 39 SK2221
Branston Booths Lincs 50 TF0668
Branstone IoW 11 SZ5583
Brant Broughton Lincs 50 SK9154
Brantham Suffk 25 TM1034
Branthwaite Cumb 58 NY0525
Branthwaite Cumb 58 NY2937
Brantingham E R Yk 56 SE9429
Branton Donc 49 SE6401
Branton Nthumb 77 NU0416
Branton Green N York 55 SE4362
Branxton Nthumb 77 NT8937
Brassington Derbys 48 SK2254
Brasted Kent 23 TQ4755
Brasted Chart Kent 23 TQ4653
Bratoft Lincs 51 TF4764
Brattleby Lincs 50 SK9480
Bratton Wilts 20 ST9152
Bratton Wrekin 37 SJ6313
Bratton Clovelly Devon 4 SX4691
Bratton Fleming Devon 7 SS6437
Bratton Seymour Somset 9 ST6729
Braughing Herts 31 TL3925
Braunston Nhants 29 SP5466
Braunston Rutlnd 40 SK8306
Braunton Devon 6 SS4836
Brawby N York 63 SE7378
Bray W & M 22 SU9079
Braybrooke Nhants 40 SP7684
Brayford Devon 7 SS6834
Bray Shop Cnwll 4 SX3374
Brayton N York 56 SE6030
Braywick W & M 22 SU8979
Breachwood Green Herts 31 TL1522
Breadsall Derbys 49 SK3639
Breadstone Gloucs 20 SO7000
Breage Cnwll 2 SW6128
Bream Gloucs 27 SO6005
Breamore Hants 10 SU1517
Brean Somset 19 ST2956
Breanais W Isls 90 NA9925
Brearton N York 55 SE3261
Breascleit W Isls 90 NB2135
Breasclete W Isls 90 NB2135
Breaston Derbys 39 SK4533
Brechfa Carmth 17 SN5230
Brechin Angus 89 NO6060
Breckles Norfk 42 TL9594
Brecon Powys 26 SO0428
Bredbury Stockp 48 SJ9291
Brede E Susx 14 TQ8218
Bredenbury Herefs 27 SO6056
Bredfield Suffk 33 TM2653
Bredgar Kent 14 TQ8860
Bredhurst Kent 14 TQ7962
Bredon Worcs 28 SO9236
Bredon's Hardwick Worcs 28 SO9135
Bredon's Norton Worcs 28 SO9339
Bredwardine Herefs 27 SO3344
Breedon on the Hill Leics 39 SK4022
Breightmet Bolton 54 SD7409
Breighton E R Yk 56 SE7033
Breinton Herefs 27 SO4739
Bremhill Wilts 20 ST9773
Brenchley Kent 14 TQ6741
Brendon Devon 18 SS7748
Brenfield Ag & B 71 NR8482
Brenish W Isls 90 NA9925
Brent Cross Gt Lon 23 TQ2286
Brent Eleigh Suffk 32 TL9448
Brentford Gt Lon 23 TQ1777
Brentingby Leics 40 SK7818
Brent Knoll Somset 19 ST3350
Brent Mill Devon 5 SX6959
Brent Pelham Herts 31 TL4330
Brentwood Essex 24 TQ5993
Brenzett Kent 15 TR0027
Brenzett Green Kent 15 TR0028
Brereton Staffs 38 SK0516
Brereton Green Ches E 47 SJ7764
Bressingham Norfk 32 TM0780
Bretby Derbys 39 SK2922
Bretford Warwks 39 SP4377
Bretforton Worcs 28 SP0943
Bretherton Lancs 53 SD4720
Brettenham Norfk 32 TL9383
Brettenham Suffk 32 TL9654
Bretton C Pete 40 TF1600
Bretton Flints 46 SJ3563
Brewood Staffs 38 SJ8808
Briantspuddle Dorset 9 SY8193
Brickendon Herts 23 TL3208
Bricket Wood Herts 22 TL1202
Brick Houses Sheff 49 SK3081
Bricklehampton Worcs 28 SO9742
Bride IoM 52 NX4401
Bridekirk Cumb 58 NY1133
Bridestowe Devon 4 SX5189
Bridford Devon 5 SX8186
Bridge Kent 15 TR1854
Bridgefoot Angus 83 NO3735
Bridgehampton Somset 9 ST5624
Bridge Hewick N York 55 SE3370
Bridgehill Dur 68 NZ0951
Bridgemary Hants 11 SU5803
Bridgend Ag & B 70 NR3362
Bridgend Ag & B 72 NR7937
Bridgend Brdgnd 18 SS9079
Bridgend Cerdgn 17 SN1745
Bridgend Devon 5 SX5548
Bridgend P & K 82 NO1224
Bridgend W Loth 75 NT0475
Bridgend of Lintrathen Angus 88 NO2854
Bridge of Allan Stirlg 81 NS7997
Bridge of Cally P & K 88 NO1351
Bridge of Canny Abers 89 NO6597
Bridge of Dee D & G 65 NX7359
Bridge of Don C Aber 95 NJ9409
Bridge of Earn P & K 82 NO1318
Bridge of Orchy Ag & B 80 NN2939
Bridge of Weir Rens 73 NS3965
Bridgerule Devon 6 SS2702
Bridge Sollers Herefs 27 SO4142
Bridge Street Suffk 32 TL8749
Bridgetown Somset 7 SS9233
Bridge Trafford Ches W 46 SJ4571
Bridgham Norfk 32 TL9685
Bridgnorth Shrops 37 SO7193
Bridgwater Somset 19 ST2937
Bridgwater Services Somset 8 ST3034
Bridlington E R Yk 57 TA1866
Bridport Dorset 8 SY4692
Bridstow Herefs 27 SO5824
Brierfield Lancs 54 SD8436
Brierley Barns 55 SE4010
Brierley Gloucs 27 SO6215
Brierley Hill Dudley 38 SO9186
Brigg N Linc 56 SE1000
Briggate Norfk 43 TG3127
Briggswath N York 63 NZ8608
Brigham Cumb 58 NY0830
Brigham E R Yk 57 TA0753
Brighouse Calder 55 SE1422
Brighstone IoW 10 SZ4282
Brighthampton Oxon 21 SP3803
Brightley Devon 7 SX6097
Brightling E Susx 14 TQ6820
Brightlingsea Essex 25 TM0817
Brighton Br & H 12 TQ3104
Brighton City Airport W Susx 12 TQ1905
Brighton le Sands Sefton 46 SJ3098
Brightons Falk 82 NS9277
Brightwalton W Berk 21 SU4279
Brightwell Suffk 33 TM2543
Brightwell Baldwin Oxon 21 SU6595
Brightwell-cum-Sotwell Oxon 21 SU5790
Brightwell Upperton Oxon 22 SU6594
Brignall Dur 61 NZ0712
Brig o'Turk Stirlg 81 NN5306
Brigsley NE Lin 51 TA2501
Brigsteer Cumb 59 SD4889
Brigstock Nhants 40 SP9485
Brill Bucks 29 SP6513
Brill Cnwll 2 SW7229
Brilley Herefs 27 SO2648
Brimfield Herefs 27 SO5267
Brimfield Cross Herefs 27 SO5368
Brimington Derbys 49 SK4073
Brimley Devon 5 SX8077
Brimpsfield Gloucs 28 SO9312
Brimpton W Berk 21 SU5564
Brimscombe Gloucs 20 SO8702
Brimstage Wirral 46 SJ3082
Brincliffe Sheff 49 SK3284
Brind E R Yk 56 SE7430
Brindister Shet 100 HU2857
Brindle Lancs 54 SD5924
Brineton Staffs 37 SJ8013
Bringhurst Leics 40 SP8492
Bringsty Common Herefs 28 SO7055
Brington Cambs 30 TL0875
Brininghan Norfk 42 TG0434
Brinkhill Lincs 51 TF3773
Brinkley Cambs 32 TL6354
Brinklow Warwks 39 SP4379
Brinkworth Wilts 20 SU0184
Brinscall Lancs 54 SD6221
Brinsley Notts 49 SK4548
Brinsworth Rothm 49 SK4189
Brinton Norfk 42 TG0335
Brinyan Ork 100 HY4327
Brisley Norfk 42 TF9421
Brislington Bristl 19 ST6270
Brissenden Green Kent 14 TQ9439
Bristol Bristl 19 ST5972
Bristol Airport N Som 19 ST5065
Briston Norfk 42 TG0632
Britford Wilts 10 SU1527
Brithdir Caerph 19 SO1401
Brithdir Gwynd 35 SH7618
British Legion Village Kent 14 TQ7257
Briton Ferry Neath 18 SS7394
Britwell Salome Oxon 22 SU6792
Brixham Torbay 5 SX9256
Brixton Devon 5 SX5552
Brixton Gt Lon 23 TQ3175
Brixton Deverill Wilts 20 ST8638
Brixworth Nhants 30 SP7470
Brize Norton Oxon 29 SP2907
Brize Norton Airport Oxon 29 SP2905
Broad Alley Worcs 28 SO8867
Broad Blunsdon Swindn 20 SU1491
Broadbottom Tamesd 48 SJ9993
Broadbridge W Susx 11 SU8105
Broadbridge Heath W Susx 12 TQ1431
Broad Campden Gloucs 28 SP1537
Broad Carr Calder 55 SE0919
Broad Chalke Wilts 10 SU0325
Broadclyst Devon 7 SX9897
Broadfield Inver 80 NS3373
Broadford Highld 85 NG6423
Broadford Bridge W Susx 12 TQ0921
Broad Green Worcs 28 SO7756
Broad Haven Pembks 16 SM8613
Broadheath Traffd 47 SJ7689
Broadhembury Devon 8 ST1004
Broadhempston Devon 5 SX8066
Broad Hinton Wilts 20 SU1075
Broadland Row E Susx 14 TQ8319
Broad Marston Worcs 28 SP1446
Broadmayne Dorset 9 SY7286
Broad Meadow Staffs 47 SJ8348
Broadmoor Pembks 16 SN0906
Broadoak Dorset 8 SY4396
Broad Oak E Susx 13 TQ6022
Broad Oak E Susx 14 TQ8219
Broad Oak Herefs 27 SO4821
Broad Oak Kent 15 TR1761
Broad Oak St Hel 47 SJ5395
Broadsands Torbay 5 SX8957
Broad's Green Essex 24 TL6912
Broadstairs Kent 15 TR3967
Broadstone BCP 10 SZ0095
Broadstone Shrops 37 SO5489
Broad Street E Susx 14 TQ8616
Broad Street Kent 14 TQ8356
Broad Town Wilts 20 SU0977
Broadwas Worcs 28 SO7555
Broadwater Herts 31 TL2422
Broadwater W Susx 12 TQ1404
Broadwaters Worcs 38 SO8477
Broadway Pembks 16 SM8713
Broadway Somset 8 ST3215
Broadway Worcs 28 SP0937
Broadwell Gloucs 27 SO5811
Broadwell Gloucs 29 SP2027
Broadwell Oxon 29 SP2504
Broadwell Warwks 29 SP4565
Broadwindsor Dorset 8 ST4302
Broadwood Kelly Devon 7 SS6106
Broadwoodwidger Devon 4 SX4189
Brockamin Worcs 28 SO7753
Brockbridge Hants 11 SU6118
Brockdish Norfk 33 TM2179
Brockenhurst Hants 10 SU3002
Brockford Street Suffk 33 TM1167
Brockhall Nhants 29 SP6362
Brockham Surrey 12 TQ1949
Brockhampton Gloucs 28 SP0322
Brockhampton Hants 11 SU7106
Brockhampton Herefs 27 SO5931
Brockholes Kirk 55 SE1510
Brocklesby Lincs 57 TA1411
Brockley N Som 19 ST4666
Brockley Suffk 32 TL8371
Brockley Green Suffk 32 TL7247
Brockley Green Suffk 32 TL8254
Brockmoor Dudley 38 SO9088
Brockton Shrops 36 SJ3104
Brockton Shrops 36 SO3285

Brockton – Chester Services

123

Brockton Shrops 37 SO5794
Brockweir Gloucs 19 SO5401
Brockworth Gloucs 28 SO8916
Brocton Staffs 38 SJ9619
Brodick N Ayrs 72 NS0135
Brodsworth Donc 55 SE5007
Brogaig Highld 90 NG4767
Brokenborough Wilts 20 ST9189
Broken Cross Ches E 48 SJ8973
Brokerswood Wilts 20 ST8352
Bromborough Wirral 46 SJ3582
Brome Suffk 33 TM1376
Brome Street Suffk 33 TM1576
Bromeswell Suffk 33 TM3050
Bromfield Cumb 67 NY1746
Bromfield Shrops 37 SO4876
Bromham Bed 30 TL0051
Bromham Wilts 20 ST9665
Bromley Dudley 38 SO9088
Bromley Gt Lon 23 TQ4069
Bromley Shrops 37 SO7395
Bromley Cross Bolton 54 SD7213
Brompton Medway 14 TQ7668
Brompton N York 62 SE3796
Brompton-by-Sawdon N York 63 SE9482
Brompton-on-Swale N York 61 SE2199
Brompton Ralph Somset 8 ST0832
Brompton Regis Somset 7 SS9531
Bromsberrow Gloucs 28 SO7433
Bromsberrow Heath Gloucs 28 SO7333
Bromsgrove Worcs 28 SO9570
Bromyard Herefs 27 SO6554
Bronant Cerdgn 35 SN6467
Brongest Cerdgn 17 SN3245
Bronington Wrexhm 37 SJ4839
Bronllys Powys 26 SO1434
Bronwydd Carmth 17 SN4123
Bronygarth Shrops 36 SJ2637
Brook Hants 10 SU2714
Brook IoW 10 SZ3983
Brook Kent 15 TR0644
Brook Surrey 12 SU9237
Brooke Norfk 43 TM2899
Brooke Rutlnd 40 SK8405
Brookenby Lincs 51 TF2095
Brookhampton Somset 9 ST6327
Brook Hill Hants 10 SU2714
Brookhouse Lancs 53 SD5464
Brookhouse Rothm 49 SK5188
Brookhouse Green Ches E 47 SJ8161
Brookhouses Derbys 48 SK0388
Brookland Kent 15 TQ9926
Brooklands Traffd 47 SJ7890
Brookmans Park Herts 23 TL2404
Brook Street Essex 24 TQ5793
Brook Street Kent 14 TQ9333
Brookthorpe Gloucs 28 SO8312
Brookwood Surrey 22 SU9557
Broom C Beds 31 TL1742
Broom Rothm 49 SK4491
Broom Warwks 28 SP0853
Broome Norfk 33 TM3591
Broome Shrops 36 SO4080
Broome Worcs 38 SO9078
Broomedge Warrtn 47 SJ7085
Broomfield Essex 24 TL7010
Broomfield Kent 14 TQ8452
Broomfield Kent 15 TR1966
Broomfield Somset 8 ST2232
Broomfleet E R Yk 56 SE8727
Broomhaugh Nthumb 68 NZ0161
Broom Hill Barns 55 SE4102
Broom Hill Notts 49 SK5447
Broomhill Nthumb 69 NU2400
Broompark Dur 61 NZ2441
Brora Highld 97 NC9103
Broseley Shrops 37 SJ6701
Brotherlee Dur 61 NY9237
Brotherton N York 55 SE4825
Brotton R & Cl 62 NZ6819
Brough Cumb 60 NY7914
Brough E R Yk 56 SE9326
Brough Notts 50 SK8458
Brough Shet 100 HU5665
Broughall Shrops 37 SJ5741
Brough Sowerby Cumb 60 NY7912
Broughton Border 75 NT1136
Broughton Cambs 31 TL2878
Broughton Flints 46 SJ3363
Broughton Hants 10 SU3033
Broughton Lancs 53 SD5234
Broughton M Keyn 30 SP8939
Broughton N Linc 56 SE9608
Broughton N York 54 SD9451
Broughton N York 63 SE7673
Broughton Nhants 30 SP8375
Broughton Oxon 29 SP4138
Broughton Salfd 47 SD8201
Broughton V Glam 18 SS9270
Broughton Astley Leics 39 SP5292
Broughton Gifford Wilts 20 ST8763
Broughton Green Worcs 28 SO9561
Broughton Hackett Worcs 28 SO9254
Broughton-in-Furness Cumb 58 SD2187
Broughton Mills Cumb 58 SD2290
Broughton Moor Cumb 58 NY0533
Broughton Poggs Oxon 29 SP2303
Broughty Ferry C Dund 83 NO4630
Brown Candover Hants 11 SU5739
Brown Edge Staffs 48 SJ9053
Brownhills Fife 83 NO5215
Brownhills Wsall 38 SK0405
Browninghill Green Hants 21 SU5859
Brown Lees Staffs 47 SJ8756
Brown's Green Birm 38 SP0491
Browns Hill Gloucs 20 SO8802
Brownston Devon 5 SX6952
Broxa N York 63 SE9491
Broxbourne Herts 23 TL3606
Broxburn E Loth 76 NT6977
Broxburn W Loth 75 NT0872
Broxted Essex 24 TL5727
Bruichladdich Ag & B 70 NR2661
Bruisyard Suffk 33 TM3266
Bruisyard Street Suffk 33 TM3365
Brumby N Linc 56 SE8909
Brund Staffs 48 SK1061
Brundall Norfk 43 TG3308
Brundish Suffk 33 TM2769
Brundish Street Suffk 33 TM2671
Brunswick Village N u Ty 69 NZ2272
Brunthwaite C Brad 55 SE0446
Bruntingthorpe Leics 39 SP6089
Brunton Fife 83 NO3220
Brunton Wilts 21 SU2456
Brushford Devon 7 SS6707
Brushford Somset 7 SS9225
Bruton Somset 9 ST6835
Bryan's Green Worcs 28 SO8868
Bryanston Dorset 9 ST8607
Brydekirk D & G 67 NY1870
Brympton Somset 8 ST5115
Bryn Carmth 17 SN5400
Bryn Neath 18 SS8192
Bryn Wigan 47 SD5600
Brynamman Carmth 26 SN7114
Brynberian Pembks 16 SN1035
Bryncir Gwynd 44 SH4844
Bryn-côch Neath 18 SS7499
Bryncroes Gwynd 44 SH2231
Bryncrug Gwynd 35 SH6103
Bryneglwys Denbgs 46 SJ1447
Brynford Flints 46 SJ1774
Bryn Gates Wigan 47 SD5901
Bryngwran IoA 44 SH3577
Bryngwyn Mons 27 SO3909
Bryngwyn Powys 27 SO1849
Bryn-Henllan Pembks 16 SN0139
Brynhoffnant Cerdgn 17 SN3351
Brynmawr Blae G 27 SO1911
Bryn-mawr Gwynd 44 SH2433
Brynmenyn Brdgnd 18 SS9084
Brynmill Swans 17 SS6392
Brynna Rhondd 18 SS9883
Brynrefail Gwynd 44 SH5562
Brynsadler Rhondd 18 ST0280
Bryn Saith Marchog Denbgs 46 SJ0750
Brynsiencyn IoA 44 SH4867
Brynteg IoA 44 SH4982
Bryn-y-Maen Conwy 45 SH8376
Bubbenhall Warwks 39 SP3672
Bubwith E R Yk 56 SE7136
Buchanhaven Abers 95 NK1247
Buchanty P & K 82 NN9328
Buchany Stirlg 81 NN7102
Buchlyvie Stirlg 81 NS5793
Buckabank Cumb 67 NY3749
Buckden Cambs 31 TL1967
Buckden N York 61 SD9477
Buckenham Norfk 43 TG3505
Buckerell Devon 8 ST1200
Buckfast Devon 5 SX7467
Buckfastleigh Devon 5 SX7366
Buckhaven Fife 83 NT3598
Buckholt Mons 27 SO5016
Buckhorn Weston Dorset 9 ST7524
Buckhurst Hill Essex 23 TQ4194
Buckie Moray 94 NJ4265
Buckingham Bucks 30 SP6933
Buckland Bucks 30 SP8812
Buckland Devon 5 SX6743
Buckland Gloucs 28 SP0835
Buckland Herts 31 TL3533
Buckland Kent 15 TR3042
Buckland Oxon 21 SU3498
Buckland Surrey 12 TQ2150
Buckland Brewer Devon 6 SS4220
Buckland Common Bucks 22 SP9207
Buckland Dinham Somset 20 ST7551
Buckland Filleigh Devon 6 SS4609
Buckland in the Moor Devon 5 SX7273
Buckland Monachorum Devon 4 SX4968
Buckland Newton Dorset 9 ST6805
Buckland Ripers Dorset 9 SY6582
Buckland St Mary Somset 8 ST2613
Buckland-Tout-Saints Devon 5 SX7645
Bucklebury W Berk 21 SU5570
Bucklers Hard Hants 10 SU4000
Bucklesham Suffk 33 TM2441
Buckley Flints 46 SJ2763
Bucklow Hill Ches E 47 SJ7383
Buckminster Leics 40 SK8722
Bucknall C Stke 48 SJ9047
Bucknall Lincs 50 TF1668
Bucknell Oxon 29 SP5625
Bucknell Shrops 36 SO3574
Buckpool Moray 94 NJ4165
Bucksburn C Aber 95 NJ8909
Buck's Cross Devon 6 SS3522
Bucks Green W Susx 12 TQ0833
Buckshaw Village Lancs 53 SD5620
Bucks Horn Oak Hants 11 SU8041
Buck's Mills Devon 6 SS3523
Buckton E R Yk 57 TA1872
Buckton Nthumb 77 NU0838
Buckworth Cambs 30 TL1476
Budby Notts 49 SK6169
Bude Cnwll 6 SS2105
Budge's Shop Cnwll 4 SX3259
Budleigh Salterton Devon 8 SY0682
Budock Water Cnwll 2 SW7831
Buerton Ches E 47 SJ6843
Bugbrooke Nhants 30 SP6757
Bugle Cnwll 3 SX0158
Bugley Dorset 9 ST7824
Bugthorpe E R Yk 56 SE7757
Buildwas Shrops 37 SJ6204
Builth Wells Powys 26 SO0350
Bulbridge Wilts 10 SU0830
Bulford Wilts 21 SU1643
Bulkeley Ches E 47 SJ5354
Bulkington Warwks 39 SP3986
Bulkington Wilts 20 ST9458
Bulkworthy Devon 6 SS3914
Bullbrook Br For 22 SU8869
Bullington Hants 21 SU4541
Bullington Lincs 50 TF0877
Bulmer Essex 32 TL8440
Bulmer N York 56 SE6967
Bulmer Tye Essex 32 TL8438
Bulphan Thurr 24 TQ6385
Bulwell C Nott 49 SK5343
Bulwick Nhants 40 SP9694
Bumble's Green Essex 23 TL4005
Bunbury Ches E 47 SJ5657
Bunessan Ag & B 78 NM3821
Bungay Suffk 33 TM3389
Bunnahabhain Ag & B 70 NR4173
Bunny Notts 39 SK5829
Buntingford Herts 31 TL3629
Bunwell Norfk 43 TM1293
Burbage Leics 39 SP4492
Burbage Wilts 21 SU2261
Burchett's Green W & M 22 SU8381
Burcombe Wilts 10 SU0730
Burcott Bucks 30 SP8823
Bures Essex 24 TL9033
Burford Oxon 29 SP2512
Burford Shrops 27 SO5868
Burgess Hill W Susx 12 TQ3118
Burgh Suffk 33 TM2351
Burgh by Sands Cumb 67 NY3259
Burgh Castle Norfk 43 TG4705
Burghclere Hants 21 SU4761
Burghead Moray 93 NJ1168
Burghfield W Berk 22 SU6668
Burghfield Common W Berk 21 SU6566
Burgh Heath Surrey 23 TQ2457
Burghill Herefs 27 SO4844
Burgh le Marsh Lincs 51 TF5065
Burgh next Aylsham Norfk 43 TG2125
Burgh on Bain Lincs 51 TF2186
Burgh St Margaret Norfk 43 TG4413
Burgh St Peter Norfk 43 TM4693
Burghwallis Donc 56 SE5311
Burham Kent 14 TQ7262
Buriton Hants 11 SU7419
Burland Ches E 47 SJ6153
Burlawn Cnwll 3 SW9970
Burleigh Gloucs 20 SO8601
Burlescombe Devon 8 ST0716
Burleston Dorset 9 SY7794
Burley Hants 10 SU2102
Burley Rutlnd 40 SK8810
Burleydam Ches E 47 SJ6042
Burley Gate Herefs 27 SO5947
Burley in Wharfedale C Brad 55 SE1646
Burley Street Hants 10 SU2004
Burley Wood Head C Brad 55 SE1544
Burlton Shrops 36 SJ4526
Burmarsh Kent 15 TR1032
Burmington Warwks 29 SP2637
Burn N York 56 SE5928
Burnage Manch 47 SJ8692
Burnaston Derbys 39 SK2832
Burnby E R Yk 56 SE8346
Burneside Cumb 59 SD5095
Burneston N York 61 SE3084
Burnett BaNES 20 ST6665
Burnfoot Border 67 NT4113
Burnfoot P & K 82 NN9904
Burnham Bucks 22 SU9282
Burnham Deepdale Norfk 42 TF8044
Burnham Market Norfk 42 TF8342
Burnham Norton Norfk 42 TF8343
Burnham-on-Crouch Essex 25 TQ9496
Burnham-on-Sea Somset 19 ST3049
Burnham Overy Norfk 42 TF8442
Burnham Overy Staithe Norfk 42 TF8444
Burnham Thorpe Norfk 42 TF8541
Burnhead D & G 66 NX8695
Burnhill Green Staffs 37 SJ7800
Burnhope Dur 69 NZ1948
Burnhouse N Ayrs 73 NS3850
Burniston N York 63 TA0193
Burnley Lancs 54 SD8432
Burnmouth Border 77 NT9560
Burnopfield Dur 69 NZ1757
Burnsall N York 55 SE0361
Burntisland Fife 83 NT2385
Burntwood Staffs 38 SK0509
Burntwood Green Staffs 38 SK0608
Burnt Yates N York 55 SE2561
Burnworthy Somset 8 ST1915
Burpham Surrey 12 TQ0152
Burpham W Susx 12 TQ0308
Burradon Nthumb 68 NT9806
Burrafirth Shet 100 HP6113
Burravoe Shet 100 HU5180
Burrells Cumb 60 NY6718
Burrelton P & K 82 NO2037
Burridge Devon 8 ST3106
Burridge Hants 11 SU5110
Burrill N York 61 SE2387
Burringham N Linc 56 SE8309
Burrington Devon 7 SS6416
Burrington Herefs 36 SO4472
Burrington N Som 19 ST4859
Burrough Green Cambs 32 TL6355
Burrough on the Hill Leics 40 SK7510
Burrow Lancs 59 SD6174
Burrow Somset 7 SS9342
Burrow Bridge Somset 8 ST3530
Burrowhill Surrey 22 SU9662
Burry Green Swans 17 SS4591
Burry Port Carmth 17 SN4400
Burscough Lancs 53 SD4411
Burscough Bridge Lancs 53 SD4412
Bursea E R Yk 56 SE8033
Bursledon Hants 11 SU4809
Burstall Suffk 33 TM0944
Burstock Dorset 8 ST4202
Burston Norfk 33 TM1383
Burstow Surrey 12 TQ3141
Burstwick E R Yk 57 TA2227
Burtersett N York 60 SD8989
Burtholme Cumb 67 NY5463
Burthorpe Green Suffk 32 TL7764
Burtoft Lincs 41 TF2635
Burton BCP 10 SZ1694
Burton Ches W 46 SJ3174
Burton Ches W 46 SJ5063
Burton Pembks 16 SM9805
Burton Somset 19 ST1944
Burton Wilts 20 ST8179
Burton Agnes E R Yk 57 TA1062
Burton Bradstock Dorset 8 SY4889
Burton-by-Lincoln Lincs 50 SK9574
Burton Coggles Lincs 40 SK9725
Burton End Essex 31 TL5323
Burton Fleming E R Yk 57 TA0871
Burton Hastings Warwks 39 SP4189
Burton-in-Kendal Cumb 59 SD5376
Burton-in-Kendal Services Cumb 59 SD5275
Burton in Lonsdale N York 54 SD6572
Burton Joyce Notts 49 SK6443
Burton Latimer Nhants 30 SP9074
Burton Lazars Leics 40 SK7716
Burton Leonard N York 55 SE3263
Burton on the Wolds Leics 39 SK5821
Burton Overy Leics 39 SP6798
Burton Pedwardine Lincs 50 TF1142
Burton Pidsea E R Yk 57 TA2431
Burton Salmon N York 55 SE4927
Burton's Green Essex 24 TL8226
Burton upon Stather N Linc 56 SE8617
Burton upon Trent Staffs 39 SK2323
Burton Waters Lincs 50 SK9372
Burtonwood Warrtn 47 SJ5692
Burtonwood Services Warrtn 47 SJ5791
Burwardsley Ches W 46 SJ5156
Burwarton Shrops 37 SO6185
Burwash E Susx 14 TQ6724
Burwash Common E Susx 13 TQ6323
Burwash Weald E Susx 13 TQ6523
Burwell Cambs 31 TL5866
Burwell Lincs 51 TF3579
Burwen IoA 44 SH4293
Burwick Ork 100 ND4484
Bury Bury 54 SD8011
Bury Cambs 41 TL2883
Bury Somset 7 SS9427
Bury W Susx 12 TQ0113
Bury Green Herts 31 TL4521
Bury St Edmunds Suffk 32 TL8564
Burythorpe N York 56 SE7964
Buscot Oxon 21 SU2298
Bush Bank Herefs 27 SO4551
Bushbury Wolves 38 SJ9202
Bushey Herts 22 TQ1395
Bushey Heath Herts 22 TQ1494
Bush Hill Park Gt Lon 23 TQ3395
Bushley Worcs 28 SO8734
Bushmoor Shrops 36 SO4387
Bushton Wilts 20 SU0677
Bussage Gloucs 28 SO8803
Bussex Somset 8 ST3535
Butcombe N Som 19 ST5161
Butleigh Somset 8 ST5233
Butleigh Wootton Somset 8 ST5035
Butlers Marston Warwks 29 SP3250
Butley Suffk 33 TM3650
Buttercrambe N York 56 SE7358
Butterknowle Dur 61 NZ1025
Butterleigh Devon 7 SS9708
Buttermere Cumb 58 NY1717
Buttershaw C Brad 55 SE1329
Butterstone P & K 88 NO0645
Butterton Staffs 38 SJ8242
Butterton Staffs 48 SK0756
Butterwick Lincs 51 TF3845
Butterwick N York 56 SE9871
Butterwick N York 63 SE7277
Buttington Powys 36 SJ2408
Buttonoak Shrops 37 SO7578
Buxhall Suffk 32 TM0057
Buxted E Susx 13 TQ4923
Buxton Derbys 48 SK0572
Buxton Norfk 43 TG2222
Buxton Heath Norfk 43 TG1821
Bwlch Powys 27 SO1522
Bwlchgwyn Wrexhm 46 SJ2653
Bwlchllan Cerdgn 34 SN5758
Bwlchtocyn Gwynd 34 SH3125
Bwlch-y-cibau Powys 36 SJ1717
Bwlch-y-ffridd Powys 36 SO0795
Bwlch-y-groes Pembks 17 SN2436
Bwlch-y-sarnau Powys 36 SO0374
Byers Green Dur 61 NZ2233
Byfield Nhants 29 SP5152
Byfleet Surrey 22 TQ0661
Byford Herefs 27 SO3942
Byker N u Ty 69 NZ2764
Bylchau Conwy 45 SH9762
Byley Ches W 47 SJ7269
Byrness Nthumb 68 NT7602
Bystock Devon 5 SY0283
Bythorn Cambs 30 TL0575
Byton Herefs 27 SO3764
Bywell Nthumb 68 NZ0461
Byworth W Susx 12 SU9821

C

Cabourne Lincs 50 TA1401
Cabrach Moray 94 NJ3826
Cabus Lancs 53 SD4948
Cadbury Devon 7 SS9105
Cadder E Duns 74 NS6072
Caddington C Beds 30 TL0619
Cadeby Donc 49 SE5100
Cadeby Leics 39 SK4202
Cadeleigh Devon 7 SS9108
Cade Street E Susx 13 TQ6020
Cadgwith Cnwll 2 SW7214
Cadham Fife 83 NO2801
Cadishead Salfd 47 SJ7091
Cadle Swans 17 SS6296
Cadley Lancs 53 SD5231
Cadley Wilts 21 SU2066
Cadley Wilts 21 SU2453
Cadmore End Bucks 22 SU7892
Cadnam Hants 10 SU3013
Cadney N Linc 56 TA0103
Cadoxton V Glam 18 ST1269
Cadoxton Juxta-Neath Neath 18 SS7598
Caeathro Gwynd 44 SH5061
Caenby Lincs 50 SK9989
Caerau Brdgnd 18 SS8694
Caerau Cardif 18 ST1375
Caer Farchell Pembks 16 SM7927
Caergeiliog IoA 44 SH3178
Caergwrle Flints 46 SJ3057
Caerleon Newpt 19 ST3490
Caernarfon Gwynd 44 SH4862
Caerphilly Caerph 19 ST1587
Caersws Powys 36 SO0392
Caerwedros Cerdgn 34 SN3755
Caerwent Mons 19 ST4790
Caerwys Flints 46 SJ1272
Caio Carmth 26 SN6739
Cairinis W Isls 90 NF8260
Cairndow Ag & B 80 NN1810
Cairneyhill Fife 82 NT0486
Cairngarroch D & G 64 NX0549
Cairnie Abers 94 NJ4844
Cairnryan D & G 64 NX0668
Caister-on-Sea Norfk 43 TG5112
Caistor Lincs 50 TA1101
Caistor St Edmund Norfk 43 TG2303
Calanais W Isls 90 NB2133
Calbourne IoW 10 SZ4286
Calcoed Flints 46 SJ1674
Calcot Gloucs 28 SP0810
Calcot Row W Berk 22 SU6771
Caldbeck Cumb 59 NY3240
Caldecote Cambs 31 TL3456
Caldecote Cambs 40 TL1488
Caldecote Highfields Cambs 31 TL3559
Caldecott Nhants 30 SP9868
Caldecott Oxon 21 SU4996
Caldecott Rutlnd 40 SP8693
Calderbank N Lans 74 NS7663
Calder Bridge Cumb 58 NY0306
Caldercruix N Lans 74 NS8167
Calder Grove Wakefd 55 SE3016
Calder Vale Lancs 53 SD5345
Calderwood S Lans 74 NS6555
Caldicot Mons 19 ST4888
Caldmore Wsall 38 SP0197
Caldwell N York 61 NZ1613
Calfsound Ork 100 HY5738
Calgary Ag & B 78 NM3751
California Falk 75 NS9076
California Norfk 43 TG5115
Calke Derbys 39 SK3721
Callander Stirlg 81 NN6207
Callanish W Isls 90 NB2133
Callestick Cnwll 2 SW7750
Callington Cnwll 4 SX3669
Callow Herefs 27 SO4934
Callow End Worcs 28 SO8350
Callow Hill Wilts 20 SU0384
Calmore Hants 10 SU3414
Calmsden Gloucs 28 SP0408
Calne Wilts 20 ST9971
Calshot Hants 11 SU4701
Calstock Cnwll 4 SX4368
Calstone Wellington Wilts 20 SU0268
Calthorpe Norfk 43 TG1831
Calthorpe Street Norfk 43 TG4025
Calthwaite Cumb 59 NY4640
Calton Staffs 48 SK1049
Calveley Ches E 47 SJ5958
Calver Derbys 48 SK2374
Calverhall Shrops 37 SJ6037
Calverleigh Devon 7 SS9214
Calverton M Keyn 30 SP7939
Calverton Notts 49 SK6149
Calvine P & K 87 NN8065
Cam Gloucs 20 ST7599
Camber E Susx 15 TQ9618
Camberley Surrey 22 SU8860
Camberwell Gt Lon 23 TQ3276
Camblesforth N York 56 SE6425
Cambo Nthumb 68 NZ0285
Camborne Cnwll 2 SW6440
Cambourne Cambs 31 TL3159
Cambridge Cambs 31 TL4558
Cambridge Gloucs 28 SO7403
Cambridge Airport Cambs 31 TL4858
Cambrose Cnwll 2 SW6845
Cambus Clacks 82 NS8593
Cambusbarron Stirlg 81 NS7792
Cambuslang S Lans 74 NS6460
Camden Town Gt Lon 23 TQ2883
Cameley BaNES 19 ST6157
Camelford Cnwll 3 SX1083
Camelon Falk 82 NS8680
Camerton BaNES 20 ST6857
Camerton Cumb 58 NY0330
Camghouran P & K 87 NN5556
Cammachmore Abers 89 NO9195
Cammeringham Lincs 50 SK9481
Campbeltown Ag & B 72 NR7120
Campbeltown Airport Ag & B 72 NR6622
Campsall Donc 56 SE5413
Campsea Ash Suffk 33 TM3356
Campton C Beds 30 TL1238
Camptown Border 68 NT6713
Camrose Pembks 16 SM9220
Camserney P & K 87 NN8149
Canada Hants 10 SU2818
Candlesby Lincs 51 TF4567
Cane End Oxon 22 SU6779
Canewdon Essex 24 TQ9094
Canford Cliffs BCP 10 SZ0589
Canford Heath BCP 10 SZ0293
Canisbay Highld 100 ND3472
Canley Covtry 39 SP3077
Cann Dorset 9 ST8721
Cann Common Dorset 9 ST8820
Cannich Highld 92 NH3331
Cannington Somset 19 ST2539
Canning Town Gt Lon 23 TQ4081
Cannock Staffs 38 SJ9810
Cannon Bridge Herefs 27 SO4340
Canonbie D & G 67 NY3976
Canon Frome Herefs 27 SO6443
Canon Pyon Herefs 27 SO4548
Canons Ashby Nhants 29 SP5750
Canonstown Cnwll 2 SW5335
Canterbury Kent 15 TR1457
Cantley Norfk 43 TG3704
Canton Cardif 19 ST1676
Cantsfield Lancs 54 SD6272
Canvey Island Essex 24 TQ7983
Canwick Lincs 50 SK9869
Canworthy Water Cnwll 4 SX2291
Caol Highld 86 NN1175
Caoles Ag & B 78 NM0848
Capel Kent 13 TQ6344
Capel Surrey 12 TQ1740
Capel Bangor Cerdgn 35 SN6580
Capel Coch IoA 44 SH4682
Capel Curig Conwy 45 SH7258
Capel Dewi Carmth 17 SN4720
Capel Dewi Cerdgn 17 SN4542
Capel-Dewi Cerdgn 35 SN6282
Capel Garmon Conwy 45 SH8155
Capel Hendre Carmth 17 SN5911
Capel Iwan Carmth 17 SN2936
Capel-le-Ferne Kent 15 TR2539
Capel Parc IoA 44 SH4486
Capel St Andrew Suffk 33 TM3748
Capel St Mary Suffk 25 TM0838
Capel Seion Cerdgn 35 SN6379
Capelulo Conwy 45 SH7476
Capenhurst Ches W 46 SJ3673
Capheaton Nthumb 68 NZ0380
Capton Devon 5 SX8353
Caputh P & K 82 NO0840
Carbis Bay Cnwll 2 SW5238
Carbost Highld 84 NG3731
Carbrook Sheff 49 SK3889
Carbrooke Norfk 42 TF9402
Car Colston Notts 49 SK7142
Carcroft Donc 56 SE5409
Cardenden Fife 82 NT2195
Cardiff Cardif 19 ST1876
Cardiff Airport V Glam 18 ST0766
Cardiff Gate Services Cardif 19 ST2182
Cardiff West Services Cardif 18 ST0979
Cardigan Cerdgn 17 SN1746
Cardington Bed 30 TL0847
Cardington Shrops 37 SO5095
Cardinham Cnwll 3 SX1268
Cardross Ag & B 80 NS3477
Cardurnock Cumb 67 NY1758
Careby Lincs 40 TF0216
Carew Pembks 16 SN0403
Carew Cheriton Pembks 16 SN0402
Carew Newton Pembks 16 SN0404
Carey Herefs 27 SO5730
Carfraemill Border 76 NT5053
Cargate Green Norfk 43 TG3912
Cargo Cumb 67 NY3659
Cargreen Cnwll 4 SX4362
Carham Nthumb 76 NT7938
Carhampton Somset 7 ST0042
Carharrack Cnwll 2 SW7341
Carinish W Isls 90 NF8260
Carisbrooke IoW 11 SZ4888
Cark Cumb 59 SD3676
Carkeel Cnwll 4 SX4160
Càrlabhagh W Isls 90 NB2043
Carlbury Darltn 61 NZ2115
Carlby Lincs 40 TF0413
Carleen Cnwll 2 SW6130
Carleton Forehoe Norfk 43 TG0905
Carleton-in-Craven N York 54 SD9749
Carleton Rode Norfk 43 TM1093
Carleton St Peter Norfk 43 TG3402
Carlingcott BaNES 20 ST6958
Carlisle Cumb 67 NY4056
Carlisle Airport Cumb 67 NY4860
Carlops Border 75 NT1656
Carloway W Isls 90 NB2043
Carlton Barns 55 SE3610
Carlton Bed 30 SP9555
Carlton Cambs 32 TL6452
Carlton Leeds 55 SE3327
Carlton Leics 39 SK3904
Carlton N York 56 SE6423
Carlton N York 61 SE0684
Carlton N York 62 SE6086
Carlton Notts 49 SK6041
Carlton S on T 62 NZ3921
Carlton Suffk 33 TM3764
Carlton Colville Suffk 33 TM5189
Carlton Curlieu Leics 40 SP6997
Carlton Green Cambs 32 TL6451
Carlton Husthwaite N York 62 SE4976
Carlton-in-Cleveland N York 62 NZ5004
Carlton in Lindrick Notts 49 SK5883
Carlton-le-Moorland Lincs 50 SK9058
Carlton Miniott N York 62 SE3981
Carlton-on-Trent Notts 50 SK7964
Carlton Scroop Lincs 50 SK9445
Carluke S Lans 74 NS8450
Carmarthen Carmth 17 SN4120
Carmel Carmth 17 SN5816
Carmel Flints 46 SJ1676
Carmel Gwynd 44 SH4954
Carmunnock C Glas 74 NS5957
Carnaby E R Yk 57 TA1465
Carnbee Fife 83 NO5206
Carnbo P & K 82 NO0503
Carn Brea Cnwll 2 SW6841
Carnforth Lancs 53 SD4970
Carnhell Green Cnwll 2 SW6137
Carnkie Cnwll 2 SW6840
Carnkie Cnwll 2 SW7134
Carno Powys 35 SN9696
Carnock Fife 82 NT0489
Carnon Downs Cnwll 2 SW7940
Carnoustie Angus 83 NO5534
Carnwath S Lans 75 NS9846
Carol Green Solhll 39 SP2577
Carperby N York 61 SE0089
Carradale Ag & B 72 NR8138
Carrbridge Highld 93 NH9022
Carreglefn IoA 44 SH3889
Carr Gate Wakefd 55 SE3123
Carrhouse N Linc 56 SE7706
Carrick Ag & B 71 NR9086
Carrick Castle Ag & B 80 NS1994
Carriden Falk 82 NT0181
Carrington Mdloth 75 NT3160
Carrington Traffd 47 SJ7492
Carrog Denbgs 46 SJ1043
Carron Falk 82 NS8882
Carronbridge D & G 66 NX8698
Carronshore Falk 82 NS8983
Carr Shield Nthumb 68 NY8047
Carrutherstown D & G 67 NY1071
Carrville Dur 69 NZ3043
Carseriggan D & G 64 NX3167
Carsethorn D & G 66 NX9959
Carshalton Gt Lon 23 TQ2764
Carsington Derbys 49 SK2553
Carsphairn D & G 65 NX5693
Carstairs S Lans 75 NS9345
Carstairs Junction S Lans 75 NS9545
Carterton Oxon 29 SP2806
Carthew Cnwll 3 SX0056
Carthorpe N York 61 SE3083
Cartmel Cumb 59 SD3878
Carway Carmth 17 SN4606
Cashe's Green Gloucs 28 SO8205
Cassington Oxon 29 SP4511
Cassop Dur 62 NZ3438
Casterton Cumb 60 SD6279
Castle Acre Norfk 42 TF8115
Castle Ashby Nhants 30 SP8659
Castlebay W Isls 90 NL6698
Castle Bolton N York 61 SE0391
Castle Bromwich Solhll 38 SP1489
Castle Bytham Lincs 40 SK9818
Castlebythe Pembks 16 SN0229
Castle Caereinion Powys 36 SJ1605
Castle Camps Cambs 32 TL6242
Castle Carrock Cumb 67 NY5455
Castle Cary Somset 9 ST6432
Castle Combe Wilts 20 ST8477
Castle Donington Leics 39 SK4427
Castle Douglas D & G 66 NX7662
Castle Eaton Swindn 20 SU1496
Castle Eden Dur 62 NZ4238
Castleford Wakefd 55 SE4225
Castle Frome Herefs 28 SO6645
Castle Gresley Derbys 39 SK2717
Castle Hedingham Essex 24 TL7835
Castle Hill Suffk 33 TM1446
Castlehill W Duns 80 NS3875
Castle Kennedy D & G 64 NX1159
Castlemartin Pembks 16 SR9198
Castlemilk C Glas 74 NS5958
Castlemorton Worcs 28 SO7937
Castlemorton Common Worcs 28 SO7838
Castle Rising Norfk 42 TF6624
Castleside Dur 68 NZ0748
Castlethorpe M Keyn 30 SP8044
Castleton Derbys 48 SK1582
Castleton N York 62 NZ6807
Castleton Newpt 19 ST2583
Castleton Rochdl 54 SD8810
Castletown Highld 100 ND1967
Castletown IoM 52 SC2667
Castletown Sundld 69 NZ3658
Castley N York 55 SE2646
Caston Norfk 42 TL9597
Castor C Pete 40 TL1298
Catcliffe Rothm 49 SK4288
Catcomb Wilts 20 SU0076
Catcott Somset 19 ST3939
Catcott Burtle Somset 19 ST4043
Caterham Surrey 23 TQ3455
Catfield Norfk 43 TG3821
Catford Gt Lon 23 TQ3773
Catforth Lancs 53 SD4735
Cathcart C Glas 74 NS5860
Cathedine Powys 26 SO1425
Catherington Hants 11 SU6914
Catherston Leweston Dorset 8 SY3694
Catisfield Hants 11 SU5506
Catmere End Essex 31 TL4939
Catmore W Berk 21 SU4580
Caton Lancs 53 SD5364
Caton Green Lancs 53 SD5565
Catrine E Ayrs 74 NS5225
Catsfield E Susx 14 TQ7213
Catsgore Somset 8 ST5025
Catshill Worcs 38 SO9573
Cattal N York 55 SE4454
Cattawade Suffk 25 TM1033
Catterall Lancs 53 SD4942
Catterick N York 61 SE2397
Catterick Bridge N York 61 SE2299
Catterlen Cumb 59 NY4833
Catterline Abers 89 NO8678
Catterton N York 55 SE5145
Catteshall Surrey 12 SU9844
Catthorpe Leics 39 SP5578
Cattistock Dorset 9 SY5999
Catton N York 62 SE3678
Catton Nthumb 68 NY8257
Catwick E R Yk 57 TA1345
Catworth Cambs 30 TL0873
Caudle Green Gloucs 28 SO9410
Caulcott Oxon 29 SP5024
Cauldhame Stirlg 81 NS6494
Cauldmill Border 76 NT5315
Cauldon Staffs 48 SK0749
Cauldwell Derbys 39 SK2517
Caundle Marsh Dorset 9 ST6713
Caunton Notts 50 SK7460
Causeway End Essex 24 TL6819
Causey Park Bridge Nthumb 69 NZ1894
Cavendish Suffk 32 TL8046
Cavenham Suffk 32 TL7670
Caversfield Oxon 29 SP5825
Caversham Readg 22 SU7274
Caverswall Staffs 48 SJ9542
Cawdor Highld 93 NH8450
Cawood N York 56 SE5737
Cawsand Cnwll 4 SX4350
Cawston Norfk 43 TG1323
Cawthorne Barns 55 SE2808
Caxton Cambs 31 TL3058
Caynham Shrops 37 SO5573
Caythorpe Lincs 50 SK9348
Caythorpe Notts 49 SK6845
Cayton N York 63 TA0583
Cefn Newpt 19 ST2788
Cefn-brîth Conwy 45 SH9350
Cefn-bryn-brain Carmth 26 SN7413
Cefn Cribwr Brdgnd 18 SS8582
Cefneithin Carmth 17 SN5513
Cefngorwydd Powys 26 SN9045
Cefn-mawr Wrexhm 36 SJ2842
Cefn-y-pant Carmth 17 SN1925
Cellardyke Fife 83 NO5704
Cellarhead Staffs 48 SJ9547
Cemaes IoA 44 SH3793
Cemmaes Powys 35 SH8406
Cemmaes Road Powys 35 SH8204
Cenarth Cerdgn 17 SN2641
Ceres Fife 83 NO4011
Cerne Abbas Dorset 9 ST6601
Cerney Wick Gloucs 20 SU0796
Cerrigydrudion Conwy 45 SH9548
Ceunant Gwynd 44 SH5361
Chaceley Gloucs 28 SO8530
Chacewater Cnwll 2 SW7544
Chackmore Bucks 30 SP6835
Chacombe Nhants 29 SP4944
Chadbury Worcs 28 SP0146
Chadderton Oldham 54 SD9005
Chaddesden C Derb 49 SK3836
Chaddesley Corbett Worcs 38 SO8973
Chaddlehanger Devon 4 SX4678
Chaddleworth W Berk 21 SU4178
Chadlington Oxon 29 SP3321
Chadshunt Warwks 29 SP3452
Chadwell Leics 40 SK7824
Chadwell Heath Gt Lon 23 TQ4888
Chadwell St Mary Thurr 24 TQ6478
Chadwick Worcs 28 SO8369
Chadwick End Solhll 39 SP2073
Chaffcombe Somset 8 ST3510
Chafford Hundred Thurr 24 TQ6079
Chagford Devon 5 SX7087
Chailey E Susx 13 TQ3919
Chainhurst Kent 14 TQ7248
Chaldon Surrey 23 TQ3155
Chaldon Herring Dorset 9 SY7983
Chale IoW 11 SZ4877
Chale Green IoW 11 SZ4879
Chalfont Common Bucks 22 TQ0092
Chalfont St Giles Bucks 22 SU9893
Chalfont St Peter Bucks 22 TQ0090
Chalford Gloucs 20 SO8903
Chalford Wilts 20 ST8650
Chalgrove Oxon 21 SU6396
Chalk Kent 14 TQ6773
Chalkwell Kent 14 TQ8963
Challacombe Devon 7 SS6940
Challock Kent 15 TR0050
Chalton C Beds 30 TL0326
Chalton Hants 11 SU7315
Chalvey Slough 22 SU9679
Chalvington E Susx 13 TQ5109
Chandler's Cross Herts 22 TQ0698
Chandler's Ford Hants 10 SU4319
Channel Tunnel Terminal Kent 15 TR1937
Chantry Somset 20 ST7146
Chantry Suffk 33 TM1443
Chapel Fife 83 NT2593
Chapel Allerton Leeds 55 SE3037
Chapel Allerton Somset 19 ST4050
Chapel Amble Cnwll 3 SW9975
Chapel Brampton Nhants 30 SP7266
Chapel Chorlton Staffs 37 SJ8137
Chapelend Way Essex 32 TL7039
Chapel-en-le-Frith Derbys 48 SK0580
Chapel Green Warwks 29 SP4660
Chapel Haddlesey N York 56 SE5826
Chapelhall N Lans 74 NS7862
Chapel Hill Lincs 51 TF2054
Chapel Hill N York 55 SE3446
Chapelhope Border 75 NT2318
Chapelknowe D & G 67 NY3173
Chapel Lawn Shrops 36 SO3176
Chapel-le-Dale N York 60 SD7377
Chapel Leigh Somset 8 ST1229
Chapel of Garioch Abers 95 NJ7124
Chapel Row W Berk 21 SU5769
Chapel St Leonards Lincs 51 TF5672
Chapel Stile Cumb 59 NY3205
Chapelton Angus 89 NO6247
Chapelton Devon 6 SS5726
Chapelton S Lans 74 NS6848
Chapeltown Bl w D 54 SD7315
Chapeltown Sheff 49 SK3596
Chapmanslade Wilts 20 ST8247
Chapmans Well Devon 4 SX3593
Chapmore End Herts 31 TL3216
Chappel Essex 24 TL8928
Chard Somset 8 ST3208
Chard Junction Somset 8 ST3404
Chardleigh Green Somset 8 ST3110
Chardstock Devon 8 ST3004
Charfield S Glos 20 ST7292
Charing Kent 14 TQ9549
Charingworth Gloucs 29 SP1939
Charlbury Oxon 29 SP3519
Charlcombe BaNES 20 ST7467
Charlcutt Wilts 20 ST9875
Charlecote Warwks 29 SP2656
Charlemont Sandw 38 SP0193
Charles Devon 7 SS6832
Charleston Angus 88 NO3845
Charlestown C Brad 55 SE1638
Charlestown Calder 54 SD9726
Charlestown Cnwll 3 SX0351
Charlestown Fife 82 NT0683
Charlestown Salfd 47 SD8100
Charlestown of Aberlour Moray 94 NJ2642
Charles Tye Suffk 32 TM0252
Charlesworth Derbys 48 SK0092
Charlinch Somset 19 ST2338
Charlton Gt Lon 23 TQ4178
Charlton Nhants 29 SP5335
Charlton Nthumb 68 NY8184
Charlton Oxon 21 SU4088
Charlton Somset 8 ST2926
Charlton Somset 20 ST6852
Charlton W Susx 11 SU8812
Charlton Wilts 9 ST9022
Charlton Wilts 20 ST9588
Charlton Worcs 28 SP0045
Charlton Wrekin 37 SJ5911
Charlton Abbots Gloucs 28 SP0324
Charlton Adam Somset 8 ST5328
Charlton All Saints Wilts 10 SU1723
Charlton Down Dorset 9 SY6895
Charlton Horethorne Somset 9 ST6623
Charlton Kings Gloucs 28 SO9621
Charlton Mackrell Somset 8 ST5328
Charlton Marshall Dorset 9 ST9004
Charlton Musgrove Somset 9 ST7229
Charlton-on-Otmoor Oxon 29 SP5616
Charlton on the Hill Dorset 9 ST8903
Charlton St Peter Wilts 20 SU1156
Charlwood Hants 11 SU6731
Charlwood Surrey 12 TQ2441
Charminster Dorset 9 SY6792
Charmouth Dorset 8 SY3693
Charndon Bucks 30 SP6724
Charney Bassett Oxon 21 SU3894
Charnock Richard Lancs 53 SD5515
Charnock Richard Services Lancs 53 SD5415
Charsfield Suffk 33 TM2556
Charter Alley Hants 21 SU5958
Charterhouse Somset 19 ST4955
Chartham Kent 15 TR1054
Chartham Hatch Kent 15 TR1056
Chartridge Bucks 22 SP9303
Chart Sutton Kent 14 TQ8049
Charvil Wokham 22 SU7775
Charwelton Nhants 29 SP5356
Chase Terrace Staffs 38 SK0309
Chasetown Staffs 38 SK0408
Chastleton Oxon 29 SP2429
Chasty Devon 6 SS3402
Chatburn Lancs 54 SD7644
Chatcull Staffs 37 SJ7934
Chatham Medway 14 TQ7567
Chatham Green Essex 24 TL7115
Chathill Nthumb 77 NU1827
Chattenden Medway 14 TQ7572
Chatteris Cambs 41 TL3985
Chatterton Lancs 54 SD7918
Chattisham Suffk 33 TM0942
Chatton Nthumb 77 NU0528
Chawleigh Devon 7 SS7112
Chawton Hants 11 SU7037
Cheadle Staffs 48 SK0043
Cheadle Stockp 47 SJ8688
Cheadle Hulme Stockp 47 SJ8786
Cheam Gt Lon 23 TQ2463
Chearsley Bucks 22 SP7110
Chebsey Staffs 38 SJ8528
Checkendon Oxon 22 SU6683
Checkley Ches E 47 SJ7346
Checkley Staffs 48 SK0237
Chedburgh Suffk 32 TL7957
Cheddar Somset 19 ST4553
Cheddington Bucks 30 SP9217
Cheddleton Staffs 48 SJ9752
Cheddon Fitzpaine Somset 8 ST2427
Chedgrave Norfk 43 TM3699
Chedington Dorset 8 ST4805
Chediston Suffk 33 TM3577
Chedworth Gloucs 28 SP0512
Chedzoy Somset 19 ST3437
Cheetham Hill Manch 47 SD8401
Cheldon Devon 7 SS7313
Chelford Ches E 47 SJ8174
Chellaston C Derb 39 SK3730
Chellington Bed 30 SP9555
Chelmarsh Shrops 37 SO7288
Chelmondiston Suffk 25 TM2037
Chelmorton Derbys 48 SK1169
Chelmsford Essex 24 TL7007
Chelmsley Wood Solhll 39 SP1887
Chelsea Gt Lon 23 TQ2778
Chelsfield Gt Lon 23 TQ4864
Chelsworth Suffk 32 TL9748
Cheltenham Gloucs 28 SO9422
Chelveston Nhants 30 SP9969
Chelvey N Som 19 ST4668
Chelwood BaNES 19 ST6361
Chelwood Gate E Susx 13 TQ4130
Cheney Longville Shrops 36 SO4284
Chenies Bucks 22 TQ0198
Chepstow Mons 19 ST5393
Cherhill Wilts 20 SU0370
Cherington Gloucs 20 ST9098
Cherington Warwks 29 SP2936
Cheriton Hants 11 SU5828
Cheriton Kent 15 TR2037
Cheriton Pembks 16 SR9897
Cheriton Swans 17 SS4593
Cheriton Bishop Devon 5 SX7793
Cheriton Fitzpaine Devon 7 SS8606
Cherrington Wrekin 37 SJ6619
Cherry Burton E R Yk 56 SE9841
Cherry Hinton Cambs 31 TL4856
Cherry Orchard Worcs 28 SO8553
Cherry Willingham Lincs 50 TF0272
Chertsey Surrey 22 TQ0466
Cherwell Valley Services Oxon 29 SP5428
Cheselbourne Dorset 9 SY7699
Chesham Bucks 22 SP9601
Chesham Bury 54 SD8012
Chesham Bois Bucks 22 SU9699
Cheshunt Herts 23 TL3502
Cheslyn Hay Staffs 38 SJ9707
Chessetts Wood Warwks 39 SP1873
Chessington Gt Lon 23 TQ1863
Chester Ches W 46 SJ4066
Chesterblade Somset 20 ST6641
Chesterfield Derbys 49 SK3871
Chesterfield Staffs 38 SK0905
Chester-le-Street Dur 69 NZ2751
Chester Moor Dur 69 NZ2649
Chesters Border 68 NT6210
Chester Services Ches W 46 SJ4674

Crowhurst – Eday Airport

125

Crowhurst E Susx 14 TQ7512
Crowhurst Surrey 13 TQ3847
Crowland Lincs 41 TF2410
Crowland Suffk 32 TM0170
Crowlas Cnwll 2 SW5133
Crowle N Linc 56 SE7712
Crowle Worcs 28 SO9256
Crowle Green Worcs 28 SO9156
Crowmarsh Gifford Oxon 21 SU6189
Crown Corner Suffk 33 TM2570
Crownhill C Plym 4 SX4858
Crownpits Surrey 12 SU9743
Crownthorpe Norfk 43 TG0803
Crowntown Cnwll 2 SW6330
Crows-an-Wra Cnwll 2 SW3927
Crowthorne Wokham 22 SU8464
Crowton Ches W 47 SJ5774
Croxdale Dur 61 NZ2636
Croxden Staffs 48 SK0639
Croxley Green Herts 22 TQ0795
Croxteth Lpool 46 SJ4096
Croxton Cambs 31 TL2460
Croxton N Linc 57 TA0912
Croxton Norfk 32 TL8786
Croxton Norfk 42 TF9831
Croxton Staffs 37 SJ7832
Croxton Kerrial Leics 40 SK8329
Croy Highld 93 NH7949
Croy N Lans 74 NS7275
Croyde Devon 6 SS4439
Croydon Cambs 31 TL3149
Croydon Gt Lon 23 TQ3265
Cruckmeole Shrops 36 SJ4309
Cruckton Shrops 36 SJ4310
Cruden Bay Abers 95 NK0836
Crudgington Wrekin 37 SJ6318
Crudwell Wilts 20 ST9593
Crumlin Caerph 19 ST2197
Crumplehorn Cnwll 4 SX2051
Crumpsall Manch 47 SD8402
Crundale Kent 15 TR0749
Crux Easton Hants 21 SU4256
Crwbin Carmth 17 SN4713
Cryers Hill Bucks 22 SU8796
Crymych Pembks 17 SN1834
Crynant Neath 26 SN7904
Crystal Palace Gt Lon 23 TQ3371
Cubert Cnwll 2 SW7857
Cublington Bucks 30 SP8422
Cublington Herefs 27 SO4038
Cuckfield W Susx 12 TQ3025
Cucklington Somset 9 ST7527
Cuckney Notts 49 SK5671
Cuddesdon Oxon 21 SP5903
Cuddington Bucks 22 SP7311
Cuddington Ches W 47 SJ5971
Cuddington Heath Ches W 46 SJ4746
Cudham Gt Lon 23 TQ4459
Cudliptown Devon 4 SX5279
Cudnell BCP 10 SZ0696
Cudworth Barns 55 SE3808
Cudworth Somset 8 ST3810
Cuffley Herts 23 TL3003
Culbokie Highld 92 NH6059
Culcabock Highld 93 NH6844
Culcheth Warrtn 47 SJ6694
Culford Suffk 32 TL8370
Culgaith Cumb 59 NY6029
Culham Oxon 21 SU5095
Culkerton Gloucs 20 ST9395
Cullen Moray 94 NJ5167
Cullercoats N Tyne 69 NZ3570
Cullingworth C Brad 55 SE0636
Culloden Highld 93 NH7246
Cullompton Devon 7 ST0207
Cullompton Services Devon 7 ST0208
Culm Davy Devon 8 ST1215
Culmington Shrops 37 SO4982
Culmstock Devon 8 ST1013
Culross Fife 82 NS9886
Culroy S Ayrs 73 NS3114
Culsalmond Abers 94 NJ6532
Cultercullen Abers 95 NJ9223
Cults C Aber 89 NJ8903
Culverstone Green Kent 14 TQ6362
Culverthorpe Lincs 50 TF0240
Culworth Nhants 29 SP5446
Cumbernauld N Lans 74 NS7674
Cumberworth Lincs 51 TF5073
Cuminestown Abers 95 NJ8050
Cummersdale Cumb 67 NY3953
Cummertrees D & G 67 NY1366
Cummingston Moray 93 NJ1368
Cumnock E Ayrs 74 NS5620
Cumnor Oxon 29 SP4504
Cumrew Cumb 67 NY5550
Cumwhinton Cumb 67 NY4552
Cumwhitton Cumb 67 NY5052
Cundall N York 55 SE4272
Cunningsburgh Shet 100 HU4330
Cupar Fife 83 NO3714
Cupar Muir Fife 83 NO3613
Curbar Derbys 49 SK2574
Curbridge Hants 11 SU5211
Curbridge Oxon 29 SP3308
Curdridge Hants 11 SU5213
Curdworth Warwks 38 SP1792
Curland Somset 8 ST2717
Curridge W Berk 21 SU4972
Currie C Edin 75 NT1867
Curry Mallet Somset 8 ST3221
Curry Rivel Somset 8 ST3925
Curtisden Green Kent 14 TQ7440
Curtisknowle Devon 5 SX7353
Cury Cnwll 2 SW6721
Cushnie Abers 94 NJ5211
Cusworth Donc 56 SE5404
Cutcombe Somset 7 SS9339
Cutnall Green Worcs 28 SO8868
Cutsdean Gloucs 28 SP0830
Cutthorpe Derbys 49 SK3473
Cuxham Oxon 22 SU6695
Cuxton Medway 14 TQ7066
Cuxwold Lincs 50 TA1701
Cwm Denbgs 46 SJ0677
Cwmafan Neath 18 SS7791
Cwmaman Rhondd 18 ST0099
Cwmbach Carmth 17 SN2526
Cwmbâch Powys 27 SO1639
Cwmbach Rhondd 18 SO0201
Cwmbach Llechrhyd Powys 26 SO0254
Cwmbran Torfn 19 ST2994
Cwmcarn Caerph 19 ST2193
Cwmcarvan Mons 27 SO4707
Cwm-cou Cerdgn 17 SN2942
Cwm Crawnon Powys 27 SO1419
Cwmdare Rhondd 26 SN9803
Cwmdu Powys 27 SO1823
Cwmdu Swans 17 SS6494
Cwmduad Carmth 17 SN3731
Cwmfelin Brdgnd 18 SS8589
Cwmfelin Myr Td 18 SO0901
Cwmfelin Boeth Carmth 17 SN1919
Cwmfelinfach Caerph 19 ST1891
Cwmffrwd Carmth 17 SN4217
Cwmgiedd Powys 26 SN7911
Cwmgorse Carmth 26 SN7010
Cwmgwili Carmth 17 SN5710
Cwmhiraeth Carmth 17 SN3437
Cwm Llinau Powys 35 SH8408
Cwmllynfell Neath 26 SN7412
Cwmmawr Carmth 17 SN5312
Cwmparc Rhondd 18 SS9495
Cwmpengraig Carmth 17 SN3536
Cwmtillery Blae G 27 SO2105
Cwm-twrch Isaf Powys 26 SN7610
Cwm-twrch Uchaf Powys 26 SN7511
Cwm-y-glo Gwynd 44 SH5562
Cwmystwyth Cerdgn 35 SN7874
Cwrt-newydd Cerdgn 17 SN4947
Cyffylliog Denbgs 45 SJ0557
Cylibebyll Neath 26 SN7404
Cymmer Neath 18 SS8695
Cymmer Rhondd 18 ST0290
Cynghordy Carmth 26 SN8040
Cynonville Neath 18 SS8395
Cynwyd Denbgs 36 SJ0541
Cynwyl Elfed Carmth 17 SN3727

D

Daccombe Devon 5 SX9068
Dacre Cumb 59 NY4526
Dacre N York 55 SE1960
Dacre Banks N York 55 SE1962
Daddry Shield Dur 60 NY8937
Dadford Bucks 30 SP6638
Dadlington Leics 39 SP4097
Dafen Carmth 17 SN5201
Dagenham Gt Lon 23 TQ5084
Daglingworth Gloucs 28 SO9905
Dagnall Bucks 30 SP9916
Dailly S Ayrs 73 NS2701
Dairsie Fife 83 NO4117
Dalbeattie D & G 66 NX8361
Dalby IoM 52 SC2178
Dalby N York 56 SE6371
Dalcapon P & K 88 NN9754
Dalcrue P & K 82 NO0427
Dalditch Devon 8 SY0483
Dale Derbys 49 SK4338
Dale Pembks 16 SM8005
Dalgety Bay Fife 82 NT1683
Dalginross P & K 81 NN7721
Dalguise P & K 88 NN9847
Dalhalvaig Highld 99 NC8954
Dalham Suffk 32 TL7261
Dalkeith Mdloth 75 NT3367
Dallas Moray 93 NJ1252
Dallinghoo Suffk 33 TM2655
Dallington E Susx 13 TQ6519
Dallington Nhants 30 SP7362
Dalmally Ag & B 80 NN1627
Dalmellington E Ayrs 73 NS4705
Dalmeny C Edin 75 NT1477
Dalry N Ayrs 73 NS2949
Dalrymple E Ayrs 73 NS3514
Dalserf S Lans 74 NS7950
Dalston Cumb 67 NY3650
Dalston Gt Lon 23 TQ3384
Dalswinton D & G 66 NX9385
Dalton D & G 67 NY1173
Dalton N York 61 NZ1108
Dalton N York 62 SE4376
Dalton Nthumb 69 NZ1172
Dalton-in-Furness Cumb 58 SD2273
Dalton-le-Dale Dur 69 NZ4048
Dalton-on-Tees N York 61 NZ2907
Dalton Piercy Hartpl 62 NZ4631
Dalveich Stirlg 81 NN6124
Dalwhinnie Highld 87 NN6384
Dalwood Devon 8 ST2400
Damerham Hants 10 SU1016
Damgate Norfk 43 TG4009
Damnaglaur D & G 64 NX1235
Danbury Essex 24 TL7805
Danby N York 63 NZ7008
Danby Wiske N York 62 SE3398
Danebridge Ches E 48 SJ9665
Dane End Herts 31 TL3321
Danehill E Susx 13 TQ4027
Dane Hills C Leic 39 SK5604
Dane Street Kent 15 TR0552
Darenth Kent 14 TQ5671
Daresbury Halton 47 SJ5882
Darfield Barns 55 SE4104
Dargate Kent 15 TR0861
Darite Cnwll 4 SX2569
Darlaston Wsall 38 SO9796
Darlaston Green Wsall 38 SO9797
Darley N York 55 SE2059
Darley Abbey C Derb 49 SK3538
Darley Bridge Derbys 49 SK2661
Darley Dale Derbys 49 SK2663
Darley Green Solhll 38 SP1774
Darleyhall Herts 30 TL1422
Darley Head N York 55 SE1959
Darlingscott Warwks 29 SP2342
Darlington Darltn 61 NZ2814
Darlton Notts 50 SK7773
Darowen Powys 35 SH8201
Darracott Devon 6 SS2317
Darracott Devon 6 SS4739
Darras Hall Nthumb 69 NZ1570
Darrington Wakefd 55 SE4819
Darsham Suffk 33 TM4169
Darshill Somset 19 ST6144
Dartford Kent 23 TQ5474
Dartford Crossing Kent 14 TQ5675
Dartington Devon 5 SX7862
Dartmouth Devon 5 SX8751
Darton Barns 55 SE3110
Darvel E Ayrs 74 NS5637
Darwen Bl w D 54 SD6922
Datchet W & M 22 SU9877
Datchworth Herts 31 TL2619
Daubhill Bolton 47 SD7007
Dauntsey Wilts 20 ST9981
Dava Highld 93 NJ0038
Davenham Ches W 47 SJ6571
Daventry Nhants 29 SP5762
Davidson's Mains C Edin 75 NT2175
Davidstow Cnwll 4 SX1587
Davington D & G 67 NT2302
Davington Hill Kent 15 TR0161
Daviot Abers 95 NJ7428
Daviot Highld 93 NH7239
Davyhulme Traffd 47 SJ7595
Daw End Wsall 38 SK0300
Dawesgreen Surrey 12 TQ2147
Dawley Wrekin 37 SJ6808
Dawlish Devon 5 SX9576
Dawlish Warren Devon 5 SX9778
Daybrook Notts 49 SK5745
Daylesford Gloucs 29 SP2425
Deal Kent 15 TR3752
Dean Cumb 58 NY0725
Dean Devon 5 SX7264
Dean Devon 18 SS7048
Dean Hants 11 SU5619
Dean Oxon 29 SP3422
Dean Somset 20 ST6743
Dean Bottom Kent 14 TQ5868
Deancombe Devon 5 SX7264
Dean Court Oxon 29 SP4705
Deane Bolton 47 SD6907
Deane Hants 21 SU5450
Deanhead Kirk 55 SE0416
Deanland Dorset 9 ST9918
Dean Prior Devon 5 SX7363
Deanraw Nthumb 68 NY8162
Deans W Loth 75 NT0369
Deanscales Cumb 58 NY0926
Deanshanger Nhants 30 SP7639
Deanston Stirlg 81 NN7101
Dearham Cumb 58 NY0736
Debach Suffk 33 TM2454
Debden Essex 23 TQ4496
Debden Essex 24 TL5533
Debenham Suffk 33 TM1763
Deblin's Green Worcs 28 SO8148
Dechmont W Loth 75 NT0370
Deddington Oxon 29 SP4631
Dedham Essex 25 TM0533
Dedworth W & M 22 SU9476
Deene Nhants 40 SP9492
Deenethorpe Nhants 40 SP9591
Deepcar Sheff 49 SK2897
Deeping Gate C Pete 40 TF1409
Deeping St James Lincs 40 TF1609
Deeping St Nicholas Lincs 41 TF2115
Deerhurst Gloucs 28 SO8630
Defford Worcs 28 SO9143
Defynnog Powys 26 SN9227
Deganwy Conwy 45 SH7779
Deighton C York 56 SE6244
Deighton N York 62 NZ3801
Deiniolen Gwynd 44 SH5763
Delabole Cnwll 3 SX0683
Delamere Ches W 47 SJ5668
Dell Quay W Susx 11 SU8302
Delph Oldham 54 SD9807
Delves Dur 69 NZ1249
Dembleby Lincs 40 TF0437
Denaby Donc 49 SK4899
Denbigh Denbgs 45 SJ0566
Denbury Devon 5 SX8268
Denby Derbys 49 SK3946
Denby Dale Kirk 55 SE2208
Denchworth Oxon 21 SU3891
Dendron Cumb 53 SD2470
Denford Nhants 30 SP9976
Dengie Essex 25 TL9802
Denham Bucks 22 TQ0487
Denham Suffk 32 TL7561
Denham Suffk 33 TM1974
Denham Green Bucks 22 TQ0488
Denholm Border 76 NT5718
Denholme C Brad 55 SE0734
Denmead Hants 11 SU6512
Denmore C Aber 95 NJ9411
Dennington Suffk 33 TM2867
Denny Falk 81 NS8082
Dennyloanhead Falk 81 NS8080
Den of Lindores Fife 83 NO2517
Denshaw Oldham 54 SD9710
Densole Kent 15 TR2141
Denston Suffk 32 TL7652
Denstone Staffs 48 SK0940
Denstroude Kent 15 TR1061
Dent Cumb 60 SD7086
Denton Cambs 40 TL1587
Denton Darltn 61 NZ2118
Denton E Susx 13 TQ4502
Denton Kent 15 TR2147
Denton Lincs 40 SK8632
Denton N York 55 SE1448
Denton Nhants 30 SP8358
Denton Norfk 33 TM2788
Denton Tamesd 48 SJ9295
Denver Norfk 41 TF6001
Denwick Nthumb 69 NU2014
Deopham Norfk 42 TG0400
Deopham Green Norfk 42 TM0499
Depden Suffk 32 TL7856
Deptford Gt Lon 23 TQ3777
Deptford Wilts 10 SU0138
Derby C Derb 39 SK3536
Derby Devon 6 SS5633
Derbyhaven IoM 52 SC2867
Dereham Norfk 42 TF9913
Deri Caerph 18 SO1201
Derringstone Kent 15 TR2049
Derrington Staffs 38 SJ8922
Derry Hill Wilts 20 ST9670
Derrythorpe N Linc 56 SE8208
Dersingham Norfk 42 TF6830
Dervaig Ag & B 79 NM4352
Derwen Denbgs 46 SJ0750
Derwenlas Powys 35 SN7298
Desborough Nhants 40 SP8083
Desford Leics 39 SK4703
Deskford Moray 94 NJ5061
Detling Kent 14 TQ7958
Devauden Mons 19 ST4898
Devil's Bridge Cerdgn 35 SN7376
Devizes Wilts 20 SU0061
Devonport C Plym 4 SX4554
Devonside Clacks 82 NS9196
Devoran Cnwll 2 SW7939
Dewlish Dorset 9 SY7798
Dewsbury Kirk 55 SE2421
Dewsbury Moor Kirk 55 SE2321
Deytheur Powys 36 SJ2317
Dibden Hants 10 SU4008
Dibden Purlieu Hants 10 SU4106
Dickleburgh Norfk 33 TM1682
Didbrook Gloucs 28 SP0531
Didcot Oxon 21 SU5290
Diddington Cambs 31 TL1965
Diddlebury Shrops 37 SO5085
Didling W Susx 11 SU8318
Didmarton Gloucs 20 ST8287
Didsbury Manch 47 SJ8491
Digby Lincs 50 TF0854
Diggle Oldham 54 SE0007
Digmoor Lancs 46 SD4905
Dihewyd Cerdgn 34 SN4855
Dilham Norfk 43 TG3325
Dilhorne Staffs 48 SJ9743
Dill Hall Lancs 54 SD7529
Dillington Cambs 30 TL1365
Dilston Nthumb 68 NY9763
Dilton Wilts 20 ST8548
Dilton Marsh Wilts 20 ST8449
Dilwyn Herefs 27 SO4154
Dinas Gwynd 44 SH2735
Dinas Cross Pembks 16 SN0138
Dinas-Mawddwy Gwynd 35 SH8515
Dinas Powys V Glam 19 ST1571
Dinder Somset 19 ST5744
Dinedor Herefs 27 SO5336
Dingestow Mons 27 SO4510
Dingle Lpool 46 SJ3687
Dingley Nhants 40 SP7787
Dingwall Highld 92 NH5458
Dinnington N u Ty 69 NZ2073
Dinnington Rothm 49 SK5285
Dinnington Somset 8 ST4012
Dinorwic Gwynd 44 SH5861
Dinton Bucks 22 SP7610
Dinton Wilts 10 SU0131
Dinworthy Devon 6 SS3015
Dipford Somset 8 ST2021
Dippen Ag & B 72 NR8037
Dippertown Devon 4 SX4284
Diptford Devon 5 SX7256
Dipton Dur 69 NZ1553
Dirleton E Loth 83 NT5183
Dirt Pot Nthumb 68 NY8545
Diseworth Leics 39 SK4524
Dishforth N York 62 SE3873
Disley Ches E 48 SJ9784
Diss Norfk 33 TM1180
Distington Cumb 58 NY0023
Ditchampton Wilts 10 SU0831
Ditcheat Somset 19 ST6236
Ditchingham Norfk 33 TM3391
Ditchling E Susx 12 TQ3215
Ditherington Shrops 37 SJ5014
Ditteridge Wilts 20 ST8169
Dittisham Devon 5 SX8655
Ditton Kent 14 TQ7158
Ditton Green Cambs 32 TL6558
Ditton Priors Shrops 37 SO6089
Dixton Mons 27 SO5113
Dobcross Oldham 54 SD9906
Dobwalls Cnwll 4 SX2165
Doccombe Devon 5 SX7786
Docking Norfk 42 TF7636
Docklow Herefs 27 SO5657
Dockray Cumb 59 NY3921
Doddinghurst Essex 24 TQ5999
Doddington Cambs 41 TL4090
Doddington Kent 14 TQ9357
Doddington Lincs 50 SK8970
Doddington Nthumb 77 NT9932
Doddington Shrops 37 SO6176
Doddiscombsleigh Devon 5 SX8586
Dodd's Green Ches E 47 SJ6043
Dodford Nhants 29 SP6160
Dodford Worcs 38 SO9373
Dodington S Glos 20 ST7580
Dodington Somset 19 ST1740
Dodleston Ches W 46 SJ3661
Dod's Leigh Staffs 38 SK0134
Dodworth Barns 55 SE3105
Doe Bank Birm 38 SP1197
Dogdyke Lincs 51 TF2055
Dogmersfield Hants 22 SU7852
Dogsthorpe C Pete 40 TF1901
Dolanog Powys 36 SJ0612
Dolbenmaen Gwynd 44 SH5043
Dolfach Powys 35 SH9101
Dolfor Powys 36 SO1087
Dolgarrog Conwy 45 SH7767
Dolgellau Gwynd 35 SH7217
Dollar Clacks 82 NS9698
Dolphin Flints 46 SJ1973
Dolphinholme Lancs 53 SD5253
Dolphinton S Lans 75 NT1046
Dolton Devon 6 SS5712
Dolwen Conwy 45 SH8874
Dolwyddelan Conwy 45 SH7352
Domgay Powys 36 SJ2818
Doncaster Donc 56 SE5703
Doncaster North Services Donc 56 SE6610
Doncaster Sheffield Airport Donc 49 SK6598
Donhead St Andrew Wilts 9 ST9124
Donhead St Mary Wilts 9 ST9024
Doniford Somset 18 ST0842
Donington Lincs 41 TF2035
Donington on Bain Lincs 51 TF2382
Donington Park Services Leics 39 SK4625
Donisthorpe Leics 39 SK3113
Donnington Gloucs 29 SP1928
Donnington Shrops 37 SJ5708
Donnington W Berk 21 SU4668
Donnington W Susx 11 SU8501
Donnington Wrekin 37 SJ7114
Donnington Wood Wrekin 37 SJ7112
Donyatt Somset 8 ST3314
Dorchester Dorset 9 SY6990
Dorchester-on-Thames Oxon 21 SU5794
Dordon Warwks 39 SK2500
Dore Sheff 49 SK3181
Dores Highld 92 NH5934
Dorking Surrey 12 TQ1649
Dormansland Surrey 13 TQ4041
Dormington Herefs 27 SO5840
Dormston Worcs 28 SO9857
Dorney Bucks 22 SU9379
Dornie Highld 85 NG8826
Dornoch Highld 97 NH7989
Dornock D & G 67 NY2366
Dorridge Solhll 38 SP1775
Dorrington Lincs 50 TF0852
Dorrington Shrops 37 SJ4702
Dorrington Shrops 37 SJ7340
Dorsington Warwks 28 SP1349
Dorstone Herefs 27 SO3141
Dorton Bucks 30 SP6714
Douglas IoM 52 SC3775
Douglas S Lans 74 NS8330
Douglas and Angus C Dund 83 NO4233
Douglastown Angus 88 NO4147
Douglas Water S Lans 74 NS8736
Doulting Somset 19 ST6443
Dounby Ork 100 HY2920
Doune Stirlg 81 NN7201
Dounepark S Ayrs 64 NX1897
Dousland Devon 4 SX5369
Dove Holes Derbys 48 SK0777
Dovenby Cumb 58 NY0933
Dover Kent 15 TR3241
Dovercourt Essex 25 TM2431
Doverdale Worcs 28 SO8666
Doveridge Derbys 38 SK1133
Doversgreen Surrey 12 TQ2548
Dowally P & K 88 NO0048
Dowdeswell Gloucs 28 SP0019
Dowlais Myr Td 26 SO0607
Dowland Devon 6 SS5610
Dowlish Wake Somset 8 ST3712
Down Ampney Gloucs 20 SU0996
Downderry Cnwll 4 SX3154
Downe Gt Lon 23 TQ4361
Downend Gloucs 20 ST8398
Downend S Glos 19 ST6577
Downfield C Dund 83 NO3833
Downgate Cnwll 4 SX3672
Downham Essex 24 TQ7296
Downham Gt Lon 23 TQ3871
Downham Lancs 54 SD7844
Downham Market Norfk 41 TF6103
Down Hatherley Gloucs 28 SO8622
Downhead Somset 9 ST5625
Downhead Somset 20 ST6945
Downholme N York 61 SE1197
Downies Abers 89 NO9294
Downley Bucks 22 SU8495
Down St Mary Devon 7 SS7404
Downside Surrey 22 TQ1057
Down Thomas Devon 4 SX5050
Downton Wilts 10 SU1821
Dowsby Lincs 40 TF1129
Doynton S Glos 20 ST7274
Draethen Caerph 19 ST2287
Draffan S Lans 74 NS7945
Drakeholes Notts 49 SK7090
Drakemyre N Ayrs 73 NS2950
Drakes Broughton Worcs 28 SO9248
Draughton N York 55 SE0352
Draughton Nhants 30 SP7676
Drax N York 56 SE6726
Draycote Warwks 29 SP4470
Draycott Derbys 39 SK4433
Draycott Gloucs 29 SP1835
Draycott Somset 19 ST4751
Draycott in the Clay Staffs 38 SK1528
Draycott in the Moors Staffs 48 SJ9840
Drayton C Port 11 SU6605
Drayton Leics 40 SP8392
Drayton Norfk 43 TG1813
Drayton Oxon 21 SU4894
Drayton Oxon 29 SP4241
Drayton Somset 8 ST4024
Drayton Worcs 38 SO9075
Drayton Bassett Staffs 39 SK1900
Drayton Beauchamp Bucks 22 SP9011
Drayton Parslow Bucks 30 SP8328
Drayton St Leonard Oxon 21 SU5996
Dreen Hill Pembks 16 SM9214
Drefach Carmth 17 SN3538
Drefach Carmth 17 SN5213
Drefach Cerdgn 17 SN4945
Dreghorn N Ayrs 73 NS3538
Drellingore Kent 15 TR2441
Drem E Loth 83 NT5079
Dresden C Stke 48 SJ9142
Drewsteignton Devon 5 SX7391
Driffield E R Yk 56 TA0257
Driffield Gloucs 20 SU0799
Drift Cnwll 2 SW4328
Drigg Cumb 58 SD0699
Drighlington Leeds 55 SE2228
Drimnin Highld 79 NM5554
Drimpton Dorset 8 ST4104
Dringhouses C York 56 SE5849
Drinkstone Suffk 32 TL9561
Drinkstone Green Suffk 32 TL9660
Drointon Staffs 38 SK0226
Droitwich Spa Worcs 28 SO8963
Dron P & K 82 NO1316
Dronfield Derbys 49 SK3578
Drongan E Ayrs 73 NS4418
Dronley Angus 83 NO3435
Droop Dorset 9 ST7508
Droxford Hants 11 SU6018
Droylsden Tamesd 48 SJ9097
Druid Denbgs 45 SJ0443
Druidston Pembks 16 SM8716
Drum P & K 82 NO0400
Drumbeg Highld 98 NC1232
Drumburgh Cumb 67 NY2659
Drumburn D & G 66 NX8854
Drumchapel C Glas 74 NS5270
Drumclog S Lans 74 NS6438
Drumelzier Border 75 NT1334
Drumgley Angus 88 NO4250
Drumleaning Cumb 67 NY2751
Drumlithie Abers 89 NO7880
Drummore D & G 64 NX1336
Drummuir Moray 94 NJ3843
Drumnadrochit Highld 92 NH5030
Drunzie P & K 82 NO1308
Drybeck Cumb 60 NY6615
Drybridge N Ayrs 73 NS3536
Drybrook Gloucs 27 SO6417
Dryburgh Border 76 NT5932
Dry Doddington Lincs 50 SK8546
Dry Drayton Cambs 31 TL3861
Drymen Stirlg 81 NS4788
Drynoch Highld 84 NG4031
Ducklington Oxon 29 SP3507
Duddenhoe End Essex 31 TL4536
Duddingston C Edin 75 NT2872
Duddington Nhants 40 SK9800
Duddlestone Somset 8 ST2321
Duddo Nthumb 77 NT9342
Duddon Ches W 46 SJ5164
Dudleston Shrops 36 SJ3438
Dudleston Heath Shrops 36 SJ3736
Dudley Dudley 38 SO9490
Dudley N Tyne 69 NZ2573
Dudley Port Sandw 38 SO9691
Dudsbury Dorset 10 SZ0798
Duffield Derbys 49 SK3443
Duffryn Neath 18 SS8495
Dufftown Moray 94 NJ3240
Duffus Moray 94 NJ1668
Dufton Cumb 60 NY6825
Duggleby N York 56 SE8767
Duirinish Highld 85 NG7831
Duisky Highld 85 NN0077
Dukestown Blae G 26 SO1410
Duke Street Suffk 32 TM0742
Dukinfield Tamesd 48 SJ9397
Dulcote Somset 19 ST5644
Dulford Devon 8 ST0706
Dull P & K 87 NN8049
Dullingham Cambs 32 TL6357
Dulnain Bridge Highld 93 NH9925
Duloe Bed 31 TL1560
Duloe Cnwll 4 SX2358
Dulverton Somset 7 SS9127
Dulwich Gt Lon 23 TQ3373
Dumbarton W Duns 81 NS4075
Dumbleton Gloucs 28 SP0135
Dumfries D & G 66 NX9776
Dummer Hants 21 SU5846
Dumpton Kent 15 TR3966
Dun Angus 89 NO6659
Dunan Ag & B 80 NS1571
Dunan Highld 84 NG5828
Dunball Somset 19 ST3141
Dunbar E Loth 83 NT6778
Dunbeath Highld 100 ND1629
Dunbeg Ag & B 79 NM8833
Dunblane Stirlg 81 NN7801
Dunbog Fife 83 NO2817
Duncanstone Abers 94 NJ5726
Dunchideock Devon 5 SX8787
Dunchurch Warwks 39 SP4871
Duncow D & G 66 NX9683
Duncrievie P & K 82 NO1309
Duncton W Susx 12 SU9617
Dundee C Dund 83 NO4030
Dundee Airport C Dund 83 NO3729
Dundon Somset 8 ST4832
Dundonald S Ayrs 73 NS3634
Dundonnell Highld 91 NH0987
Dundraw Cumb 67 NY2149
Dundrennan D & G 65 NX7447
Dundry N Som 19 ST5666
Dunecht Abers 95 NJ7509
Dunfermline Fife 82 NT0987
Dunfield Gloucs 20 SU1497
Dunham-on-the-Hill Ches W 46 SJ4772
Dunham-on-Trent Notts 50 SK8074
Dunhampton Worcs 28 SO8466
Dunham Town Traffd 47 SJ7387
Dunham Woodhouses Traffd 47 SJ7287
Dunholme Lincs 50 TF0279
Dunino Fife 83 NO5311
Dunipace Falk 81 NS8083
Dunkeld P & K 88 NO0242
Dunkerton BaNES 20 ST7159
Dunkeswell Devon 8 ST1407
Dunkeswick N York 55 SE3047
Dunkirk Kent 15 TR0759
Dunkirk S Glos 20 ST7885
Dunk's Green Kent 13 TQ6152
Dunley Worcs 28 SO7869
Dunlop E Ayrs 73 NS4049
Dunmore Falk 82 NS8989
Dunnet Highld 100 ND2171
Dunnichen Angus 89 NO5048
Dunning P & K 82 NO0114
Dunnington C York 56 SE6652
Dunnington E R Yk 57 TA1551
Dunnington Warwks 28 SP0654
Dunoon Ag & B 80 NS1776
Dunragit D & G 64 NX1557
Duns Border 76 NT7853
Dunsby Lincs 40 TF1026
Dunscore D & G 66 NX8684
Dunscroft Donc 56 SE6409
Dunsdale R & Cl 62 NZ6019
Dunsden Green Oxon 22 SU7377
Dunsdon Devon 6 SS3008
Dunsfold Surrey 12 TQ0035
Dunsford Devon 5 SX8189
Dunshalt Fife 83 NO2410
Dunsill Notts 49 SK4661
Dunsley N York 63 NZ8511
Dunsley Staffs 38 SO8583
Dunsmore Bucks 22 SP8605
Dunsop Bridge Lancs 54 SD6549
Dunstable C Beds 30 TL0122
Dunstall Staffs 39 SK1820
Dunstan Nthumb 77 NU2419
Dunster Somset 7 SS9943
Duns Tew Oxon 29 SP4528
Dunston Gatesd 69 NZ2362
Dunston Lincs 50 TF0662
Dunston Norfk 43 TG2202
Dunston Staffs 38 SJ9217
Dunstone Devon 5 SX5951
Dunstone Devon 5 SX7175
Dunsville Donc 56 SE6407
Dunswell E R Yk 57 TA0735
Dunsyre S Lans 75 NT0748
Dunterton Devon 4 SX3779
Duntisbourne Abbots Gloucs 28 SO9608
Duntisbourne Rouse Gloucs 28 SO9805
Duntish Dorset 9 ST6906
Duntocher W Duns 74 NS4872
Dunton Bucks 30 SP8224
Dunton C Beds 31 TL2344
Dunton Norfk 42 TF8830
Dunton Bassett Leics 39 SP5490
Dunton Green Kent 23 TQ5157
Dunure S Ayrs 73 NS2515
Dunvant Swans 17 SS5993
Dunvegan Highld 90 NG2547
Dunwich Suffk 33 TM4770
Durgan Cnwll 2 SW7727
Durham Dur 61 NZ2742
Durham Services Dur 61 NZ3037
Durham Tees Valley Airport S on T 62 NZ3713
Durisdeer D & G 66 NS8903
Durleigh Somset 19 ST2736
Durley Hants 11 SU5116
Durley Wilts 21 SU2364
Durley Street Hants 11 SU5217
Durlock Kent 15 TR2757
Durlock Kent 15 TR3164
Durness Highld 98 NC4068
Durno Abers 95 NJ7128
Duror Highld 86 NM9955
Durrington W Susx 12 TQ1105
Durrington Wilts 20 SU1544
Durris Abers 89 NO7796
Dursley Gloucs 20 ST7598
Dursley Cross Gloucs 28 SO6920
Durston Somset 8 ST2928
Durweston Dorset 9 ST8508
Duston Nhants 30 SP7261
Duthil Highld 93 NH9324
Dutton Ches W 47 SJ5779
Duxford Cambs 31 TL4846
Duxford Oxon 21 SU3610
Dwygyfylchi Conwy 45 SH7376
Dwyran IoA 44 SH4465
Dyce C Aber 95 NJ8812
Dyffryn Ardudwy Gwynd 34 SH5823
Dyffryn Cellwen Neath 26 SN8510
Dyke Lincs 40 TF1022
Dyke Moray 93 NH9858
Dykehead Angus 88 NO3859
Dykehead N Lans 74 NS8659
Dymchurch Kent 15 TR1029
Dymock Gloucs 28 SO7031
Dyrham S Glos 20 ST7475
Dysart Fife 83 NT3093
Dyserth Denbgs 45 SJ0578

E

Eagland Hill Lancs 53 SD4345
Eagle Lincs 50 SK8766
Eaglesfield Cumb 58 NY0928
Eaglesfield D & G 67 NY2374
Eaglesham E Rens 74 NS5751
Eagley Bolton 54 SD7112
Eakring Notts 49 SK6762
Ealand N Linc 56 SE7811
Ealing Gt Lon 23 TQ1780
Eals Nthumb 68 NY6756
Eamont Bridge Cumb 59 NY5228
Earby Lancs 54 SD9046
Earcroft Bl w D 54 SD6824
Eardington Shrops 37 SO7290
Eardisland Herefs 27 SO4158
Eardisley Herefs 27 SO3149
Eardiston Shrops 36 SJ3725
Eardiston Worcs 28 SO6968
Earith Cambs 31 TL3875
Earlestown St Hel 47 SJ5795
Earley Wokham 22 SU7472
Earlham Norfk 43 TG1908
Earls Barton Nhants 30 SP8563
Earls Colne Essex 24 TL8528
Earls Common Worcs 28 SO9559
Earl's Croome Worcs 28 SO8742
Earlsdon Covtry 39 SP3278
Earlsferry Fife 83 NO4800
Earlsfield Gt Lon 23 TQ2573
Earlsheaton Kirk 55 SE2621
Earl Shilton Leics 39 SP4697
Earl Soham Suffk 33 TM2363
Earl Sterndale Derbys 48 SK0966
Earlston Border 76 NT5738
Earlswood Surrey 12 TQ2749
Earlswood Warwks 38 SP1174
Earnley W Susx 11 SZ8196
Earsdon N Tyne 69 NZ3272
Earsham Norfk 33 TM3288
Eartham W Susx 12 SU9309
Easby N York 62 NZ5708
Easdale Ag & B 79 NM7417
Easebourne W Susx 11 SU9023
Easenhall Warwks 39 SP4679
Eashing Surrey 12 SU9443
Easington Bucks 22 SP6810
Easington Dur 69 NZ4143
Easington E R Yk 57 TA3919
Easington R & Cl 63 NZ7417
Easington Colliery Dur 69 NZ4344
Easington Lane Sundld 69 NZ3645
Easingwold N York 56 SE5269
Eassie and Nevay Angus 88 NO3344
East Aberthaw V Glam 18 ST0366
East Allington Devon 5 SX7748
East Anstey Devon 7 SS8626
East Ashey IoW 11 SZ5888
East Ashling W Susx 11 SU8107
East Ayton N York 63 SE9985
East Barkwith Lincs 50 TF1681
East Barming Kent 14 TQ7254
East Barnby N York 63 NZ8212
East Barnet Gt Lon 23 TQ2795
East Barsham Norfk 42 TF9133
East Beckham Norfk 43 TG1639
East Bedfont Gt Lon 22 TQ0873
East Bergholt Suffk 25 TM0734
East Bilney Norfk 42 TF9519
East Blatchington E Susx 13 TQ4800
East Boldon S Tyne 69 NZ3661
East Boldre Hants 10 SU3700
Eastbourne Darltn 61 NZ3013
Eastbourne E Susx 13 TV6199
East Bradenham Norfk 42 TF9308
East Brent Somset 19 ST3451
Eastbridge Suffk 33 TM4566
East Bridgford Notts 49 SK6943
East Buckland Devon 7 SS6831
East Budleigh Devon 8 SY0684
Eastburn C Brad 55 SE0144
Eastbury W Berk 21 SU3477
East Butterwick N Linc 56 SE8306
Eastby N York 55 SE0154
East Calder W Loth 75 NT0867
East Carleton Norfk 43 TG1701
East Carlton Leeds 55 SE2143
East Carlton Nhants 40 SP8389
East Chaldon Dorset 9 SY7983
East Challow Oxon 21 SU3888
East Charleton Devon 5 SX7642
East Chelborough Dorset 9 ST5505
East Chiltington E Susx 13 TQ3715
East Chinnock Somset 8 ST4913
East Chisenbury Wilts 20 SU1452
Eastchurch Kent 15 TQ9871
East Clandon Surrey 12 TQ0651
East Claydon Bucks 30 SP7325
East Coker Somset 9 ST5412
Eastcombe Gloucs 28 SO8904
East Compton Somset 19 ST6141
East Cornworthy Devon 5 SX8455
Eastcote Gt Lon 22 TQ1088
Eastcote Nhants 30 SP6853
Eastcote Solhll 39 SP1979
Eastcott Wilts 20 SU0255
East Cottingwith E R Yk 56 SE7042
Eastcourt Wilts 21 SU2361
East Cowes IoW 11 SZ5095
East Cowick E R Yk 56 SE6621
East Cowton N York 61 NZ3003
East Cranmore Somset 20 ST6743
East Dean E Susx 13 TV5598
East Dean Gloucs 28 SO6520
East Dean Hants 10 SU2726
East Dean W Susx 11 SU9012
East Drayton Notts 50 SK7775
East Dulwich Gt Lon 23 TQ3375
East Dundry N Som 19 ST5766
East Ella C KuH 57 TA0529
Eastend Essex 25 TQ9492
East End Hants 10 SZ3696
East End Hants 21 SU4161
East End Kent 14 TQ8335
East End Oxon 29 SP3915
East End Somset 20 ST6746
Easter Compton S Glos 19 ST5782
Eastergate W Susx 12 SU9405
Easterhouse C Glas 74 NS6865
Eastern Green Covtry 39 SP2879
Easter Skeld Shet 100 HU3144
Easterton Wilts 20 SU0254
East Everleigh Wilts 21 SU2053
East Farleigh Kent 14 TQ7353
East Farndon Nhants 40 SP7184
East Ferry Lincs 50 SK8199
Eastfield N Lans 74 NS8964
Eastfield N York 63 TA0484
East Garston W Berk 21 SU3576
Eastgate Dur 61 NY9538
Eastgate Lincs 40 TF1019
Eastgate Norfk 43 TG1423
East Goscote Leics 39 SK6413
East Grafton Wilts 21 SU2560
East Grimstead Wilts 10 SU2227
East Grinstead W Susx 13 TQ3938
East Guldeford E Susx 14 TQ9321
East Haddon Nhants 30 SP6668
East Hagbourne Oxon 21 SU5288
East Halton N Linc 57 TA1319
East Ham Gt Lon 23 TQ4283
Easthampton Herefs 27 SO4063
East Hanney Oxon 21 SU4193
East Hanningfield Essex 24 TL7701
East Hardwick Wakefd 55 SE4618
East Harling Norfk 32 TL9986
East Harlsey N York 62 SE4299
East Harnham Wilts 10 SU1428
East Harptree BaNES 19 ST5655
East Harting W Susx 11 SU7919
East Hatch Wilts 9 ST9228
East Hatley Cambs 31 TL2850
East Hauxwell N York 61 SE1693
East Haven Angus 83 NO5836
East Heckington Lincs 50 TF1944
East Hedleyhope Dur 61 NZ1540
East Hendred Oxon 21 SU4588
East Heslerton N York 63 SE9276
East Hoathly E Susx 13 TQ5216
East Holme Dorset 9 SY8986
Easthope Shrops 37 SO5695
Easthorpe Essex 24 TL9121
East Horrington Somset 19 ST5846
East Horsley Surrey 12 TQ0952
East Howe BCP 10 SZ0795
East Huntington C York 56 SE6155
East Huntspill Somset 19 ST3445
East Ilsley W Berk 21 SU4981
Eastington Devon 7 SS7408
Eastington Gloucs 28 SO7705
Eastington Gloucs 28 SP1213
East Keal Lincs 51 TF3863
East Kennett Wilts 20 SU1167
East Keswick Leeds 55 SE3644
East Kilbride S Lans 74 NS6354
East Kirkby Lincs 51 TF3362
East Knighton Dorset 9 SY8185
East Knoyle Wilts 9 ST8830
East Lambrook Somset 8 ST4318
East Langdon Kent 15 TR3346
East Langton Leics 40 SP7292
East Lavant W Susx 11 SU8608
East Lavington W Susx 12 SU9416
East Layton N York 61 NZ1609
Eastleach Martin Gloucs 29 SP2004
Eastleach Turville Gloucs 29 SP1905
East Leake Notts 39 SK5526
Eastleigh Devon 6 SS4827
Eastleigh Hants 10 SU4519
East Lexham Norfk 42 TF8517
Eastling Kent 15 TQ9656
East Linton E Loth 76 NT5977
East Lockinge Oxon 21 SU4287
East Lound N Linc 50 SK7899
East Lulworth Dorset 9 SY8682
East Lutton N York 56 SE9469
East Lydford Somset 9 ST5731
East Malling Kent 14 TQ7056
East Marden W Susx 11 SU8014
East Markham Notts 50 SK7373
East Martin Hants 10 SU0719
East Marton N York 54 SD9050
East Meon Hants 11 SU6722
East Mersea Essex 25 TM0414
East Midlands Airport Leics 39 SK4525
East Molesey Surrey 22 TQ1467
East Morden Dorset 9 SY9194
East Morton C Brad 55 SE0942
East Ness N York 62 SE6978
Eastney C Port 11 SZ6698
Eastnor Herefs 28 SO7237
East Norton Leics 40 SK7800
Eastoft N Linc 56 SE8016
East Ogwell Devon 5 SX8370
Easton Cambs 30 TL1371
Easton Devon 5 SX7289
Easton Dorset 9 SY6971
Easton Hants 11 SU5132
Easton Lincs 40 SK9326
Easton Norfk 43 TG1310
Easton Somset 19 ST5147
Easton Suffk 33 TM2858
Easton Wilts 20 ST8970
Easton Grey Wilts 20 ST8887
Easton-in-Gordano N Som 19 ST5175
Easton Maudit Nhants 30 SP8858
Easton-on-the-Hill Nhants 40 TF0104
Easton Royal Wilts 21 SU2060
East Orchard Dorset 9 ST8317
East Peckham Kent 14 TQ6648
East Pennard Somset 19 ST5937
East Perry Cambs 31 TL1566
East Portlemouth Devon 5 SX7538
East Prawle Devon 5 SX7836
East Preston W Susx 12 TQ0602
East Putford Devon 6 SS3616
East Quantoxhead Somset 18 ST1343
East Rainton Sundld 69 NZ3347
East Ravendale NE Lin 51 TF2399
East Raynham Norfk 42 TF8825
Eastrea Cambs 41 TL2997
Eastriggs D & G 67 NY2466
East Rigton Leeds 55 SE3743
Eastrington E R Yk 56 SE7929
Eastrop Swindn 21 SU2092
East Rounton N York 62 NZ4203
East Rudham Norfk 42 TF8228
East Runton Norfk 43 TG1942
East Ruston Norfk 43 TG3427
Eastry Kent 15 TR3054
East Saltoun E Loth 76 NT4767
East Sheen Gt Lon 23 TQ2075
East Shefford W Berk 21 SU3874
East Stockwith Lincs 50 SK7894
East Stoke Dorset 9 SY8686
East Stoke Notts 50 SK7549
East Stour Dorset 9 ST8022
East Stourmouth Kent 15 TR2662
East Stowford Devon 7 SS6326
East Stratton Hants 21 SU5440
East Studdal Kent 15 TR3149
East Taphouse Cnwll 4 SX1863
East-the-Water Devon 6 SS4526
East Thirston Nthumb 69 NU1900
East Tilbury Thurr 24 TQ6778
East Tisted Hants 11 SU7032
East Torrington Lincs 50 TF1483
East Tuddenham Norfk 42 TG0711
East Tytherley Hants 10 SU2929
East Tytherton Wilts 20 ST9674
East Village Devon 7 SS8405
Eastville Bristl 19 ST6174
Eastville Lincs 51 TF4056
East Walton Norfk 42 TF7416
East Week Devon 5 SX6692
Eastwell Leics 40 SK7728
East Wellow Hants 10 SU3020
East Wemyss Fife 83 NT3497
Eastwick Herts 23 TL4311
East Wickham Gt Lon 23 TQ4677
East Williamston Pembks 16 SN0904
East Winch Norfk 42 TF6916
East Winterslow Wilts 10 SU2434
East Wittering W Susx 11 SZ7997
East Witton N York 61 SE1486
Eastwood Notts 49 SK4646
Eastwood Sthend 24 TQ8488
East Woodburn Nthumb 68 NY9086
East Woodhay Hants 21 SU4061
East Worldham Hants 11 SU7538
East Wretham Norfk 32 TL9190
Eathorpe Warwks 29 SP3969
Eaton Ches E 47 SJ8765
Eaton Ches W 47 SJ5763
Eaton Leics 40 SK7928
Eaton Norfk 43 TG2106
Eaton Notts 49 SK7077
Eaton Oxon 21 SP4403
Eaton Shrops 37 SO5089
Eaton Bray C Beds 30 SP9720
Eaton Constantine Shrops 37 SJ5906
Eaton Green C Beds 30 SP9621
Eaton Hastings Oxon 21 SU2598
Eaton Mascott Shrops 37 SJ5305
Eaton Socon Cambs 31 TL1759
Eaton upon Tern Shrops 37 SJ6523
Ebberston N York 63 SE8982
Ebbesborne Wake Wilts 9 ST9924
Ebbw Vale Blae G 27 SO1609
Ebchester Dur 69 NZ1055
Ebford Devon 5 SX9887
Ebley Gloucs 28 SO8205
Ebnal Ches W 46 SJ4948
Ebrington Gloucs 29 SP1840
Ecchinswell Hants 21 SU4959
Ecclefechan D & G 67 NY1974
Eccles Border 76 NT7641
Eccles Kent 14 TQ7360
Eccles Salfd 47 SJ7798
Ecclesall Sheff 49 SK3284
Ecclesfield Sheff 49 SK3593
Eccleshall Staffs 38 SJ8329
Eccleshill C Brad 55 SE1736
Ecclesmachan W Loth 75 NT0573
Eccles Road Norfk 32 TM0189
Eccleston Ches W 46 SJ4162
Eccleston Lancs 53 SD5217
Eccleston St Hel 46 SJ4895
Echt Abers 89 NJ7405
Eckford Border 76 NT7026
Eckington Derbys 49 SK4379
Eckington Worcs 28 SO9241
Ecton Nhants 30 SP8263
Edale Derbys 48 SK1285
Eday Airport Ork 100 HY5634

126 Edburton – Gilmerton

Edburton W Susx 12 TQ2311
Edderton Highld 97 NH7084
Eddleston Border 75 NT2447
Eddlewood S Lans 74 NS7153
Edenbridge Kent 13 TQ4446
Edenfield Lancs 54 SD8019
Edenhall Cumb 59 NY5632
Edenham Lincs 40 TF0621
Eden Park Gt Lon 23 TQ3667
Edensor Derbys 48 SK2469
Edenthorpe Donc 56 SE6206
Edern Gwynd 44 SH2739
Edgbaston Birm 38 SP0684
Edgcott Bucks 30 SP6722
Edgcott Somset 7 SS8438
Edge Gloucs 28 SO8409
Edgefield Norfk 43 TG0934
Edgefield Green Norfk 43 TG0934
Edgerton Kirk 55 SE1317
Edgeworth Gloucs 28 SO9406
Edgmond Wrekin 37 SJ7119
Edgton Shrops 36 SO3885
Edgware Gt Lon 23 TQ1991
Edgworth Bl w D 54 SD7416
Edinbane Highld 90 NG3450
Edinburgh C Edin 75 NT2573
Edinburgh Airport C Edin 75 NT1473
Edingale Staffs 39 SK2111
Edingley Notts 49 SK6655
Edingthorpe Norfk 43 TG3132
Edingthorpe Green Norfk 43 TG3031
Edington Nthumb 69 NZ1582
Edington Somset 19 ST3839
Edington Wilts 20 ST9253
Edington Burtle Somset 19 ST3943
Edingworth Somset 19 ST3653
Edithmead Somset 19 ST3249
Edith Weston Rutlnd 40 SK9205
Edlesborough Bucks 30 SP9719
Edlingham Nthumb 69 NU1109
Edlington Lincs 51 TF2371
Edmondsham Dorset 10 SU0611
Edmondsley Dur 69 NZ2349
Edmondthorpe Leics 40 SK8517
Edmonton Gt Lon 23 TQ3492
Edmundbyers Dur 68 NZ0150
Ednam Border 76 NT7337
Edrom Border 77 NT8255
Edstaston Shrops 37 SJ5132
Edstone Warwks 29 SP1861
Edwalton Notts 39 SK5935
Edwinstowe Notts 49 SK6266
Edworth C Beds 31 TL2241
Edwyn Ralph Herefs 27 SO6457
Edzell Angus 89 NO6068
Efail-fach Neath 18 SS7895
Efail Isaf Rhondd 18 ST0884
Efailnewydd Gwynd 44 SH3535
Efailwen Carmth 16 SN1325
Efenechtyd Denbgs 46 SJ1155
Effingham Surrey 22 TQ1153
Egerton Bolton 54 SD7014
Egerton Kent 14 TQ9147
Eggborough N York 56 SE5523
Eggbuckland C Plym 4 SX4957
Eggesford Devon 7 SS6811
Eggington C Beds 30 SP9525
Egginton Derbys 39 SK2628
Eggleston Dur 61 NY9923
Egham Surrey 22 TQ0071
Egleton Rutlnd 40 SK8707
Eglingham Nthumb 77 NU1019
Egloshayle Cnwll 3 SX0072
Egloskerry Cnwll 4 SX2786
Eglwysbach Conwy 45 SH8070
Eglwys Cross Wrexhm 37 SJ4740
Eglwyswrw Pembks 16 SN1438
Egmanton Notts 50 SK7368
Egremont Cumb 58 NY0110
Egremont Wirral 46 SJ3192
Egton N York 63 NZ8006
Egton Bridge N York 63 NZ8004
Egypt Bucks 22 SU9586
Eight Ash Green Essex 25 TL9425
Elan Village Powys 35 SN9364
Elberton S Glos 19 ST6088
Elburton C Plym 4 SX5353
Elcombe Swindn 20 SU1280
Eldersfield Worcs 28 SO7931
Elderslie Rens 73 NS4463
Eldon Dur 61 NZ2328
Elerch Cerdgn 35 SN6886
Elford Staffs 39 SK1810
Elgin Moray 94 NJ2162
Elgol Highld 84 NG5213
Elham Kent 15 TR1744
Elie Fife 83 NO4900
Elim IoA 44 SH3584
Eling Hants 10 SU3612
Elkesley Notts 49 SK6975
Elkstone Gloucs 28 SO9612
Ellacombe Torbay 5 SX9164
Elland Calder 55 SE1120
Ellary Ag & B 71 NR7376
Ellastone Staffs 48 SK1143
Ellel Lancs 53 SD4856
Ellemford Border 76 NT7260
Ellenhall Staffs 38 SJ8426
Ellen's Green Surrey 12 TQ0935
Ellerbeck N York 62 SE4396
Ellerby N York 63 NZ7914
Ellerdine Heath Wrekin 37 SJ6122
Ellerker E R Yk 56 SE9229
Ellerton E R Yk 56 SE7039
Ellerton N York 61 SE2598
Ellesborough Bucks 22 SP8306
Ellesmere Shrops 36 SJ3934
Ellesmere Port Ches W 46 SJ4076
Ellingham Norfk 33 TM3792
Ellingham Nthumb 77 NU1725
Ellingstring N York 61 SE1783
Ellington Cambs 31 TL1671
Ellington Nthumb 69 NZ2791
Elliots Green Somset 20 ST7945
Ellisfield Hants 21 SU6446
Ellistown Leics 39 SK4310
Ellon Abers 95 NJ9530
Ellonby Cumb 59 NY4235
Elloughton E R Yk 56 SE9427
Ellwood Gloucs 27 SO5907
Elm Cambs 41 TF4707
Elmbridge Worcs 28 SO9068
Elmdon Essex 31 TL4639
Elmdon Solhll 38 SP1783
Elmer W Susx 12 SU9800
Elmers End Gt Lon 23 TQ3668
Elmer's Green Lancs 46 SD5006
Elmesthorpe Leics 39 SP4696
Elmhurst Staffs 38 SK1112
Elmley Castle Worcs 28 SO9841
Elmley Lovett Worcs 28 SO8769
Elmore Gloucs 28 SO7815
Elmore Back Gloucs 28 SO7616
Elm Park Gt Lon 23 TQ5385
Elmsett Suffk 32 TM0546
Elmstead Market Essex 25 TM0624
Elmsted Kent 15 TR1144
Elmstone Kent 15 TR2660
Elmstone Hardwicke Gloucs 28 SO9125
Elmswell E R Yk 56 SE9958
Elmswell Suffk 32 TL9964
Elmton Derbys 49 SK5073
Elphin Highld 96 NC2111
Elphinstone E Loth 76 NT3970
Elrig D & G 64 NX3247
Elrington Nthumb 68 NY8563
Elsdon Nthumb 68 NY9393
Elsenham Essex 24 TL5326
Elsfield Oxon 29 SP5410
Elsham N Linc 57 TA0312
Elsing Norfk 42 TG0516
Elslack N York 54 SD9349
Elson Hants 11 SU6002
Elsrickle S Lans 75 NT0643
Elstead Surrey 22 SU9043
Elsted W Susx 11 SU8119
Elsthorpe Lincs 40 TF0623
Elston Notts 50 SK7647
Elstow Bed 30 TL0546
Elstree Herts 23 TQ1795
Elstronwick E R Yk 57 TA2232
Elswick Lancs 53 SD4238
Elswick N u Ty 69 NZ2263
Elsworth Cambs 31 TL3163
Elterwater Cumb 59 NY3204
Eltham Gt Lon 23 TQ4274
Eltisley Cambs 31 TL2759
Elton Cambs 40 TL0893
Elton Ches W 46 SJ4575
Elton Derbys 48 SK2260
Elton Herefs 36 SO4570
Elton S on T 62 NZ4017
Elton-on-the-Hill Notts 40 SK7638
Eltringham Nthumb 68 NZ0762
Elvanfoot S Lans 75 NS9517
Elvaston Derbys 39 SK4032
Elveden Suffk 32 TL8280
Elvetham Heath Hants 22 SU8055
Elvington C York 56 SE6947
Elvington Kent 15 TR2750
Elwick Hartpl 62 NZ4532
Elworth Ches E 47 SJ7361
Elworthy Somset 8 ST0834
Ely Cambs 41 TL5480
Ely Cardif 18 ST1476
Emberton M Keyn 30 SP8849
Embleton Cumb 58 NY1730
Embleton Nthumb 77 NU2322
Embo Highld 97 NH8192
Emborough Somset 19 ST6151
Embsay N York 54 SE0053
Emery Down Hants 10 SU2808
Emley Kirk 55 SE2413
Emmington Oxon 22 SP7402
Emneth Norfk 41 TF4807
Emneth Hungate Norfk 41 TF5107
Empingham Rutlnd 40 SK9408
Empshott Hants 11 SU7531
Emsworth Hants 11 SU7406
Enborne W Berk 21 SU4365
Enborne Row W Berk 21 SU4463
Enderby Leics 39 SP5399
Endmoor Cumb 59 SD5384
Endon Staffs 48 SJ9253
Endon Bank Staffs 48 SJ9253
Enfield Gt Lon 23 TQ3597
Enfield Lock Gt Lon 23 TQ3698
Enfield Wash Gt Lon 23 TQ3598
Enford Wilts 20 SU1351
Engine Common S Glos 20 ST6984
Englefield W Berk 21 SU6272
Englefield Green Surrey 22 SU9971
English Bicknor Gloucs 27 SO5815
Englishcombe BaNES 20 ST7162
English Frankton Shrops 36 SJ4529
Enham Alamein Hants 21 SU3649
Enmore Somset 8 ST2435
Enmore Green Dorset 9 ST8523
Ennerdale Bridge Cumb 58 NY0615
Ensbury BCP 10 SZ0896
Ensdon Shrops 36 SJ4017
Enstone Oxon 29 SP3724
Enville Staffs 38 SO8286
Epney Gloucs 28 SO7611
Epperstone Notts 49 SK6548
Epping Essex 23 TL4502
Epping Green Essex 23 TL4305
Epping Upland Essex 23 TL4404
Eppleby N York 61 NZ1713
Epsom Surrey 23 TQ2160
Epwell Oxon 29 SP3540
Epworth N Linc 56 SE7803
Erbistock Wrexhm 36 SJ3541
Erdington Birm 38 SP1191
Eridge Green E Susx 13 TQ5535
Eriswell Suffk 32 TL7278
Erith Gt Lon 23 TQ5177
Erlestoke Wilts 20 ST9653
Ermington Devon 5 SX6353
Erpingham Norfk 43 TG1931
Errogie Highld 92 NH5622
Errol P & K 83 NO2422
Erskine Rens 73 NS4770
Erwarton Suffk 25 TM2234
Erwood Powys 26 SO0942
Eryholme N York 62 NZ3208
Eryrys Denbgs 46 SJ2057
Escomb Dur 61 NZ1830
Escrick N York 56 SE6242
Esgairgeiliog Powys 35 SH7606
Esh Dur 69 NZ1944
Esher Surrey 22 TQ1364
Eshott Nthumb 69 NZ2097
Esh Winning Dur 61 NZ1942
Eskadale Highld 92 NH4540
Eskdale Green Cumb 58 NY1400
Eskdalemuir D & G 67 NY2597
Esprick Lancs 53 SD4036
Essendine Rutlnd 40 TF0412
Essendon Herts 23 TL2708
Essington Staffs 38 SJ9503
Eston R & Cl 62 NZ5418
Etal Nthumb 77 NT9339
Etchilhampton Wilts 20 SU0460
Etchingham E Susx 14 TQ7126
Etchinghill Kent 15 TR1639
Etchinghill Staffs 38 SK0218
Eton W & M 22 SU9677
Eton Wick W & M 22 SU9478
Etruria C Stke 47 SJ8647
Ettersgill Dur 60 NY8829
Ettiley Heath Ches E 47 SJ7360
Ettingshall Wolves 38 SO9396
Ettington Warwks 29 SP2749
Etton C Pete 40 TF1406
Etton E R Yk 56 SE9743
Ettrick Border 67 NT2714
Ettrickbridge Border 76 NT3824
Etwall Derbys 39 SK2631
Euston Suffk 32 TL8979
Euxton Lancs 53 SD5519
Evanton Highld 92 NH6066
Evedon Lincs 50 TF0947
Evenjobb Powys 27 SO2662
Evenley Nhants 29 SP5834
Evenlode Gloucs 29 SP2129
Evenwood Dur 61 NZ1524
Evercreech Somset 19 ST6438
Everingham E R Yk 56 SE8042
Everleigh Wilts 21 SU2053
Eversholt C Beds 30 SP9833
Evershot Dorset 9 ST5704
Eversley Hants 22 SU7762
Eversley Cross Hants 22 SU7961
Everthorpe E R Yk 56 SE9031
Everton C Beds 31 TL2051
Everton Hants 10 SZ2894
Everton Lpool 46 SJ3491
Everton Notts 49 SK6990
Evertown D & G 67 NY3576
Evesbatch Herefs 28 SO6948
Evesham Worcs 28 SP0344
Evington C Leic 39 SK6203
Ewden Village Sheff 49 SK2796
Ewell Surrey 23 TQ2262
Ewell Minnis Kent 15 TR2643
Ewelme Oxon 21 SU6491
Ewen Gloucs 20 SU0097
Ewenny V Glam 18 SS9077
Ewerby Lincs 50 TF1247
Ewhurst Surrey 12 TQ0940
Ewhurst Green E Susx 14 TQ7924
Ewhurst Green Surrey 12 TQ0939
Ewloe Flints 46 SJ3066
Ewood Bl w D 54 SD6725
Eworthy Devon 6 SX4495
Ewshot Hants 22 SU8149
Ewyas Harold Herefs 27 SO3828
Exbourne Devon 7 SS6002
Exbury Hants 10 SU4200
Exebridge Somset 7 SS9324
Exelby N York 61 SE2987
Exeter Devon 5 SX9292
Exeter Airport Devon 5 SX9993
Exeter Services Devon 5 SX9691
Exford Somset 7 SS8538
Exfordsgreen Shrops 36 SJ4505
Exhall Warwks 28 SP1055
Exhall Warwks 39 SP3585
Exlade Street Oxon 22 SU6581
Exminster Devon 5 SX9487
Exmouth Devon 5 SY0081
Exning Suffk 32 TL6265
Exton Devon 5 SX9886
Exton Hants 11 SU6120
Exton Rutlnd 40 SK9211
Exton Somset 7 SS9233
Exwick Devon 5 SX9093
Eyam Derbys 48 SK2176
Eydon Nhants 29 SP5449
Eye C Pete 41 TF2202
Eye Herefs 27 SO4964
Eye Suffk 33 TM1473
Eyemouth Border 77 NT9464
Eyeworth C Beds 31 TL2545
Eyhorne Street Kent 14 TQ8354
Eyke Suffk 33 TM3151
Eynesbury Cambs 31 TL1859
Eynsford Kent 23 TQ5465
Eynsham Oxon 29 SP4309
Eype Dorset 8 SY4491
Eythorne Kent 15 TR2849
Eyton Herefs 27 SO4761
Eyton Shrops 36 SJ4422
Eyton on Severn Shrops 37 SJ5706
Eyton upon the Weald Moors Wrekin 37 SJ6515

F

Faccombe Hants 21 SU3857
Faceby N York 62 NZ4903
Fachwen Powys 36 SJ0316
Faddiley Ches E 47 SJ5852
Fadmoor N York 62 SE6789
Faerdre Swans 18 SN6901
Faifley W Duns 74 NS4973
Failand N Som 19 ST5171
Failsworth Oldham 48 SD8901
Fairbourne Gwynd 35 SH6113
Fairburn N York 55 SE4727
Fairfield Derbys 48 SK0673
Fairfield Worcs 38 SO9475
Fairford Gloucs 20 SP1501
Fairgirth D & G 66 NX8756
Fair Green Norfk 42 TF6517
Fairhaven Lancs 53 SD3227
Fair Isle Airport Shet 100 HZ2072
Fairlands Surrey 12 SU9652
Fairlie N Ayrs 73 NS2054
Fairlight E Susx 14 TQ8511
Fairmile Devon 8 SY0897
Fairmile Surrey 22 TQ1161
Fairnilee Border 76 NT4532
Fair Oak Hants 11 SU4918
Fairoak Staffs 37 SJ7632
Fair Oak Green Hants 22 SU6660
Fairseat Kent 14 TQ6261
Fairstead Essex 24 TL7616
Fairstead Norfk 42 TF6420
Fairwarp E Susx 13 TQ4626
Fairwater Cardif 18 ST1377
Fairy Cross Devon 6 SS4024
Fakenham Norfk 42 TF9229
Fakenham Magna Suffk 32 TL9176
Fala Mdloth 76 NT4460
Fala Dam Mdloth 76 NT4361
Faldingworth Lincs 50 TF0684
Falfield S Glos 20 ST6893
Falkenham Suffk 33 TM2939
Falkirk Falk 82 NS8880
Falkland Fife 83 NO2507
Fallin Stirlg 82 NS8391
Fallodon Nthumb 77 NU1922
Fallowfield Manch 47 SJ8593
Fallowfield Nthumb 68 NY9268
Falmer E Susx 12 TQ3508
Falmouth Cnwll 2 SW8032
Falsgrave N York 63 TA0288
Falstone Nthumb 68 NY7287
Fancott C Beds 30 TL0127
Fangdale Beck N York 62 SE5694
Fangfoss E R Yk 56 SE7653
Far Bletchley M Keyn 30 SP8533
Farcet Cambs 41 TL2094
Far Cotton Nhants 30 SP7559
Fareham Hants 11 SU5606
Farewell Staffs 38 SK0811
Faringdon Oxon 21 SU2895
Farington Lancs 53 SD5325
Farlam Cumb 67 NY5558
Farleigh N Som 19 ST4969
Farleigh Surrey 23 TQ3760
Farleigh Hungerford Somset 20 ST8057
Farleigh Wallop Hants 21 SU6247
Farlesthorpe Lincs 51 TF4774
Farleton Cumb 59 SD5380
Farleton Lancs 54 SD5767
Farley Staffs 48 SK0644
Farley Wilts 10 SU2229
Farley Green Surrey 12 TQ0545
Farley Hill Wokham 22 SU7464
Farleys End Gloucs 28 SO7614
Farlington C Port 11 SU6805
Farlington N York 56 SE6167
Farlow Shrops 37 SO6380
Farmborough BaNES 20 ST6660
Farmcote Gloucs 28 SP0628
Farmington Gloucs 28 SP1315
Farmoor Oxon 29 SP4506
Far Moor Wigan 46 SD5204
Farnborough Gt Lon 23 TQ4464
Farnborough Hants 22 SU8753
Farnborough W Berk 21 SU4381
Farnborough Warwks 29 SP4349
Farnborough Park Hants 22 SU8755
Farncombe Surrey 12 SU9744
Farndish Bed 30 SP9263
Farndon Ches W 46 SJ4154
Farndon Notts 50 SK7651
Farnell Angus 89 NO6255
Farnham Dorset 9 ST9515
Farnham Essex 31 TL4724
Farnham N York 55 SE3460
Farnham Suffk 33 TM3660
Farnham Surrey 22 SU8346
Farnham Common Bucks 22 SU9585
Farnham Royal Bucks 22 SU9583
Farningham Kent 23 TQ5466
Farnley Leeds 55 SE2532
Farnley N York 55 SE2148
Farnley Tyas Kirk 55 SE1612
Farnsfield Notts 49 SK6456
Farnworth Bolton 47 SD7306
Farnworth Halton 46 SJ5187
Far Oakridge Gloucs 28 SO9203
Farr Highld 99 NC7163
Farringdon Devon 5 SY0191
Farrington Gurney BaNES 19 ST6355
Far Sawrey Cumb 59 SD3795
Farthinghoe Nhants 29 SP5339
Farthingstone Nhants 29 SP6154
Fartown Kirk 55 SE1518
Fasnacloich Ag & B 86 NN0247
Fatfield Sundld 69 NZ3054
Fauldhouse W Loth 75 NS9360
Faulkbourne Essex 24 TL7917
Faulkland Somset 20 ST7354
Fauls Shrops 37 SJ5832
Faversham Kent 15 TR0161
Fawdington N York 62 SE4372
Fawdon N u Ty 69 NZ2268
Fawkham Green Kent 14 TQ5865
Fawler Oxon 29 SP3717
Fawley Bucks 22 SU7586
Fawley Hants 10 SU4503
Fawley W Berk 21 SU3981
Faxfleet E R Yk 56 SE8624
Faygate W Susx 12 TQ2134
Fazakerley Lpool 46 SJ3796
Fazeley Staffs 39 SK2001
Fearby N York 61 SE1981
Fearnan P & K 87 NN7244
Fearnmore Highld 91 NG7260
Featherstone Staffs 38 SJ9305
Featherstone Wakefd 55 SE4219
Feckenham Worcs 28 SP0162
Feering Essex 24 TL8720
Feetham N York 61 SD9898
Felbridge Surrey 13 TQ3739
Felbrigg Norfk 43 TG2039
Felcourt Surrey 13 TQ3841
Felindre Carmth 17 SN3538
Felindre Carmth 17 SN5521
Felindre Powys 36 SO1681
Felindre Swans 17 SN6302
Felindre Farchog Pembks 16 SN1039
Felinfoel Carmth 17 SN5102
Felingwm Isaf Carmth 17 SN5023
Felingwm Uchaf Carmth 17 SN5024
Felixkirk N York 62 SE4684
Felixstowe Suffk 25 TM3034
Felling Gatesd 69 NZ2762
Felmersham Bed 30 SP9957
Felmingham Norfk 43 TG2529
Felpham W Susx 12 SZ9499
Felsham Suffk 32 TL9457
Felsted Essex 24 TL6720
Feltham Gt Lon 22 TQ1073
Felthamhill Surrey 22 TQ0971
Felthorpe Norfk 43 TG1618
Felton Herefs 27 SO5748
Felton N Som 19 ST5265
Felton Nthumb 69 NU1800
Felton Butler Shrops 36 SJ3917
Feltwell Norfk 32 TL7190
Fence Lancs 54 SD8237
Fence Rothm 49 SK4485
Fencott Oxon 29 SP5716
Fendike Corner Lincs 51 TF4560
Fen Ditton Cambs 31 TL4860
Fen Drayton Cambs 31 TL3368
Feniscliffe Bl w D 54 SD6526
Feniscowles Bl w D 54 SD6425
Feniton Devon 8 SY1099
Fenn Green Shrops 37 SO7783
Fenn Street Medway 14 TQ7975
Fenny Bentley Derbys 48 SK1749
Fenny Bridges Devon 8 SY1198
Fenny Compton Warwks 29 SP4152
Fenny Drayton Leics 39 SP3596
Fenstanton Cambs 31 TL3168
Fen Street Norfk 42 TL9895
Fenton Cambs 41 TL3279
Fenton Cumb 67 NY5056
Fenton Lincs 50 SK8476
Fenton Lincs 50 SK8751
Fenton Notts 50 SK7982
Fenton Nthumb 77 NT9733
Fenwick Donc 56 SE5916
Fenwick E Ayrs 73 NS4643
Fenwick Nthumb 68 NZ0572
Fenwick Nthumb 77 NU0640
Feock Cnwll 2 SW8238
Ferndale Rhondd 18 SS9996
Ferndown Dorset 10 SU0700
Ferness Highld 93 NH9645
Fernham Oxon 21 SU2991
Fernhill Heath Worcs 28 SO8659
Fernhurst W Susx 11 SU8928
Fernilee Derbys 48 SK0178
Fernwood Notts 50 SK8250
Ferrensby N York 55 SE3760
Ferring W Susx 12 TQ0902
Ferrybridge Services Wakefd 55 SE4822
Ferryden Angus 89 NO7156
Ferryhill Dur 61 NZ2832
Ferryhill Station Dur 61 NZ2931
Ferryside Carmth 17 SN3610
Fersfield Norfk 32 TM0683
Fetcham Surrey 22 TQ1455
Fetterangus Abers 95 NJ9850
Fettercairn Abers 89 NO6573
Fewston N York 55 SE1954
Ffairfach Carmth 17 SN6321
Ffair Rhos Cerdgn 35 SN7368
Ffarmers Carmth 26 SN6444
Ffestiniog Gwynd 45 SH7042
Fforest Carmth 17 SN5704
Ffostrasol Cerdgn 17 SN3747
Ffrith Flints 46 SJ2855
Ffynnongroyw Flints 46 SJ1381
Fickleshole Surrey 23 TQ3860
Fiddington Somset 19 ST2140
Fiddleford Dorset 9 ST8013
Fiddlers Green Cnwll 2 SW8155
Field Staffs 38 SK0233
Field Dalling Norfk 42 TG0038
Field Head Leics 39 SK4909
Fifehead Magdalen Dorset 9 ST7821
Fifehead Neville Dorset 9 ST7610
Fifehead St Quintin Dorset 9 ST7710
Fife Keith Moray 94 NJ4250
Fifield Oxon 29 SP2418
Fifield W & M 22 SU9076
Figheldean Wilts 20 SU1547
Filby Norfk 43 TG4613
Filey N York 63 TA1180
Filgrave M Keyn 30 SP8648
Filkins Oxon 29 SP2304
Filleigh Devon 7 SS6627
Fillingham Lincs 50 SK9485
Fillongley Warwks 39 SP2887
Filton S Glos 19 ST6079
Fimber E R Yk 56 SE8960
Fincham Norfk 42 TF6806
Finchampstead Wokham 22 SU7963
Finchdean Hants 11 SU7312
Finchingfield Essex 24 TL6832
Finchley Gt Lon 23 TQ2690
Findern Derbys 39 SK3030
Findhorn Moray 93 NJ0364
Findochty Moray 94 NJ4667
Findon Abers 89 NO9397
Findon W Susx 12 TQ1208
Finedon Nhants 30 SP9172
Fingest Bucks 22 SU7791
Finghall N York 61 SE1889
Finglesham Kent 15 TR3353
Fingringhoe Essex 25 TM0220
Finmere Oxon 29 SP6332
Finningham Suffk 32 TM0669
Finningley Donc 49 SK6799
Finsbay W Isls 90 NG0786
Finstall Worcs 28 SO9770
Finsthwaite Cumb 59 SD3687
Finstock Oxon 29 SP3616
Finstown Ork 100 HY3513
Fintry Stirlg 81 NS6186
Finzean Abers 89 NO6092
Fionnphort Ag & B 78 NM3023
Fionnsbhagh W Isls 90 NG0786
Firbank Cumb 60 SD6293
Firbeck Rothm 49 SK5688
Firby N York 56 SE7466
Firby N York 61 SE2686
Firle E Susx 13 TQ4707
Firsby Lincs 51 TF4562
Fir Tree Dur 61 NZ1434
Fishbourne IoW 11 SZ5592
Fishbourne W Susx 11 SU8304
Fishburn Dur 62 NZ3632
Fishcross Clacks 82 NS8995
Fisherrow E Loth 75 NT3472
Fisher's Pond Hants 11 SU4820
Fisherton S Ayrs 73 NS2717
Fisherton de la Mere Wilts 10 SU0038
Fishery Estate W & M 22 SU8980
Fishguard Pembks 16 SM9537
Fishlake Donc 56 SE6513
Fishponds Bristl 19 ST6375
Fishtoft Lincs 51 TF3642
Fishtoft Drove Lincs 51 TF3148
Fishwick Lancs 53 SD5529
Fiskerton Lincs 50 TF0471
Fiskerton Notts 50 SK7351
Fittleton Wilts 20 SU1449
Fittleworth W Susx 12 TQ0019
Fitz Shrops 36 SJ4417
Fitzhead Somset 8 ST1228
Fitzwilliam Wakefd 55 SE4115
Five Ash Down E Susx 13 TQ4723
Five Ashes E Susx 13 TQ5525
Fivehead Somset 8 ST3522
Fivelanes Cnwll 4 SX2280
Five Oak Green Kent 13 TQ6445
Five Oaks W Susx 12 TQ0928
Five Roads Carmth 17 SN4805
Flackwell Heath Bucks 22 SU8989
Fladbury Worcs 28 SO9946
Fladdabister Shet 100 HU4332
Flagg Derbys 48 SK1368
Flamborough E R Yk 57 TA2270
Flamstead Herts 30 TL0714
Flamstead End Herts 23 TL3403
Flansham W Susx 12 SU9601
Flanshaw Wakefd 55 SE3020
Flasby N York 54 SD9456
Flash Staffs 48 SK0266
Flaunden Herts 22 TL0100
Flawborough Notts 50 SK7842
Flawith N York 55 SE4865
Flax Bourton N Som 19 ST5069
Flaxby N York 55 SE3957
Flaxley Gloucs 28 SO6815
Flaxpool Somset 8 ST1435
Flaxton N York 56 SE6762
Fleckney Leics 39 SP6493
Flecknoe Warwks 29 SP5163
Fledborough Notts 50 SK8072
Fleet Dorset 9 SY6380
Fleet Hants 22 SU8053
Fleet Lincs 41 TF3823
Fleet Hargate Lincs 41 TF3925
Fleet Services Hants 22 SU7955
Fleetwood Lancs 53 SD3348
Fleggburgh Norfk 43 TG4413
Flemingston V Glam 18 ST0169
Flemington S Lans 74 NS6559
Flempton Suffk 32 TL8169
Fletchertown Cumb 58 NY2042
Fletching E Susx 13 TQ4223
Flexbury Cnwll 6 SS2107
Flexford Surrey 12 SU9350
Flimby Cumb 58 NY0233
Flimwell E Susx 14 TQ7131
Flint Flints 46 SJ2472
Flintham Notts 50 SK7445
Flinton E R Yk 57 TA2136
Flitcham Norfk 42 TF7326
Flitton C Beds 30 TL0535
Flitwick C Beds 30 TL0334
Flixborough N Linc 56 SE8714
Flixborough Stather N Linc 56 SE8614
Flixton N York 63 TA0479
Flixton Suffk 33 TM3186
Flixton Traffd 47 SJ7494
Flockton Kirk 55 SE2314
Flockton Green Kirk 55 SE2515
Flookburgh Cumb 59 SD3675
Flordon Norfk 43 TM1897
Flore Nhants 29 SP6460
Flowton Suffk 33 TM0846
Flushing Cnwll 2 SW8034
Fluxton Devon 8 SY0893
Flyford Flavell Worcs 28 SO9755
Fobbing Thurr 24 TQ7183
Fochabers Moray 94 NJ3458
Fochriw Caerph 26 SO1005
Fockerby N Linc 56 SE8419
Foddington Somset 9 ST5729
Foel Powys 35 SH9911
Foggathorpe E R Yk 56 SE7537
Fogo Border 76 NT7649
Fole Staffs 48 SK0437
Foleshill Covtry 39 SP3582
Folke Dorset 9 ST6513
Folkestone Kent 15 TR2336
Folkingham Lincs 40 TF0733
Folkington E Susx 13 TQ5603
Folksworth Cambs 40 TL1489
Folkton N York 63 TA0579
Follifoot N York 55 SE3452
Folly Gate Devon 6 SX5798
Fonthill Bishop Wilts 9 ST9333
Fonthill Gifford Wilts 9 ST9231
Fontmell Magna Dorset 9 ST8616
Fontmell Parva Dorset 9 ST8214
Fontwell W Susx 12 SU9407
Foolow Derbys 48 SK1976
Forcett N York 61 NZ1712
Ford Bucks 22 SP7709
Ford Derbys 49 SK4080
Ford Devon 6 SS4124
Ford Gloucs 28 SP0829
Ford Nthumb 77 NT9437
Ford Somset 8 ST0928
Ford Staffs 48 SK0653
Ford W Susx 12 SU9903
Ford Wilts 20 ST8475
Fordcombe Kent 13 TQ5240
Fordell Fife 82 NT1588
Forden Powys 36 SJ2201
Ford End Essex 24 TL6716
Forder Green Devon 5 SX7967
Fordham Cambs 32 TL6370
Fordham Essex 25 TL9228
Fordham Norfk 41 TL6199
Fordingbridge Hants 10 SU1414
Fordon E R Yk 63 TA0475
Fordoun Abers 89 NO7475
Fordstreet Essex 24 TL9226
Ford Street Somset 8 ST1518
Fordwich Kent 15 TR1859
Fordyce Abers 94 NJ5563
Forebridge Staffs 38 SJ9322
Forest Chapel Ches E 48 SJ9772
Forest Gate Gt Lon 23 TQ4085
Forest Green Surrey 12 TQ1241
Forest Hall N Tyne 69 NZ2769
Forest Hill Gt Lon 23 TQ3672
Forest Hill Oxon 29 SP5807
Forest Lane Head N York 55 SE3356
Forest Mill Clacks 82 NS9694
Forest Row E Susx 13 TQ4234
Forestside W Susx 11 SU7612
Forfar Angus 89 NO4550
Forgandenny P & K 82 NO0818
Forge Hammer Torfn 19 ST2895
Forgie Moray 94 NJ3854
Formby Sefton 46 SD3006
Forncett End Norfk 43 TM1493
Forncett St Mary Norfk 43 TM1694
Forncett St Peter Norfk 43 TM1693
Fornham All Saints Suffk 32 TL8367
Fornham St Martin Suffk 32 TL8567
Forres Moray 93 NJ0358
Forsbrook Staffs 48 SJ9641
Fort Augustus Highld 92 NH3709
Forteviot P & K 82 NO0517
Forth S Lans 75 NS9453
Forthampton Gloucs 28 SO8532
Fortingall P & K 87 NN7347
Forton Hants 21 SU4143
Forton Lancs 53 SD4851
Forton Shrops 36 SJ4316
Forton Somset 8 ST3307
Forton Staffs 37 SJ7521
Fortrose Highld 93 NH7256
Fortuneswell Dorset 9 SY6873
Fort William Highld 86 NN1074
Forty Hill Gt Lon 23 TQ3398
Fosbury Wilts 21 SU3157
Foscot Oxon 29 SP2421
Fosdyke Lincs 41 TF3133
Foss P & K 87 NN7858
Fossebridge Gloucs 28 SP0711
Foster Street Essex 23 TL4809
Foston Derbys 39 SK1931
Foston Leics 39 SP6094
Foston Lincs 50 SK8542
Foston N York 56 SE6965
Foston on the Wolds E R Yk 57 TA1055
Fotherby Lincs 51 TF3191
Fotheringhay Nhants 40 TL0593
Foulden Border 77 NT9355
Foulden Norfk 42 TL7699
Foul End Warwks 39 SP2494
Foulridge Lancs 54 SD8942
Foulsham Norfk 42 TG0324
Fountainhall Border 76 NT4249
Four Ashes Suffk 32 TM0070
Four Crosses Powys 36 SJ2618
Four Elms Kent 13 TQ4648
Four Forks Somset 19 ST2336
Four Gotes Cambs 41 TF4516
Four Lanes Cnwll 2 SW6838
Four Marks Hants 11 SU6735
Four Mile Bridge IoA 44 SH2778
Four Oaks Birm 38 SP1098
Four Oaks Solhll 39 SP2480
Four Roads Carmth 17 SN4409
Fourstones Nthumb 68 NY8867
Four Throws Kent 14 TQ7729
Fovant Wilts 10 SU0028
Fowey Cnwll 3 SX1251
Fowlhall Kent 14 TQ6946
Fowlis Angus 83 NO3133
Fowlis Wester P & K 82 NN9224
Fowlmere Cambs 31 TL4245
Fownhope Herefs 27 SO5834
Foxcote Somset 20 ST7155
Foxdale IoM 52 SC2778
Foxearth Essex 32 TL8344
Foxfield Cumb 58 SD2185
Foxhole Cnwll 3 SW9654
Foxholes N York 63 TA0173
Foxley Norfk 42 TG0422
Foxt Staffs 48 SK0348
Foxton Cambs 31 TL4148
Foxton Leics 40 SP7089
Foxton N York 62 SE4296
Foxwood Shrops 37 SO6276
Foy Herefs 27 SO5928
Foyers Highld 92 NH4921
Fraddon Cnwll 3 SW9158
Fradley Staffs 38 SK1513
Fradswell Staffs 38 SJ9931
Fraisthorpe E R Yk 57 TA1561
Framfield E Susx 13 TQ4920
Framingham Earl Norfk 43 TG2702
Framingham Pigot Norfk 43 TG2703
Framlingham Suffk 33 TM2863
Frampton Dorset 9 SY6295
Frampton Lincs 41 TF3239
Frampton Cotterell S Glos 20 ST6682
Frampton Mansell Gloucs 20 SO9202
Frampton-on-Severn Gloucs 28 SO7407
Framsden Suffk 33 TM1959
Framwellgate Moor Dur 69 NZ2644
Franche Worcs 38 SO8278
Frankby Wirral 46 SJ2486
Frankley Worcs 38 SO9980
Frankley Services Worcs 38 SO9880
Frankton Warwks 29 SP4270
Frant E Susx 13 TQ5835
Fraserburgh Abers 95 NJ9966
Frating Essex 25 TM0722
Frating Green Essex 25 TM0823
Fratton C Port 11 SU6500
Freathy Cnwll 4 SX3952
Freckenham Suffk 32 TL6672
Freckleton Lancs 53 SD4329
Freeby Leics 40 SK8020
Freefolk Hants 21 SU4848
Freeland Oxon 29 SP4112
Freethorpe Norfk 43 TG4005
Freethorpe Common Norfk 43 TG4004
Freiston Lincs 51 TF3743
Fremington Devon 6 SS5132
Fremington N York 61 SE0499
Frenchay S Glos 19 ST6377
Frensham Surrey 11 SU8441
Freshfield Sefton 46 SD2907
Freshford Wilts 20 ST7860
Freshwater IoW 10 SZ3487
Fressingfield Suffk 33 TM2677
Freston Suffk 33 TM1638
Freswick Highld 100 ND3667
Fretherne Gloucs 28 SO7210
Frettenham Norfk 43 TG2417
Freuchie Fife 83 NO2806
Freystrop Pembks 16 SM9511
Friar Park Sandw 38 SP0094
Friday Bridge Cambs 41 TF4604
Friday Street Suffk 33 TM3760
Fridaythorpe E R Yk 56 SE8759
Friern Barnet Gt Lon 23 TQ2892
Friesthorpe Lincs 50 TF0683
Frieston Lincs 50 SK9347
Frieth Bucks 22 SU7990
Frilford Oxon 21 SU4497
Frilsham W Berk 21 SU5473
Frimley Surrey 22 SU8757
Frindsbury Medway 14 TQ7469
Fring Norfk 42 TF7334
Fringford Oxon 29 SP6029
Frinsted Kent 14 TQ8957
Frinton-on-Sea Essex 25 TM2320
Friockheim Angus 89 NO5949
Frisby on the Wreake Leics 39 SK6917
Friskney Lincs 51 TF4655
Friston E Susx 13 TV5598
Friston Suffk 33 TM4160
Fritchley Derbys 49 SK3552
Fritham Hants 10 SU2314
Frithelstock Devon 6 SS4619
Frithelstock Stone Devon 6 SS4518
Frithville Lincs 51 TF3150
Frittenden Kent 14 TQ8140
Frittiscombe Devon 5 SX8043
Fritton Norfk 43 TG4600
Fritton Norfk 43 TM2293
Fritwell Oxon 29 SP5229
Frizinghall C Brad 55 SE1435
Frizington Cumb 58 NY0316
Frocester Gloucs 20 SO7803
Frodesley Shrops 37 SJ5101
Frodsham Ches W 46 SJ5177
Frog End Cambs 31 TL3946
Froggatt Derbys 48 SK2476
Froghall Staffs 48 SK0247
Frogmore Devon 5 SX7742
Frognall Lincs 40 TF1610
Frog Pool Worcs 28 SO8065
Frogwell Cnwll 4 SX3468
Frolesworth Leics 39 SP5090
Frome Somset 20 ST7747
Frome St Quintin Dorset 9 ST5902
Fromes Hill Herefs 28 SO6846
Froncysyllte Wrexhm 36 SJ2741
Fron-goch Gwynd 45 SH9039
Fron Isaf Wrexhm 36 SJ2740
Frosterley Dur 61 NZ0237
Froxfield Wilts 21 SU2968
Froxfield Green Hants 11 SU7025
Fryern Hill Hants 10 SU4320
Fryerning Essex 24 TL6300
Fulbeck Lincs 50 SK9450
Fulbourn Cambs 31 TL5256
Fulbrook Oxon 29 SP2513
Fulflood Hants 11 SU4730
Fulford C York 56 SE6149
Fulford Somset 8 ST2029
Fulford Staffs 48 SJ9537
Fulham Gt Lon 23 TQ2576
Fulking W Susx 12 TQ2411
Fullarton N Ayrs 73 NS3238
Fuller Street Essex 24 TL7416
Fullerton Hants 10 SU3739
Fulletby Lincs 51 TF2973
Fullready Warwks 29 SP2846
Full Sutton E R Yk 56 SE7455
Fulmer Bucks 22 SU9985
Fulmodeston Norfk 42 TF9930
Fulnetby Lincs 50 TF0979
Fulney Lincs 41 TF2623
Fulstow Lincs 51 TF3297
Fulwell Sundld 69 NZ3859
Fulwood Lancs 53 SD5431
Fulwood Sheff 49 SK3085
Fundenhall Norfk 43 TM1596
Funtington W Susx 11 SU8008
Furley Devon 8 ST2604
Furnace Ag & B 80 NN0200
Furnace Carmth 17 SN5001
Furness Vale Derbys 48 SK0083
Furneux Pelham Herts 31 TL4327
Furzley Hants 10 SU2816
Fyfield Essex 24 TL5707
Fyfield Hants 21 SU2946
Fyfield Oxon 21 SU4298
Fyfield Wilts 20 SU1468
Fyfield Wilts 21 SU1760
Fylingthorpe N York 63 NZ9404
Fyning W Susx 11 SU8123
Fyvie Abers 95 NJ7637

G

Gaddesby Leics 39 SK6813
Gaddesden Row Herts 30 TL0512
Gaerllwyd Mons 19 ST4496
Gaerwen IoA 44 SH4871
Gailey Staffs 38 SJ9110
Gainford Dur 61 NZ1716
Gainsborough Lincs 50 SK8189
Gainsford End Essex 24 TL7235
Gairloch Highld 91 NG8076
Gairlochy Highld 86 NN1784
Gaitsgill Cumb 67 NY3846
Galashiels Border 76 NT4936
Galgate Lancs 53 SD4855
Galhampton Somset 9 ST6329
Gallatown Fife 83 NT2994
Galleywood Essex 24 TL7003
Galmpton Devon 5 SX6840
Galmpton Torbay 5 SX8856
Galphay N York 61 SE2572
Galston E Ayrs 74 NS4936
Gamblesby Cumb 59 NY6039
Gamlingay Cambs 31 TL2452
Gamlingay Great Heath Cambs 31 TL2151
Gamston Notts 49 SK5937
Gamston Notts 49 SK7176
Ganllwyd Gwynd 35 SH7324
Ganstead E R Yk 57 TA1434
Ganthorpe N York 56 SE6870
Ganton N York 63 SE9977
Garboldisham Norfk 32 TM0081
Gardeners Green Wokham 22 SU8266
Gardenstown Abers 95 NJ8064
Garden Village Sheff 49 SK2698
Garderhouse Shet 100 HU3347
Gare Hill Somset 20 ST7840
Garelochhead Ag & B 80 NS2491
Garford Oxon 21 SU4296
Garforth Leeds 55 SE4033
Gargrave N York 54 SD9354
Gargunnock Stirlg 81 NS7094
Garlic Street Norfk 33 TM2183
Garlieston D & G 65 NX4746
Garlinge Kent 15 TR3369
Garlinge Green Kent 15 TR1152
Garlogie Abers 89 NJ7805
Garmond Abers 95 NJ8052
Garmouth Moray 94 NJ3364
Garmston Shrops 37 SJ6006
Garndolbenmaen Gwynd 44 SH4943
Garrabost W Isls 90 NB5133
Garras Cnwll 2 SW7023
Garreg Gwynd 45 SH6141
Garrigill Cumb 60 NY7441
Garrochtrie D & G 64 NX1138
Garsdale Head Cumb 60 SD7891
Garsdon Wilts 20 ST9687
Garshall Green Staffs 38 SJ9633
Garsington Oxon 21 SP5802
Garstang Lancs 53 SD4945
Garston Herts 22 TL1100
Garston Lpool 46 SJ4084
Garth Powys 26 SN9549
Garth Wrexhm 46 SJ2542
Garthamlock C Glas 74 NS6566
Garthmyl Powys 36 SO1999
Garthorpe Leics 40 SK8320
Garthorpe N Linc 56 SE8418
Garth Row Cumb 59 SD5297
Gartmore Stirlg 81 NS5297
Gartness N Lans 74 NS7864
Gartness Stirlg 81 NS5086
Gartocharn W Duns 81 NS4286
Garton-on-the-Wolds E R Yk 56 SE9759
Garvald E Loth 76 NT5870
Garvan Highld 85 NM9777
Garve Highld 92 NH3961
Garvestone Norfk 42 TG0207
Garway Herefs 27 SO4522
Garyvard W Isls 90 NB3619
Gasper Wilts 9 ST7633
Gastard Wilts 20 ST8868
Gasthorpe Norfk 32 TL9781
Gaston Green Essex 31 TL4917
Gatcombe IoW 11 SZ4985
Gate Burton Lincs 50 SK8382
Gateforth N York 56 SE5628
Gate Helmsley N York 56 SE6955
Gatehouse Nthumb 68 NY7889
Gatehouse of Fleet D & G 65 NX5956
Gateley Norfk 42 TF9624
Gatenby N York 62 SE3287
Gateshead Gatesd 69 NZ2562
Gateside E Rens 74 NS4858
Gateside Fife 82 NO1809
Gatley Stockp 47 SJ8488
Gattonside Border 76 NT5435
Gatwick Airport W Susx 12 TQ2740
Gaulby Leics 40 SK6900
Gauldry Fife 83 NO3723
Gautby Lincs 50 TF1772
Gavinton Border 76 NT7652
Gawcott Bucks 30 SP6831
Gawsworth Ches E 48 SJ8969
Gawthrop Cumb 60 SD6987
Gawthwaite Cumb 58 SD2784
Gaydon Warwks 29 SP3653
Gayhurst M Keyn 30 SP8446
Gayle N York 60 SD8688
Gayles N York 61 NZ1207
Gayton Nhants 30 SP7054
Gayton Norfk 42 TF7219
Gayton Staffs 38 SJ9828
Gayton le Marsh Lincs 51 TF4284
Gayton Thorpe Norfk 42 TF7418
Gaywood Norfk 41 TF6320
Gazeley Suffk 32 TL7264
Gearraidh Bhaird W Isls 90 NB3619
Gedding Suffk 32 TL9457
Geddington Nhants 40 SP8983
Gedling Notts 49 SK6142
Gedney Lincs 41 TF4024
Gedney Broadgate Lincs 41 TF4022
Gedney Drove End Lincs 41 TF4629
Gedney Dyke Lincs 41 TF4126
Gedney Hill Lincs 41 TF3311
Geeston Rutlnd 40 SK9803
Geldeston Norfk 33 TM3991
Gellifor Denbgs 46 SJ1262
Gelligaer Caerph 18 ST1396
Gellilydan Gwynd 45 SH6839
Gellinudd Neath 26 SN7303
Gellyburn P & K 82 NO0939
Gellywen Carmth 17 SN2723
Gelston D & G 66 NX7758
Gelston Lincs 50 SK9145
Gembling E R Yk 57 TA1057
Gentleshaw Staffs 38 SK0411
George Green Bucks 22 SU9981
Georgeham Devon 6 SS4639
George Nympton Devon 7 SS7023
Germansweek Devon 6 SX4394
Gerrans Cnwll 3 SW8735
Gerrards Cross Bucks 22 TQ0088
Gerrick R & Cl 63 NZ7012
Gestingthorpe Essex 24 TL8138
Geuffordd Powys 36 SJ2114
Gidea Park Gt Lon 23 TQ5290
Giffnock E Rens 74 NS5658
Gifford E Loth 76 NT5368
Giggleswick N York 54 SD8063
Gilberdyke E R Yk 56 SE8329
Gilcrux Cumb 58 NY1138
Gildersome Leeds 55 SE2429
Gildingwells Rothm 49 SK5585
Gilesgate Moor Dur 61 NZ2942
Gileston V Glam 18 ST0166
Gilfach Caerph 19 ST1598
Gilfach Goch Brdgnd 18 SS9790
Gilfachrheda Cerdgn 34 SN4158
Gilgarran Cumb 58 NY0323
Gillamoor N York 62 SE6889
Gilling East N York 62 SE6176
Gillingham Dorset 9 ST8026
Gillingham Medway 14 TQ7768
Gillingham Norfk 33 TM4191
Gilling West N York 61 NZ1805
Gills Highld 100 ND3272
Gilmerton C Edin 75 NT2868

Gilmerton – Hawford 127

Gilmerton P & K 82 NN8823
Gilmonby Dur 61 NY9912
Gilmorton Leics 39 SP5787
Gilsland Nthumb 68 NY6366
Gilston Herts 31 TL4412
Gilwern Mons 27 SO2414
Gimingham Norfk 43 TG2836
Gipping Suffk 32 TM0763
Gipsey Bridge Lincs 51 TF2849
Girlsta Shet 100 HU4250
Girsby N York 62 NZ3508
Girton Cambs 31 TL4262
Girton Notts 50 SK8265
Girvan S Ayrs 64 NX1897
Gisburn Lancs 54 SD8248
Gisleham Suffk 33 TM5188
Gislingham Suffk 32 TM0771
Gissing Norfk 33 TM1485
Gittisham Devon 8 SY1398
Gladestry Powys 27 SO2355
Gladsmuir E Loth 76 NT4573
Glais Swans 18 SN7000
Glaisdale N York 63 NZ7705
Glamis Angus 88 NO3846
Glanaman Carmth 26 SN6713
Glandford Norfk 42 TG0441
Glandwr Pembks 17 SN1928
Glandyfi Cerdgn 35 SN6996
Glanllynfi Brdgnd 18 SS8690
Glan-rhyd Powys 26 SN7809
Glanton Nthumb 68 NU0714
Glanvilles Wootton Dorset 9 ST6708
Glan-y-don Flints 46 SJ1679
Glapthorn Nhants 40 TL0290
Glapwell Derbys 49 SK4766
Glasbury Powys 27 SO1739
Glascote Staffs 39 SK2203
Glascwm Powys 27 SO1552
Glasfryn Conwy 45 SH9250
Glasgow C Glas 74 NS5865
Glasgow Airport Rens 73 NS4766
Glasgow Prestwick Airport S Ayrs 73 NS3627
Glasinfryn Gwynd 44 SH5868
Glassford S Lans 74 NS7247
Glasshouse Gloucs 28 SO7021
Glasshouses N York 55 SE1764
Glasson Cumb 67 NY2560
Glasson Lancs 53 SD4456
Glassonby Cumb 59 NY5738
Glaston Rutlnd 40 SK8900
Glastonbury Somset 19 ST5038
Glatton Cambs 40 TL1586
Glazebrook Warrtn 47 SJ6992
Glazebury Warrtn 47 SJ6797
Glazeley Shrops 37 SO7088
Gleaston Cumb 53 SD2570
Gledhow Leeds 55 SE3137
Gledrid Shrops 36 SJ3036
Glemsford Suffk 32 TL8348
Glenallachie Moray 94 NJ2641
Glen Auldyn IoM 52 SC4393
Glenbarr Ag & B 72 NR6736
Glenbervie Abers 89 NO7680
Glenboig N Lans 74 NS7268
Glenborrodale Highld 79 NM6061
Glenbuck E Ayrs 74 NS7429
Glencaple D & G 66 NX9968
Glencarse P & K 82 NO1921
Glencoe Highld 86 NN1058
Glencraig Fife 82 NT1894
Glendaruel Ag & B 80 NR9983
Glendevon P & K 82 NN9904
Glendoick P & K 82 NO2022
Glenelg Highld 85 NG8119
Glenfarg P & K 82 NO1310
Glenfield Leics 39 SK5406
Glenfinnan Highld 85 NM9080
Glengolly Highld 100 ND1065
Glenkindie Abers 94 NJ4314
Glenlivet Moray 94 NJ1929
Glenluce D & G 64 NX1957
Glenmavis N Lans 74 NS7567
Glen Maye IoM 52 SC2379
Glen Parva Leics 39 SP5698
Glenridding Cumb 59 NY3817
Glenrothes Fife 83 NO2700
Glentham Lincs 50 TF0090
Glentrool D & G 64 NX3578
Glentworth Lincs 50 SK9488
Glen Vine IoM 52 SC3378
Glewstone Herefs 27 SO5521
Glinton C Pete 40 TF1505
Glooston Leics 40 SP7595
Glossop Derbys 48 SK0393
Gloster Hill Nthumb 69 NU2504
Gloucester Gloucs 28 SO8318
Gloucester Services Gloucs 28 SO8413
Gloucestershire Airport Gloucs 28 SO8821
Glusburn N York 54 SE0045
Glympton Oxon 29 SP4221
Glynarthen Cerdgn 17 SN3148
Glyn Ceiriog Wrexhm 36 SJ2038
Glyncoch Rhondd 18 ST0792
Glyncorrwg Neath 18 SS8798
Glynde E Susx 13 TQ4509
Glyndyfrdwy Denbgs 46 SJ1442
Glynneath Neath 26 SN8806
Glyntawe Powys 26 SN8416
Glynteg Carmth 17 SN3637
Gnosall Staffs 38 SJ8220
Gnosall Heath Staffs 38 SJ8220
Goadby Leics 40 SP7598
Goadby Marwood Leics 40 SK7726
Goatacre Wilts 20 SU0276
Goathill Dorset 9 ST6717
Goathland N York 63 NZ8301
Goathurst Somset 8 ST2534
Goat Lees Kent 15 TR0145
Gobowen Shrops 36 SJ3033
Godalming Surrey 12 SU9643
Goddard's Green Kent 14 TQ8134
Godmanchester Cambs 31 TL2470
Godmanstone Dorset 9 SY6697
Godmersham Kent 15 TR0550
Godney Somset 19 ST4842
Godolphin Cross Cnwll 2 SW6031
Godre'r-graig Neath 26 SN7506
Godshill IoW 11 SZ5281
Godstone Surrey 12 TQ3551
Goetre Mons 27 SO3206
Goff's Oak Herts 23 TL3202
Goginan Cerdgn 35 SN6881
Golan Gwynd 44 SH5242
Golant Cnwll 3 SX1254
Golberdon Cnwll 4 SX3271
Golborne Wigan 47 SJ6097
Golcar Kirk 55 SE0915
Goldcliff Newpt 19 ST3683
Golden Green Kent 13 TQ6348
Goldenhill C Stke 47 SJ8553
Golden Pot Hants 11 SU7143
Golders Green Gt Lon 23 TQ2487
Goldhanger Essex 24 TL9008
Goldington Bed 30 TL0750
Goldsborough N York 55 SE3856
Goldsborough N York 63 NZ8314
Golds Green Sandw 38 SO9893
Goldsithney Cnwll 2 SW5430
Goldthorpe Barns 55 SE4604
Goldworthy Devon 6 SS3922
Gollanfield Highld 93 NH8053
Golspie Highld 97 NC8300
Gomeldon Wilts 10 SU1835
Gomshall Surrey 12 TQ0847
Gonalston Notts 49 SK6747
Gonerby Hill Foot Lincs 40 SK9037
Gonfirth Shet 100 HU3661
Good Easter Essex 24 TL6212
Gooderstone Norfk 42 TF7602
Goodleigh Devon 7 SS6034
Goodmanham E R Yk 56 SE8843
Goodmayes Gt Lon 23 TQ4687
Goodnestone Kent 15 TR0461
Goodnestone Kent 15 TR2554
Goodrich Herefs 27 SO5719
Goodrington Torbay 5 SX8958
Goodshaw Lancs 54 SD8125
Goodwick Pembks 16 SM9438
Goodworth Clatford Hants 21 SU3642
Goole E R Yk 56 SE7423
Goom's Hill Worcs 28 SP0154
Goonbell Cnwll 2 SW7249
Goonhavern Cnwll 2 SW7853
Goonvrea Cnwll 2 SW7149
Gooseford Devon 5 SX6792
Goose Green Essex 25 TM1325
Goose Green S Glos 20 ST6774
Gooseham Cnwll 6 SS2316
Goosey Oxon 21 SU3591
Goosnargh Lancs 53 SD5536
Goostrey Ches E 47 SJ7770
Gordano Services N Som 19 ST5175
Gordon Border 76 NT6443
Gordonstown Abers 95 NJ7138
Gorebridge Mdloth 75 NT3461
Gorefield Cambs 41 TF4112
Gores Wilts 20 SU1158
Goring Oxon 21 SU6080
Goring-by-Sea W Susx 12 TQ1102
Gorleston on Sea Norfk 43 TG5204
Gorran Churchtown Cnwll 3 SW9942
Gorran Haven Cnwll 3 SX0141
Gorsedd Flints 46 SJ1576
Gorse Hill Swindn 20 SU1586
Gorseinon Swans 17 SS5998
Gorsgoch Cerdgn 17 SN4850
Gorslas Carmth 17 SN5713
Gorsley Gloucs 28 SO6825
Gorsley Common Herefs 28 SO6725
Gorsty Hill Staffs 38 SK1028
Gorton Manch 47 SJ8896
Gosbeck Suffk 33 TM1555
Gosberton Lincs 41 TF2431
Gosfield Essex 24 TL7829
Gosforth Cumb 58 NY0603
Gosforth N u Ty 69 NZ2368
Gosport Hants 11 SZ6099
Gossington Gloucs 20 SO7302
Gotham Notts 39 SK5330
Gotherington Gloucs 28 SO9529
Gotton Somset 8 ST2428
Goudhurst Kent 14 TQ7237
Goulceby Lincs 51 TF2579
Gourdon Abers 89 NO8270
Gourock Inver 80 NS2477
Govan C Glas 74 NS5465
Goveton Devon 5 SX7546
Govilon Mons 27 SO2613
Gowdall E R Yk 56 SE6222
Gowerton Swans 17 SS5896
Gowkhall Fife 82 NT0589
Goxhill E R Yk 57 TA1844
Goxhill N Linc 57 TA1021
Grabhair W Isls 90 NB3915
Graffham W Susx 12 SU9217
Grafham Cambs 31 TL1669
Grafham Surrey 12 TQ0241
Grafton N York 55 SE4163
Grafton Oxon 21 SP2600
Grafton Shrops 36 SJ4319
Grafton Worcs 28 SO9837
Grafton Flyford Worcs 28 SO9655
Grafton Regis Nhants 30 SP7546
Grafton Underwood Nhants 40 SP9280
Grafty Green Kent 14 TQ8748
Graig Conwy 45 SH8071
Graigfechan Denbgs 46 SJ1454
Grain Medway 24 TQ8876
Grainsby Lincs 51 TF2799
Grainthorpe Lincs 51 TF3896
Grampound Cnwll 3 SW9348
Grampound Road Cnwll 3 SW9150
Gramsdal W Isls 90 NF8155
Gramsdale W Isls 90 NF8155
Granborough Bucks 30 SP7625
Granby Notts 40 SK7536
Grandborough Warwks 29 SP4966
Grange Cumb 58 NY2517
Grange Medway 14 TQ7968
Grange Hill Essex 23 TQ4492
Grangemill Derbys 48 SK2457
Grange Moor Kirk 55 SE2215
Grangemouth Falk 82 NS9281
Grange-over-Sands Cumb 59 SD4077
Grangepans Falk 82 NT0181
Grange Park Nhants 30 SP7655
Grangetown R & Cl 62 NZ5420
Grangetown Sundld 69 NZ4154
Grange Villa Dur 69 NZ2352
Gransmoor E R Yk 57 TA1259
Granston Pembks 16 SM8934
Grantchester Cambs 31 TL4355
Grantham Lincs 40 SK9135
Granton C Edin 75 NT2376
Grantown-on-Spey Highld 93 NJ0328
Grantshouse Border 76 NT8065
Grasby Lincs 57 TA0804
Grasmere Cumb 59 NY3307
Grasscroft Oldham 54 SD9704
Grassendale Lpool 46 SJ3985
Grassington N York 54 SE0063
Grassmoor Derbys 49 SK4067
Grassthorpe Notts 50 SK7967
Grateley Hants 21 SU2741
Graveley Cambs 31 TL2563
Graveley Herts 31 TL2327
Gravelly Hill Birm 38 SP1090
Graveney Kent 15 TR0562
Gravesend Kent 14 TQ6574
Gravir W Isls 90 NB3915
Grayingham Lincs 50 SK9396
Grayrigg Cumb 59 SD5796
Grays Thurr 24 TQ6177
Grayshott Hants 11 SU8735
Grayswood Surrey 12 SU9134
Greasbrough Rothm 49 SK4195
Greasby Wirral 46 SJ2587
Great Abington Cambs 31 TL5348
Great Addington Nhants 30 SP9675
Great Alne Warwks 28 SP1259
Great Altcar Lancs 46 SD3305
Great Amwell Herts 31 TL3712
Great Asby Cumb 60 NY6713
Great Ashfield Suffk 32 TL9967
Great Ayton N York 62 NZ5610
Great Baddow Essex 24 TL7304
Great Badminton S Glos 20 ST8082
Great Bardfield Essex 24 TL6730
Great Barford Bed 30 TL1351
Great Barr Sandw 38 SP0495
Great Barrington Gloucs 29 SP2113
Great Barrow Ches W 46 SJ4768
Great Barton Suffk 32 TL8967
Great Barugh N York 63 SE7479
Great Bavington Nthumb 68 NY9880
Great Bealings Suffk 33 TM2348
Great Bedwyn Wilts 21 SU2764
Great Bentley Essex 25 TM1021
Great Billing Nhants 30 SP8162
Great Bircham Norfk 42 TF7732
Great Blakenham Suffk 33 TM1150
Great Blencow Cumb 59 NY4532
Great Bolas Wrekin 37 SJ6421
Great Bookham Surrey 22 TQ1354
Great Bourton Oxon 29 SP4545
Great Bowden Leics 40 SP7488
Great Bradley Suffk 32 TL6753
Great Braxted Essex 24 TL8614
Great Bricett Suffk 32 TM0350
Great Brickhill Bucks 30 SP9030
Great Bridgeford Staffs 38 SJ8827
Great Brington Nhants 30 SP6665
Great Bromley Essex 25 TM0826
Great Broughton Cumb 58 NY0731
Great Broughton N York 62 NZ5405
Great Budworth Ches W 47 SJ6677
Great Burdon Darltn 62 NZ3116
Great Burstead Essex 24 TQ6892
Great Busby N York 62 NZ5205
Great Carlton Lincs 51 TF4085
Great Casterton Rutlnd 40 TF0008
Great Chalfield Wilts 20 ST8563
Great Chart Kent 15 TQ9841
Great Chatwell Staffs 37 SJ7914
Great Chell C Stke 47 SJ8752
Great Chesterford Essex 31 TL5042
Great Cheverell Wilts 20 ST9854
Great Chishill Cambs 31 TL4238
Great Clacton Essex 25 TM1716
Great Clifton Cumb 58 NY0429
Great Coates NE Lin 57 TA2309
Great Comberton Worcs 28 SO9542
Great Corby Cumb 67 NY4754
Great Cornard Suffk 32 TL8840
Great Cowden E R Yk 57 TA2342
Great Coxwell Oxon 21 SU2693
Great Cransley Nhants 30 SP8376
Great Cressingham Norfk 42 TF8501
Great Crosthwaite Cumb 58 NY2524
Great Cubley Derbys 48 SK1638
Great Dalby Leics 40 SK7414
Great Denham Bed 30 TL0148
Great Doddington Nhants 30 SP8864
Great Dunham Norfk 42 TF8714
Great Dunmow Essex 24 TL6222
Great Durnford Wilts 10 SU1338
Great Easton Essex 24 TL6025
Great Easton Leics 40 SP8492
Great Eccleston Lancs 53 SD4240
Great Ellingham Norfk 42 TM0196
Great Elm Somset 20 ST7449
Great Everdon Nhants 29 SP5957
Great Eversden Cambs 31 TL3653
Great Fencote N York 61 SE2893
Great Finborough Suffk 32 TM0158
Greatford Lincs 40 TF0811
Great Fransham Norfk 42 TF8913
Great Gaddesden Herts 22 TL0211
Greatgate Staffs 48 SK0539
Great Gidding Cambs 40 TL1183
Great Givendale E R Yk 56 SE8153
Great Glemham Suffk 33 TM3361
Great Glen Leics 39 SP6597
Great Gonerby Lincs 40 SK8938
Great Gransden Cambs 31 TL2655
Great Green Cambs 31 TL2844
Great Green Suffk 32 TL9155
Great Habton N York 63 SE7576
Great Hale Lincs 50 TF1442
Great Hallingbury Essex 31 TL5119
Greatham Hants 11 SU7730
Greatham Hartpl 62 NZ4927
Greatham W Susx 12 TQ0415
Great Hampden Bucks 22 SP8401
Great Harrowden Nhants 30 SP8770
Great Harwood Lancs 54 SD7332
Great Haseley Oxon 21 SP6401
Great Hatfield E R Yk 57 TA1842
Great Haywood Staffs 38 SJ9922
Great Heck N York 56 SE5920
Great Henny Essex 24 TL8637
Great Hinton Wilts 20 ST9059
Great Hockham Norfk 32 TL9592
Great Holland Essex 25 TM2019
Great Hollands Br For 22 SU8667
Great Horkesley Essex 25 TL9731
Great Hormead Herts 31 TL4029
Great Horton C Brad 55 SE1431
Great Horwood Bucks 30 SP7731
Great Houghton Barns 55 SE4206
Great Houghton Nhants 30 SP7958
Great Hucklow Derbys 48 SK1777
Great Kelk E R Yk 57 TA1058
Great Kimble Bucks 22 SP8205
Great Kingshill Bucks 22 SU8797
Great Langdale Cumb 58 NY2906
Great Langton N York 61 SE2996
Great Leighs Essex 24 TL7217
Great Limber Lincs 57 TA1308
Great Linford M Keyn 30 SP8541
Great Livermere Suffk 32 TL8871
Great Longstone Derbys 48 SK2071
Great Lumley Dur 69 NZ2949
Great Malvern Worcs 28 SO7845
Great Maplestead Essex 24 TL8034
Great Marton Bpool 53 SD3235
Great Massingham Norfk 42 TF7922
Great Milton Oxon 21 SP6202
Great Missenden Bucks 22 SP8901
Great Mitton Lancs 54 SD7138
Great Mongeham Kent 15 TR3551
Great Moulton Norfk 33 TM1690
Great Musgrave Cumb 60 NY7613
Great Ness Shrops 36 SJ3919
Great Notley Essex 24 TL7421
Great Oak Mons 27 SO3810
Great Oakley Essex 25 TM1927
Great Oakley Nhants 40 SP8785
Great Offley Herts 30 TL1427
Great Ormside Cumb 60 NY7017
Great Orton Cumb 67 NY3254
Great Ouseburn N York 55 SE4461
Great Oxendon Nhants 40 SP7383
Great Park N u Ty 69 NZ2270
Great Parndon Essex 23 TL4308
Great Paxton Cambs 31 TL2063
Great Plumpton Lancs 53 SD3833
Great Plumstead Norfk 43 TG3010
Great Ponton Lincs 40 SK9230
Great Preston Leeds 55 SE4029
Great Raveley Cambs 41 TL2581
Great Rissington Gloucs 29 SP1917
Great Rollright Oxon 29 SP3231
Great Ryburgh Norfk 42 TF9527
Great Ryton Shrops 37 SJ4803
Great Saling Essex 24 TL6925
Great Salkeld Cumb 59 NY5536
Great Sampford Essex 24 TL6435
Great Saughall Ches W 46 SJ3669
Great Shefford W Berk 21 SU3875
Great Shelford Cambs 31 TL4651
Great Smeaton N York 62 NZ3404
Great Snoring Norfk 42 TF9434
Great Somerford Wilts 20 ST9682
Great Soudley Shrops 37 SJ7229
Great Stainton Darltn 62 NZ3322
Great Stambridge Essex 24 TQ8991
Great Staughton Cambs 30 TL1264
Great Steeping Lincs 51 TF4364
Great Stoke S Glos 19 ST6280
Greatstone-on-Sea Kent 15 TR0822
Great Strickland Cumb 59 NY5522
Great Stukeley Cambs 31 TL2274
Great Sturton Lincs 51 TF2176
Great Swinburne Nthumb 68 NY9375
Great Tew Oxon 29 SP4028
Great Tey Essex 24 TL8925
Great Thurlow Suffk 32 TL6750
Great Torrington Devon 6 SS4919
Great Tosson Nthumb 68 NU0200
Great Totham Essex 24 TL8611
Great Totham Essex 24 TL8713
Great Urswick Cumb 58 SD2674
Great Wakering Essex 25 TQ9487
Great Waldingfield Suffk 32 TL9043
Great Walsingham Norfk 42 TF9437
Great Waltham Essex 24 TL6913
Great Warley Essex 24 TQ5890
Great Washbourne Gloucs 28 SO9834
Great Weeke Devon 5 SX7187
Great Wenham Suffk 32 TM0738
Great Whittington Nthumb 68 NZ0070
Great Wigborough Essex 25 TL9615
Great Wilbraham Cambs 31 TL5557
Great Wishford Wilts 10 SU0735
Great Witcombe Gloucs 28 SO9114
Great Witley Worcs 28 SO7566
Great Wolford Warwks 29 SP2534
Greatworth Nhants 29 SP5542
Great Wratting Suffk 32 TL6848
Great Wymondley Herts 31 TL2128
Great Wyrley Staffs 38 SJ9907
Great Yarmouth Norfk 43 TG5207
Great Yeldham Essex 24 TL7638
Greenburn W Loth 75 NS9360
Green End Herts 31 TL3222
Green End Herts 31 TL3333
Greenfield C Beds 30 TL0534
Greenfield Flints 46 SJ1977
Greenfield Oldham 54 SD9904
Greenford Gt Lon 22 TQ1482
Greengairs N Lans 74 NS7870
Greengates C Brad 55 SE1937
Greenham Somset 8 ST0820
Green Hammerton N York 55 SE4556
Greenhaugh Nthumb 68 NY7987
Greenhead Nthumb 68 NY6565
Green Heath Staffs 38 SJ9913
Greenhill D & G 67 NY1079
Greenhill Kent 15 TR1666
Greenhills S Lans 74 NS6252
Greenhithe Kent 14 TQ5875
Greenholm E Ayrs 74 NS5437
Greenhow Hill N York 55 SE1164
Greenland Sheff 49 SK3988
Greenlaw Border 76 NT7146
Greenlea D & G 66 NY0375
Greenloaning P & K 82 NN8307
Greenmount Bury 54 SD7714
Greenock Inver 80 NS2876
Greenodd Cumb 58 SD3182
Green Ore Somset 19 ST5750
Green Quarter Cumb 59 NY4603
Greenside Gatesd 69 NZ1362
Greenside Kirk 55 SE1716
Greens Norton Nhants 30 SP6649
Greenstead Green Essex 24 TL8227
Green Street Herts 23 TQ1998
Green Street Herts 31 TL4521
Green Tye Herts 31 TL4418
Greenway Somset 8 ST3124
Greenwich Gt Lon 23 TQ3877
Greet Gloucs 28 SP0230
Greete Shrops 37 SO5770
Greetham Lincs 51 TF3070
Greetham Rutlnd 40 SK9214
Greetland Calder 55 SE0821
Greinton Somset 19 ST4136
Grenaby IoM 52 SC2672
Grendon Nhants 30 SP8760
Grendon Warwks 39 SP2799
Grendon Underwood Bucks 30 SP6820
Grenoside Sheff 49 SK3393
Gresford Wrexhm 46 SJ3454
Gresham Norfk 43 TG1638
Gressenhall Norfk 42 TF9615
Gressenhall Green Norfk 42 TF9616
Gressingham Lancs 53 SD5769
Greta Bridge Dur 61 NZ0813
Gretna D & G 67 NY3167
Gretna Green D & G 67 NY3168
Gretna Services D & G 67 NY3068
Gretton Gloucs 28 SP0030
Gretton Nhants 40 SP8994
Gretton Shrops 37 SO5195
Grewelthorpe N York 61 SE2376
Greys Green Oxon 22 SU7182
Greysouthen Cumb 58 NY0729
Greystoke Cumb 59 NY4430
Greystone Angus 89 NO5343
Greywell Hants 22 SU7151
Griff Warwks 39 SP3689
Griffithstown Torfn 19 ST2998
Grimeford Village Lancs 54 SD6112
Grimesthorpe Sheff 49 SK3689
Grimethorpe Barns 55 SE4109
Grimley Worcs 28 SO8360
Grimoldby Lincs 51 TF3988
Grimpo Shrops 36 SJ3526
Grimsargh Lancs 54 SD5834
Grimsby NE Lin 57 TA2710
Grimscote Nhants 29 SP6553
Grimscott Cnwll 6 SS2606
Grimshader W Isls 90 NB4025
Grimsthorpe Lincs 40 TF0422
Grimston Leics 39 SK6821
Grimston Norfk 42 TF7222
Grimstone Dorset 9 SY6394
Grimstone End Suffk 32 TL9368
Grindale E R Yk 57 TA1271
Grindleford Derbys 48 SK2477
Grindleton Lancs 54 SD7545
Grindley Brook Shrops 46 SJ5242
Grindlow Derbys 48 SK1877
Grindon Staffs 48 SK0854
Gringley on the Hill Notts 50 SK7390
Grinsdale Cumb 67 NY3758
Grinshill Shrops 37 SJ5223
Grinton N York 61 SE0498
Griomaisiader W Isls 90 NB4025
Gristhorpe N York 63 TA0981
Griston Norfk 42 TL9499
Gritley Ork 100 HY5504
Grittenham Wilts 20 SU0382
Grittleton Wilts 20 ST8580
Grizebeck Cumb 58 SD2384
Grizedale Cumb 59 SD3394
Groby Leics 39 SK5207
Groes Conwy 45 SJ0064
Groes-faen Rhondd 18 ST0680
Groeslon Gwynd 44 SH4755
Groes-Wen Caerph 18 ST1286
Gronant Flints 46 SJ0983
Groombridge E Susx 13 TQ5337
Grosmont Mons 27 SO4024
Grosmont N York 63 NZ8305
Groton Suffk 32 TL9641
Grove Notts 50 SK7479
Grove Oxon 21 SU4090
Grove Green Kent 14 TQ7856
Grove Park Gt Lon 23 TQ4072
Grovesend Swans 17 SN5900
Grundisburgh Suffk 33 TM2251
Gruting Shet 100 HU2749
Guardbridge Fife 83 NO4518
Guarlford Worcs 28 SO8145
Guestling Green E Susx 14 TQ8513
Guestling Thorn E Susx 14 TQ8516
Guestwick Norfk 42 TG0626
Guide Bridge Tamesd 48 SJ9297
Guilden Morden Cambs 31 TL2744
Guilden Sutton Ches W 46 SJ4468
Guildford Surrey 12 SU9949
Guildtown P & K 82 NO1331
Guilsborough Nhants 30 SP6772
Guilsfield Powys 36 SJ2211
Guineaford Devon 6 SS5537
Guisborough R & Cl 62 NZ6015
Guiseley Leeds 55 SE1942
Guist Norfk 42 TG0025
Guiting Power Gloucs 28 SP0924
Gullane E Loth 83 NT4882
Gulval Cnwll 2 SW4831
Gulworthy Devon 4 SX4572
Gumfreston Pembks 16 SN1001
Gumley Leics 39 SP6889
Gunby Lincs 40 SK9121
Gunby Lincs 51 TF4666
Gundleton Hants 11 SU6133
Gun Hill E Susx 13 TQ5614
Gunn Devon 7 SS6333
Gunnerside N York 61 SD9598
Gunnerton Nthumb 68 NY9074
Gunness N Linc 56 SE8411
Gunnislake Cnwll 4 SX4371
Gunthorpe C Pete 40 TF1802
Gunthorpe N Linc 50 SK8096
Gunthorpe Norfk 42 TG0134
Gunthorpe Notts 49 SK6844
Gunwalloe Cnwll 2 SW6522
Gurnard IoW 11 SZ4795
Gurney Slade Somset 19 ST6249
Gurnos Powys 26 SN7709
Gussage All Saints Dorset 10 SU0010
Gussage St Andrew Dorset 9 ST9714
Gussage St Michael Dorset 9 ST9811
Guston Kent 15 TR3244
Gutcher Shet 100 HU5499
Guthrie Angus 89 NO5650
Guyhirn Cambs 41 TF4003
Guyzance Nthumb 69 NU2103
Gwaenysgor Flints 46 SJ0781
Gwalchmai IoA 44 SH3876
Gwaun-Cae-Gurwen Carmth 26 SN6911
Gweek Cnwll 2 SW7026
Gwenddwr Powys 26 SO0643
Gwennap Cnwll 2 SW7340
Gwernaffield Flints 46 SJ2065
Gwernesney Mons 19 SO4101
Gwernogle Carmth 17 SN5333
Gwernymynydd Flints 46 SJ2162
Gwespyr Flints 46 SJ1183
Gwinear Cnwll 2 SW5937
Gwithian Cnwll 2 SW5841
Gwyddelwern Denbgs 46 SJ0746
Gwyddgrug Carmth 17 SN4635
Gwytherin Conwy 45 SH8761

H

Habberley Shrops 36 SJ3903
Habberley Worcs 37 SO8177
Habergham Lancs 54 SD8033
Habertoft Lincs 51 TF5069
Habrough NE Lin 57 TA1413
Hacconby Lincs 40 TF1025
Haceby Lincs 40 TF0236
Hacheston Suffk 33 TM3059
Hackbridge Gt Lon 23 TQ2865
Hackenthorpe Sheff 49 SK4183
Hackford Norfk 42 TG0502
Hackforth N York 61 SE2492
Hackland Ork 100 HY3920
Hackleton Nhants 30 SP8055
Hacklinge Kent 15 TR3454
Hackness N York 63 SE9790
Hackney Gt Lon 23 TQ3484
Hackthorn Lincs 50 SK9982
Hackthorpe Cumb 59 NY5423
Haddenham Bucks 22 SP7308
Haddenham Cambs 31 TL4675
Haddington E Loth 76 NT5173
Haddington Lincs 50 SK9162
Haddiscoe Norfk 43 TM4497
Haddon Cambs 40 TL1392
Hadfield Derbys 48 SK0296
Hadham Ford Herts 31 TL4321
Hadleigh Essex 24 TQ8187
Hadleigh Suffk 32 TM0242
Hadley Worcs 28 SO8564
Hadley Wrekin 37 SJ6711
Hadley End Staffs 38 SK1320
Hadley Wood Gt Lon 23 TQ2698
Hadlow Kent 13 TQ6350
Hadlow Down E Susx 13 TQ5324
Hadnall Shrops 37 SJ5220
Hadstock Essex 31 TL5644
Hadzor Worcs 28 SO9162
Haggerston Nthumb 77 NU0443
Haggs Falk 81 NS7979
Hagley Herefs 27 SO5641
Hagley Worcs 38 SO9180
Hagworthingham Lincs 51 TF3469
Haile Cumb 58 NY0308
Hailey Oxon 29 SP3512
Hailsham E Susx 13 TQ5909
Hail Weston Cambs 31 TL1662
Hainault Gt Lon 23 TQ4591
Hainford Norfk 43 TG2218
Hainton Lincs 50 TF1884
Haisthorpe E R Yk 57 TA1264
Hakin Pembks 16 SM8905
Halam Notts 49 SK6754
Halberton Devon 7 ST0112
Hale Cumb 59 SD5078
Hale Halton 46 SJ4782
Hale Hants 10 SU1818
Hale Surrey 22 SU8448
Hale Traffd 47 SJ7786
Hale Barns Traffd 47 SJ7985
Hales Norfk 43 TM3797
Hales Staffs 37 SJ7134
Halesowen Dudley 38 SO9683
Hales Place Kent 15 TR1459
Hale Street Kent 14 TQ6749
Halesworth Suffk 33 TM3877
Halewood Knows 46 SJ4585
Halford Devon 5 SX8174
Halford Warwks 29 SP2645
Halfpenny Green Staffs 38 SO8291
Halfway House Shrops 36 SJ3411
Halfway Houses Kent 14 TQ9372
Halifax Calder 55 SE0925
Halkirk Highld 100 ND1359
Halkyn Flints 46 SJ2171
Halland E Susx 13 TQ4916
Hallaton Leics 40 SP7896
Hallatrow BaNES 19 ST6357
Hallbankgate Cumb 67 NY5859
Hall Dunnerdale Cumb 58 SD2195
Hallen S Glos 19 ST5580
Hallgarth Dur 69 NZ3243
Hallglen Falk 82 NS8978
Hall Green Birm 38 SP1081
Hallin Highld 90 NG2558
Halling Medway 14 TQ7063
Hallington Lincs 51 TF3085
Hallington Nthumb 68 NY9875
Halliwell Bolton 54 SD6910
Halloughton Notts 49 SK6951
Hallow Worcs 28 SO8258
Hall's Green Herts 31 TL2728
Halmore Gloucs 20 SO7002
Halnaker W Susx 11 SU9007
Halsall Lancs 53 SD3710
Halse Nhants 29 SP5640
Halse Somset 8 ST1428
Halsetown Cnwll 2 SW5038
Halsham E R Yk 57 TA2727
Halstead Essex 24 TL8130
Halstead Kent 23 TQ4861
Halstead Leics 40 SK7505
Halstock Dorset 8 ST5308
Haltham Lincs 51 TF2463
Halton Bucks 22 SP8710
Halton Halton 47 SJ5481
Halton Lancs 53 SD5064
Halton Leeds 55 SE3533
Halton Nthumb 68 NY9967
Halton Wrexhm 36 SJ3039
Halton East N York 55 SE0454
Halton Gill N York 60 SD8776
Halton Holegate Lincs 51 TF4165
Halton Lea Gate Nthumb 68 NY6458
Halton Shields Nthumb 68 NZ0168
Halton West N York 54 SD8454
Haltwhistle Nthumb 68 NY7064
Halvergate Norfk 43 TG4106
Halwell Devon 5 SX7753
Halwill Devon 6 SX4299
Halwill Junction Devon 6 SS4400
Ham Devon 8 ST2301
Ham Gloucs 20 ST6898
Ham Gt Lon 23 TQ1772
Ham Kent 15 TR3254
Ham Somset 8 ST2825
Ham Wilts 21 SU3262
Hambleden Bucks 22 SU7886
Hambledon Hants 11 SU6414
Hambledon Surrey 12 SU9638
Hamble-le-Rice Hants 11 SU4806
Hambleton Lancs 53 SD3742
Hambleton N York 56 SE5530
Hambridge Somset 8 ST3921
Hambrook W Susx 11 SU7806
Hameringham Lincs 51 TF3167
Hamerton Cambs 40 TL1379
Ham Green Worcs 28 SP0163
Hamilton S Lans 74 NS7255
Hamilton Services S Lans 74 NS7257
Hamlet Dorset 9 ST5908
Hammersmith Gt Lon 23 TQ2378
Hammerwich Staffs 38 SK0707
Hammoon Dorset 9 ST8114
Hamnavoe Shet 100 HU3735
Hampden Park E Susx 13 TQ6002
Hampnett Gloucs 28 SP0915
Hampole Donc 55 SE5010
Hampreston Dorset 10 SZ0598
Hampstead Gt Lon 23 TQ2685
Hampstead Norreys W Berk 21 SU5276
Hampsthwaite N York 55 SE2559
Hampton C Pete 40 TL1794
Hampton Gt Lon 22 TQ1369
Hampton Kent 15 TR1568
Hampton Shrops 37 SO7486
Hampton Swindn 21 SU1892
Hampton Worcs 28 SP0243
Hampton Bishop Herefs 27 SO5637
Hampton Heath Ches W 46 SJ5049
Hampton-in-Arden Solhll 39 SP2080
Hampton Lovett Worcs 28 SO8865
Hampton Lucy Warwks 29 SP2557
Hampton Magna Warwks 29 SP2665
Hampton Poyle Oxon 29 SP5015
Hampton Wick Gt Lon 23 TQ1769
Hamptworth Wilts 10 SU2419
Hamsey E Susx 13 TQ4012
Hamstall Ridware Staffs 38 SK1019
Hamstead Birm 38 SP0592
Hamstead Marshall W Berk 21 SU4165
Hamsterley Dur 61 NZ1231
Hamsterley Dur 69 NZ1156
Hamstreet Kent 15 TR0033
Ham Street Somset 9 ST5534
Hamworthy BCP 9 SY9991
Hanbury Staffs 38 SK1727
Hanbury Worcs 28 SO9664
Hanchurch Staffs 38 SJ8441
Hand and Pen Devon 7 SY0495
Handbridge Ches W 46 SJ4065
Handcross W Susx 12 TQ2629
Handforth Ches E 47 SJ8583
Handley Ches W 46 SJ4657
Handley Derbys 49 SK3761
Handsworth Birm 38 SP0489
Handsworth Sheff 49 SK4186
Hanford C Stke 38 SJ8741
Hanging Heaton Kirk 55 SE2522
Hanging Houghton Nhants 30 SP7573
Hanging Langford Wilts 10 SU0337
Hangleton Br & H 12 TQ2607
Hanham S Glos 19 ST6472
Hankelow Ches E 47 SJ6645
Hankerton Wilts 20 ST9790
Hanley C Stke 47 SJ8847
Hanley Castle Worcs 28 SO8442
Hanley Child Worcs 27 SO6565
Hanley Swan Worcs 28 SO8142
Hanley William Worcs 28 SO6766
Hanlith N York 54 SD8961
Hanmer Wrexhm 36 SJ4539
Hannaford Devon 7 SS6029
Hannington Hants 21 SU5355
Hannington Nhants 30 SP8170
Hannington Swindn 21 SU1793
Hannington Wick Swindn 21 SU1795
Hanslope M Keyn 30 SP8046
Hanthorpe Lincs 40 TF0823
Hanwell Gt Lon 23 TQ1579
Hanwell Oxon 29 SP4343
Hanwood Shrops 36 SJ4409
Hanworth Gt Lon 22 TQ1271
Hanworth Norfk 43 TG1935
Happendon Services S Lans 74 NS8533
Happisburgh Norfk 43 TG3831
Happisburgh Common Norfk 43 TG3728
Hapsford Ches W 46 SJ4774
Hapton Lancs 54 SD7931
Hapton Norfk 43 TM1796
Harberton Devon 5 SX7758
Harbertonford Devon 5 SX7856
Harbledown Kent 15 TR1357
Harborne Birm 38 SP0284
Harborough Magna Warwks 39 SP4879
Harbottle Nthumb 68 NT9304
Harbourneford Devon 5 SX7162
Harbury Warwks 29 SP3759
Harby Leics 40 SK7431
Harby Notts 50 SK8770
Harcombe Devon 5 SX8881
Harcombe Devon 8 SY1590
Harcombe Bottom Devon 8 SY3395
Harden C Brad 55 SE0838
Harden Wsall 38 SK0100
Hardenhuish Wilts 20 ST9174
Hardgate D & G 66 NX8167
Hardgate W Duns 74 NS5072
Hardham W Susx 12 TQ0317
Hardingham Norfk 42 TG0403
Hardingstone Nhants 30 SP7657
Hardington Somset 20 ST7452
Hardington Mandeville Somset 8 ST5111
Hardington Marsh Somset 8 ST5009
Hardington Moor Somset 8 ST5112
Hardisworthy Devon 6 SS2320
Hardley Hants 10 SU4204
Hardley Street Norfk 43 TG3801
Hardraw N York 60 SD8691
Hardstoft Derbys 49 SK4363
Hardway Hants 11 SU6001
Hardway Somset 9 ST7234
Hardwick Bucks 30 SP8019
Hardwick Cambs 31 TL3758
Hardwick Nhants 30 SP8469
Hardwick Norfk 33 TM2289
Hardwick Oxon 29 SP3806
Hardwick Oxon 29 SP5729
Hardwick Wsall 38 SP0798
Hardwicke Gloucs 28 SO7912
Hardwicke Gloucs 28 SO9027
Hardy's Green Essex 25 TL9320
Hare Croft C Brad 55 SE0835
Harefield Gt Lon 22 TQ0590
Hare Green Essex 25 TM1025
Hare Hatch Wokham 22 SU8077
Harehill Derbys 38 SK1735
Harehills Leeds 55 SE3234
Harescombe Gloucs 28 SO8310
Haresfield Gloucs 28 SO8010
Harestock Hants 11 SU4631
Hare Street Essex 23 TL4209
Hare Street Herts 31 TL3929
Harewood Leeds 55 SE3245
Harewood End Herefs 27 SO5227
Harford Devon 5 SX6359
Hargrave Ches W 46 SJ4862
Hargrave Nhants 30 TL0370
Hargrave Suffk 32 TL7759
Harkstead Suffk 25 TM1834
Harlaston Staffs 39 SK2110
Harlaxton Lincs 40 SK8832
Harlech Gwynd 44 SH5831
Harlescott Shrops 37 SJ4916
Harlesden Gt Lon 23 TQ2183
Harlesthorpe Derbys 49 SK4976
Harleston Devon 5 SX7945
Harleston Norfk 33 TM2483
Harleston Suffk 32 TM0160
Harlestone Nhants 30 SP7064
Harle Syke Lancs 54 SD8635
Harley Rothm 49 SK3698
Harley Shrops 37 SJ5901
Harlington C Beds 30 TL0330
Harlington Donc 55 SE4802
Harlington Gt Lon 22 TQ0877
Harlosh Highld 84 NG2841
Harlow Essex 23 TL4410
Harlow Hill Nthumb 68 NZ0768
Harlthorpe E R Yk 56 SE7337
Harlton Cambs 31 TL3852
Harlyn Cnwll 3 SW8775
Harman's Cross Dorset 9 SY9880
Harmby N York 61 SE1289
Harmer Green Herts 31 TL2515
Harmer Hill Shrops 37 SJ4822
Harmston Lincs 50 SK9662
Harnage Shrops 37 SJ5604
Harnhill Gloucs 20 SP0600
Harold Hill Gt Lon 23 TQ5392
Haroldston West Pembks 16 SM8615
Haroldswick Shet 100 HP6312
Harold Wood Gt Lon 24 TQ5590
Harome N York 62 SE6481
Harpenden Herts 30 TL1314
Harpford Devon 8 SY0990
Harpham E R Yk 57 TA0861
Harpley Norfk 42 TF7825
Harpley Worcs 28 SO6861
Harpole Nhants 30 SP6961
Harpswell Lincs 50 SK9389
Harpurhey Manch 47 SD8501
Harraby Cumb 67 NY4154
Harracott Devon 6 SS5527
Harrietfield P & K 82 NN9829
Harrietsham Kent 14 TQ8652
Harringay Gt Lon 23 TQ3188
Harrington Cumb 58 NX9825
Harrington Lincs 51 TF3671
Harrington Nhants 40 SP7780
Harringworth Nhants 40 SP9197
Harrogate N York 55 SE3055
Harrold Bed 30 SP9457
Harrow Gt Lon 23 TQ1588
Harrowbarrow Cnwll 4 SX4070
Harrowgate Village Darltn 61 NZ2917
Harrow Green Suffk 32 TL8654
Harrow on the Hill Gt Lon 23 TQ1587
Harrow Weald Gt Lon 23 TQ1591
Harston Cambs 31 TL4250
Harston Leics 40 SK8331
Harswell E R Yk 56 SE8240
Hart Hartpl 62 NZ4635
Hartburn Nthumb 68 NZ0885
Hartburn S on T 62 NZ4217
Hartest Suffk 32 TL8352
Hartfield E Susx 13 TQ4735
Hartford Cambs 31 TL2572
Hartford Ches W 47 SJ6372
Hartfordbridge Hants 22 SU7757
Hartford End Essex 24 TL6817
Hartforth N York 61 NZ1606
Hartgrove Dorset 9 ST8318
Harthill Ches W 46 SJ4955
Harthill N Lans 75 NS9064
Harthill Rothm 49 SK4980
Hartington Derbys 48 SK1260
Hartland Devon 6 SS2524
Hartland Quay Devon 6 SS2224
Hartlebury Worcs 38 SO8471
Hartlepool Hartpl 62 NZ5032
Hartley Cumb 60 NY7808
Hartley Kent 14 TQ6067
Hartley Kent 14 TQ7634
Hartley Wespall Hants 22 SU6958
Hartley Wintney Hants 22 SU7656
Hartlip Kent 14 TQ8364
Harton N York 56 SE7061
Harton S Tyne 69 NZ3765
Hartpury Gloucs 28 SO7924
Hartshead Kirk 55 SE1822
Hartshead Moor Services Calder 55 SE1723
Hartshill C Stke 47 SJ8546
Hartshill Warwks 39 SP3293
Hartshorne Derbys 39 SK3221
Hartwell Nhants 30 SP7850
Hartwith N York 55 SE2161
Harvel Kent 14 TQ6563
Harvington Worcs 28 SP0549
Harvington Worcs 38 SO8775
Harwell Notts 49 SK6891
Harwell Oxon 21 SU4989
Harwich Essex 25 TM2531
Harwood Dale N York 63 SE9695
Harworth Notts 49 SK6191
Hasbury Dudley 38 SO9582
Hascombe Surrey 12 TQ0039
Haselbech Nhants 30 SP7177
Haselbury Plucknett Somset 8 ST4710
Haseley Warwks 29 SP2367
Haselor Warwks 28 SP1257
Hasfield Gloucs 28 SO8227
Haskayne Lancs 46 SD3508
Hasketon Suffk 33 TM2450
Haslemere Surrey 11 SU9032
Haslingden Lancs 54 SD7823
Haslingfield Cambs 31 TL4052
Haslington Ches E 47 SJ7355
Hassingham Norfk 43 TG3605
Hassocks W Susx 12 TQ3015
Hassop Derbys 48 SK2272
Haster Highld 100 ND3251
Hastingleigh Kent 15 TR0945
Hastings E Susx 14 TQ8209
Hastingwood Essex 23 TL4807
Hastoe Herts 22 SP9209
Haswell Dur 69 NZ3743
Haswell Plough Dur 62 NZ3742
Hatch Beauchamp Somset 8 ST3020
Hatch End Gt Lon 22 TQ1390
Hatchmere Ches W 47 SJ5571
Hatcliffe NE Lin 51 TA2100
Hatfield Donc 56 SE6609
Hatfield Herefs 27 SO5959
Hatfield Herts 23 TL2308
Hatfield Broad Oak Essex 24 TL5416
Hatfield Heath Essex 31 TL5215
Hatfield Peverel Essex 24 TL7911
Hatfield Woodhouse Donc 56 SE6708
Hatford Oxon 21 SU3395
Hatherden Hants 21 SU3450
Hatherleigh Devon 6 SS5404
Hathern Leics 39 SK5022
Hatherop Gloucs 28 SP1505
Hathersage Derbys 48 SK2381
Hathersage Booths Derbys 48 SK2480
Hatherton Ches E 47 SJ6847
Hatherton Staffs 38 SJ9510
Hatley St George Cambs 31 TL2751
Hatt Cnwll 4 SX4062
Hattersley Tamesd 48 SJ9894
Hatton Abers 95 NK0537
Hatton Derbys 39 SK2130
Hatton Gt Lon 22 TQ0975
Hatton Lincs 50 TF1776
Hatton Shrops 37 SO4790
Hatton Warrtn 47 SJ5982
Hatton Warwks 29 SP2367
Hatton of Fintray Abers 95 NJ8316
Haugh E Ayrs 74 NS4925
Haugham Lincs 51 TF3381
Haughley Suffk 32 TM0262
Haughley Green Suffk 32 TM0264
Haugh of Urr D & G 66 NX8066
Haughton Ches E 47 SJ5756
Haughton Shrops 36 SJ3726
Haughton Staffs 38 SJ8620
Haughton le Skerne Darltn 62 NZ3116
Haultwick Herts 31 TL3323
Haunton Staffs 39 SK2310
Hauxton Cambs 31 TL4452
Havant Hants 11 SU7106
Havenstreet IoW 11 SZ5690
Havercroft Wakefd 55 SE3813
Haverfordwest Pembks 16 SM9515
Haverhill Suffk 32 TL6745
Haverigg Cumb 58 SD1578
Havering-atte-Bower Gt Lon 23 TQ5193
Haversham M Keyn 30 SP8242
Haverthwaite Cumb 59 SD3483
Havyatt N Som 19 ST4761
Hawarden Flints 46 SJ3165
Hawbush Green Essex 24 TL7820
Hawen Cerdgn 17 SN3446
Hawes N York 60 SD8789
Hawe's Green Norfk 43 TM2399
Hawford Worcs 28 SO8460

128 Hawick – Ingleton

Hawick Border 67 NT5014
Hawkchurch Devon 8 ST3400
Hawkedon Suffk 32 TL7953
Hawkeridge Wilts 20 ST8653
Hawkesbury S Glos 20 ST7686
Hawkesbury Upton S Glos 20 ST7786
Hawkhurst Kent 14 TQ7530
Hawkinge Kent 15 TR2139
Hawkley Hants 11 SU7429
Hawkridge Somset 7 SS8630
Hawkshead Cumb 59 SD3598
Hawkshead Hill Cumb 59 SD3398
Hawkstone Shrops 37 SJ5830
Hawkswick N York 54 SD9570
Hawksworth Leeds 55 SE1641
Hawksworth Notts 50 SK7543
Hawkwell Essex 24 TQ8591
Hawley Hants 22 SU8657
Hawling Gloucs 28 SP0622
Hawnby N York 62 SE5489
Haworth C Brad 55 SE0337
Hawstead Suffk 32 TL8559
Hawthorn Dur 69 NZ4145
Hawthorn Hill Lincs 51 TF2155
Hawton Notts 50 SK7851
Haxby C York 56 SE6058
Haxey N Linc 50 SK7799
Haydock St Hel 47 SJ5697
Haydon Bridge Nthumb 68 NY8464
Haydon Wick Swindn 20 SU1387
Hayes Gt Lon 22 TQ0980
Hayes Gt Lon 23 TQ4066
Hayes End Gt Lon 22 TQ0882
Hayfield Derbys 48 SK0386
Hayle Cnwll 2 SW5537
Hayley Green Dudley 38 SO9582
Hayne Devon 5 SX7685
Haynes C Beds 30 TL0941
Haynes Church End C Beds 30 TL0740
Haynes West End C Beds 30 TL0640
Hay-on-Wye Powys 27 SO2342
Hayscastle Pembks 16 SM8925
Hayscastle Cross Pembks 16 SM9125
Hay Street Herts 31 TL3926
Hayton Cumb 58 NY1041
Hayton Cumb 67 NY5157
Hayton E R Yk 56 SE8245
Hayton Notts 50 SK7284
Haytor Vale Devon 5 SX7777
Haytown Devon 6 SS3814
Haywards Heath W Susx 12 TQ3324
Haywood Donc 56 SE5812
Hazelbank S Lans 74 NS8345
Hazelbury Bryan Dorset 9 ST7408
Hazeleigh Essex 24 TL8203
Hazel Grove Stockp 48 SJ9287
Hazelwood Derbys 49 SK3245
Hazlemere Bucks 22 SU8895
Hazlerigg N u Ty 69 NZ2371
Hazleton Gloucs 28 SP0718
Heacham Norfk 42 TF6737
Headbourne Worthy Hants 11 SU4832
Headcorn Kent 14 TQ8344
Headingley Leeds 55 SE2836
Headington Oxon 29 SP5407
Headlam Dur 61 NZ1818
Headlesscross N Lans 75 NS9158
Headless Cross Worcs 28 SP0365
Headley Hants 11 SU8236
Headley Hants 21 SU5162
Headley Surrey 23 TQ2054
Headley Down Hants 11 SU8336
Headon Notts 50 SK7476
Heads Nook Cumb 67 NY5054
Heage Derbys 49 SK3750
Healaugh N York 55 SE5047
Healaugh N York 61 SE0199
Heald Green Stockp 47 SJ8486
Heale Somset 8 ST2420
Heale Somset 8 ST3825
Healey N York 61 SE1780
Healeyfield Dur 68 NZ0648
Healing NE Lin 57 TA2110
Heamoor Cnwll 2 SW4631
Heanor Derbys 49 SK4346
Heanton Punchardon Devon 6 SS5035
Heapham Lincs 50 SK8788
Heart of Scotland Services N Lans 75 NS9064
Heasley Mill Devon 7 SS7332
Heath Derbys 49 SK4466
Heath Wakefd 55 SE3520
Heath and Reach C Beds 30 SP9228
Heathcote Derbys 48 SK1460
Heather Leics 39 SK3910
Heathfield E Susx 13 TQ5821
Heathfield Somset 8 ST1626
Heath Green Worcs 38 SP0771
Heath Hayes & Wimblebury Staffs 38 SK0110
Heath Hill Shrops 37 SJ7613
Heathrow Airport Gt Lon 22 TQ0775
Heathton Shrops 37 SO8192
Heath Town Wolves 38 SO9399
Heatley Warrtn 47 SJ7088
Heaton C Brad 55 SE1335
Heaton N u Ty 69 NZ2666
Heaton Staffs 48 SJ9562
Heaton Chapel Stockp 47 SJ8891
Heaton Mersey Stockp 47 SJ8690
Heaton Norris Stockp 47 SJ8890
Heaton's Bridge Lancs 53 SD4011
Heaverham Kent 14 TQ5758
Heavitree Devon 5 SX9492
Hebburn S Tyne 69 NZ3164
Hebden N York 55 SE0263
Hebden Bridge Calder 54 SD9927
Hebing End Herts 31 TL3122
Hebron Carmth 17 SN1827
Hebron Nthumb 69 NZ1989
Heckfield Hants 22 SU7260
Heckfield Green Suffk 33 TM1875
Heckfordbridge Essex 25 TL9421
Heckington Lincs 50 TF1444
Heckmondwike Kirk 55 SE2123
Heddington Wilts 20 ST9966
Heddon-on-the-Wall Nthumb 69 NZ1366
Hedenham Norfk 43 TM3193
Hedge End Hants 11 SU4912
Hedgerley Bucks 22 SU9687
Hedging Somset 8 ST3029
Hedley on the Hill Nthumb 68 NZ0759
Hednesford Staffs 38 SJ9912
Hedon E R Yk 57 TA1928
Hedsor Bucks 22 SU9086
Heeley Sheff 49 SK3684
Heighington Darltn 61 NZ2422
Heighington Lincs 50 TF0269
Heightington Worcs 37 SO7671
Heiton Border 76 NT7130
Hele Devon 6 SS5347
Hele Devon 7 SS9902
Helensburgh Ag & B 80 NS2982
Helford Cnwll 2 SW7526
Helford Passage Cnwll 2 SW7626
Helhoughton Norfk 42 TF8626
Helions Bumpstead Essex 32 TL6541
Helland Cnwll 3 SX0771
Hellescott Cnwll 4 SX2888
Hellesdon Norfk 43 TG2012
Hellidon Nhants 29 SP5158
Hellifield N York 54 SD8556
Hellingly E Susx 13 TQ5812
Helmdon Nhants 29 SP5943
Helme Kirk 55 SE0912
Helmingham Suffk 33 TM1857
Helmsdale Highld 97 ND0315
Helmshore Lancs 54 SD7821
Helmsley N York 62 SE6183
Helperby N York 55 SE4469
Helperthorpe N York 56 SE9570
Helpringham Lincs 50 TF1440
Helpston C Pete 40 TF1205
Helsby Ches W 46 SJ4975
Helston Cnwll 2 SW6527
Helstone Cnwll 3 SX0881
Helton Cumb 59 NY5021
Hemel Hempstead Herts 22 TL0507
Hemerdon Devon 5 SX5657
Hemingbrough N York 56 SE6730
Hemingby Lincs 51 TF2374
Hemingford Abbots Cambs 31 TL2871
Hemingford Grey Cambs 31 TL2970
Hemingstone Suffk 33 TM1454
Hemington Leics 39 SK4527
Hemington Nhants 40 TL0985
Hemington Somset 20 ST7253
Hemley Suffk 33 TM2842
Hemlington Middsb 62 NZ5014
Hempnall Norfk 43 TM2494
Hempnall Green Norfk 43 TM2493
Hempriggs Moray 93 NJ1063
Hempstead Essex 24 TL6338
Hempstead Medway 14 TQ7964
Hempstead Norfk 43 TG1037
Hempstead Norfk 43 TG4028
Hempton Norfk 42 TF9129
Hempton Oxon 29 SP4431
Hemsby Norfk 43 TG4917
Hemswell Lincs 50 SK9290
Hemswell Cliff Lincs 50 SK9489
Hemsworth Wakefd 55 SE4213
Hemyock Devon 8 ST1313
Henbury Bristl 19 ST5678
Hendon Gt Lon 23 TQ2389
Hendon Sundld 69 NZ4055
Hendy Carmth 17 SN5803
Henfield W Susx 12 TQ2115
Hengoed Caerph 19 ST1594
Hengoed Powys 27 SO2253
Hengrave Suffk 32 TL8268
Henham Essex 24 TL5428
Heniarth Powys 36 SJ1208
Henlade Somset 8 ST2623
Henley Dorset 9 ST6904
Henley Somset 8 ST4332
Henley Suffk 33 TM1551
Henley W Susx 11 SU8925
Henley Green Covtry 39 SP3681
Henley-in-Arden Warwks 28 SP1566
Henley-on-Thames Oxon 22 SU7682
Henley's Down E Susx 14 TQ7312
Henllan Cerdgn 17 SN3540
Henllan Denbgs 45 SJ0268
Henllys Torfn 19 ST2691
Henlow C Beds 31 TL1738
Hennock Devon 5 SX8381
Henny Street Essex 24 TL8738
Henryd Conwy 45 SH7774
Henry's Moat (Castell Hendre) Pembks 16 SN0427
Hensall N York 56 SE5923
Henshaw Nthumb 68 NY7564
Hensingham Cumb 58 NX9816
Henstead Suffk 33 TM4885
Hensting Hants 11 SU4922
Henstridge Somset 9 ST7219
Henstridge Ash Somset 9 ST7220
Henton Oxon 22 SP7602
Henton Somset 19 ST4945
Henwick Worcs 28 SO8355
Henwood Cnwll 4 SX2673
Heol-y-Cyw Brdgnd 18 SS9484
Hepple Nthumb 68 NT9901
Hepscott Nthumb 69 NZ2284
Heptonstall Calder 54 SD9828
Hepworth Kirk 55 SE1606
Hepworth Suffk 32 TL9874
Herbrandston Pembks 16 SM8707
Hereford Herefs 27 SO5139
Hereson Kent 15 TR3865
Hermitage Dorset 9 ST6506
Hermitage W Berk 21 SU5072
Hermon Carmth 17 SN3630
Hermon Pembks 17 SN2031
Herne Kent 15 TR1865
Herne Bay Kent 15 TR1768
Herne Hill Gt Lon 23 TQ3274
Herne Pound Kent 14 TQ6654
Hernhill Kent 15 TR0660
Herodsfoot Cnwll 4 SX2160
Herriard Hants 22 SU6646
Herringfleet Suffk 43 TM4797
Herringswell Suffk 32 TL7270
Herringthorpe Rothm 49 SK4492
Herrington Sundld 69 NZ3553
Hersden Kent 15 TR2062
Hersham Surrey 22 TQ1164
Herstmonceux E Susx 13 TQ6312
Herston Ork 100 ND4191
Hertford Herts 31 TL3212
Hertford Heath Herts 23 TL3510
Hertingfordbury Herts 23 TL3012
Hesketh Bank Lancs 53 SD4423
Hesketh Lane Lancs 54 SD6141
Hesket Newmarket Cumb 59 NY3438
Hesleden Dur 62 NZ4438
Heslington C York 56 SE6250
Hessay C York 56 SE5253
Hessenford Cnwll 4 SX3057
Hessett Suffk 32 TL9361
Hessle E R Yk 56 TA0226
Hessle Wakefd 55 SE4317
Hest Bank Lancs 53 SD4666
Heston Gt Lon 22 TQ1277
Heston Services Gt Lon 22 TQ1177
Heswall Wirral 46 SJ2681
Hethe Oxon 29 SP5929
Hethersett Norfk 43 TG1404
Hethersgill Cumb 67 NY4767
Hett Dur 61 NZ2836
Hetton N York 54 SD9658
Hetton-le-Hole Sundld 69 NZ3547
Heugh Nthumb 68 NZ0873
Heugh Head Border 77 NT8762
Heveningham Suffk 33 TM3372
Hever Kent 13 TQ4745
Heversham Cumb 59 SD4983
Hevingham Norfk 43 TG1921
Hewas Water Cnwll 3 SW9649
Hewelsfield Gloucs 19 SO5602
Hewish Somset 8 ST4208
Hewood Dorset 8 ST3502
Hexham Nthumb 68 NY9363
Hextable Kent 23 TQ5170
Hexthorpe Donc 56 SE5602
Hexton Herts 30 TL1030
Hexworthy Cnwll 4 SX3581
Hexworthy Devon 5 SX6572
Heybridge Essex 24 TL8508
Heybridge Essex 24 TQ6398
Heybrook Bay Devon 4 SX4949
Heydon Cambs 31 TL4339
Heydon Norfk 43 TG1127
Heydour Lincs 40 TF0039
Heylor Shet 100 HU2980
Heysham Lancs 53 SD4160
Heyshott W Susx 11 SU8917
Heytesbury Wilts 20 ST9242
Heythrop Oxon 29 SP3527
Heywood Rochdl 54 SD8510
Heywood Wilts 20 ST8753
Hibaldstow N Linc 56 SE9702
Hickleton Donc 55 SE4805
Hickling Norfk 43 TG4124
Hickling Notts 40 SK6928
Hickling Green Norfk 43 TG4123
Hickstead W Susx 12 TQ2620
Hidcote Bartrim Gloucs 29 SP1742
Hidcote Boyce Gloucs 29 SP1742
High Ackworth Wakefd 55 SE4417
Higham Barns 55 SE3107
Higham Derbys 49 SK3859
Higham Kent 13 TQ6048
Higham Kent 14 TQ7171
Higham Lancs 54 SD8136
Higham Suffk 25 TM0335
Higham Suffk 32 TL7465
Higham Ferrers Nhants 30 SP9668
Higham Gobion C Beds 30 TL1032
Higham Hill Gt Lon 23 TQ3590
Higham on the Hill Leics 39 SP3895
Highampton Devon 6 SS4804
Highams Park Gt Lon 23 TQ3891
High Bankhill Cumb 59 NY5542
High Beach Essex 23 TQ4198
High Bentham N York 54 SD6669
High Bickington Devon 7 SS6020
High Biggins Cumb 59 SD6078
High Blantyre S Lans 74 NS6756
High Bray Devon 7 SS6934
Highbridge Somset 19 ST3247
Highbrook W Susx 12 TQ3630
High Brooms Kent 13 TQ5941
Highburton Kirk 55 SE1813
Highbury Gt Lon 23 TQ3185
Highbury Somset 20 ST6949
High Catton E R Yk 56 SE7153
Highclere Hants 21 SU4359
Highcliffe BCP 10 SZ2193
High Coniscliffe Darltn 61 NZ2215
High Crosby Cumb 67 NY4559
High Cross Hants 11 SU7126
High Cross Herts 31 TL3618
High Cross Warwks 29 SP2067
High Easter Essex 24 TL6214
High Ellington N York 61 SE1983
Higher Ansty Dorset 9 ST7604
Higher Bartle Lancs 53 SD5033
Higher Bockhampton Dorset 9 SY7292
Higher Brixham Torbay 5 SX9155
High Ercall Wrekin 37 SJ5917
Higher Chillington Somset 8 ST3810
Higher Folds Wigan 47 SD6800
Higher Gabwell Devon 5 SX9169
Higher Heysham Lancs 53 SD4160
Higher Irlam Salfd 47 SJ7295
Higher Kinnerton Flints 46 SJ3261
Higher Muddiford Devon 6 SS5638
Higher Penwortham Lancs 53 SD5128
Higher Prestacott Devon 6 SX3896
Higher Town Cnwll 2 SW8044
Higher Town Cnwll 3 SX0061
Higher Town IoS 2 SV9215
Higher Walton Lancs 54 SD5727
Higher Walton Warrtn 47 SJ5985
Higher Wambrook Somset 8 ST2908
Higher Waterston Dorset 9 SY7295
Higher Wheelton Lancs 54 SD6022
Higher Whitley Ches W 47 SJ6180
Higher Wincham Ches W 47 SJ6876
Higher Wraxhall Dorset 9 ST5601
Higher Wych Ches W 46 SJ4943
High Etherley Dur 61 NZ1728
Highfield Gatesd 69 NZ1458
High Garrett Essex 24 TL7727
Highgate Gt Lon 23 TQ2887
Highgate Kent 14 TQ7630
High Grantley N York 55 SE2369
High Green Norfk 33 TM1689
High Green Norfk 43 TG1305
High Green Sheff 49 SK3397
High Halden Kent 14 TQ8937
High Halstow Medway 14 TQ7875
High Ham Somset 8 ST4231
High Harrington Cumb 58 NY0025
High Harrogate N York 55 SE3155
High Hatton Shrops 37 SJ6124
High Hauxley Nthumb 69 NU2703
High Hawsker N York 63 NZ9207
High Hesket Cumb 67 NY4744
High Hoyland Barns 55 SE2710
High Hurstwood E Susx 13 TQ4926
High Hutton N York 56 SE7568
High Ireby Cumb 58 NY2237
High Kilburn N York 62 SE5179
High Lands Dur 61 NZ1226
Highlane Derbys 49 SK4081
High Lane Stockp 48 SJ9585
High Lanes Cnwll 2 SW5637
Highleadon Gloucs 28 SO7623
High Legh Ches E 47 SJ7084
Highleigh W Susx 11 SZ8498
High Leven S on T 62 NZ4512
Highley Shrops 37 SO7483
High Littleton BaNES 20 ST6458
High Lorton Cumb 58 NY1625
High Marnham Notts 50 SK8070
High Melton Donc 49 SE5001
High Mickley Nthumb 68 NZ0761
Highmoor Oxon 22 SU7084
Highmoor Cross Oxon 22 SU7084
Highnam Gloucs 28 SO7819
High Newport Sundld 69 NZ3754
High Newton Cumb 59 SD4082
High Nibthwaite Cumb 58 SD2989
High Offley Staffs 37 SJ7826
High Ongar Essex 24 TL5603
High Onn Staffs 38 SJ8216
High Park Corner Essex 25 TM0320
High Roding Essex 24 TL6017
High Salvington W Susx 12 TQ1206
High Spen Gatesd 69 NZ1359
Highsted Kent 14 TQ9061
High Street Cnwll 3 SW9653
Highstreet Kent 15 TR0862
Highstreet Green Surrey 12 SU9835
Hightae D & G 67 NY0978
Highter's Heath Birm 38 SP0879
Hightown Sefton 46 SD3003
Hightown Green Suffk 32 TL9756
High Toynton Lincs 51 TF2869
High Valleyfield Fife 82 NS1008
Highweek Devon 5 SX8472
Highwood Essex 24 TL6404
Highwood Hill Gt Lon 23 TQ2193
Highworth Swindn 21 SU2092
High Wray Cumb 59 SD3799
High Wych Herts 31 TL4614
High Wycombe Bucks 22 SU8693
Hilborough Norfk 42 TF8100
Hilcott Wilts 20 SU1158
Hildenborough Kent 13 TQ5648
Hilden Park Kent 13 TQ5747
Hildersham Cambs 31 TL5448
Hilderstone Staffs 38 SJ9534
Hilderthorpe E R Yk 57 TA1766
Hilgay Norfk 41 TL6298
Hill S Glos 19 ST6495
Hill Warwks 29 SP4566
Hillam N York 55 SE5028
Hill Brow Hants 11 SU7926
Hillbutts Dorset 9 ST9901
Hill Chorlton Staffs 37 SJ7939
Hillcliffiane Derbys 49 SK2947
Hill Common Somset 8 ST1426
Hilldyke Lincs 51 TF3447
Hill End Fife 82 NT0395
Hillend Fife 82 NT1483
Hill End Gloucs 28 SO9037
Hillesden Bucks 30 SP6828
Hillesley Gloucs 20 ST7689
Hillfarrance Somset 8 ST1624
Hill Green Kent 14 TQ8362
Hill Head Hants 11 SU5402
Hillingdon Gt Lon 22 TQ0782
Hillington C Glas 74 NS5164
Hillington Norfk 42 TF7225
Hillmorton Warwks 39 SP5373
Hill of Fearn Highld 97 NH8378
Hill Ridware Staffs 38 SK0817
Hillside Angus 89 NO7061
Hill Side Kirk 55 SE1717
Hills Town Derbys 49 SK4869
Hillstreet Hants 10 SU3416
Hillswick Shet 100 HU2877
Hill Top Sandw 38 SO9993
Hill Top Wakefd 55 SE3315
Hillwell Shet 100 HU3714
Hilmarton Wilts 20 SU0175
Hilperton Wilts 20 ST8759
Hilsea C Port 11 SU6503
Hilston E R Yk 57 TA2833
Hilton Cambs 31 TL2966
Hilton Cumb 60 NY7320
Hilton Derbys 39 SK2430
Hilton Dorset 9 ST7802
Hilton Dur 61 NZ1622
Hilton S on T 62 NZ4611
Hilton Shrops 37 SO7795
Hilton Park Services Staffs 38 SJ9604
Himbleton Worcs 28 SO9458
Himley Staffs 38 SO8891
Hincaster Cumb 59 SD5084
Hinchley Wood Surrey 23 TQ1565
Hinckley Leics 39 SP4294
Hinderclay Suffk 32 TM0276
Hinderwell N York 63 NZ7916
Hindhead Surrey 11 SU8835
Hindhead Tunnel Surrey 11 SU8935
Hindley Wigan 47 SD6104
Hindlip Worcs 28 SO8858
Hindolveston Norfk 42 TG0329
Hindon Wilts 9 ST9132
Hindringham Norfk 42 TF9836
Hingham Norfk 42 TG0202
Hinstock Shrops 37 SJ6925
Hintlesham Suffk 33 TM0843
Hinton Herefs 27 SO3338
Hinton S Glos 20 ST7376
Hinton Shrops 36 SJ4008
Hinton Ampner Hants 11 SU6027
Hinton Blewett BaNES 19 ST5956
Hinton Charterhouse BaNES 20 ST7758
Hinton-in-the-Hedges Nhants 29 SP5636
Hinton Martell Dorset 10 SU0106
Hinton on the Green Worcs 28 SP0240
Hinton Parva Swindn 21 SU2383
Hinton St George Somset 8 ST4212
Hinton St Mary Dorset 9 ST7816
Hinton Waldrist Oxon 21 SU3799
Hints Staffs 38 SK1502
Hinwick Bed 30 SP9361
Hinxhill Kent 15 TR0442
Hinxton Cambs 31 TL4945
Hinxworth Herts 31 TL2340
Hipperholme Calder 55 SE1225
Hipswell N York 61 SE1898
Hirn Abers 89 NJ7200
Hirnant Powys 36 SJ0422
Hirst Nthumb 69 NZ2787
Hirst Courtney N York 56 SE6124
Hirwaun Rhondd 26 SN9505
Hiscott Devon 6 SS5426
Histon Cambs 31 TL4463
Hitcham Suffk 32 TL9851
Hitcham Causeway Suffk 32 TL9852
Hitcham Street Suffk 32 TL9851
Hitchin Herts 31 TL1829
Hither Green Gt Lon 23 TQ3874
Hittisleigh Devon 7 SX7395
Hive E R Yk 56 SE8230
Hixon Staffs 38 SK0025
Hoaden Kent 15 TR2759
Hoar Cross Staffs 38 SK1323
Hoarwithy Herefs 27 SO5429
Hoath Kent 15 TR2064
Hobarris Shrops 36 SO3178
Hobson Dur 69 NZ1756
Hoby Leics 39 SK6617
Hockering Norfk 42 TG0713
Hockerton Notts 49 SK7156
Hockley Essex 24 TQ8392
Hockley Heath Solhll 38 SP1572
Hockliffe C Beds 30 SP9726
Hockwold cum Wilton Norfk 32 TL7388
Hockworthy Devon 7 ST0319
Hoddesdon Herts 23 TL3708
Hoddlesden Bl w D 54 SD7122
Hoddom Mains D & G 67 NY1572
Hodgeston Pembks 16 SS0399
Hodnet Shrops 37 SJ6128
Hodsock Notts 49 SK6185
Hodsoll Street Kent 14 TQ6262
Hodson Swindn 21 SU1780
Hodthorpe Derbys 49 SK5376
Hoe Norfk 42 TF9916
Hogben's Hill Kent 15 TR0356
Hoggeston Bucks 30 SP8024
Hoggrill's End Warwks 39 SP2292
Hoghton Lancs 54 SD6127
Hognaston Derbys 48 SK2350
Hogsthorpe Lincs 51 TF5372
Holbeach Lincs 41 TF3624
Holbeach Bank Lincs 41 TF3527
Holbeach Clough Lincs 41 TF3526
Holbeach Drove Lincs 41 TF3212
Holbeach Hurn Lincs 41 TF3926
Holbeach St Johns Lincs 41 TF3518
Holbeach St Mark's Lincs 41 TF3731
Holbeach St Matthew Lincs 41 TF4132
Holbeck Notts 49 SK5473
Holberrow Green Worcs 28 SP0259
Holbeton Devon 5 SX6150
Holborn Gt Lon 23 TQ3181
Holbrook Derbys 49 SK3644
Holbrook Suffk 25 TM1636
Holbrooks Covtry 39 SP3382
Holbury Hants 10 SU4303
Holcombe Devon 5 SX9574
Holcombe Somset 20 ST6749
Holcombe Rogus Devon 7 ST0518
Holcot Nhants 30 SP7969
Holden Lancs 54 SD7749
Holdenby Nhants 30 SP6967
Holder's Green Essex 24 TL6328
Holdgate Shrops 37 SO5689
Holdingham Lincs 50 TF0547
Holditch Dorset 8 ST3402
Holemoor Devon 6 SS4205
Holford Somset 19 ST1541
Holgate C York 56 SE5851
Holker Cumb 59 SD3676
Holkham Norfk 42 TF8943
Hollacombe Devon 6 SS3702
Holland Fen Lincs 51 TF2349
Holland-on-Sea Essex 25 TM1916
Hollandstoun Ork 100 HY7553
Hollee D & G 67 NY2669
Hollesley Suffk 33 TM3544
Hollicombe Torbay 5 SX8962
Hollingbourne Kent 14 TQ8455
Hollingbury Br & H 12 TQ3107
Hollingdon Bucks 30 SP8727
Hollington Derbys 48 SK2239
Hollington Staffs 48 SK0538
Hollingworth Tamesd 48 SK0096
Hollinsclough Staffs 48 SK0666
Hollins End Sheff 49 SK3883
Hollins Green Warrtn 47 SJ6990
Hollinswood Wrekin 37 SJ7008
Hollocombe Devon 7 SS6311
Holloway Derbys 49 SK3256
Holloway Gt Lon 23 TQ3086
Hollowell Nhants 30 SP6971
Hollowmoor Heath Ches W 46 SJ4868
Hollybush Caerph 19 SO1603
Hollybush E Ayrs 73 NS3915
Hollybush Herefs 28 SO7536
Hollym E R Yk 57 TA3425
Holmbridge Kirk 55 SE1206
Holmbury St Mary Surrey 12 TQ1143
Holmbush Cnwll 3 SX0352
Holmcroft Staffs 38 SJ9024
Holme Cambs 40 TL1987
Holme Cumb 59 SD5278
Holme Kirk 55 SE1105
Holme N York 62 SE3582
Holme Notts 50 SK8059
Holme Chapel Lancs 54 SD8728
Holme Hale Norfk 42 TF8807
Holme Lacy Herefs 27 SO5535
Holme Marsh Herefs 27 SO3454
Holme next the Sea Norfk 42 TF7043
Holme on the Wolds E R Yk 56 SE9646
Holme Pierrepont Notts 49 SK6238
Holmer Herefs 27 SO5042
Holmer Green Bucks 22 SU9097
Holme St Cuthbert Cumb 67 NY1047
Holmes Chapel Ches E 47 SJ7667
Holmesfield Derbys 49 SK3277
Holmeswood Lancs 53 SD4316
Holmethorpe Surrey 12 TQ2851
Holme upon Spalding Moor E R Yk 56 SE8038
Holmewood Derbys 49 SK4365
Holmfirth Kirk 55 SE1408
Holmpton E R Yk 57 TA3623
Holmrook Cumb 58 SD0799
Holmside Dur 69 NZ2149
Holne Devon 5 SX7069
Holnicote Somset 18 SS9146
Holsworthy Devon 6 SS3403
Holsworthy Beacon Devon 6 SS3608
Holt Dorset 10 SU0303
Holt Norfk 43 TG0838
Holt Wilts 20 ST8661
Holt Worcs 28 SO8362
Holt Wrexhm 46 SJ4053
Holtby C York 56 SE6754
Holt End Worcs 28 SP0769
Holt Heath Worcs 28 SO8163
Holton Oxon 29 SP6006
Holton Somset 9 ST6826
Holton Suffk 33 TM4077
Holton cum Beckering Lincs 50 TF1181
Holton le Clay Lincs 57 TA2802
Holton le Moor Lincs 50 TF0897
Holton St Mary Suffk 25 TM0536
Holwell Dorset 9 ST6911
Holwell Herts 31 TL1633
Holwell Leics 40 SK7323
Holwell Oxon 29 SP2309
Holwick Dur 60 NY9126
Holybourne Hants 11 SU7340
Holyhead IoA 44 SH2482
Holy Island Nthumb 77 NU1241
Holymoorside Derbys 49 SK3369
Holyport W & M 22 SU8977
Holystone Nthumb 68 NT9502
Holytown N Lans 74 NS7660
Holywell C Beds 30 TL0117
Holywell Cambs 31 TL3370
Holywell Cnwll 2 SW7659
Holywell Dorset 9 ST5904
Holywell Flints 46 SJ1875
Holywell Green Calder 55 SE0819
Holywell Lake Somset 8 ST1020
Holywell Row Suffk 32 TL7177
Holywood D & G 66 NX9480
Homer Shrops 37 SJ6101
Homersfield Suffk 33 TM2885
Homington Wilts 10 SU1226
Honeybourne Worcs 28 SP1144
Honeychurch Devon 7 SS6303
Honeystreet Wilts 20 SU1061
Honey Tye Suffk 25 TL9535
Honiley Warwks 39 SP2372
Honing Norfk 43 TG3227
Honingham Norfk 43 TG1011
Honington Lincs 50 SK9443
Honington Suffk 32 TL9174
Honington Warwks 29 SP2642
Honiton Devon 8 ST1600
Honley Kirk 55 SE1311
Hooe C Plym 4 SX5052
Hooe E Susx 14 TQ6910
Hoo Green Ches E 47 SJ7182
Hoohill Bpool 53 SD3237
Hook E R Yk 56 SE7625
Hook Gt Lon 23 TQ1864
Hook Hants 22 SU7254
Hook Pembks 16 SM9711
Hook Wilts 20 SU0784
Hooke Dorset 8 ST5300
Hook Green Kent 13 TQ6535
Hook Norton Oxon 29 SP3533
Hookway Devon 7 SX8598
Hooley Surrey 23 TQ2856
Hoo St Werburgh Medway 14 TQ7872
Hooton Levitt Rothm 49 SK5291
Hooton Pagnell Donc 55 SE4807
Hooton Roberts Rothm 49 SK4897
Hope Derbys 48 SK1783
Hope Devon 5 SX6740
Hope Flints 46 SJ3058
Hope Staffs 48 SK1254
Hope Bagot Shrops 37 SO5873
Hope Bowdler Shrops 37 SO4792
Hopeman Moray 93 NJ1469
Hope Mansell Herefs 27 SO6219
Hopesay Shrops 36 SO3983
Hope under Dinmore Herefs 27 SO5052
Hopgrove C York 56 SE6354
Hopperton N York 55 SE4256
Hopstone Shrops 37 SO7894
Hopton Derbys 49 SK2653
Hopton Staffs 38 SJ9425
Hopton Suffk 32 TL9979
Hopton Cangeford Shrops 37 SO5480
Hopton Castle Shrops 36 SO3678
Hoptonheath Shrops 36 SO3877
Hopton on Sea Norfk 43 TM5299
Hopton Wafers Shrops 37 SO6376
Hopwas Staffs 39 SK1804
Hopwood Worcs 38 SP0375
Hopwood Park Services Worcs 38 SP0373
Horam E Susx 13 TQ5717
Horbling Lincs 40 TF1135
Horbury Wakefd 55 SE2918
Horden Dur 62 NZ4440
Hordle Hants 10 SZ2795
Hordley Shrops 36 SJ3831
Horfield Bristl 19 ST5976
Horham Suffk 33 TM2072
Horkesley Heath Essex 25 TL9829
Horkstow N Linc 56 SE9817
Horley Oxon 29 SP4144
Horley Surrey 12 TQ2842
Hornblotton Green Somset 9 ST5833
Hornby Lancs 54 SD5868
Hornby N York 61 SE2293
Hornby N York 62 NZ3605
Horncastle Lincs 51 TF2669
Hornchurch Gt Lon 24 TQ5387
Horncliffe Nthumb 77 NT9249
Horndean Border 77 NT9049
Horndean Hants 11 SU7013
Horndon Devon 4 SX5280
Horndon on the Hill Thurr 24 TQ6683
Horne Surrey 12 TQ3344
Horner Somset 7 SS9045
Horning Norfk 43 TG3417
Horninghold Leics 40 SP8097
Horninglow Staffs 39 SK2425
Horningsea Cambs 31 TL4962
Horningsham Wilts 20 ST8141
Horningtoft Norfk 42 TF9323
Horns Cross Devon 6 SS3823
Hornsea E R Yk 57 TA1947
Hornsey Gt Lon 23 TQ3089
Hornton Oxon 29 SP3945
Horra Shet 100 HU4693
Horrabridge Devon 4 SX5169
Horringer Suffk 32 TL8261
Horrocksford Lancs 54 SD7543
Horsebridge Devon 4 SX4075
Horsebridge E Susx 13 TQ5811
Horsebridge Hants 10 SU3430
Horsehay Wrekin 37 SJ6707
Horseheath Cambs 31 TL6147
Horsehouse N York 61 SE0480
Horsell Surrey 22 SU9959
Horseman's Green Wrexhm 36 SJ4441
Horsey Norfk 43 TG4622
Horsey Somset 19 ST3239
Horsford Norfk 43 TG1916
Horsforth Leeds 55 SE2338
Horsham W Susx 12 TQ1731
Horsham Worcs 28 SO7358
Horsham St Faith Norfk 43 TG2115
Horsington Lincs 50 TF1968
Horsington Somset 9 ST7023
Horsley Derbys 49 SK3744
Horsley Gloucs 20 ST8497
Horsley Nthumb 68 NY8496
Horsley Nthumb 68 NZ0965
Horsleycross Street Essex 25 TM1228
Horsley Woodhouse Derbys 49 SK3944
Horsmonden Kent 14 TQ7040
Horspath Oxon 29 SP5705
Horstead Norfk 43 TG2619
Horsted Keynes W Susx 13 TQ3828
Horton Bucks 30 SP9219
Horton Dorset 10 SU0307
Horton Lancs 54 SD8550
Horton Nhants 30 SP8154
Horton S Glos 20 ST7584
Horton Somset 8 ST3214
Horton Staffs 48 SJ9457
Horton Swans 17 SS4785
Horton W & M 22 TQ0175
Horton Wilts 20 SU0463
Horton Wrekin 37 SJ6814
Horton-cum-Studley Oxon 29 SP5912
Horton Green Ches W 46 SJ4549
Horton-in-Ribblesdale N York 54 SD8071
Horton Kirby Kent 14 TQ5668
Horwich Bolton 54 SD6311
Horwood Devon 6 SS5027
Hose Leics 40 SK7329
Hosh P & K 82 NN8523
Hoswick Shet 100 HU4123
Hotham E R Yk 56 SE8934
Hothfield Kent 15 TQ9644
Hoton Leics 39 SK5722
Hough Ches E 47 SJ7151
Hougham Lincs 50 SK8844
Hough Green Halton 46 SJ4886
Hough-on-the-Hill Lincs 50 SK9246
Houghton Cambs 31 TL2872
Houghton Hants 10 SU3432
Houghton Pembks 16 SM9807
Houghton W Susx 12 TQ0111
Houghton Conquest C Beds 30 TL0441
Houghton Green E Susx 14 TQ9222
Houghton-le-Spring Sundld 69 NZ3449
Houghton on the Hill Leics 39 SK6703
Houghton Regis C Beds 30 TL0123
Houghton St Giles Norfk 42 TF9235
Hound Green Hants 22 SU7359
Houndslow Border 76 NT6347
Hounslow Gt Lon 22 TQ1375
Houses Hill Kirk 55 SE1916
Houston Rens 73 NS4066
Houton Ork 100 HY3104
Hove Br & H 12 TQ2804
Hoveringham Notts 49 SK6946
Hoveton Norfk 43 TG3018
Hovingham N York 62 SE6675
How Caple Herefs 27 SO6030
Howden E R Yk 56 SE7428
Howden-le-Wear Dur 61 NZ1633
Howe N York 62 SE3580
Howe Norfk 43 TM2799
Howe Green Essex 24 TL7403
Howegreen Essex 24 TL8301
Howell Lincs 50 TF1346
Howe Street Essex 24 TL6914
Howe Street Essex 24 TL6934
Howey Powys 26 SO0558
Howgate Cumb 58 NX9921
Howgate Mdloth 75 NT2457
Howick Nthumb 77 NU2517
Howlett End Essex 24 TL5834
Howley Somset 8 ST2609
How Mill Cumb 67 NY5056
Howmore W Isls 90 NF7536
Hownam Border 76 NT7719
Howsham N Linc 57 TA0404
Howsham N York 56 SE7362
Howtel Nthumb 77 NT8934
How Wood Herts 22 TL1403
Howwood Rens 73 NS3960
Hoxne Suffk 33 TM1777
Hoylake Wirral 46 SJ2189
Hoyland Barns 49 SE3700
Hoylandswaine Barns 55 SE2604
Hubberston Pembks 16 SM8906
Huby N York 55 SE2747
Huby N York 56 SE5665
Hucclecote Gloucs 28 SO8717
Hucking Kent 14 TQ8458
Hucknall Notts 49 SK5349
Huddersfield Kirk 55 SE1416
Huddington Worcs 28 SO9457
Hudswell N York 61 NZ1400
Huggate E R Yk 56 SE8855
Hughenden Valley Bucks 22 SU8697
Hughley Shrops 37 SO5698
Hugh Town IoS 2 SV9010
Huish Devon 6 SS5311
Huish Wilts 20 SU1463
Huish Champflower Somset 7 ST0529
Huish Episcopi Somset 8 ST4326
Hulcott Bucks 30 SP8516
Hulham Devon 5 SY0183
Hulland Derbys 48 SK2446
Hulland Ward Derbys 49 SK2546
Hullavington Wilts 20 ST8981
Hullbridge Essex 24 TQ8095
Hull, Kingston upon C KuH 57 TA0829
Hulme Manch 47 SJ8396
Hulme Staffs 48 SJ9345
Hulme Warrtn 47 SJ6091
Hulme End Staffs 48 SK1059
Hulme Walfield Ches E 47 SJ8465
Hulverstone IoW 10 SZ3984
Hulver Street Suffk 33 TM4686
Humber Bridge N Linc 56 TA0224
Humberside Airport N Linc 57 TA0910
Humberston NE Lin 57 TA3105
Humberstone C Leic 39 SK6305
Humbie E Loth 76 NT4662
Humbleton E R Yk 57 TA2234
Humby Lincs 40 TF0032
Hume Border 76 NT7041
Humshaugh Nthumb 68 NY9171
Huncote Leics 39 SP5197
Hunderthwaite Dur 61 NY9821
Hundleby Lincs 51 TF3966
Hundleton Pembks 16 SM9600
Hundon Suffk 32 TL7348
Hundred House Powys 26 SO1154
Hungarton Leics 40 SK6907
Hungerford Somset 7 ST0440
Hungerford W Berk 21 SU3368
Hungerford Newtown W Berk 21 SU3571
Hungerstone Herefs 27 SO4435
Hunmanby N York 63 TA0977
Hunningham Warwks 29 SP3767
Hunsbury Hill Nhants 30 SP7357
Hunsdon Herts 31 TL4114
Hunsingore N York 55 SE4253
Hunslet Leeds 55 SE3130
Hunsonby Cumb 59 NY5835
Hunstanton Norfk 42 TF6740
Hunstanworth Dur 68 NY9448
Hunsterson Ches E 47 SJ6946
Hunston Suffk 32 TL9768
Hunston W Susx 11 SU8601
Hunstrete BaNES 20 ST6462
Hunsworth Kirk 55 SE1827
Hunter's Quay Ag & B 80 NS1879
Huntham Somset 8 ST3426
Huntingdon Cambs 31 TL2471
Huntingfield Suffk 33 TM3374
Huntington C York 56 SE6156
Huntington Ches W 46 SJ4264
Huntington Herefs 27 SO2553
Huntington Staffs 38 SJ9712
Huntley Gloucs 28 SO7219
Huntly Abers 94 NJ5339
Hunton Kent 14 TQ7149
Hunton N York 61 SE1892
Huntscott Somset 7 SS9144
Huntsham Devon 7 ST0020
Huntshaw Devon 6 SS5023
Huntspill Somset 19 ST3145
Huntstile Somset 8 ST2633
Huntworth Somset 8 ST3134
Hunwick Dur 61 NZ1832
Hunworth Norfk 42 TG0635
Hurdcott Wilts 10 SU1733
Hurdsfield Ches E 48 SJ9274
Hurley W & M 22 SU8283
Hurley Warwks 39 SP2495
Hurley Common Warwks 39 SP2496
Hurlford E Ayrs 73 NS4536
Hurn BCP 10 SZ1296
Hursley Hants 10 SU4225
Hurst Wokham 22 SU7973
Hurstbourne Priors Hants 21 SU4346
Hurstbourne Tarrant Hants 21 SU3853
Hurst Green E Susx 14 TQ7327
Hurst Green Essex 25 TM0916
Hurst Green Lancs 54 SD6838
Hurst Green Surrey 13 TQ4050
Hurst Hill Dudley 38 SO9393
Hurstpierpoint W Susx 12 TQ2716
Hurstwood Lancs 54 SD8831
Hurworth-on-Tees Darltn 61 NZ3009
Hurworth Place Darltn 61 NZ2909
Husbands Bosworth Leics 39 SP6484
Husborne Crawley C Beds 30 SP9635
Husthwaite N York 62 SE5175
Huthwaite Notts 49 SK4659
Huttoft Lincs 51 TF5176
Hutton Border 77 NT9053
Hutton E R Yk 56 TA0253
Hutton Essex 24 TQ6395
Hutton Lancs 53 SD4926
Hutton N Som 19 ST3558
Hutton Buscel N York 63 SE9784
Hutton Conyers N York 62 SE3273
Hutton Cranswick E R Yk 56 TA0252
Hutton End Cumb 59 NY4538
Hutton Henry Dur 62 NZ4236
Hutton-le-Hole N York 63 SE7090
Hutton Lowcross R & Cl 62 NZ5914
Hutton Magna Dur 61 NZ1212
Hutton Roof Cumb 59 NY3734
Hutton Roof Cumb 59 SD5677
Hutton Rudby N York 62 NZ4606
Hutton Sessay N York 62 SE4776
Hutton Wandesley N York 55 SE5050
Huxham Devon 7 SX9497
Huxley Ches W 46 SJ5061
Huyton Knows 46 SJ4490
Hycemoor Cumb 58 SD0989
Hyde Tamesd 48 SJ9494
Hyde Heath Bucks 22 SP9300
Hyde Lea Staffs 38 SJ9119
Hynish Ag & B 78 NL9839
Hyssington Powys 36 SO3194
Hythe Essex 25 TM0125
Hythe Hants 10 SU4207
Hythe Kent 15 TR1634
Hythe End W & M 22 TQ0172

I

Ibberton Dorset 9 ST7807
Ible Derbys 48 SK2457
Ibsley Hants 10 SU1509
Ibstock Leics 39 SK4009
Ibstone Bucks 22 SU7593
Ibthorpe Hants 21 SU3753
Iburndale N York 63 NZ8707
Ibworth Hants 21 SU5654
Ickburgh Norfk 42 TL8195
Ickenham Gt Lon 22 TQ0786
Ickford Bucks 29 SP6407
Ickham Kent 15 TR2258
Ickleford Herts 31 TL1831
Icklesham E Susx 14 TQ8716
Ickleton Cambs 31 TL4943
Icklingham Suffk 32 TL7772
Ickornshaw N York 54 SD9642
Ickwell Green C Beds 31 TL1545
Icomb Gloucs 29 SP2122
Idbury Oxon 29 SP2319
Iddesleigh Devon 6 SS5708
Ide Devon 5 SX8990
Ideford Devon 5 SX8977
Ide Hill Kent 13 TQ4851
Iden E Susx 14 TQ9123
Iden Green Kent 14 TQ7437
Iden Green Kent 14 TQ8031
Idle C Brad 55 SE1737
Idless Cnwll 2 SW8147
Idlicote Warwks 29 SP2844
Idmiston Wilts 10 SU1937
Idole Carmth 17 SN4215
Idridgehay Derbys 49 SK2849
Idrigill Highld 90 NG3863
Idstone Oxon 21 SU2584
Iffley Oxon 29 SP5203
Ifield W Susx 12 TQ2537
Ifold W Susx 12 TQ0231
Iford BCP 10 SZ1393
Iford E Susx 13 TQ4007
Ifton Mons 19 ST4688
Ightfield Shrops 37 SJ5938
Ightham Kent 14 TQ5956
Ilam Staffs 48 SK1350
Ilchester Somset 8 ST5222
Ilderton Nthumb 77 NU0121
Ilford Gt Lon 23 TQ4486
Ilford Somset 8 ST3617
Ilfracombe Devon 6 SS5247
Ilkeston Derbys 49 SK4641
Ilketshall St Andrew Suffk 33 TM3887
Ilketshall St Margaret Suffk 33 TM3485
Ilkley C Brad 55 SE1147
Illand Cnwll 4 SX2878
Illey Dudley 38 SO9881
Illogan Cnwll 2 SW6743
Illston on the Hill Leics 40 SP7099
Ilmer Bucks 22 SP7605
Ilmington Warwks 29 SP2143
Ilminster Somset 8 ST3614
Ilsington Devon 5 SX7875
Ilston Swans 17 SS5590
Ilton N York 61 SE1978
Ilton Somset 8 ST3517
Immingham NE Lin 57 TA1814
Immingham Dock NE Lin 57 TA1916
Impington Cambs 31 TL4463
Ince Ches W 46 SJ4576
Ince Blundell Sefton 46 SD3203
Ince-in-Makerfield Wigan 47 SD5904
Inchinnan Rens 73 NS4769
Inchnadamph Highld 96 NC2521
Inchture P & K 83 NO2728
Indian Queens Cnwll 3 SW9159
Ingatestone Essex 24 TQ6499
Ingbirchworth Barns 55 SE2205
Ingestre Staffs 38 SJ9724
Ingham Lincs 50 SK9483
Ingham Norfk 43 TG3926
Ingham Suffk 32 TL8570
Ingham Corner Norfk 43 TG3927
Ingleby Derbys 39 SK3426
Ingleby Arncliffe N York 62 NZ4400
Ingleby Barwick S on T 62 NZ4414
Ingleby Greenhow N York 62 NZ5706
Ingleigh Green Devon 7 SS6007
Inglesbatch BaNES 20 ST7061
Inglesham Swindn 21 SU2098
Ingleton Dur 61 NZ1720
Ingleton N York 60 SD6972

Luscombe Devon....5 SX7957
Luss Ag & B....80 NS3692
Lusta Highld....90 NG2656
Lustleigh Devon....5 SX7881
Luston Herefs....27 SO4863
Luthermuir Abers....89 NO6568
Luthrie Fife....83 NO3219
Luton Devon....5 SX9076
Luton Devon....8 ST0802
Luton Luton....30 TL0921
Luton Medway....14 TQ7766
Luton Airport Luton....30 TL1221
Lutterworth Leics....39 SP5484
Lutton Devon....5 SX5959
Lutton Devon....5 SX6961
Lutton Lincs....41 TF4325
Lutton Nhants....40 TL1187
Luxborough Somset....17 SS9738
Luxulyan Cnwll....3 SX0558
Lybster Highld....100 ND2635
Lydbury North Shrops....36 SO3486
Lydd Kent....15 TR0420
Lydd Airport Kent....15 TR0621
Lydden Kent....15 TR2645
Lydden Kent....15 TR3567
Lyddington Rutlnd....40 SP8797
Lydeard St Lawrence Somset....8 ST1332
Lydford Devon....4 SX5185
Lydford on Fosse Somset....9 ST5630
Lydgate Calder....54 SD9225
Lydham Shrops....36 SO3391
Lydiard Millicent Wilts....20 SU0986
Lydiard Tregoze Swindn....20 SU1084
Lydiate Sefton....46 SD3604
Lydiate Ash Worcs....38 SO9775
Lydlinch Dorset....9 ST7413
Lydney Gloucs....19 SO6303
Lydstep Pembks....16 SS0898
Lye Dudley....38 SO9284
Lye Green E Susx....13 TQ5134
Lye Green Warwks....29 SP1965
Lye's Green Wilts....20 ST8146
Lyford Oxon....21 SU3994
Lymbridge Green Kent....15 TR1244
Lyme Regis Dorset....8 SY3492
Lyminge Kent....15 TR1641
Lymington Hants....10 SZ3295
Lyminster W Susx....12 TQ0204
Lymm Warrtn....47 SJ6887
Lymm Services Warrtn....47 SJ6684
Lympne Kent....15 TR1135
Lympsham Somset....19 ST3354
Lympstone Devon....5 SX9984
Lynch Green Norfk....43 TG1505
Lyndhurst Hants....10 SU3008
Lyndon Rutlnd....40 SK9004
Lyndon Green Birm....38 SP1485
Lyne Surrey....22 TQ0166
Lyneal Shrops....45 SJ4433
Lyneham Oxon....29 SP2720
Lyneham Wilts....20 SU0278
Lynemouth Nthumb....69 NZ2991
Lyne of Skene Abers....95 NJ7610
Lyness Ork....100 ND3094
Lyng Norfk....42 TG0617
Lyng Somset....8 ST3329
Lynmouth Devon....18 SS7249
Lynsted Kent....14 TQ9460
Lynton Devon....18 SS7249
Lyon's Gate Dorset....9 ST6505
Lyonshall Herefs....27 SO3355
Lytchett Matravers Dorset....9 SY9495
Lytchett Minster Dorset....9 SY9693
Lytham Lancs....53 SD3627
Lytham St Annes Lancs....53 SD3427
Lythe N York....63 NZ8413

M

Mabe Burnthouse Cnwll....2 SW7634
Mablethorpe Lincs....51 TF5085
Macclesfield Ches E....48 SJ9173
Macduff Abers....95 NJ7064
Machen Caerph....19 ST2189
Machrihanish Ag & B....72 NR6320
Machynlleth Powys....35 SH7400
Machynys Carmth....17 SS5198
Mackworth Derbys....49 SK3137
Macmerry E Loth....76 NT4372
Maddaford Devon....75 NS9476
Maddiston Falk....75 NS9476
Madeley Staffs....47 SJ7744
Madeley Wrekin....37 SJ6904
Madingley Cambs....31 TL3960
Madley Herefs....27 SO4238
Madresfield Worcs....28 SO8047
Madron Cnwll....2 SW4531
Maenclochog Pembks....16 SN0827
Maendy V Glam....18 ST0076
Maentwrog Gwynd....45 SH6640
Maen-y-groes Cerdgn....34 SN3858
Maer Staffs....47 SJ7938
Maerdy Conwy....45 SJ0144
Maerdy Rhondd....18 SS9798
Maesbrook Shrops....36 SJ3021
Maesbury Shrops....45 SJ3026
Maesbury Marsh Shrops....36 SJ3125
Maeslyn Cerdgn....17 SN3644
Maesteg Brdgnd....18 SS8590
Maesmynis Powys....26 SO0349
Maesycwmmer Caerph....19 ST1594
Maggieknockater Moray....94 NJ3145
Magham Down E Susx....13 TQ6011
Maghull Sefton....46 SD3702
Magna Park Leics....39 SP5184
Magor Mons....19 ST4287
Magor Services Mons....19 ST4188
Maiden Bradley Wilts....20 ST8038
Maidencombe Torbay....5 SX9268
Maidenhayne Devon....8 SY2795
Maiden Head N Som....19 ST5666
Maidenhead W & M....22 SU8980
Maiden Newton Dorset....9 SY5997
Maidens S Ayrs....80 NS2107
Maiden's Green Br For....22 SU9072
Maiden Wells Pembks....16 SR9799
Maidford Nhants....29 SP6052
Maids Moreton Bucks....30 SP7035
Maidstone Kent....14 TQ7555
Maidstone Services Kent....14 TQ8255
Maidwell Nhants....39 SP7476
Mail Shet....100 HU4990
Maindee Newpt....19 ST3288
Mainsforth Dur....62 NZ3131
Mainsriddle D & G....66 NX9456
Mainstone Shrops....36 SO2787
Maisemore Gloucs....28 SO8121
Major's Green Worcs....38 SP1077
Malborough Devon....5 SX7139
Maldon Essex....24 TL8406
Malham N York....58 SD9063
Maligar Highld....85 NM6796
Malltraeth IoA....44 SH4068
Mallwyd Gwynd....35 SH8612

Malmesbury Wilts....20 ST9387
Malmsmead Devon....18 SS7947
Malpas Ches W....46 SJ4947
Malpas Cnwll....3 SW8442
Malpas Newpt....19 ST3090
Maltby Rothm....49 SK5392
Maltby S on T....62 NZ4613
Maltby le Marsh Lincs....51 TF4681
Maltman's Hill Kent....14 TQ9043
Malton N York....56 SE7871
Malvern Worcs....28 SO7946
Malvern Link Worcs....28 SO7947
Malvern Wells Worcs....28 SO7742
Mamble Worcs....37 SO6871
Mamhilad Mons....19 SO3003
Manaccan Cnwll....2 SW7624
Manafon Powys....36 SJ1102
Manais W Isls....90 NG1089
Manaton Devon....5 SX7581
Manby Lincs....51 TF3986
Mancetter Warwks....39 SP3296
Manchester Manch....47 SJ8397
Manchester Airport Manch....47 SJ8184
Mancot Flints....48 SJ3167
Manea Cambs....41 TL4789
Maney Birm....38 SP1195
Manfield N York....62 NZ2113
Mangotsfield S Glos....20 ST6676
Manish W Isls....90 NG1089
Manley Ches W....48 SJ5071
Manmoel Caerph....19 SO1803
Manningford Bohune Wilts....20 SU1357
Manningford Bruce Wilts....20 SU1358
Manningham C Brad....55 SE1435
Mannings Heath W Susx....12 TQ2028
Mannington Dorset....10 SU0605
Manningtree Essex....35 TM1031
Mannofield C Aber....89 NJ9104
Manorbier Pembks....16 SS0697
Manorbier Newton Pembks....16 SN0400
Manorowen Pembks....16 SM9336
Manor Park Gt Lon....23 TQ4285
Mansell Gamage Herefs....27 SO3944
Mansell Lacy Herefs....27 SO4245
Mansfield Notts....49 SK5361
Mansfield Woodhouse Notts....49 SK5363
Manston Dorset....9 ST8115
Manston Kent....15 TR3466
Manston Leeds....55 SE3634
Manswood Dorset....9 ST9708
Manthorpe Lincs....40 TF0715
Manton N Linc....50 SE9302
Manton Rutlnd....40 SK8704
Manton Wilts....20 SU1768
Manuden Essex....31 TL4926
Maperton Somset....9 ST6726
Maplebeck Notts....49 SK7060
Mapledurham Oxon....22 SU6776
Mapledurwell Hants....22 SU6851
Maplehurst W Susx....12 TQ1824
Maplescombe Kent....14 TQ5664
Mapleton Derbys....48 SK1647
Mapperley Derbys....49 SK4342
Mapperley Park C Nott....49 SK5842
Mapperton Dorset....8 SY5099
Mappleborough Green Warwks....28 SP0866
Mappleton E R Yk....57 TA2244
Mapplewell Barns....55 SE3210
Mappowder Dorset....9 ST7306
Marazion Cnwll....2 SW5130
Marbury Ches E....45 SJ5645
March Cambs....41 TL4196
Marcham Oxon....21 SU4596
Marchamley Shrops....37 SJ5929
Marchington Staffs....38 SK1330
Marchros Gwynd....44 SH3125
Marchwiel Wrexhm....46 SJ3547
Marchwood Hants....10 SU3810
Marcross V Glam....18 SS9269
Marden Herefs....27 SO5247
Marden Kent....14 TQ7444
Marden Wilts....20 SU0857
Marden Thorn Kent....14 TQ7642
Mardy Mons....27 SO3015
Mareham le Fen Lincs....51 TF2761
Mareham on the Hill Lincs....51 TF2867
Marehill W Susx....12 TQ0618
Maresfield E Susx....12 TQ4624
Marfleet C Hull....57 TA1429
Marford Wrexhm....46 SJ3556
Margam Neath....18 SS7887
Margaret Marsh Dorset....9 ST8218
Margaretting Essex....24 TL6701
Margaretting Tye Essex....24 TL6800
Margate Kent....15 TR3571
Margnaheglish N Ayrs....72 NS0332
Margrove Park R & CI....62 NZ6515
Marham Norfk....42 TF7009
Marhamchurch Cnwll....7 SS2203
Marholm C Pete....40 TF1401
Marianleigh Devon....7 SS7422
Marine Town Kent....14 TQ9274
Maristow Devon....4 SX4764
Mark Somset....19 ST3847
Markbeech Kent....13 TQ4742
Markby Lincs....51 TF4878
Mark Cross E Susx....13 TQ5831
Market Bosworth Leics....39 SK4002
Market Deeping Lincs....40 TF1310
Market Drayton Shrops....37 SJ6734
Market Harborough Leics....40 SP7387
Market Lavington Wilts....20 SU0154
Market Overton Rutlnd....40 SK8816
Market Rasen Lincs....50 TF1089
Market Stainton Lincs....51 TF2279
Market Warsop Notts....49 SK5667
Market Weighton E R Yk....56 SE8741
Market Weston Suffk....32 TL9877
Markfield Leics....39 SK4809
Markham Caerph....19 SO1601
Markham Moor Notts....49 SK7173
Markinch Fife....83 NO2901
Markington N York....55 SE2865
Marksbury BaNES....20 ST6662
Marks Tey Essex....24 TL9023
Markyate Herts....30 TL0616
Marlborough Wilts....21 SU1868
Marlcliff Warwks....28 SP0850
Marldon Devon....5 SX8663
Marlesford Suffk....33 TM3258
Marley Green Ches E....45 SJ5845
Marlingford Norfk....43 TG1309
Marloes Pembks....16 SM7908
Marlow Bucks....22 SU8486
Marlow Bottom Bucks....22 SU8486
Marlpit Hill Kent....13 TQ4347
Marnhull Dorset....9 ST7718
Marple Stockp....48 SJ9588
Marr Donc....55 SE5105
Marrick N York....61 SE0798
Marsden Kirk....55 SE0411

Marsden S Tyne....69 NZ3964
Marshalswick Herts....23 TL1608
Marsham Norfk....43 TG1923
Marsh Baldon Oxon....21 SU5699
Marshborough Kent....15 TR3057
Marshbrook Shrops....36 SO4489
Marshchapel Lincs....51 TF3599
Marsh Farm Luton....30 TL0625
Marshfield Newpt....19 ST2582
Marshfield S Glos....20 ST7873
Marshgate Cnwll....4 SX1592
Marsh Gibbon Bucks....29 SP6422
Marsh Green Devon....8 SY0493
Marsh Green Kent....13 TQ4344
Marshland St James Norfk....41 TF5209
Marsh Lane Derbys....49 SK4079
Marsh Street Somset....18 SS9944
Marshwood Dorset....8 SY3899
Marske N York....61 NZ1000
Marske-by-the-Sea R & CI....62 NZ1422
Marston Herefs....27 SO3657
Marston Lincs....50 SK8943
Marston Oxon....29 SP5208
Marston Staffs....38 SJ9227
Marston Wilts....20 ST9656
Marston Green Solhll....38 SP1785
Marston Magna Somset....9 ST5922
Marston Meysey Wilts....20 SU1297
Marston Montgomery Derbys....48 SK1337
Marston Moretaine C Beds....30 SP9941
Marston on Dove Derbys....39 SK2329
Marston St Lawrence Nhants....29 SP5341
Marston Trussell Nhants....40 SP6985
Marstow Herefs....27 SO5518
Marsworth Bucks....30 SP9114
Marten Wilts....21 SU2860
Martham Norfk....43 TG4518
Martin Hants....10 SU0619
Martin Kent....15 TR3447
Martin Lincs....50 TF1259
Martinhoe Devon....18 SS6648
Martin Hussingtree Worcs....28 SO8860
Martinstown Dorset....9 SY6489
Martlesham Suffk....33 TM2446
Martlesham Heath Suffk....33 TM2445
Martletwy Pembks....16 SN0310
Martley Worcs....28 SO7560
Martock Somset....8 ST4619
Marton Ches E....47 SJ8568
Marton Cumb....62 SD2275
Marton E R Yk....57 TA1739
Marton Lincs....50 SK8381
Marton Middsb....62 NZ5115
Marton N York....55 SE4162
Marton N York....63 SE7383
Marton Shrops....36 SJ2802
Marton Warwks....29 SP4068
Marton-le-Moor N York....55 SE3770
Martyr Worthy Hants....11 SU5132
Marwood Devon....6 SS5437
Maryburgh Highld....92 NH5456
Maryhill C Glas....74 NS5669
Marykirk Abers....89 NO6864
Marylebone Gt Lon....23 TQ2782
Marylebone Wigan....47 SD5807
Maryport Cumb....58 NY0336
Maryport D & G....64 NX1434
Marystow Devon....4 SX4382
Mary Tavy Devon....4 SX5079
Marywell Abers....89 NO5895
Marywell Angus....89 NO6544
Masham N York....61 SE2280
Masongill N York....60 SD6675
Mastin Moor Derbys....49 SK4575
Matching Essex....24 TL5311
Matching Green Essex....24 TL5311
Matching Tye Essex....24 TL5111
Matfen Nthumb....68 NZ0371
Matfield Kent....13 TQ6541
Mathern Mons....19 ST5290
Mathon Herefs....28 SO7346
Mathry Pembks....16 SM8832
Matlask Norfk....43 TG1534
Matlock Derbys....49 SK3059
Matlock Bath Derbys....48 SK2958
Matson Gloucs....28 SO8515
Mattersey Notts....49 SK6889
Mattingley Hants....22 SU7357
Mattishall Norfk....42 TG0510
Mattishall Burgh Norfk....42 TG0512
Mauchline E Ayrs....74 NS4927
Maud Abers....95 NJ9248
Maugersbury Gloucs....29 SP2025
Maughold IoM....52 SC4991
Maulden C Beds....30 TL0538
Maulds Meaburn Cumb....60 NY6216
Maunby N York....62 SE3586
Maundown Somset....18 ST0628
Mautby Norfk....43 TG4812
Mavesyn Ridware Staffs....38 SK0816
Mavis Enderby Lincs....51 TF3666
Mawbray Cumb....67 NY0846
Mawdesley Lancs....53 SD4914
Mawdlam Brdgnd....18 SS8081
Mawgan Cnwll....2 SW7025
Mawgan Porth Cnwll....3 SW8567
Mawla Cnwll....2 SW7045
Mawnan Cnwll....2 SW7827
Mawnan Smith Cnwll....2 SW7728
Mawsley Nhants....40 SP8076
Maxey C Pete....40 TF1208
Maxstoke Warwks....39 SP2386
Maxton Kent....15 TR3041
Maxworthy Cnwll....4 SX2593
May Bank Staffs....47 SJ8547
Maybole S Ayrs....73 NS2909
Maybury Surrey....22 TQ0158
Mayfield E Susx....13 TQ5826
Mayfield Mdloth....77 NT3565
Mayfield Staffs....48 SK1545
Mayford Surrey....22 SU9956
May Hill Gloucs....28 SO7020
Mayland Essex....24 TL9101
Maylandsea Essex....24 TL9002
Maynard's Green E Susx....12 TQ5826
Maypole Birm....38 SP0778
Maypole Kent....15 TR2064
Maypole Mons....27 SO4716
Maypole Green Norfk....43 TM4195
Maypole Green Suffk....33 TL9159
Meadgate BaNES....20 ST6658
Meadle Bucks....22 SP8005
Meadowfield Dur....61 NZ2439
Meadwell Devon....4 SX4081
Meanwood Leeds....55 SE2837
Meare Somset....19 ST4541
Meare Green Somset....8 ST3326
Meare Green Somset....8 ST3022
Mears Ashby Nhants....30 SP8366
Measham Leics....39 SK3311
Meath Green Surrey....12 TQ2643
Meathop Cumb....59 SD4380
Meavaig W Isls....90 NB0834
Meavy Devon....4 SX5467

Medbourne Leics....40 SP8093
Meddon Devon....6 SS2717
Meden Vale Notts....49 SK5869
Medmenham Bucks....22 SU8084
Medomsley Dur....69 NZ1154
Medstead Hants....11 SU6537
Medway Services Medway....14 TQ8163
Meerbrook Staffs....48 SJ9860
Meesden Herts....31 TL4332
Meeth Devon....6 SS5408
Meeting House Hill Norfk....43 TG3028
Meidrim Carmth....17 SN2920
Meifod Powys....36 SJ1513
Meigle P & K....88 NO2844
Meikle Earnock S Lans....74 NS7053
Meikleour P & K....82 NO1539
Meinciau Carmth....17 SN4610
Meir C Stke....48 SJ9342
Melbourn Cambs....31 TL3844
Melbourne Derbys....39 SK3825
Melbourne E R Yk....56 SE7543
Melbury Abbas Dorset....9 ST8820
Melbury Bubb Dorset....9 ST5906
Melbury Osmond Dorset....9 ST5707
Melchbourne Bed....30 TL0265
Melcombe Bingham Dorset....9 ST7602
Meldon Devon....6 SX5692
Meldon Nthumb....69 NZ1183
Meldreth Cambs....31 TL3746
Meliden Denbgs....45 SJ0680
Melin-y-wig Denbgs....45 SJ0448
Melkinthorpe Cumb....59 NY5525
Melkridge Nthumb....67 NY7364
Melksham Wilts....20 ST9063
Melling Lancs....54 SD5970
Melling Sefton....46 SD3800
Mellis Suffk....33 TM0974
Mellor Lancs....54 SD6530
Mellor Stockp....48 SJ9888
Mellor Brook Lancs....54 SD6431
Mells Somset....20 ST7248
Melmerby N York....59 SE0785
Melmerby N York....62 SE3376
Melmerby Cumb....67 NY6137
Melness Highld....99 NC5861
Melplash Dorset....8 SY4898
Melrose Border....76 NT5434
Melsetter Ork....100 ND2689
Melsonby N York....62 NZ1908
Meltham Kirk....55 SE1010
Melton E R Yk....56 SE9726
Melton Suffk....33 TM2850
Melton Constable Norfk....42 TG0432
Melton Mowbray Leics....40 SK7518
Melton Ross N Linc....50 TA0610
Melvaig Highld....91 NG7486
Melverley Shrops....36 SJ3316
Melvich Highld....99 NC8764
Membury Devon....8 ST2803
Membury Services W Berk....21 SU3175
Memsie Abers....95 NJ9762
Memus Angus....88 NO4358
Menai Bridge IoA....44 SH5571
Mendham Suffk....33 TM2782
Mendlesham Suffk....33 TM1065
Mendlesham Green Suffk....33 TM0963
Menheniot Cnwll....4 SX2863
Mennock D & G....66 NS8107
Menston C Brad....55 SE1643
Menstrie Clacks....82 NS8597
Mentmore Bucks....30 SP9019
Meole Brace Shrops....37 SJ4810
Meonstoke Hants....11 SU6119
Meopham Kent....14 TQ6466
Mepal Cambs....41 TL4481
Meppershall C Beds....30 TL1336
Mere Ches E....47 SJ7281
Mere Wilts....20 ST8132
Mere Brow Lancs....53 SD4218
Mereclough Lancs....54 SD8730
Mere Green Birm....38 SP1198
Mereworth Kent....14 TQ6653
Merrden Solhll....39 SP2482
Merrion Pembks....16 SR9397
Merriott Somset....8 ST4412
Merrow Surrey....12 TQ0250
Merry Hill Herts....22 TQ1394
Merryhill Wolves....38 SO8897
Merrymeet Cnwll....4 SX2766
Mersey Crossing Halton....56 SJ5183
Mersham Kent....15 TR0540
Merstham Surrey....12 TQ2953
Merston W Susx....11 SU8902
Merstone IoW....11 SZ5285
Merther Cnwll....3 SW8644
Merthyr Cynog Powys....26 SN9837
Merthyr Mawr Brdgnd....18 SS8877
Merthyr Tydfil Myr Td....26 SO0406
Merthyr Vale Myr Td....18 ST0799
Merton Devon....6 SS5212
Merton Gt Lon....23 TQ2570
Merton Norfk....42 TL9197
Merton Oxon....29 SP5717
Meshaw Devon....7 SS7519
Messing Essex....24 TL8918
Messingham N Linc....50 SE8904
Metfield Suffk....33 TM2980
Metherell Cnwll....4 SX4069
Metheringham Lincs....50 TF0661
Methil Fife....83 NT3799
Methilhill Fife....83 NT3500
Methlem Gwynd....44 SH1827
Methley Leeds....55 SE3926
Methlick Abers....95 NJ8537
Methven P & K....82 NO0226
Methwold Norfk....42 TL7394
Methwold Hythe Norfk....42 TL7194
Mettingham Suffk....33 TM3689
Metton Norfk....43 TG1937
Mevagissey Cnwll....3 SX0144
Mexborough Donc....49 SE4700
Mey Highld....100 ND2872
Meysey Hampton Gloucs....20 SP1100
Miabhaig W Isls....90 NB0834
Michaelchurch Herefs....27 SO5225
Michaelchurch Escley Herefs....27 SO3134
Michaelstone-y-Fedw Newpt....19 ST2484
Michaelstow Cnwll....3 SX0778
Michaelwood Services Gloucs....20 ST7095
Micheldever Hants....11 SU5139
Micheldever Station Hants....21 SU5143
Michelmersh Hants....10 SU3426
Mickfield Suffk....33 TM1361
Micklebring Donc....49 SK5194
Mickleby N York....63 NZ8012
Micklefield Leeds....55 SE4433
Mickleham Surrey....23 TQ1653
Mickleover Derbys....48 SK3033
Micklethwaite Cumb....67 NY2751
Mickleton Dur....61 NY9623
Mickleton Gloucs....28 SP1643
Mickletown Leeds....55 SE4027
Mickle Trafford Ches W....46 SJ4469
Mickley N York....62 SE2576

Mickley Square Nthumb....68 NZ0762
Midbea Ork....100 HY4444
Mid Calder W Loth....75 NT0767
Middle Aston Oxon....29 SP4726
Middle Barton Oxon....29 SP4325
Middlebie D & G....67 NY2176
Middle Chinnock Somset....8 ST4713
Middle Claydon Bucks....30 SP7225
Middleham N York....61 SE1287
Middle Handley Derbys....49 SK4077
Middlehill Wilts....20 ST8168
Middlehope Shrops....37 SO4988
Middle Littleton Worcs....28 SP0847
Middlemarsh Dorset....9 ST6707
Middle Mayfield Staffs....48 SK1444
Middle Rasen Lincs....50 TF0889
Middle Rocombe Devon....5 SX9069
Middlesbrough Middsb....62 NZ4919
Middleshaw Cumb....59 SD5589
Middlesmoor N York....61 SE0973
Middlestone Dur....61 NZ2531
Middlestown Wakefd....55 SE2617
Middlethird Border....78 NT6743
Middleton Ag & B....78 NM2562
Middleton Cumb....60 SD6286
Middleton Derbys....49 SK2755
Middleton Derbys....48 SK1963
Middleton Essex....32 TL8639
Middleton Hants....21 SU4244
Middleton Herefs....27 SO5469
Middleton Leeds....55 SE3028
Middleton N York....55 SE1287
Middleton N York....56 SE7885
Middleton Nhants....40 SP8389
Middleton Norfk....42 TF6616
Middleton Nthumb....68 NZ0585
Middleton Nthumb....81 NU1035
Middleton P & K....82 NO1207
Middleton Rochdl....54 SD8705
Middleton Shrops....37 SO5477
Middleton Suffk....33 TM4267
Middleton Swans....17 SS4287
Middleton Warwks....38 SP1798
Middleton Cheney Nhants....29 SP4941
Middleton-in-Teesdale Dur....61 NY9425
Middleton Moor Suffk....33 TM4167
Middleton One Row Darltn....62 NZ3512
Middleton-on-Sea W Susx....12 SU9600
Middleton on the Hill Herefs....27 SO5364
Middleton on the Wolds E R Yk....56 SE9449
Middleton Park C Aber....95 NJ9211
Middleton Quernhow N York....62 SE3378
Middleton St George Darltn....62 NZ3412
Middleton Scriven Shrops....37 SO6887
Middleton Stoney Oxon....29 SP5323
Middleton Tyas N York....62 NZ2205
Middle Town IoS....2 SV8808
Middletown Powys....36 SJ3012
Middle Tysoe Warwks....29 SP3444
Middle Wallop Hants....10 SU2937
Middlewich Ches E....47 SJ7066
Middle Winterslow Wilts....10 SU2333
Middle Woodford Wilts....10 SU1136
Middlewood Green Suffk....33 TM0961
Middleyzoy Somset....8 ST3733
Midford BaNES....20 ST7660
Midgham W Berk....21 SU5567
Midgley Calder....55 SE0226
Midgley Wakefd....55 SE2714
Midhopestones Sheff....48 SK2399
Midhurst W Susx....11 SU8821
Mid Lavant W Susx....11 SU8508
Midlem Border....76 NT5227
Midsomer Norton BaNES....20 ST6654
Mid Yell Shet....100 HU5190
Milborne Port Somset....9 ST6718
Milborne St Andrew Dorset....9 SY8097
Milborne Wick Somset....9 ST6620
Milbourne Nthumb....69 NZ1175
Milbourne Wilts....20 ST9587
Milburn Cumb....60 NY6529
Milbury Heath S Glos....20 ST6790
Milby N York....55 SE4067
Milcombe Oxon....29 SP4134
Milden Suffk....32 TL9546
Mildenhall Suffk....32 TL7174
Mildenhall Wilts....21 SU2069
Mileham Norfk....42 TF9119
Mile Oak Br & H....12 TQ2407
Milesmark Fife....82 NT0688
Miles Platting Manch....47 SJ8599
Mile Town Kent....14 TQ9274
Milfield Nthumb....77 NT9333
Milford Derbys....49 SK3545
Milford Devon....6 SS2322
Milford Powys....36 SO1291
Milford Staffs....38 SJ9720
Milford Surrey....11 SU9442
Milford Haven Pembks....16 SM9005
Milford on Sea Hants....10 SZ2891
Milkwall Gloucs....27 SO5809
Milland W Susx....11 SU8328
Mill Bank Calder....55 SE0321
Millbreck Abers....95 NK0044
Millbridge Surrey....11 SU8442
Millbrook C Beds....30 TL0138
Millbrook C Sotn....10 SU3813
Millbrook Cnwll....4 SX4252
Mill Brow Stockp....48 SJ9789
Millbuie Abers....95 NJ7408
Millcombe Devon....5 SX8050
Mill Common Suffk....33 TM4081
Mill Cross Devon....5 SX7361
Mill End Bucks....22 SU7885
Mill End Herts....31 TL3332
Millerhill Mdloth....75 NT3269
Miller's Dale Derbys....48 SK1473
Mill Green Cambs....32 TL6655
Mill Green Essex....24 TL6301
Mill Green Lincs....41 TF2223
Mill Green Norfk....33 TM1690
Mill Green Suffk....32 TL9542
Mill Green W Susx....33 TM1360

Mill Hill Gt Lon....23 TQ2292
Millhouse Ag & B....71 NR9570
Millhouse Green Barns....55 SE2203
Millhouses Sheff....49 SK3484
Milliken Park Rens....73 NS4162
Millington E R Yk....56 SE8351
Millmeece Staffs....38 SJ8333
Mill of Haldane W Duns....80 NS3982
Millom Cumb....58 SD1780
Millport N Ayrs....73 NS1654
Mill Side Cumb....59 SD4484
Mill Street Norfk....42 TG0617
Millthrop Cumb....60 SD6591
Milltimber C Aber....89 NJ8501
Milltown D & G....67 NY3375
Milltown Derbys....49 SK3561
Milltown Devon....6 SS5538
Milltown of Edinvillie Moray....94 NJ2640
Milltown of Rothiemay Moray....94 NJ5548
Milnathort P & K....82 NO1204
Milngavie E Duns....75 NS5574
Milnrow Rochdl....54 SD9212
Milnthorpe Cumb....59 SD4981
Milson Shrops....37 SO6472
Milstead Kent....14 TQ9058
Milston Wilts....21 SU1645
Milthorpe Nhants....29 SP5946
Milton C Stke....48 SJ9050
Milton Cambs....31 TL4762
Milton Cumb....67 NY5560
Milton D & G....64 NX1154
Milton D & G....66 NX8470
Milton Derbys....39 SK3126
Milton Highld....92 NH4930
Milton Highld....97 NH7674
Milton Highld....101 NH5749
Milton Highld....101 ND3451
Milton Moray....101 NJ2863
Milton N Som....19 ST3462
Milton Notts....50 SK7173
Milton Oxon....21 SU4892
Milton Oxon....29 SP4535
Milton Pembks....16 SN0403
Milton Somset....8 ST4621
Milton Stirlg....81 NS4490
Milton W Duns....81 NS4274
Milton Abbas Dorset....9 ST8001
Milton Abbot Devon....4 SX4079
Milton Bryan C Beds....30 SP9730
Milton Clevedon Somset....20 ST6637
Milton Combe Devon....4 SX4866
Milton Damerel Devon....6 SS3810
Milton Ernest Bed....30 TL0156
Milton Green Ches W....46 SJ4658
Milton Hill Oxon....21 SU4790
Milton Keynes M Keyn....30 SP8537
Milton Lilbourne Wilts....21 SU1960
Milton Malsor Nhants....30 SP7355
Milton of Balgonie Fife....83 NO3200
Milton of Campsie E Duns....74 NS6576
Milton of Murtle C Aber....89 NJ8702
Milton on Stour Dorset....9 ST7928
Milton Regis Kent....14 TQ9064
Milton-under-Wychwood Oxon....29 SP2618
Milverton Somset....18 ST1225
Milverton Warwks....29 SP3066
Milwich Staffs....38 SJ9632
Minchinhampton Gloucs....20 SO8700
Mindrum Nthumb....77 NT8432
Minehead Somset....18 SS9646
Minera Wrexhm....46 SJ2751
Minety Wilts....20 SU0290
Minffordd Gwynd....44 SH5938
Miningsby Lincs....51 TF3264
Minions Cnwll....4 SX2671
Minllyn Gwynd....35 SH8514
Minnigaff D & G....64 NX4166
Minskip N York....55 SE3864
Minstead Hants....10 SU2811
Minsted W Susx....11 SU8520
Minster Kent....14 TR3064
Minster Kent....15 TR3171
Minsterley Shrops....36 SJ3705
Minster Lovell Oxon....29 SP3110
Minster-on-Sea Kent....14 TQ9573
Minsterworth Gloucs....28 SO7717
Minterne Magna Dorset....9 ST6504
Minting Lincs....50 TF1873
Mintlaw Abers....95 NJ9948
Minto Border....76 NT5620
Minton Shrops....36 SO4390
Mirehouse Cumb....58 NX9715
Mirfield Kirk....55 SE2019
Miserden Gloucs....28 SO9308
Miskin Rhondd....18 ST0480
Misson Notts....49 SK6895
Misterton Leics....39 SP5583
Misterton Notts....50 SK7694
Misterton Somset....8 ST4508
Mistley Essex....35 TM1131
Mitcham Gt Lon....23 TQ2768
Mitcheldean Gloucs....28 SO6618
Mitchell Cnwll....3 SW8554
Mitchel Troy Mons....27 SO4910
Mitford Nthumb....69 NZ1786
Mithian Cnwll....2 SW7450
Mixbury Oxon....29 SP6033
Mobberley Ches E....47 SJ7879
Mobberley Staffs....48 SK0041
Mochdre Powys....36 SO0788
Mochrum D & G....64 NX3446
Mockbeggar Kent....14 TQ7146
Mockerkin Cumb....58 NY0923
Modbury Devon....5 SX6651
Moddershall Staffs....38 SJ9236
Moelfre IoA....44 SH5186
Moelfre Powys....36 SJ1828
Moffat D & G....67 NT0805
Moggerhanger C Beds....30 TL1449
Moira Leics....39 SK3115
Molash Kent....15 TR0251
Mold Flints....46 SJ2363
Moldgreen Kirk....55 SE1516
Molehill Green Essex....24 TL5624
Molescroft E R Yk....56 TA0340
Molesworth Cambs....30 TL0775
Molland Devon....7 SS8028
Mollington Ches W....46 SJ3870
Mollington Oxon....29 SP4447
Mollinsburn N Lans....75 NS7171
Monewden Suffk....33 TM2358
Moniaive D & G....66 NX7890
Monifieth Angus....83 NO4932
Monikie Angus....83 NO4938
Monimail Fife....83 NO2914
Monk Bretton Barns....55 SE3607
Monken Hadley Gt Lon....23 TQ2497
Monk Fryston N York....55 SE5029
Monkhide Herefs....27 SO6143
Monkhill Cumb....67 NY3458
Monkhopton Shrops....37 SO6293
Monkland Herefs....27 SO4557
Monkleigh Devon....6 SS4520
Monknash V Glam....18 SS9170
Monkokehampton Devon....6 SS5805
Monkseaton N Tyne....69 NZ3472
Monks Eleigh Suffk....32 TL9647
Monk's Gate W Susx....12 TQ2028
Monk Sherborne Hants....21 SU6156
Monksilver Somset....18 ST0737
Monks Kirby Warwks....39 SP4683
Monk Soham Suffk....33 TM2165
Monks Risborough Bucks....22 SP8104
Monkspath Solhll....38 SP1276
Monksthorpe Lincs....51 TF4465
Monk Street Essex....24 TL6128
Monkswood Mons....19 SO3402
Monkton Devon....8 ST1803
Monkton Kent....15 TR2964
Monkton S Ayrs....73 NS3527
Monkton S Tyne....69 NZ3363
Monkton V Glam....18 SS9167
Monkton Combe BaNES....20 ST7762
Monkton Deverill Wilts....20 ST8537
Monkton Farleigh Wilts....20 ST8065
Monkton Heathfield Somset....8 ST2526
Monkton Wyld Dorset....8 SY3396

Monkwearmouth Sundld....69 NZ3958
Monkwood Hants....11 SU6630
Monmore Green Wolves....38 SO9297
Monmouth Mons....27 SO5012
Monnington on Wye Herefs....27 SO3743
Monreith D & G....64 NX3641
Montacute Somset....8 ST4916
Montford Shrops....36 SJ4114
Montford Bridge Shrops....36 SJ4215
Montgarrie Abers....94 NJ5717
Montgomery Powys....36 SO2296
Montrose Angus....89 NO7157
Monxton Hants....21 SU3144
Monyash Derbys....48 SK1566
Monymusk Abers....95 NJ6815
Monzie P & K....82 NN8825
Moodiesburn N Lans....74 NS6970
Moonzie Fife....83 NO3317
Moor Allerton Leeds....55 SE3038
Moorby Lincs....51 TF2964
Moor Crichel Dorset....9 ST9908
Moordown BCP....10 SZ0994
Moore Halton....47 SJ5784
Moor End Calder....55 SE0828
Moorends Donc....56 SE6915
Moorgreen Hants....10 SU4815
Moorhead C Brad....55 SE1337
Moorhouse Cumb....67 NY3356
Moorhouse Notts....50 SK7766
Moorhouse Bank Surrey....13 TQ4353
Moorlinch Somset....19 ST3936
Moor Monkton N York....55 SE5156
Moorsholm R & CI....62 NZ6814
Moorside Dorset....9 ST7919
Moor Street Birm....38 SO9982
Moorswater Cnwll....4 SX2364
Moorthorpe Wakefd....55 SE4611
Moortown Leeds....55 SE2939
Moortown Lincs....50 TF0798
Morangie Highld....97 NH7782
Morar Highld....84 NM6793
Morborne Cambs....40 TL1391
Morchard Bishop Devon....7 SS7707
Morcombelake Dorset....8 SY4094
Morcott Rutlnd....40 SK9200
Morda Shrops....36 SJ2827
Morden Dorset....9 SY9195
Morden Gt Lon....23 TQ2568
Mordiford Herefs....27 SO5737
Mordon Dur....62 NZ3226
More Shrops....36 SO3491
Morebath Devon....7 SS9525
Morebattle Border....76 NT7724
Morecambe Lancs....53 SD4364
Moredon Swindn....20 SU1387
Morefield Highld....96 NH1195
Morehall Kent....15 TR2136
Moreleigh Devon....5 SX7652
Morenish P & K....81 NN6035
Morestead Hants....11 SU5025
Moreton Dorset....9 SY8089
Moreton Essex....23 TL5307
Moreton Herefs....27 SO5064
Moreton Oxon....20 SP6904
Moreton Wirral....46 SJ2689
Moreton Corbet Shrops....37 SJ5623
Moretonhampstead Devon....5 SX7586
Moreton-in-Marsh Gloucs....29 SP2032
Moreton Jeffries Herefs....27 SO6048
Moreton Morrell Warwks....29 SP3155
Moreton on Lugg Herefs....27 SO5045
Moreton Pinkney Nhants....29 SP5749
Moreton Say Shrops....37 SJ6334
Moreton Valence Gloucs....28 SO7709
Morfa Nefyn Gwynd....44 SH2840
Morham E Loth....78 NT5571
Moriah Cerdgn....35 SN6279
Morland Cumb....59 NY6022
Morley Ches E....47 SJ8282
Morley Derbys....49 SK3940
Morley Leeds....55 SE2627
Morley Green Ches E....47 SJ8281
Morley St Botolph Norfk....42 TM0799
Morningside C Edin....77 NT2470
Morningside N Lans....75 NS8355
Morningthorpe Norfk....33 TM2192
Morpeth Nthumb....69 NZ1986
Morrey Staffs....38 SK1218
Morriston Swans....18 SS6698
Morston Norfk....42 TG0043
Mortehoe Devon....6 SS4545
Morthen Rothm....49 SK4788
Mortimer W Berk....21 SU6564
Mortimer West End Hants....21 SU6363
Mortlake Gt Lon....23 TQ2075
Morton Cumb....67 NY3854
Morton Derbys....49 SK4060
Morton Lincs....40 TF0924
Morton Lincs....50 SK8091
Morton Notts....50 SK7251
Morton Shrops....36 SJ2924
Morton-on-Swale N York....62 SE3291
Morvah Cnwll....2 SW4035
Morvich Highld....84 NG9621
Morville Shrops....37 SO6794
Morwenstow Cnwll....6 SS2015
Mosborough Sheff....49 SK4281
Moscow E Ayrs....74 NS4840
Mosedale Cumb....67 NY3532
Moseley Birm....38 SP0783
Moseley Wolves....38 SO9198
Moseley Worcs....28 SO8159
Moss Donc....56 SE5914
Moss Bank St Hel....46 SJ5197
Mossbay Cumb....58 NX9927
Mossblown S Ayrs....73 NS4024
Moss Edge Lancs....53 SD4143
Mossend N Lans....75 NS7460
Mossley Ches E....47 SJ8360
Mossley Tamesd....48 SD9701
Moss-side Highld....93 NH8155
Mosstodloch Moray....94 NJ3259
Mossy Lea Lancs....53 SD5312
Mosterton Dorset....8 ST4505
Moston Manch....47 SD8701
Mostyn Flints....46 SJ1580
Motcombe Dorset....9 ST8525
Mothecombe Devon....5 SX6047
Motherby Cumb....67 NY4228
Motherwell N Lans....75 NS7457
Motspur Park Gt Lon....23 TQ2267
Mottingham Gt Lon....23 TQ4272
Mottisfont Hants....10 SU3226
Mottistone IoW....10 SZ4083
Mottram in Longdendale Tamesd....48 SJ9995
Mottram St Andrew Ches E....47 SJ8778
Mouldsworth Ches W....46 SJ5071
Moulin P & K....87 NN9459
Moulsecoomb Br & H....12 TQ3307
Moulsford Oxon....21 SU5883
Moulsoe M Keyn....30 SP9141
Moulton Ches W....46 SJ6569
Moulton Lincs....41 TF3023
Moulton N York....62 NZ2303

Moulton Nhants....30 SP7866
Moulton Suffk....32 TL6964
Moulton V Glam....18 ST0770
Moulton Chapel Lincs....41 TF2918
Moulton St Mary Norfk....43 TG3907
Moulton Seas End Lincs....41 TF3227
Mount Cnwll....3 SX1468
Mount Cnwll....3 SX1457
Mountain Ash Rhondd....18 ST0499
Mountain Cross Border....75 NT1547
Mountbenger Border....76 NT3125
Mount Bures Essex....34 TL9032
Mount Hawke Cnwll....2 SW7147
Mount Lothian Mdloth....75 NT2757
Mountnessing Essex....24 TQ6297
Mounton Mons....19 ST5193
Mount Pleasant Derbys....49 SK3448
Mount Pleasant Suffk....32 TL7347
Mountsorrel Leics....39 SK5814
Mount Tabor Calder....55 SE0627
Mousehole Cnwll....2 SW4626
Mouswald D & G....66 NY0672
Mow Cop Ches E....47 SJ8557
Mowmacre Hill C Leic....39 SK5807
Mowsley Leics....39 SP6489
Moy Highld....86 NN4282
Moy Highld....93 NH7634
Moylegrove Pembks....16 SN1144
Muasdale Ag & B....71 NR6840
Muchalls Abers....89 NO9092
Much Birch Herefs....27 SO5030
Much Cowarne Herefs....27 SO6147
Much Dewchurch Herefs....27 SO4831
Muchelney Somset....8 ST4224
Muchelney Ham Somset....8 ST4223
Much Hadham Herts....31 TL4219
Much Hoole Lancs....53 SD4723
Muchlarnick Cnwll....4 SX2156
Much Marcle Herefs....28 SO6532
Much Wenlock Shrops....37 SO6299
Mucklestone Staffs....37 SJ7237
Muckton Lincs....51 TF3781
Muddiford Devon....6 SS5638
Muddles Green E Susx....13 TQ5413
Mudeford BCP....10 SZ1892
Mudford Somset....8 ST5719
Mudford Sock Somset....8 ST5519
Mugginton Derbys....49 SK2842
Muirdrum Angus....83 NO5637
Muirhead Angus....83 NO3334
Muirhead Fife....83 NO2805
Muirhead N Lans....74 NS6869
Muirkirk E Ayrs....74 NS6927
Muir of Fowlis Abers....94 NJ5612
Muir of Ord Highld....92 NH5250
Muirton P & K....82 NN9211
Muirtown P & K....82 NN8018
Muker N York....61 SD9097
Mulbarton Norfk....43 TG1901
Mullion Cnwll....2 SW6719
Mullion Cove Cnwll....2 SW6617
Mumby Lincs....51 TF5174
Munderfield Row Herefs....27 SO6451
Munderfield Stocks Herefs....27 SO6550
Mundesley Norfk....43 TG3136
Mundford Norfk....42 TL8093
Mundham Norfk....43 TM3397
Mundon Hill Essex....24 TL8602
Mungrisdale Cumb....59 NY3630
Munlochy Highld....93 NH6453
Munsley Herefs....28 SO6640
Munslow Shrops....37 SO5287
Murchington Devon....5 SX6888
Murcott Oxon....29 SP5815
Murrow Cambs....41 TF3707
Mursley Bucks....30 SP8128
Murthly P & K....82 NO1038
Murton C York....56 SE6452
Murton Cumb....60 NY7221
Murton Dur....62 NZ3947
Murton Nthumb....77 NT9748
Murton Swan....17 SS5988
Musbury Devon....8 SY2794
Musselburgh E Loth....75 NT3472
Muston Leics....40 SK8237
Muston N York....57 TA0979
Muswell Hill Gt Lon....23 TQ2889
Mutehill D & G....65 NX6848
Mutford Suffk....33 TM4888
Muthill P & K....82 NN8717
Mybster Highld....100 ND1652
Myddfai Carmth....26 SN7730
Myddle Shrops....37 SJ4623
Mydroilyn Cerdgn....34 SN4555
Mylor Cnwll....3 SW8235
Mylor Bridge Cnwll....2 SW8036
Mynachlog ddu Pembks....16 SN1430
Mynydd-bach Mons....19 ST4894
Mynydd-bach Swans....18 SS6597
Mynyddgarreg Carmth....17 SN4208
Mynydd Isa Flints....46 SJ2563
Mytchett Surrey....22 SU8855
Mytholm Calder....54 SD9827
Mytholmroyd Calder....55 SE0126
Myton-on-Swale N York....55 SE4366

N

Naburn C York....56 SE5945
Nackington Kent....15 TR1554
Nacton Suffk....33 TM2240
Nafferton E R Yk....57 TA0559
Nailbourne Somset....8 ST2128
Nailsea N Som....19 ST4770
Nailstone Leics....39 SK4106
Nailsworth Gloucs....28 ST8499
Nairn Highld....93 NH8856
Nannerch Flints....46 SJ1669
Nanpantan Leics....39 SK5017
Nanpean Cnwll....3 SW9656
Nanstallon Cnwll....3 SX0367
Nanternis Cerdgn....34 SN3756
Nantgaredig Carmth....17 SN4921
Nantglyn Denbgs....45 SJ0061
Nantmel Powys....26 SO0366
Nantmor Gwynd....45 SH6046
Nant Peris Gwynd....45 SH6058
Nantwich Ches E....45 SJ6552
Nantyglo Blae G....27 SO1910
Nant-y-moel Brdgnd....18 SS9392
Naphill Bucks....22 SU8496
Napton on the Hill Warwks....29 SP4661
Narberth Pembks....16 SN1015
Narborough Leics....39 SP5497
Narborough Norfk....42 TF7412
Nasareth Gwynd....44 SH4749
Naseby Nhants....39 SP6978
Nash Bucks....30 SP7833
Nash Herefs....27 SO3062
Nash Newpt....19 ST3483
Nash Shrops....37 SO6071
Nash V Glam....18 SS9469
Nash Lee Bucks....22 SP8408
Nassington Nhants....40 TL0696
Nateby Cumb....60 NY7706
Nateby Lancs....53 SD4644
Natland Cumb....59 SD5289
Naughton Suffk....32 TM0249
Naunton Gloucs....29 SP1123
Naunton Worcs....28 SO8739

132 Naunton Beauchamp – Padstow

Naunton Beauchamp Worcs 28 SO9652
Navenby Lincs 50 SK9858
Navestock Essex 23 TQ5397
Navestock Side Essex 24 TQ5697
Nawton N York 62 SE6584
Nayland Suffk 25 TL9734
Nazeing Essex 23 TL4106
Neap Shet 100 HU5058
Near Cotton Staffs 48 SK0646
Near Sawrey Cumb 59 SD3795
Neasden Gt Lon 23 TQ2185
Neasham Darltn 62 NZ3210
Neath Neath 18 SS7597
Neatham Hants 11 SU7440
Neatishead Norfk 43 TG3420
Nebo Cerdgn 34 SN5465
Nebo Conwy 45 SH8355
Nebo Gwynd 44 SH4850
Nebo IoA 44 SH4690
Necton Norfk 42 TF8709
Nedd Highld 98 NC1331
Nedging Suffk 32 TL9948
Nedging Tye Suffk 32 TM0149
Needham Norfk 33 TM2281
Needham Market Suffk 33 TM0855
Needingworth Cambs 31 TL3472
Neen Savage Shrops 37 SO6777
Neen Sollars Shrops 37 SO6672
Neenton Shrops 37 SO6387
Nefyn Gwynd 44 SH3040
Neilston E Rens 73 NS4857
Nelson Caerph 18 ST1195
Nelson Lancs 54 SD8638
Nemphlar S Lans 74 NS8544
Nempnett Thrubwell BaNES 19 ST5260
Nenthead Cumb 68 NY7743
Nenthorn Border 76 NT6837
Nercwys Flints 46 SJ2360
Nesbit Nthumb 77 NT9833
Nesfield N York 55 SE0949
Nesscliffe Shrops 36 SJ3819
Neston Ches W 46 SJ2977
Neston Wilts 20 ST8668
Netchwood Shrops 37 SO6291
Nether Alderley Ches E 47 SJ8476
Netheravon Wilts 20 SU1448
Nether Broughton Leics 40 SK6925
Netherbury Dorset 8 SY4799
Netherby N York 55 SE3346
Nether Cerne Dorset 9 SY6798
Nether Compton Dorset 9 ST5917
Nether Dallachy Moray 94 NJ3563
Netherend Gloucs 19 SO5900
Netherfield E Susx 14 TQ7019
Netherfield Notts 49 SK6140
Netherhampton Wilts 10 SU1029
Nether Haugh Rothm 49 SK4196
Netherhay Dorset 8 ST4105
Nether Headon Notts 50 SK7477
Nether Heage Derbys 49 SK3650
Nether Heyford Nhants 30 SP6658
Nether Kellet Lancs 53 SD5068
Nether Langwith Notts 49 SK5370
Netherne-on-the-Hill Surrey 23 TQ2956
Netheroyd Hill Kirk 55 SE1419
Nether Padley Derbys 48 SK2478
Nether Poppleton C York 56 SE5654
Netherseal Derbys 39 SK2812
Nether Silton N York 62 SE4592
Nether Stowey Somset 19 ST1939
Netherthong Kirk 55 SE1309
Netherton Devon 5 SX8971
Netherton Dudley 38 SO9488
Netherton Kirk 55 SE1213
Netherton Nthumb 68 NT9807
Netherton Sefton 46 SJ3599
Netherton Wakefd 55 SE2816
Nethertown Cumb 58 NX9907
Nethertown Staffs 38 SK1017
Nether Wallop Hants 10 SU3036
Nether Wasdale Cumb 58 NY1204
Nether Westcote Gloucs 29 SP2220
Nether Whitacre Warwks 39 SP2392
Nether Winchendon Bucks 30 SP7312
Netherwitton Nthumb 68 NZ0990
Nethy Bridge Highld 93 NJ0020
Netley Hants 10 SU4508
Netley Marsh Hants 10 SU3313
Nettlebed Oxon 22 SU6986
Nettlebridge Somset 19 ST6448
Nettlecombe Dorset 8 SY5195
Nettleden Herts 22 TL0210
Nettleham Lincs 50 TF0075
Nettlestead Kent 14 TQ6852
Nettlestead Green Kent 14 TQ6750
Nettlestone IoW 11 SZ6290
Nettlesworth Dur 69 NZ2547
Nettleton Lincs 50 TA1100
Nettleton Wilts 20 ST8278
Netton Wilts 10 SU1236
Nevern Pembks 16 SN0840
Nevill Holt Leics 40 SP8193
New Abbey D & G 66 NX9666
New Aberdour Abers 95 NJ8863
New Addington Gt Lon 23 TQ3763
Newall Leeds 55 SE1946
New Alresford Hants 11 SU5832
New Alyth P & K 88 NO2447
Newark C Pete 41 TF2100
Newark Ork 100 HY7142
Newark-on-Trent Notts 50 SK7953
Newarthill N Lans 74 NS7859
New Ash Green Kent 14 TQ6065
New Balderton Notts 50 SK8152
New Barn Kent 14 TQ6169
New Barnet Gt Lon 23 TQ2695
Newbattle Mdloth 75 NT3365
New Bewick Nthumb 77 NU0620
Newbiggin Cumb 59 NY4729
Newbiggin Cumb 60 NY6228
Newbiggin Cumb 67 NY5549
Newbiggin Dur 60 NY9127
Newbiggin N York 61 SE0086
Newbiggin-by-the-Sea Nthumb 69 NZ3087
Newbigging Angus 83 NO4936
Newbigging Angus 88 NO2841
Newbigging S Lans 75 NT0145
Newbiggin-on-Lune Cumb 60 NY7005
New Bilton Warwks 39 SP4875
Newbold Derbys 49 SK3672
Newbold on Avon Warwks 39 SP4977
Newbold on Stour Warwks 29 SP2446
Newbold Pacey Warwks 29 SP2957
Newbold Verdon Leics 39 SK4403
New Bolingbroke Lincs 51 TF3057
Newborough C Pete 41 TF2005
Newborough IoA 44 SH4265
Newborough Staffs 38 SK1325
New Boultham Lincs 50 SK9670
Newbourne Suffk 33 TM2743
New Bradwell M Keyn 30 SP8341
New Brampton Derbys 49 SK3771
New Brancepeth Dur 61 NZ2241
Newbridge C Edin 75 NT1272
Newbridge Caerph 19 ST2097
Newbridge Cnwll 2 SW4231
Newbridge D & G 66 NX9479
Newbridge Hants 10 SU2915
Newbridge IoW 10 SZ4187
Newbridge Green Worcs 28 SO8439
Newbridge-on-Wye Powys 26 SO0158
New Brighton Wirral 46 SJ3093
Newbrough Nthumb 68 NY8767
New Buckenham Norfk 33 TM0890
Newbuildings Devon 7 SS7903
Newburgh Abers 95 NJ9925
Newburgh Fife 83 NO2318
Newburgh Lancs 53 SD4810
Newburn N u Ty 69 NZ1665
Newbury Somset 20 ST6949
Newbury W Berk 21 SU4766
Newbury Park Gt Lon 23 TQ4488
Newby Cumb 59 NY5921
Newby Lancs 54 SD8146
Newby N York 54 SD7269
Newby N York 62 NZ5012
Newby Bridge Cumb 59 SD3686
Newby East Cumb 67 NY4758
Newby West Cumb 67 NY3753
Newcastle Mons 27 SO4417
Newcastle Shrops 36 SO2582
Newcastle Airport Nthumb 69 NZ1871
Newcastle Emlyn Carmth 17 SN3040
Newcastleton Border 67 NY4887
Newcastle-under-Lyme Staffs 47 SJ8445
Newcastle upon Tyne N u Ty 69 NZ2464
Newchapel Pembks 17 SN2239
Newchapel Surrey 12 TQ3641
Newchurch IoW 11 SZ5685
Newchurch Kent 15 TR0531
Newchurch Mons 19 ST4597
Newchurch Powys 27 SO2150
Newchurch Staffs 38 SK1423
New Costessey Norfk 43 TG1810
Newcraighall C Edin 75 NT3272
New Crofton Wakefd 55 SE3817
New Cross Gt Lon 23 TQ3676
New Cross Somset 8 ST4119
New Cumnock E Ayrs 66 NS6213
New Deer Abers 95 NJ8847
New Denham Bucks 22 TQ0484
Newdigate Surrey 12 TQ1942
New Duston Nhants 30 SP7162
New Earswick C York 56 SE6155
New Edlington Donc 49 SK5398
New Ellerby E R Yk 57 TA1639
Newell Green Br For 22 SU8770
New Eltham Gt Lon 23 TQ4472
New End Worcs 28 SP0560
Newenden Kent 14 TQ8327
New England C Pete 40 TF1801
Newent Gloucs 28 SO7225
New Ferry Wirral 46 SJ3385
Newfield Dur 61 NZ2033
New Fletton C Pete 40 TL1997
Newgale Pembks 16 SM8522
New Galloway D & G 65 NX6377
Newgate Street Herts 23 TL3005
New Gilston Fife 83 NO4308
New Grimsby IoS 2 SV8815
Newhall Ches E 47 SJ6145
New Hartley Nthumb 69 NZ3076
Newhaven C Edin 75 NT2576
Newhaven E Susx 13 TQ4401
New Haw Surrey 22 TQ0563
New Hedges Pembks 16 SN1202
New Holland N Linc 57 TA0823
Newholm N York 63 NZ8610
New Houghton Derbys 49 SK4965
New Houghton Norfk 42 TF7927
New Hutton Cumb 59 SD5691
Newick E Susx 13 TQ4121
Newington Kent 14 TQ8564
Newington Kent 15 TR1837
Newington Oxon 21 SU6096
New Inn Carmth 17 SN4736
New Inn Torfn 19 ST3099
New Invention Shrops 36 SO2976
New Lakenham Norfk 43 TG2307
New Lanark S Lans 74 NS8842
Newland C KuH 57 TA0831
Newland Gloucs 27 SO5509
Newland N York 56 SE6824
Newland Somset 7 SS8238
Newland Worcs 28 SO7948
Newlands Nthumb 68 NZ0855
New Leake Lincs 51 TF4057
New Leeds Abers 95 NJ9954
New Lodge Barns 55 SE3508
New Longton Lancs 53 SD5025
New Luce D & G 64 NX1764
Newlyn Cnwll 2 SW4628
Newmachar Abers 95 NJ8819
Newmains N Lans 74 NS8256
New Malden Gt Lon 23 TQ2168
Newman's Green Suffk 32 TL8843
Newmarket Suffk 32 TL6463
New Marske R & Cl 62 NZ6121
New Marston Oxon 29 SP5207
Newmill Border 67 NT4510
New Mill Cnwll 2 SW4534
New Mill Kirk 55 SE1609
Newmill Moray 94 NJ4352
Newmillerdam Wakefd 55 SE3315
New Mills Derbys 48 SK0085
Newmills Mons 27 SO5107
New Mills Powys 36 SJ0901
Newmilns E Ayrs 74 NS5337
New Milton Hants 10 SZ2495
New Mistley Essex 25 TM1231
New Moat Pembks 16 SN0625
Newney Green Essex 24 TL6507
Newnham Hants 22 SU7053
Newnham Herts 31 TL2437
Newnham Kent 14 TQ9557
Newnham Nhants 29 SP5859
Newnham Bridge Worcs 27 SO6469
Newnham on Severn Gloucs 28 SO6911
New Ollerton Notts 49 SK6667
New Oscott Birm 38 SP0994
New Pitsligo Abers 95 NJ8855
Newport Cnwll 4 SX3285
Newport E R Yk 56 SE8530
Newport Essex 31 TL5234
Newport Gloucs 20 ST7097
Newport Highld 100 ND1224
Newport IoW 11 SZ5089
Newport Newpt 19 ST3188
Newport Pembks 16 SN0539
Newport Wrekin 37 SJ7419
Newport-on-Tay Fife 83 NO4227
Newport Pagnell M Keyn 30 SP8743
Newport Pagnell Services M Keyn 30 SP8543
New Prestwick S Ayrs 73 NS3424
New Quay Cerdgn 34 SN3959
Newquay Cnwll 2 SW8161
New Rackheath Norfk 43 TG2812
New Radnor Powys 27 SO2161
New Ridley Nthumb 68 NZ0559
New Romney Kent 15 TR0624
New Rossington Donc 49 SK6198
New Sauchie Clacks 82 NS8994
Newsham Lancs 53 SD5136
Newsham N York 61 NZ1010
Newsham N York 62 SE3784
Newsham Nthumb 69 NZ3080
New Sharlston Wakefd 55 SE3819
Newsholme E R Yk 56 SE7129
New Silksworth Sundld 69 NZ3853
Newsome Kirk 55 SE1514
New Somerby Lincs 40 SK9235
Newstead Border 76 NT5634
Newstead Notts 49 SK5152
Newstead Nthumb 77 NU1527
New Stevenston N Lans 74 NS7659
Newthorpe Notts 49 SK4745
New Thundersley Essex 24 TQ7789
Newton Brdgnd 18 SS8377
Newton C Beds 31 TL2344
Newton Cambs 31 TL4349
Newton Cambs 41 TF4314
Newton Ches W 46 SJ4167
Newton Ches W 46 SJ5059
Newton Cumb 53 SD2271
Newton Derbys 49 SK4459
Newton Herefs 27 SO3432
Newton Herefs 27 SO5153
Newton Lincs 40 TF0436
Newton Nhants 40 SP8883
Newton Norfk 42 TF8315
Newton Notts 49 SK6841
Newton Nthumb 68 NZ0364
Newton Sandw 38 SP0393
Newton Staffs 38 SK0325
Newton Suffk 32 TL9240
Newton W Loth 75 NT0977
Newton Warwks 39 SP5378
Newton Abbot Devon 5 SX8571
Newton Arlosh Cumb 67 NY2055
Newton Aycliffe Dur 61 NZ2724
Newton Bewley Hartpl 62 NZ4626
Newton Blossomville M Keyn 30 SP9251
Newton Bromswold Nhants 30 SP9966
Newton Burgoland Leics 39 SK3708
Newton-by-the-Sea Nthumb 77 NU2325
Newton by Toft Lincs 50 TF0487
Newton Ferrers Devon 5 SX5548
Newton Ferry W Isls 90 NF8977
Newton Flotman Norfk 43 TM2198
Newtongrange Mdloth 75 NT3364
Newton Green Mons 19 ST5191
Newton Harcourt Leics 39 SP6497
Newton Heath Manch 47 SD8700
Newtonhill Abers 89 NO9193
Newton-in-Bowland Lancs 54 SD6950
Newton Kyme N York 55 SE4644
Newton-le-Willows N York 61 SE2189
Newton-le-Willows St Hel 47 SJ5995
Newtonloan Mdloth 75 NT3362
Newton Longville Bucks 30 SP8431
Newton Mearns E Rens 74 NS5355
Newtonmore Highld 87 NN7098
Newton Morrell N York 61 NZ2309
Newton of Balcanquhal P & K 82 NO1610
Newton-on-Ouse N York 55 SE5159
Newton-on-Rawcliffe N York 63 SE8090
Newton-on-the-Moor Nthumb 69 NU1705
Newton on Trent Lincs 50 SK8373
Newton Poppleford Devon 8 SY0889
Newton Purcell Oxon 29 SP6230
Newton Regis Warwks 39 SK2707
Newton Reigny Cumb 59 NY4731
Newton St Cyres Devon 7 SX8898
Newton St Faith Norfk 43 TG2217
Newton St Loe BaNES 20 ST7064
Newton St Petrock Devon 6 SS4112
Newton Solney Derbys 39 SK2825
Newton Stacey Hants 21 SU4140
Newton Stewart D & G 64 NX4065
Newton Tony Wilts 21 SU2140
Newton Tracey Devon 6 SS5226
Newton under Roseberry R & Cl 62 NZ5713
Newton upon Derwent E R Yk 56 SE7149
Newton Valence Hants 11 SU7232
Newton Wamphray D & G 67 NY1195
Newton with Scales Lancs 53 SD4530
Newtown BCP 10 SZ0393
Newtown Cumb 67 NY1048
Newtown Cumb 67 NY5062
Newtown Devon 7 SS7625
Newtown Devon 7 SY0699
New Town E Susx 13 TQ4720
Newtown Gloucs 20 SO6702
Newtown Hants 11 SU6013
Newtown Herefs 27 SO6145
Newtown IoW 10 SZ4290
Newtown Nthumb 77 NU0425
Newtown Powys 36 SO1091
Newtown Shrops 37 SJ4731
Newtown Somset 8 ST2712
Newtown Staffs 48 SJ9060
Newtown Wigan 47 SD5604
Newtown Worcs 28 SO8755
Newtown Linford Leics 39 SK5209
Newtown St Boswells Border 76 NT5732
New Tredegar Caerph 18 SO1402
New Trows S Lans 74 NS8038
Newtyle Angus 88 NO2941
New Walsoken Cambs 41 TF4609
New Waltham NE Lin 57 TA2804
New Winton E Loth 76 NT4271
New York Lincs 51 TF2455
New York N Tyne 69 NZ3270
Neyland Pembks 16 SM9605
Nicholashayne Devon 8 ST1016
Nicholaston Swans 17 SS5288
Nidd N York 55 SE3060
Nigg C Aber 89 NJ9402
Nigg Highld 93 NH8071
Ninebanks Nthumb 68 NY7853
Nine Elms Swindn 20 SU1186
Ninfield E Susx 14 TQ7012
Ningwood IoW 10 SZ3989
Nisbet Border 76 NT6725
Nisbet Hill Border 76 NT7950
Niton IoW 11 SZ5076
Nitshill C Glas 74 NS5260
Nocton Lincs 50 TF0564
Noke Oxon 29 SP5413
Nolton Pembks 16 SM8618
Nolton Haven Pembks 16 SM8618
No Man's Heath Ches W 46 SJ5148
No Man's Heath Warwks 39 SK2808
Nomansland Devon 7 SS8313
Nomansland Wilts 10 SU2517
Noneley Shrops 37 SJ4828
Nonington Kent 15 TR2552
Nook Cumb 59 SD5481
Norbiton Gt Lon 23 TQ1969
Norbury Ches E 47 SJ5547
Norbury Derbys 48 SK1241
Norbury Gt Lon 23 TQ3069
Norbury Shrops 36 SO3692
Norbury Staffs 37 SJ7823
Norchard Worcs 28 SO8468
Nordelph Norfk 41 TF5501
Nordley Shrops 37 SO6996
Norham Nthumb 77 NT9047
Norley Ches W 47 SJ5772
Norleywood Hants 10 SZ3597
Normanby Lincs 50 SK9988
Normanby N Linc 56 SE8816
Normanby N York 63 SE7381
Normanby R & Cl 62 NZ5418
Normanby le Wold Lincs 50 TF1295
Normandy Surrey 12 SU9351
Norman's Green Devon 7 ST0503
Normanton C Derb 39 SK3433
Normanton Leics 50 SK8140
Normanton Notts 49 SK7054
Normanton Wakefd 55 SE3822
Normanton le Heath Leics 39 SK3712
Normanton on Cliffe Lincs 50 SK9446
Normanton on Soar Notts 39 SK5122
Normanton on the Wolds Notts 39 SK6232
Normanton on Trent Notts 50 SK7868
Norris Green Lpool 46 SJ3994
Norris Hill Leics 39 SK3216
Norristhorpe Kirk 55 SE2123
Northall Bucks 30 SP9520
Northallerton N York 62 SE3694
Northam C Sotn 10 SU4312
Northam Devon 6 SS4529
Northampton Nhants 30 SP7560
Northampton Worcs 28 SO8365
Northampton Services Nhants 30 SP7257
North Anston Rothm 49 SK5184
North Ascot Br For 22 SU9169
North Aston Oxon 29 SP4828
Northaw Herts 23 TL2702
Northay Somset 8 ST2811
North Baddesley Hants 10 SU3920
North Ballachulish Highld 86 NN0560
North Barrow Somset 9 ST6129
North Barsham Norfk 42 TF9135
Northbay W Isls 90 NF7003
North Benfleet Essex 24 TQ7588
North Berwick E Loth 83 NT5485
North Boarhunt Hants 11 SU6010
Northborough C Pete 40 TF1507
Northbourne Kent 15 TR3352
North Bovey Devon 5 SX7484
North Bradley Wilts 20 ST8555
North Brentor Devon 4 SX4881
North Brewham Somset 20 ST7236
Northbrook Hants 11 SU5139
North Buckland Devon 6 SS4840
North Burlingham Norfk 43 TG3609
North Cadbury Somset 9 ST6327
North Carlton Lincs 50 SK9477
North Carlton Notts 49 SK5984
North Cave E R Yk 56 SE8932
North Cerney Gloucs 28 SP0107
North Chailey E Susx 13 TQ3921
Northchapel W Susx 12 SU9529
North Charford Hants 10 SU1919
North Charlton Nthumb 77 NU1622
North Cheam Gt Lon 23 TQ2365
North Cheriton Somset 9 ST6925
North Chideock Dorset 8 SY4294
Northchurch Herts 22 SP9708
North Cliffe E R Yk 56 SE8736
North Clifton Notts 50 SK8272
North Cockerington Lincs 51 TF3790
North Cornelly Brdgnd 18 SS8181
North Cotes Lincs 51 TA3400
Northcott Devon 4 SX3392
Northcourt Oxon 21 SU4998
North Cove Suffk 33 TM4689
North Cowton N York 61 NZ2803
North Crawley M Keyn 30 SP9244
North Creake Norfk 42 TF8538
North Curry Somset 8 ST3125
North Dalton E R Yk 56 SE9351
North Deighton N York 55 SE3951
Northdown Kent 15 TR3770
North Duffield N York 56 SE6837
North Elmham Norfk 42 TF9820
North Elmsall Wakefd 55 SE4712
North End C Port 11 SU6502
North End Essex 24 TL6618
North End Hants 10 SU1016
North End Nhants 30 SP9668
North End W Susx 12 SU9703
Northend Warwks 29 SP3952
Northenden Manch 47 SJ8289
North Erradale Highld 91 NG7480
North Evington C Leic 39 SK6204
North Fambridge Essex 24 TQ8597
North Ferriby E R Yk 56 SE9826
Northfield Birm 38 SP0279
Northfield C Aber 95 NJ9008
Northfield E R Yk 57 TA0326
Northfields Lincs 40 TF0208
Northfleet Kent 14 TQ6374
North Frodingham E R Yk 57 TA1053
North Gorley Hants 10 SU1611
North Green Suffk 33 TM3162
North Greetwell Lincs 50 TF0173
North Grimston N York 56 SE8467
North Hayling Hants 11 SU7303
North Hill Cnwll 4 SX2776
North Hillingdon Gt Lon 22 TQ0784
North Hinksey Village Oxon 29 SP4905
North Holmwood Surrey 12 TQ1647
North Huish Devon 5 SX7156
North Hykeham Lincs 50 SK9465
Northiam E Susx 14 TQ8324
Northill C Beds 30 TL1446
Northington Hants 11 SU5637
North Kelsey Lincs 50 TA0401
North Kessock Highld 93 NH6548
North Killingholme N Linc 57 TA1417
North Kilvington N York 62 SE4285
North Kilworth Leics 39 SP6183
North Kyme Lincs 50 TF1552
North Landing E R Yk 57 TA2471
Northlands Lincs 51 TF3453
Northleach Gloucs 28 SP1114
North Lee Bucks 22 SP8308
Northleigh Devon 8 SY1995
North Leigh Oxon 29 SP3813
North Leverton with Habblesthorpe Notts 50 SK7882
Northlew Devon 6 SX5099
North Littleton Worcs 28 SP0847
North Lopham Norfk 32 TM0382
North Luffenham Rutlnd 40 SK9303
North Marden W Susx 11 SU8016
North Marston Bucks 30 SP7722
North Middleton Mdloth 76 NT3559
North Molton Devon 7 SS7329
Northmoor Oxon 21 SP4202
North Moreton Oxon 21 SU5689
Northmuir Angus 88 NO3855
North Mundham W Susx 11 SU8702
North Muskham Notts 50 SK7958
North Newbald E R Yk 56 SE9136
North Newington Oxon 29 SP4240
North Newnton Wilts 20 SU1257
North Newton Somset 8 ST3031
Northney Hants 11 SU7303
North Nibley Gloucs 20 ST7495
Northolt Gt Lon 22 TQ1384
Northolt Airport Gt Lon 22 TQ0985
Northop Flints 46 SJ2468
Northop Hall Flints 46 SJ2667
North Ormesby Middsb 62 NZ5119
North Ormsby Lincs 51 TF2893
Northorpe Kirk 55 SE2121
Northorpe Lincs 41 TF2036
Northorpe Lincs 50 SK8997
North Otterington N York 62 SE3689
North Owersby Lincs 50 TF0594
Northowram Calder 55 SE1126
North Perrott Somset 8 ST4709
North Petherton Somset 8 ST2833
North Petherwin Cnwll 4 SX2789
North Pickenham Norfk 42 TF8606
North Piddle Worcs 28 SO9654
North Poorton Dorset 8 SY5298
Northport Dorset 9 SY9288
North Queensferry Fife 82 NT1380
North Rauceby Lincs 50 TF0246
Northrepps Norfk 43 TG2439
North Reston Lincs 51 TF3883
North Rigton N York 55 SE2749
North Rode Ches E 47 SJ8866
North Ronaldsay Airport Ork 100 HY7554
North Runcton Norfk 42 TF6416
North Scarle Lincs 50 SK8466
North Shields N Tyne 69 NZ3568
North Shoebury Sthend 25 TQ9286
North Shore Bpool 53 SD3037
North Side C Pete 41 TL2799
North Somercotes Lincs 51 TF4296
North Stainley N York 61 SE2876
North Stifford Thurr 24 TQ6080
North Stoke BaNES 20 ST7069
North Stoke Oxon 21 SU6186
North Stoke W Susx 12 TQ0110
North Street Kent 15 TR0157
North Street W Berk 21 SU6371
North Sunderland Nthumb 77 NU2131
North Tamerton Cnwll 6 SX3197
North Tawton Devon 7 SS6601
North Thoresby Lincs 51 TF2998
North Tolsta W Isls 90 NB5347
North Town Devon 6 SS5109
North Town Somset 19 ST5642
North Town W & M 22 SU8882
North Tuddenham Norfk 42 TG0314
North Walsham Norfk 43 TG2830
North Waltham Hants 21 SU5646
North Warnborough Hants 22 SU7351
North Weald Bassett Essex 23 TL4904
North Wheatley Notts 50 SK7585
Northwich Ches W 47 SJ6673
Northwick Worcs 28 SO8458
North Widcombe BaNES 19 ST5758
North Willingham Lincs 50 TF1688
North Wingfield Derbys 49 SK4065
North Witham Lincs 40 SK9221
Northwold Norfk 42 TL7597
Northwood C Stke 48 SJ8949
Northwood Gt Lon 22 TQ0991
Northwood IoW 11 SZ4893
Northwood Shrops 37 SJ4633
Northwood Green Gloucs 28 SO7216
North Wootton Dorset 9 ST6514
North Wootton Norfk 42 TF6424
North Wootton Somset 19 ST5641
North Wraxall Wilts 20 ST8175
Norton Donc 56 SE5415
Norton E Susx 13 TQ4701
Norton Gloucs 28 SO8524
Norton Halton 47 SJ5581
Norton Nhants 29 SP5963
Norton Notts 49 SK5671
Norton Powys 27 SO3067
Norton S on T 62 NZ4421
Norton Sheff 49 SK3681
Norton Shrops 37 SJ7200
Norton Suffk 32 TL9565
Norton Swans 17 SS6188
Norton W Susx 12 SU9206
Norton Wilts 20 ST8884
Norton Worcs 28 SO8751
Norton Worcs 28 SP0447
Norton Bavant Wilts 20 ST9043
Norton Canes Staffs 38 SK0108
Norton Canes Services Staffs 38 SK0207
Norton Canon Herefs 27 SO3847
Norton Disney Lincs 50 SK8859
Norton Fitzwarren Somset 8 ST1925
Norton Green IoW 10 SZ3488
Norton Hawkfield BaNES 19 ST5964
Norton Heath Essex 24 TL6004
Norton in Hales Shrops 37 SJ7038
Norton-Juxta-Twycross Leics 39 SK3207
Norton-le-Clay N York 55 SE4071
Norton-le-Moors C Stke 48 SJ8951
Norton Lindsey Warwks 29 SP2263
Norton Little Green Suffk 32 TL9766
Norton Malreward BaNES 19 ST6064
Norton-on-Derwent N York 56 SE7971
Norton St Philip Somset 20 ST7755
Norton Subcourse Norfk 43 TM4198
Norton sub Hamdon Somset 8 ST4615
Norwell Notts 50 SK7761
Norwell Woodhouse Notts 50 SK7362
Norwich Norfk 43 TG2308
Norwich Airport Norfk 43 TG2113
Norwick Shet 100 HP6414
Norwood Clacks 82 NS8793
Norwood Green Gt Lon 22 TQ1378
Norwood Hill Surrey 12 TQ2343
Norwoodside Cambs 41 TL4197
Noss Mayo Devon 5 SX5547
Nosterfield N York 61 SE2780
Notgrove Gloucs 28 SP1020
Nottage Brdgnd 18 SS8177
Nottingham C Nott 49 SK5739
Notton Wakefd 55 SE3413
Notton Wilts 20 ST9169
Noutard's Green Worcs 28 SO8066
Nuffield Oxon 22 SU6687
Nunburnholme E R Yk 56 SE8447
Nuneaton Warwks 39 SP3691
Nunhead Gt Lon 23 TQ3475
Nun Monkton N York 55 SE5057
Nunney Somset 20 ST7345
Nunnington N York 62 SE6679
Nunsthorpe NE Lin 57 TA2607
Nunthorpe C York 56 SE6050
Nunthorpe Middsb 62 NZ5314
Nunthorpe Village Middsb 62 NZ5413
Nunton Wilts 10 SU1526
Nunwick N York 62 SE3274
Nursling Hants 10 SU3716
Nutbourne W Susx 11 SU7705
Nutbourne W Susx 12 TQ0718
Nutfield Surrey 12 TQ3050
Nuthall Notts 49 SK5243
Nuthampstead Herts 31 TL4034
Nuthurst W Susx 12 TQ1925
Nutley E Susx 13 TQ4427
Nuttall Bury 54 SD7915
Nyetimber W Susx 11 SZ8998
Nyewood W Susx 11 SU8021
Nymet Rowland Devon 7 SS7108
Nymet Tracey Devon 7 SS7200
Nympsfield Gloucs 20 SO8000
Nynehead Somset 8 ST1422
Nyton W Susx 12 SU9305

O

Oadby Leics 39 SK6200
Oad Street Kent 14 TQ8762
Oakamoor Staffs 48 SK0444
Oak Cross Devon 6 SX5399
Oakdale Caerph 19 ST1898
Oake Somset 8 ST1525
Oaken Staffs 38 SJ8502
Oakenclough Lancs 53 SD5447
Oakengates Wrekin 37 SJ7011
Oakenshaw Dur 61 NZ1937
Oakenshaw Kirk 55 SE1727
Oakford Cerdgn 34 SN4558
Oakford Devon 7 SS9121
Oakham Rutlnd 40 SK8608
Oakhanger Hants 11 SU7635
Oakhill Somset 19 ST6347
Oakington Cambs 31 TL4164
Oakle Street Gloucs 28 SO7517
Oakley Bed 30 TL0153
Oakley Bucks 29 SP6412
Oakley Fife 82 NT0289
Oakley Hants 21 SU5650
Oakley Suffk 33 TM1677
Oakridge Lynch Gloucs 28 SO9103
Oaksey Wilts 20 ST9993
Oakthorpe Leics 39 SK3212
Oakwood C Derb 49 SK3738
Oakworth C Brad 55 SE0338
Oare Kent 15 TR0063
Oare Somset 18 SS7947
Oare Wilts 20 SU1563
Oasby Lincs 40 TF0039
Oath Somset 8 ST3827
Oathlaw Angus 89 NO4756
Oatlands Park Surrey 22 TQ0865
Oban Ag & B 79 NM8629
Oban Airport Ag & B 79 NM9035
Obley Shrops 36 SO3377
Oborne Dorset 9 ST6518
Occold Suffk 33 TM1570
Ochiltree E Ayrs 74 NS5021
Ockbrook Derbys 39 SK4235
Ocker Hill Sandw 38 SO9793
Ockham Surrey 22 TQ0756
Ockley Surrey 12 TQ1440
Ocle Pychard Herefs 27 SO5945
Odcombe Somset 8 ST5015
Odd Down BaNES 20 ST7462
Oddingley Worcs 28 SO9159
Oddington Gloucs 29 SP2225
Oddington Oxon 29 SP5515
Odell Bed 30 SP9657
Odiham Hants 22 SU7451
Odsal C Brad 55 SE1529
Odsey Cambs 31 TL2938
Odstock Wilts 10 SU1426
Odstone Leics 39 SK3907
Offchurch Warwks 29 SP3565
Offenham Worcs 28 SP0546
Offerton Stockp 48 SJ9189
Offham E Susx 13 TQ4012
Offham Kent 14 TQ6557
Offham W Susx 12 TQ0208
Offord Cluny Cambs 31 TL2267
Offord D'Arcy Cambs 31 TL2266
Offton Suffk 32 TM0649
Offwell Devon 8 SY1999
Ogbourne Maizey Wilts 21 SU1871
Ogbourne St Andrew Wilts 21 SU1872
Ogbourne St George Wilts 21 SU2074
Ogle Nthumb 69 NZ1378
Oglet Lpool 46 SJ4481
Ogmore V Glam 18 SS8876
Ogmore-by-Sea V Glam 18 SS8675
Ogmore Vale Brdgnd 18 SS9390
Okeford Fitzpaine Dorset 9 ST8010
Okehampton Devon 6 SX5995
Oker Side Derbys 49 SK2760
Okewood Hill Surrey 12 TQ1337
Old Nhants 30 SP7872
Old Aberdeen C Aber 95 NJ9407
Old Alresford Hants 11 SU5834
Old Basford C Nott 49 SK5543
Old Basing Hants 22 SU6652
Old Beetley Norfk 42 TF9718
Oldberrow Warwks 28 SP1265
Old Bewick Nthumb 77 NU0621
Old Bolingbroke Lincs 51 TF3565
Old Bramhope Leeds 55 SE2343
Old Brampton Derbys 49 SK3371
Old Buckenham Norfk 32 TM0691
Old Burghclere Hants 21 SU4657
Oldbury Sandw 38 SO9988
Oldbury Shrops 37 SO7192
Oldbury Warwks 39 SP3194
Oldbury-on-Severn S Glos 19 ST6092
Oldbury on the Hill Gloucs 20 ST8188
Old Byland N York 62 SE5585
Old Cantley Donc 49 SE6202
Oldcastle Mons 27 SO3224
Old Catton Norfk 43 TG2312
Old Clee NE Lin 57 TA2808
Old Cleeve Somset 7 ST0441
Old Colwyn Conwy 45 SH8678
Oldcotes Notts 49 SK5888
Old Coulsdon Gt Lon 23 TQ3157
Old Dailly S Ayrs 64 NX2299
Old Dalby Leics 39 SK6723
Old Deer Abers 95 NJ9747
Old Edlington Donc 49 SK5397
Old Ellerby E R Yk 57 TA1637
Old Felixstowe Suffk 25 TM3135
Oldfield Worcs 28 SO8464
Old Fletton C Pete 41 TL1997
Oldford Somset 20 ST7850
Old Forge Herefs 27 SO5518
Old Grimsby IoS 2 SV8915
Old Hall Green Herts 31 TL3722
Oldham Oldham 54 SD9204
Oldhamstocks E Loth 76 NT7470
Old Harlow Essex 23 TL4711
Old Hunstanton Norfk 42 TF6842
Old Hurst Cambs 31 TL3077
Old Hutton Cumb 59 SD5688
Old Inns Services N Lans 74 NS7777
Old Kilpatrick W Duns 81 NS4672
Old Knebworth Herts 31 TL2320
Old Lakenham Norfk 43 TG2205
Oldland S Glos 20 ST6771
Old Langho Lancs 54 SD7035
Old Leake Lincs 51 TF4050
Old Malton N York 63 SE7972
Oldmeldrum Abers 95 NJ8127
Oldmill Cnwll 4 SX3673
Old Milverton Warwks 29 SP2967
Oldmixon N Som 19 ST3358
Old Newton Suffk 32 TM0562
Old Radford C Nott 49 SK5540
Old Radnor Powys 27 SO2558
Old Rayne Abers 95 NJ6728
Old Romney Kent 15 TR0325
Old Shoreham W Susx 12 TQ2006
Old Sodbury S Glos 20 ST7581
Old Somerby Lincs 40 SK9633
Oldstead N York 62 SE5379
Old Stratford Nhants 30 SP7741
Old Swinford Dudley 38 SO9083
Old Thirsk N York 62 SE4382
Old Town Cumb 59 SD5982
Old Town E Susx 13 TV5999
Old Town IoS 2 SV9110
Old Trafford Traffd 47 SJ8196
Oldwall Cumb 67 NY4761
Oldwalls Swans 17 SS4891
Old Warden C Beds 30 TL1343
Old Weston Cambs 30 TL0977
Old Wick Highld 100 ND3649
Old Windsor W & M 22 SU9874
Old Wives Lees Kent 15 TR0754
Old Woking Surrey 22 TQ0157
Olive Green Staffs 38 SK1118
Oliver's Battery Hants 10 SU4527
Ollaberry Shet 100 HU3680
Ollerton Ches E 47 SJ7776
Ollerton Notts 49 SK6567
Ollerton Shrops 37 SJ6425
Olney M Keyn 30 SP8951
Olton Solhll 38 SP1382
Olveston S Glos 19 ST6086
Ombersley Worcs 28 SO8464
Ompton Notts 49 SK6865
Onchan IoM 52 SC3978
Onecote Staffs 48 SK0455
Onibury Shrops 36 SO4579
Onich Highld 86 NN0261
Onllwyn Neath 26 SN8410
Onneley Staffs 47 SJ7542
Onslow Green Essex 24 TL6518
Onslow Village Surrey 12 SU9849
Onston Ches W 47 SJ5873
Opinan Highld 91 NG7472
Orby Lincs 51 TF4967
Orchard Portman Somset 8 ST2421
Orcheston Wilts 20 SU0545
Orcop Herefs 27 SO4726
Orcop Hill Herefs 27 SO4727
Ordhead Abers 95 NJ6610
Ordie Abers 89 NJ4501
Ordsall Notts 49 SK7079
Ore E Susx 14 TQ8311
Orford Suffk 33 TM4250
Orford Warrtn 47 SJ6190
Organford Dorset 9 SY9392
Orlestone Kent 15 TR0034
Orleton Herefs 27 SO4967
Orleton Worcs 28 SO7067
Orlingbury Nhants 30 SP8572
Ormesby R & Cl 62 NZ5317
Ormesby St Margaret Norfk 43 TG4914
Ormesby St Michael Norfk 43 TG4714
Ormiston E Loth 76 NT4169
Ormskirk Lancs 53 SD4108
Orphir Ork 100 HY3404
Orpington Gt Lon 23 TQ4666
Orrell Sefton 46 SJ3496
Orrell Wigan 47 SD5303
Orsett Thurr 24 TQ6482
Orslow Staffs 37 SJ8015
Orston Notts 50 SK7740
Orton Cumb 60 NY6208
Orton Nhants 40 SP8079
Orton Staffs 38 SO8795
Orton Longueville C Pete 40 TL1796
Orton-on-the-Hill Leics 39 SK3003
Orton Waterville C Pete 40 TL1595
Orwell Cambs 31 TL3650
Osbaldeston Lancs 54 SD6431
Osbaldwick C York 56 SE6251
Osbaston Leics 39 SK4204
Osbaston Shrops 36 SJ3222
Osbournby Lincs 40 TF0638
Oscroft Ches W 46 SJ5067
Osgathorpe Leics 39 SK4319
Osgodby Lincs 50 TF0792
Osgodby N York 56 SE6433
Osgodby N York 63 TA0584
Osmaston Derbys 48 SK1943
Osmington Dorset 9 SY7283
Osmington Mills Dorset 9 SY7381
Osmondthorpe Leeds 55 SE3333
Osmotherley N York 62 SE4596
Osney Oxon 29 SP4906
Ospringe Kent 15 TR0060
Ossett Wakefd 55 SE2720
Ossington Notts 50 SK7564
Osterley Gt Lon 23 TQ1577
Oswaldkirk N York 62 SE6278
Oswaldtwistle Lancs 54 SD7327
Oswestry Shrops 36 SJ2929
Otford Kent 23 TQ5359
Otham Kent 14 TQ7953
Othery Somset 8 ST3831
Otley Leeds 55 SE2045
Otley Suffk 33 TM2055
Otterbourne Hants 10 SU4522
Otterburn N York 54 SD8857
Otterburn Nthumb 68 NY8893
Otter Ferry Ag & B 71 NR9384
Otterham Cnwll 4 SX1690
Otterhampton Somset 19 ST2443
Ottershaw Surrey 22 TQ0263
Otterton Devon 8 SY0885
Ottery St Mary Devon 8 SY1095
Ottinge Kent 15 TR1642
Ottringham E R Yk 57 TA2624
Oughterside Cumb 58 NY1140
Oughtibridge Sheff 49 SK3093
Oughtrington Warrtn 47 SJ6987
Oulston N York 62 SE5474
Oulton Cumb 67 NY2450
Oulton Norfk 43 TG1328
Oulton Staffs 38 SJ9035
Oulton Suffk 43 TM5294
Oulton Broad Suffk 33 TM5192
Oulton Street Norfk 43 TG1527
Oundle Nhants 40 TL0388
Ounsdale Staffs 38 SO8693
Ousby Cumb 59 NY6134
Ousden Suffk 32 TL7459
Ousefleet E R Yk 56 SE8323
Ouston Dur 69 NZ2554
Outgate Cumb 59 SD3599
Outhgill Cumb 60 NY7801
Outhill Warwks 28 SP1066
Outlane Kirk 55 SE0817
Out Rawcliffe Lancs 53 SD4041
Outwell Norfk 41 TF5103
Outwood Surrey 12 TQ3145
Outwoods Staffs 37 SJ7817
Ouzlewell Green Leeds 55 SE3326
Over Cambs 31 TL3770
Overbury Worcs 28 SO9537
Overcombe Dorset 9 SY6982
Over Compton Dorset 9 ST5816
Over Haddon Derbys 48 SK2066
Over Kellet Lancs 53 SD5169
Over Kiddington Oxon 29 SP4021
Overleigh Somset 8 ST4835
Over Norton Oxon 29 SP3128
Over Peover Ches E 47 SJ7873
Overpool Ches W 46 SJ3877
Overseal Derbys 39 SK2915
Over Silton N York 62 SE4493
Oversland Kent 15 TR0557
Overstone Nhants 30 SP7966
Over Stowey Somset 19 ST1838
Overstrand Norfk 43 TG2440
Over Stratton Somset 8 ST4315
Overthorpe Nhants 29 SP4840
Overton Hants 21 SU5149
Overton Lancs 53 SD4358
Overton N York 56 SE5555
Overton Shrops 37 SO5072
Overton Swans 17 SS4685
Overton Wakefd 55 SE2516
Overton Wrexhm 36 SJ3741
Overtown N Lans 74 NS8053
Over Wallop Hants 10 SU2838
Over Whitacre Warwks 39 SP2590
Over Worton Oxon 29 SP4329
Oving Bucks 30 SP7821
Oving W Susx 11 SU9004
Ovingdean Br & H 12 TQ3503
Ovingham Nthumb 68 NZ0863
Ovington Dur 61 NZ1314
Ovington Essex 32 TL7642
Ovington Hants 11 SU5631
Ovington Norfk 42 TF9202
Ovington Nthumb 68 NZ0663
Ower Hants 10 SU3216
Owermoigne Dorset 9 SY7685
Owlerton Sheff 49 SK3389
Owlsmoor Br For 22 SU8462
Owlswick Bucks 22 SP7806
Owmby Lincs 50 TF0087
Owmby Lincs 57 TA0704
Owslebury Hants 11 SU5123
Owston Donc 56 SE5511
Owston Leics 40 SK7707
Owston Ferry N Linc 50 SE8000
Owstwick E R Yk 57 TA2732
Owthorne E R Yk 57 TA3328
Owthorpe Notts 39 SK6733
Owton Manor Hartpl 62 NZ4829
Oxborough Norfk 42 TF7401
Oxcombe Lincs 51 TF3177
Oxenholme Cumb 59 SD5389
Oxenhope C Brad 55 SE0334
Oxen Park Cumb 58 SD3187
Oxenpill Somset 19 ST4441
Oxenton Gloucs 28 SO9531
Oxenwood Wilts 21 SU3058
Oxford Oxon 29 SP5106
Oxford Airport Oxon 29 SP4615
Oxford Services Oxon 29 SP6204
Oxhey Herts 22 TQ1295
Oxhill Dur 69 NZ1852
Oxhill Warwks 29 SP3146
Oxley Wolves 38 SJ9001
Oxley Green Essex 24 TL9014
Oxlode Cambs 41 TL4886
Oxnam Border 76 NT6918
Oxnead Norfk 43 TG2224
Oxshott Surrey 22 TQ1460
Oxspring Barns 49 SE2601
Oxted Surrey 13 TQ3952
Oxton Border 76 NT4953
Oxton N York 55 SE5042
Oxton Notts 49 SK6351
Oxton Wirral 46 SJ3087
Oxwich Swans 17 SS4986
Oxwich Green Swans 17 SS4985
Oyne Abers 95 NJ6725
Oystermouth Swans 17 SS6187

P

Pabail W Isls 90 NB5231
Packington Leics 39 SK3614
Packmoor C Stke 47 SJ8654
Padanaram Angus 88 NO4251
Padbury Bucks 30 SP7230
Paddington Gt Lon 23 TQ2681
Paddlesworth Kent 14 TQ6862
Paddlesworth Kent 15 TR1939
Paddock Wood Kent 14 TQ6644
Padiham Lancs 54 SD7933
Padside N York 55 SE1659
Padstow Cnwll 3 SW9175

134 Rickerscote – Shiptonthorpe

Rickerscote Staffs 38 SJ9220
Rickford N Som 19 ST4859
Rickham Devon 5 SX7537
Rickinghall Suffk 32 TM0475
Rickling Green Essex 31 TL5129
Rickmansworth Herts 22 TQ0694
Riddlecombe Devon 7 SS6113
Riddlesden C Brad 55 SE0742
Ridge Dorset 9 SY9386
Ridge Herts 23 TL2100
Ridge Wilts 9 ST9531
Ridge Lane Warwks 39 SP2994
Ridgeway Derbys 49 SK4081
Ridgewell Essex 32 TL7340
Ridgewood E Susx 13 TQ4719
Ridgmont C Beds 30 SP9736
Riding Mill Nthumb 68 NZ0261
Ridlington Norfk 43 TG3430
Ridlington Rutlnd 40 SK8402
Ridsdale Nthumb 68 NY9084
Rievaulx N York 62 SE5785
Rigg D & G 67 NY2966
Rigsby Lincs 51 TF4375
Riley Green Lancs 54 SD6225
Rilla Mill Cnwll 4 SX2973
Rillington N York 63 SE8574
Rimington Lancs 54 SD8045
Rimpton Somset 9 ST6121
Rimswell E R Yk 57 TA3028
Rinaston Pembks 16 SM9825
Rindleford Shrops 37 SO7395
Ringford D & G 65 NX6957
Ringland Norfk 43 TG1313
Ringmer E Susx 13 TQ4412
Ringmore Devon 5 SX6546
Ringmore Devon 5 SX9272
Ringsfield Suffk 33 TM4088
Ringsfield Corner Suffk 33 TM4087
Ringshall Herts 30 SP9814
Ringshall Suffk 32 TM0452
Ringshall Stocks Suffk 32 TM0551
Ringstead Nhants 30 SP9875
Ringstead Norfk 42 TF7040
Ringwood Hants 10 SU1505
Ringwould Kent 15 TR3548
Ripe E Susx 13 TQ5110
Ripley Derbys 49 SK3950
Ripley Hants 10 SZ1698
Ripley N York 55 SE2860
Ripley Surrey 22 TQ0556
Riplington Hants 11 SU6623
Ripon N York 55 SE3171
Rippingale Lincs 40 TF0927
Ripple Kent 15 TR3550
Ripple Worcs 28 SO8737
Ripponden Calder 55 SE0319
Risbury Herefs 27 SO5455
Risby Suffk 32 TL8066
Risca Caerph 19 ST2391
Rise E R Yk 57 TA1542
Risegate Lincs 41 TF2129
Riseley Bed 30 TL0462
Riseley Wokham 22 SU7263
Rishangles Suffk 33 TM1668
Rishton Lancs 54 SD7230
Rishworth Calder 55 SE0318
Risley Derbys 39 SK4535
Risley Warrtn 47 SJ6592
Risplith N York 55 SE2468
River Kent 15 TR2943
River W Susx 12 SU9323
Riverhead Kent 23 TQ5156
Rivington Lancs 54 SD6214
Rivington Services Lancs 54 SD6211
Roade Nhants 30 SP7651
Roadmeetings S Lans 74 NS8649
Roadwater Somset 7 ST0338
Roath Cardif 19 ST1977
Roberton Border 67 NT4214
Roberton S Lans 75 NS9428
Robertsbridge E Susx 14 TQ7423
Roberttown Kirk 55 SE1922
Robeston Wathen Pembks 16 SN0815
Robin Hood's Bay N York 63 NZ9505
Roborough Devon 4 SX5062
Roborough Devon 6 SS5717
Robroyston C Glas 74 NS6368
Roby Knows 46 SJ4390
Rocester Staffs 48 SK1039
Roch Pembks 16 SM8821
Rochdale Rochdl 54 SD8913
Roche Cnwll 3 SW9860
Rochester Medway 14 TQ7468
Rochester Nthumb 68 NY8298
Rochford Essex 24 TQ8790
Rochford Worcs 27 SO6268
Rock Cnwll 3 SW9375
Rock Nthumb 77 NU2020
Rock Worcs 37 SO7371
Rockbeare Devon 7 SY0194
Rockbourne Hants 10 SU1118
Rockcliffe Cumb 67 NY3561
Rockcliffe D & G 66 NX8454
Rockend Torbay 5 SX9263
Rock Ferry Wirral 46 SJ3386
Rockfield Mons 27 SO4814
Rockford Devon 18 SS7547
Rockhampton S Glos 20 ST6593
Rockhill Shrops 36 SO2978
Rockingham Nhants 40 SP8691
Rockland All Saints Norfk 42 TL9996
Rockland St Mary Norfk 43 TG3104
Rockland St Peter Norfk 42 TL9897
Rockley Notts 49 SK7174
Rockwell End Bucks 22 SU7988
Rodborough Gloucs 28 SO8404
Rodbourne Swindn 20 SU1485
Rodbourne Wilts 20 ST9383
Rodden Dorset 9 SY6184
Rode Somset 20 ST8053
Rode Heath Ches E 47 SJ8056
Roden Wrekin 37 SJ5716
Rodhuish Somset 7 ST0139
Rodington Wrekin 37 SJ5814
Rodington Heath Wrekin 37 SJ5814
Rodley Gloucs 28 SO7411
Rodmarton Gloucs 20 ST9498
Rodmell E Susx 13 TQ4106
Rodmersham Kent 14 TQ9261
Rodmersham Green Kent 14 TQ9161
Rodney Stoke Somset 19 ST4849
Rodsley Derbys 48 SK2040
Roecliffe N York 55 SE3765
Roe Green Herts 23 TL2107
Roe Green Herts 31 TL3133
Roehampton Gt Lon 23 TQ2273
Roffey W Susx 12 TQ1932
Rogate W Susx 11 SU8023
Rogerstone Newpt 19 ST2787
Rogiet Mons 19 ST4587
Roke Oxon 21 SU6293
Roker Sundld 69 NZ4058
Rollesby Norfk 43 TG4416
Rolleston Leics 40 SK7300
Rolleston Notts 50 SK7452
Rolleston on Dove Staffs 39 SK2327
Rolston E R Yk 57 TA2144
Rolvenden Kent 14 TQ8431
Rolvenden Layne Kent 14 TQ8530
Romaldkirk Dur 61 NY9922
Romanby N York 62 SE3693
Romanno Bridge Border 75 NT1647
Romansleigh Devon 7 SS7220
Romford Dorset 10 SU0709
Romford Gt Lon 23 TQ5188
Romiley Stockp 48 SJ9490
Romsey Cambs 31 TL4757
Romsey Hants 10 SU3521
Romsley Shrops 37 SO7883
Romsley Worcs 38 SO9680
Rookhope Dur 61 NY9342
Rookley IoW 11 SZ5084
Rooks Bridge Somset 19 ST3652
Rooks Nest Somset 8 ST0933
Rookwith N York 61 SE2086
Roos E R Yk 57 TA2830
Roothams Green Bed 30 TL0957
Ropley Hants 11 SU6431
Ropley Dean Hants 11 SU6232
Ropsley Lincs 40 SK9933
Rora Abers 95 NK0650
Rorrington Shrops 36 SJ3000
Rose Cnwll 2 SW7754
Rose Ash Devon 7 SS7921
Rosebush Pembks 16 SN0729
Rosedale Abbey N York 63 SE7296
Rose Green Essex 24 TL9028
Rose Green Suffk 25 TL9337
Rose Green Suffk 32 TL9744
Rose Green W Susx 11 SZ9099
Rosehall Highld 96 NC4702
Rosehearty Abers 95 NJ9267
Rose Hill Lancs 54 SD8231
Roselands E Susx 13 TQ6200
Rosemarket Pembks 16 SM9508
Rosemarkie Highld 93 NH7357
Rosemary Lane Devon 8 ST1514
Rosemount P & K 88 NO1843
Rosenannon Cnwll 3 SW9566
Rosewell Mdloth 75 NT2862
Roseworth S on T 62 NZ4221
Rosgill Cumb 59 NY5316
Rosley Cumb 67 NY3245
Roslin Mdloth 75 NT2763
Rosliston Derbys 39 SK2416
Rosneath Ag & B 80 NS2583
Ross D & G 65 NX6444
Rossett Wrexhm 46 SJ3657
Rossett Green N York 55 SE2952
Rossington Donc 49 SK6298
Ross-on-Wye Herefs 27 SO5923
Rostherne Ches E 47 SJ7483
Rosthwaite Cumb 58 NY2514
Roston Derbys 48 SK1340
Rosyth Fife 82 NT1183
Rothbury Nthumb 68 NU0501
Rotherby Leics 39 SK6716
Rotherfield E Susx 13 TQ5529
Rotherfield Greys Oxon 22 SU7282
Rotherfield Peppard Oxon 22 SU7182
Rotherham Rothm 49 SK4392
Rothersthorpe Nhants 30 SP7156
Rotherwick Hants 22 SU7156
Rothes Moray 94 NJ2749
Rothesay Ag & B 73 NS0864
Rothienorman Abers 95 NJ7235
Rothley Leics 39 SK5812
Rothwell Leeds 55 SE3428
Rothwell Lincs 50 TF1499
Rothwell Nhants 40 SP8181
Rottingdean Br & H 13 TQ3602
Rottington Cumb 58 NX9613
Roucan D & G 66 NY0277
Rougham Norfk 42 TF8320
Rougham Suffk 32 TL9061
Rough Common Kent 15 TR1259
Roughton Lincs 51 TF2464
Roughton Norfk 43 TG2136
Roughton Shrops 37 SO7594
Roundbush Green Essex 24 TL5814
Round Green Luton 30 TL1022
Roundham Somset 8 ST4209
Roundhay Leeds 55 SE3337
Rounds Green Sandw 38 SO9889
Roundswell Devon 6 SS5431
Roundway Wilts 20 SU0163
Rousdon Devon 8 SY2991
Rousham Oxon 29 SP4724
Rous Lench Worcs 28 SP0153
Routh E R Yk 57 TA0942
Row Cumb 59 SD4589
Rowanburn D & G 67 NY4177
Rowarth Derbys 48 SK0189
Rowberrow Somset 19 ST4558
Rowde Wilts 20 ST9762
Rowen Conwy 45 SH7671
Rowfoot Nthumb 68 NY6860
Rowhedge Essex 25 TM0221
Rowington Warwks 29 SP2069
Rowland Derbys 48 SK2172
Rowland's Castle Hants 11 SU7310
Rowlands Gill Gatesd 69 NZ1658
Rowledge Surrey 11 SU8243
Rowley Dur 68 NZ0848
Rowley Regis Sandw 38 SO9787
Rowlstone Herefs 27 SO3727
Rowly Surrey 12 TQ0440
Rowner Hants 11 SU5801
Rowney Green Worcs 38 SP0471
Rownhams Hants 10 SU3817
Rownhams Services Hants 10 SU3917
Rowrah Cumb 58 NY0518
Rowsham Bucks 30 SP8417
Rowsley Derbys 49 SK2565
Rowston Lincs 50 TF0856
Rowton Ches W 46 SJ4464
Rowton Wrekin 37 SJ6119
Roxburgh Border 76 NT6930
Roxby N Linc 56 SE9116
Roxton Bed 31 TL1554
Roxwell Essex 24 TL6408
Royal Leamington Spa Warwks 29 SP3265
Royal Sutton Coldfield Birm 38 SP1295
Royal Tunbridge Wells Kent 13 TQ5839
Royal Wootton Bassett Wilts 20 SU0682
Roydon Essex 23 TL4010
Roydon Norfk 33 TM1080
Roydon Norfk 42 TF7023
Roydon Hamlet Essex 23 TL4107
Royston Barns 55 SE3611
Royston Herts 31 TL3540
Royton Oldham 54 SD9107
Ruabon Wrexhm 46 SJ3043
Ruaig Ag & B 78 NM0747
Ruan Lanihorne Cnwll 3 SW8942
Ruan Major Cnwll 2 SW7016
Ruan Minor Cnwll 2 SW7115
Ruardean Gloucs 27 SO6217
Ruardean Hill Gloucs 27 SO6317
Ruardean Woodside Gloucs 27 SO6216
Rubery Birm 38 SO9977
Rubha Ban W Isls 90 NF7811
Ruckhall Herefs 27 SO4539
Ruckinge Kent 15 TR0233
Ruckley Shrops 37 SJ5300
Rudby N York 62 NZ4706
Rudchester Nthumb 69 NZ1167
Ruddington Notts 39 SK5632
Rudge Somset 20 ST8251
Rudgeway S Glos 19 ST6386
Rudgwick W Susx 12 TQ0834
Rudheath Ches W 47 SJ6772
Rudley Green Essex 24 TL8303
Rudloe Wilts 20 ST8470
Rudry Caerph 19 ST2086
Rudston E R Yk 57 TA0967
Rudyard Staffs 48 SJ9557
Rufford Lancs 53 SD4615
Rufforth C York 56 SE5251
Rugby Warwks 39 SP5075
Rugeley Staffs 38 SK0418
Ruishton Somset 8 ST2625
Ruislip Gt Lon 22 TQ0987
Rumbling Bridge P & K 82 NT0199
Rumburgh Suffk 33 TM3481
Rumford Cnwll 3 SW8970
Rumford Falk 75 NS9377
Rumney Cardif 19 ST2178
Runcorn Halton 46 SJ5182
Runcton W Susx 11 SU8802
Runcton Holme Norfk 41 TF6109
Runfold Surrey 22 SU8647
Runhall Norfk 42 TG0507
Runham Norfk 43 TG4610
Runnington Somset 8 ST1221
Runswick N York 63 NZ8016
Runwell Essex 24 TQ7594
Ruscombe Wokham 22 SU7976
Rushall Herefs 27 SO6435
Rushall Norfk 33 TM1982
Rushall Wilts 20 SU1255
Rushall Wsall 38 SK0200
Rushbrooke Suffk 32 TL8961
Rushbury Shrops 37 SO5191
Rushden Herts 31 TL3031
Rushden Nhants 30 SP9566
Rushenden Kent 14 TQ9071
Rushford Norfk 32 TL9281
Rush Green Essex 25 TM1515
Rush Green Gt Lon 23 TQ5187
Rush Green Warrtn 47 SJ6987
Rushlake Green E Susx 13 TQ6218
Rushmere Suffk 33 TM4986
Rushmoor Surrey 11 SU8740
Rushock Worcs 38 SO8871
Rusholme Manch 47 SJ8594
Rushton Nhants 40 SP8482
Rushton Spencer Staffs 48 SJ9362
Rushwick Worcs 28 SO8254
Rushyford Dur 61 NZ2728
Ruskington Lincs 50 TF0851
Rusland Cross Cumb 59 SD3488
Rusper W Susx 12 TQ2037
Ruspidge Gloucs 28 SO6611
Russell's Water Oxon 22 SU7089
Russ Hill Surrey 12 TQ2240
Rusthall Kent 13 TQ5639
Rustington W Susx 12 TQ0402
Ruston N York 63 SE9583
Ruston Parva E R Yk 57 TA0661
Ruswarp N York 63 NZ8809
Rutherford Border 76 NT6430
Rutherglen S Lans 74 NS6161
Ruthernbridge Cnwll 3 SX0166
Ruthin Denbgs 46 SJ1258
Ruthrieston C Aber 89 NJ9204
Ruthven Abers 94 NJ5046
Ruthven Angus 88 NO2848
Ruthvoes Cnwll 3 SW9260
Ruthwell D & G 67 NY0967
Ruyton-XI-Towns Shrops 36 SJ3922
Ryal Nthumb 68 NZ0174
Ryall Dorset 8 SY4095
Ryall Worcs 28 SO8640
Ryarsh Kent 14 TQ6660
Rydal Cumb 59 NY3606
Ryde IoW 11 SZ5992
Rye E Susx 14 TQ9220
Rye Foreign E Susx 14 TQ8922
Rye Street Worcs 28 SO7835
Ryhall Rutlnd 40 TF0310
Ryhill Wakefd 55 SE3814
Ryhope Sundld 69 NZ4152
Ryland Lincs 50 TF0179
Rylands Notts 39 SK5335
Rylstone N York 54 SD9658
Ryme Intrinseca Dorset 9 ST5810
Ryther N York 56 SE5539
Ryton Gatesd 69 NZ1564
Ryton Shrops 37 SJ7602
Ryton-on-Dunsmore Warwks 39 SP3874

S

Sabden Lancs 54 SD7837
Sacombe Herts 31 TL3319
Sacriston Dur 69 NZ2447
Sadberge Darltn 62 NZ3416
Saddell Ag & B 72 NR7832
Saddington Leics 39 SP6691
Saddlebow Norfk 41 TF6015
Saddlescombe W Susx 12 TQ2711
Saffron Walden Essex 24 TL5438
Sageston Pembks 16 SN0503
Saham Hills Norfk 42 TF9003
Saham Toney Norfk 42 TF8901
Saighton Ches W 46 SJ4462
St Abbs Border 77 NT9167
St Agnes Cnwll 2 SW7150
St Albans Herts 22 TL1407
St Allen Cnwll 2 SW8250
St Andrews Fife 83 NO5116
St Andrews Major V Glam 18 ST1371
St Andrews Well Dorset 8 SY4793
St Anne's Lancs 53 SD3228
St Ann's Chapel Cnwll 4 SX4170
St Ann's Chapel Devon 5 SX6647
St Anthony-in-Meneage Cnwll 2 SW7825
St Anthony's Hill E Susx 13 TQ6201
St Arvans Mons 19 ST5296
St Asaph Denbgs 45 SJ0374
St Athan V Glam 18 ST0167
St Austell Cnwll 3 SX0152
St Bees Cumb 58 NX9711
St Blazey Cnwll 3 SX0654
St Boswells Border 76 NT5930
St Breock Cnwll 3 SW9771
St Breward Cnwll 3 SX0976
St Briavels Gloucs 27 SO5604
St Bride's Major V Glam 18 SS8974
St Brides-super-Ely V Glam 18 ST0977
St Brides Wentlooge Newpt 19 ST2982
St Budeaux C Plym 4 SX4558
Saintbury Gloucs 28 SP1139
St Buryan Cnwll 2 SW4025
St Catherines Ag & B 80 NN1207
St Chloe Gloucs 20 SO8401
St Clears Carmth 17 SN2816
St Cleer Cnwll 4 SX2468
St Clement Cnwll 3 SW8543
St Clether Cnwll 4 SX2084
St Columb Major Cnwll 3 SW9163
St Columb Minor Cnwll 3 SW8362
St Columb Road Cnwll 3 SW9159
St Combs Abers 95 NK0563
St Cross South Elmham Suffk 33 TM2984
St Cyrus Abers 89 NO7464
St David's P & K 82 NN9420
St Davids Pembks 16 SM7525
St Day Cnwll 2 SW7242
St Dennis Cnwll 3 SW9557
St Dogmaels Pembks 17 SN1645
St Dominick Cnwll 4 SX4067
St Donats V Glam 18 SS9368
St Endellion Cnwll 3 SW9978
St Enoder Cnwll 3 SW8956
St Erme Cnwll 3 SW8449
St Erney Cnwll 4 SX3759
St Erth Cnwll 2 SW5535
St Erth Praze Cnwll 2 SW5735
St Ervan Cnwll 3 SW8970
St Eval Cnwll 3 SW8868
St Ewe Cnwll 3 SW9746
St Fagans Cardif 18 ST1277
St Fergus Abers 95 NK0952
St Fillans P & K 81 NN6924
St Florence Pembks 16 SN0801
St Gennys Cnwll 6 SX1497
St George Conwy 45 SH9775
St Georges N Som 19 ST3762
St George's V Glam 18 ST1076
St Germans Cnwll 4 SX3657
St Giles in the Wood Devon 6 SS5319
St Giles-on-the-Heath Devon 4 SX3690
St Harmon Powys 35 SN9872
St Helen Auckland Dur 61 NZ1826
St Helen's E Susx 14 TQ8212
St Helens IoW 11 SZ6289
St Helens St Hel 46 SJ5095
St Helier Gt Lon 23 TQ2666
St Hilary Cnwll 2 SW5431
St Hilary V Glam 18 ST0173
St Ippolyts Herts 31 TL1927
St Ishmael's Pembks 16 SM8307
St Issey Cnwll 3 SW9271
St Ive Cnwll 4 SX3167
St Ives Cambs 31 TL3171
St Ives Cnwll 2 SW5140
St James's End Nhants 30 SP7460
St James South Elmham Suffk 33 TM3281
St Jidgey Cnwll 3 SW9469
St John Cnwll 4 SX4053
St John's E Susx 13 TQ5031
St John's IoM 52 SC2781
St John's Kent 23 TQ5356
St Johns Surrey 22 SU9958
St Johns Worcs 28 SO8454
St John's Chapel Devon 6 SS5329
St John's Chapel Dur 60 NY8837
St John's Fen End Norfk 41 TF5312
St John's Town of Dalry D & G 65 NX6281
St John's Wood Gt Lon 23 TQ2683
St Judes IoM 52 SC3996
St Just Cnwll 2 SW3731
St Just-in-Roseland Cnwll 3 SW8435
St Keverne Cnwll 2 SW7921
St Kew Cnwll 3 SX0276
St Kew Highway Cnwll 3 SX0375
St Keyne Cnwll 4 SX2461
St Lawrence Essex 25 TL9604
St Lawrence IoW 11 SZ5376
St Lawrence Kent 15 TR3665
St Leonards Bucks 22 SP9007
St Leonards Dorset 10 SU1103
St Leonards E Susx 14 TQ8009
St Levan Cnwll 2 SW3822
St Lythans V Glam 18 ST1072
St Mabyn Cnwll 3 SX0473
St Margarets Herefs 27 SO3533
St Margarets Herts 23 TL3811
St Margaret's at Cliffe Kent 15 TR3544
St Margaret's Hope Ork 100 ND4493
St Margaret South Elmham Suffk 33 TM3183
St Marks IoM 52 SC2974
St Martin Cnwll 2 SW7323
St Martin Cnwll 4 SX2555
St Martin's Shrops 36 SJ3236
St Mary Bourne Hants 21 SU4250
St Marychurch Torbay 5 SX9166
St Mary Church V Glam 18 ST0071
St Mary Cray Gt Lon 23 TQ4768
St Mary in the Marsh Kent 15 TR0627
St Mary's Ork 100 HY4701
St Mary's Bay Kent 15 TR0827
St Mary's Hoo Medway 24 TQ8076
St Mary's Platt Kent 14 TQ6257
St Maughans Green Mons 27 SO4717
St Mawes Cnwll 3 SW8433
St Mawgan Cnwll 3 SW8765
St Mellion Cnwll 4 SX3965
St Mellons Cardif 19 ST2281
St Merryn Cnwll 3 SW8873
St Michael Caerhays Cnwll 3 SW9642
St Michael Church Somset 8 ST3030
St Michael Penkevil Cnwll 3 SW8541
St Michaels Kent 14 TQ8835
St Michaels Worcs 27 SO5865
St Michael's on Wyre Lancs 53 SD4641
St Minver Cnwll 3 SW9677
St Monans Fife 83 NO5201
St Neot Cnwll 4 SX1868
St Neots Cambs 31 TL1860
St Newlyn East Cnwll 3 SW8256
St Nicholas Pembks 16 SM9035
St Nicholas V Glam 18 ST0974
St Nicholas-at-Wade Kent 15 TR2666
St Ninians Stirlg 81 NS7991
St Olaves Norfk 43 TM4599
St Osyth Essex 25 TM1215
St Owen's Cross Herefs 27 SO5324
St Paul's Cray Gt Lon 23 TQ4768
St Paul's Walden Herts 31 TL1922
St Peter's Kent 15 TR3868
St Peter's Hill Cambs 31 TL2372
St Pinnock Cnwll 4 SX2063
St Stephen Cnwll 3 SW9453
St Stephens Cnwll 4 SX3285
St Stephens Cnwll 4 SX4158
St Teath Cnwll 3 SX0680
St Thomas Devon 5 SX9091
St Tudy Cnwll 3 SX0676
St Twynnells Pembks 16 SR9597
St Veep Cnwll 3 SX1455
St Vigeans Angus 89 NO6443
St Wenn Cnwll 3 SW9664
St Weonards Herefs 27 SO4924
Salcombe Devon 5 SX7439
Salcombe Regis Devon 8 SY1588
Salcott-cum-Virley Essex 25 TL9413
Sale Traffd 47 SJ7991
Saleby Lincs 51 TF4578
Sale Green Worcs 28 SO9358
Salehurst E Susx 14 TQ7524
Salem Cerdgn 35 SN6684
Salen Ag & B 79 NM5743
Salen Highld 79 NM6864
Salford C Beds 30 SP9339
Salford Oxon 29 SP2828
Salford Salfd 47 SJ8197
Salford Priors Warwks 28 SP0751
Salfords Surrey 12 TQ2846
Salhouse Norfk 43 TG3114
Saline Fife 82 NT0292
Salisbury Wilts 10 SU1430
Salkeld Dykes Cumb 59 NY5437
Salle Norfk 43 TG1024
Salmonby Lincs 51 TF3273
Salperton Gloucs 28 SP0720
Salsburgh N Lans 74 NS8262
Salt Staffs 38 SJ9527
Saltaire C Brad 55 SE1438
Saltash Cnwll 4 SX4258
Saltburn Highld 93 NH7270
Saltburn-by-the-Sea R & Cl 62 NZ6621
Saltby Leics 40 SK8526
Saltcoats N Ayrs 73 NS2441
Saltdean Br & H 13 TQ3802
Salterbeck Cumb 58 NX9926
Salterforth Lancs 54 SD8845
Salterton Wilts 10 SU1236
Saltfleet Lincs 51 TF4593
Saltfleetby All Saints Lincs 51 TF4590
Saltfleetby St Clement Lincs 51 TF4691
Saltfleetby St Peter Lincs 51 TF4489
Saltford BaNES 20 ST6867
Salthouse Norfk 42 TG0743
Saltley Birm 38 SP1088
Saltmarshe E R Yk 56 SE7824
Saltney Flints 46 SJ3864
Salton N York 63 SE7179
Saltrens Devon 6 SS4522
Saltwood Kent 15 TR1535
Salvington W Susx 12 TQ1205
Salwarpe Worcs 28 SO8762
Salway Ash Dorset 8 SY4596
Sambourne Warwks 28 SP0562
Sambrook Wrekin 37 SJ7124
Sampford Arundel Somset 8 ST1118
Sampford Brett Somset 18 ST0840
Sampford Courtenay Devon 7 SS6301
Sampford Moor Somset 8 ST1118
Sampford Peverell Devon 7 ST0314
Sampford Spiney Devon 4 SX5372
Samsonlane Ork 100 HY6526
Samuelston E Loth 76 NT4870
Sanaigmore Ag & B 70 NR2370
Sancreed Cnwll 2 SW4129
Sancton E R Yk 56 SE8939
Sandal Magna Wakefd 55 SE3417
Sanday Airport Ork 100 HY6740
Sandbach Ches E 47 SJ7560
Sandbach Services Ches E 47 SJ7760
Sandbank Ag & B 80 NS1680
Sandbanks BCP 10 SZ0487
Sandend Abers 94 NJ5566
Sanderstead Gt Lon 23 TQ3461
Sandford Cumb 60 NY7316
Sandford Devon 7 SS8202
Sandford Dorset 9 SY9289
Sandford Hants 10 SU1601
Sandford IoW 11 SZ5381
Sandford N Som 19 ST4259
Sandford-on-Thames Oxon 21 SP5301
Sandford Orcas Dorset 9 ST6220
Sandford St Martin Oxon 29 SP4226
Sandgate Kent 15 TR2035
Sandhaven Abers 95 NJ9667
Sandhead D & G 64 NX0949
Sand Hills Leeds 55 SE3739
Sandhills Oxon 29 SP5507
Sandhills Surrey 12 SU9337
Sandhoe Nthumb 68 NY9666
Sand Hole E R Yk 56 SE8036
Sandholme E R Yk 56 SE8230
Sandhurst Br For 22 SU8361
Sandhurst Gloucs 28 SO8223
Sandhurst Kent 14 TQ8028
Sand Hutton N York 56 SE6958
Sandhutton N York 62 SE3881
Sandiacre Derbys 39 SK4736
Sandilands Lincs 51 TF5280
Sandleheath Hants 10 SU1215
Sandleigh Oxon 21 SP4701
Sandley Dorset 9 ST7724
Sandness Shet 100 HU1957
Sandon Essex 24 TL7404
Sandon Herts 31 TL3234
Sandon Staffs 38 SJ9429
Sandon Bank Staffs 38 SJ9428
Sandown IoW 11 SZ5984
Sandplace Cnwll 4 SX2557
Sandridge Herts 23 TL1710
Sandringham Norfk 42 TF6928
Sandsend N York 63 NZ8612
Sandtoft N Linc 56 SE7408
Sandway Kent 14 TQ8950
Sandwich Kent 15 TR3358
Sandwick Shet 100 HU4323
Sandwith Cumb 58 NX9614
Sandy C Beds 31 TL1649
Sandygate Devon 5 SX8674
Sandygate IoM 52 SC3797
Sandyhills D & G 66 NX8855
Sandylands Lancs 53 SD4263
Sandy Lane Wilts 20 ST9668
Sandy Park Devon 5 SX7189
Sankyn's Green Worcs 28 SO7965
Sanquhar D & G 66 NS7809
Santon Bridge Cumb 58 NY1101
Santon Downham Suffk 32 TL8187
Sapcote Leics 39 SP4893
Sapey Common Herefs 28 SO7064
Sapiston Suffk 32 TL9175
Sapley Cambs 31 TL2474
Sapperton Gloucs 20 SO9403
Sapperton Lincs 40 TF0133
Saracen's Head Lincs 41 TF3427
Sarisbury Hants 11 SU5008
Sarn Powys 36 SO2090
Sarnau Cerdgn 17 SN3150
Sarnau Powys 36 SJ2315
Sarn Mellteyrn Gwynd 44 SH2432
Sarn Park Services Brdgnd 18 SS9082
Saron Carmth 17 SN6012
Saron Gwynd 44 SH5365
Sarratt Herts 22 TQ0499
Sarre Kent 15 TR2565
Sarsden Oxon 29 SP2822
Satley Dur 69 NZ1143
Satterleigh Devon 7 SS6622
Satterthwaite Cumb 59 SD3392
Sauchen Abers 95 NJ7011
Saul Gloucs 28 SO7409
Saundby Notts 50 SK7888
Saundersfoot Pembks 16 SN1304
Saunderton Bucks 22 SP7901
Saunton Devon 6 SS4637
Sausthorpe Lincs 51 TF3868
Savile Town Kirk 55 SE2420
Sawbridge Warwks 29 SP5065
Sawbridgeworth Herts 31 TL4814
Sawdon N York 63 SE9485
Sawley Lancs 54 SD7746
Sawley N York 55 SE2467
Sawston Cambs 31 TL4849
Sawtry Cambs 40 TL1683
Saxby Leics 40 SK8219
Saxby Lincs 50 TF0086
Saxby All Saints N Linc 56 SE9816
Saxelbye Leics 40 SK6921
Saxham Street Suffk 33 TM0861
Saxilby Lincs 50 SK8975
Saxlingham Norfk 42 TG0239
Saxlingham Green Norfk 43 TM2396
Saxlingham Nethergate Norfk 43 TM2297
Saxlingham Thorpe Norfk 43 TM2197
Saxmundham Suffk 33 TM3863
Saxondale Notts 49 SK6839
Saxon Street Cambs 32 TL6759
Saxtead Suffk 33 TM2665
Saxtead Green Suffk 33 TM2564
Saxtead Little Green Suffk 33 TM2466
Saxthorpe Norfk 43 TG1130
Saxton N York 55 SE4736
Sayers Common W Susx 12 TQ2618
Scackleton N York 62 SE6472
Scaftworth Notts 49 SK6691
Scagglethorpe N York 63 SE8372
Scalasaig Ag & B 70 NR3993
Scalby E R Yk 56 SE8429
Scalby N York 63 TA0090
Scaldwell Nhants 30 SP7672
Scaleby Cumb 67 NY4463
Scalebyhill Cumb 67 NY4463
Scales Cumb 53 SD2772
Scales Cumb 59 NY3426
Scalford Leics 40 SK7624
Scaling N York 63 NZ7413
Scalloway Shet 100 HU4039
Scamblesby Lincs 51 TF2778
Scampston N York 63 SE8575
Scampton Lincs 50 SK9579
Scapegoat Hill Kirk 55 SE0916
Scarborough N York 63 TA0488
Scarcewater Cnwll 3 SW9154
Scarcliffe Derbys 49 SK4968
Scarcroft Leeds 55 SE3541
Scarinish Ag & B 78 NM0444
Scarisbrick Lancs 53 SD3713
Scarning Norfk 42 TF9512
Scarrington Notts 50 SK7341
Scartho NE Lin 57 TA2606
Scatsta Airport Shet 100 HU3872
Scaur D & G 66 NX8354
Scawby N Linc 56 SE9605
Scawsby Donc 56 SE5404
Scawthorpe Donc 56 SE5506
Scawton N York 62 SE5483
Scayne's Hill W Susx 13 TQ3623
Scethrog Powys 26 SO1025
Scholar Green Ches E 47 SJ8357
Scholes Kirk 55 SE1507
Scholes Leeds 55 SE3736
Scholes Rothm 49 SK3895
Scholes Wigan 47 SD5905
Scissett Kirk 55 SE2410
Scleddau Pembks 16 SM9434
Scofton Notts 49 SK6380
Scole Norfk 33 TM1579
Scone P & K 82 NO1326
Sconser Highld 84 NG5131
Scoonie Fife 83 NO3801
Scopwick Lincs 50 TF0757
Scorborough E R Yk 56 TA0145
Scorrier Cnwll 2 SW7244
Scorton Lancs 53 SD5048
Scorton N York 61 NZ2500
Scotby Cumb 67 NY4455
Scotch Corner N York 61 NZ2105
Scotch Corner Rest Area N York 61 NZ2205
Scotforth Lancs 53 SD4859
Scothern Lincs 50 TF0377
Scotlandwell P & K 82 NO1801
Scot's Gap Nthumb 68 NZ0386
Scotstoun C Glas 74 NS5267
Scotswood N u Ty 69 NZ2063
Scotter Lincs 50 SE8800
Scotterthorpe Lincs 50 SE8701
Scotton Lincs 50 SK8899
Scotton N York 55 SE3259
Scotton N York 61 SE1895
Scoulton Norfk 42 TF9800
Scourie Highld 98 NC1544
Scousburgh Shet 100 HU3717
Scrabster Highld 100 ND1070
Scraesburgh Border 76 NT6718
Scrane End Lincs 51 TF3841
Scraptoft Leics 39 SK6405
Scratby Norfk 43 TG5015
Scrayingham N York 56 SE7359
Scredington Lincs 50 TF0940
Scremby Lincs 51 TF4467
Scremerston Nthumb 77 NU0049
Screveton Notts 50 SK7343
Scriven N York 55 SE3458
Scrooby Notts 49 SK6590
Scropton Derbys 39 SK1930
Scrub Hill Lincs 51 TF2355
Scruton N York 61 SE2992
Sculthorpe Norfk 42 TF8930
Scunthorpe N Linc 56 SE8910
Seaborough Dorset 8 ST4206
Seabridge Staffs 47 SJ8343
Seabrook Kent 15 TR1835
Seaburn Sundld 69 NZ4059
Seacombe Wirral 46 SJ3290
Seacroft Leeds 55 SE3536
Seaford E Susx 13 TV4899
Seaforth Sefton 46 SJ3297
Seagrave Leics 39 SK6117
Seaham Dur 69 NZ4149
Seahouses Nthumb 77 NU2231
Seal Kent 23 TQ5556
Sealand Flints 46 SJ3568
Seale Surrey 22 SU8947
Seamer N York 62 NZ4910
Seamer N York 63 TA0183
Seamill N Ayrs 73 NS2047
Sea Palling Norfk 43 TG4226
Searby Lincs 57 TA0705
Seasalter Kent 15 TR0864
Seascale Cumb 58 NY0301
Seathwaite Cumb 58 SD2295
Seatoller Cumb 58 NY2413
Seaton Cnwll 4 SX3054
Seaton Cumb 58 NY0130
Seaton Devon 8 SY2490
Seaton E R Yk 57 TA1646
Seaton Kent 15 TR2258
Seaton Nthumb 69 NZ3276
Seaton Rutlnd 40 SP9098
Seaton Carew Hartpl 62 NZ5229
Seaton Delaval Nthumb 69 NZ3075
Seaton Ross E R Yk 56 SE7840
Seaton Sluice Nthumb 69 NZ3376
Seatown Dorset 8 SY4291
Seave Green N York 62 NZ5500
Seaview IoW 11 SZ6291
Seaville Cumb 67 NY1553
Seavington St Mary Somset 8 ST4014
Seavington St Michael Somset 8 ST4015
Sebergham Cumb 59 NY3641
Seckington Warwks 39 SK2507
Second Severn Crossing Mons 19 ST5186
Sedbergh Cumb 60 SD6591
Sedbury Gloucs 19 ST5493
Sedbusk N York 60 SD8891
Sedgeberrow Worcs 28 SP0238
Sedgebrook Lincs 40 SK8537
Sedgefield Dur 62 NZ3528
Sedgeford Norfk 42 TF7036
Sedgehill Wilts 9 ST8627
Sedgemoor Services Somset 19 ST3552
Sedgley Dudley 38 SO9193
Sedgley Park Bury 47 SD8202
Sedgwick Cumb 59 SD5186
Sedlescombe E Susx 14 TQ7818
Sedrup Bucks 22 SP8011
Seend Wilts 20 ST9460
Seend Cleeve Wilts 20 ST9360
Seer Green Bucks 22 SU9692
Seething Norfk 43 TM3197
Sefton Sefton 46 SD3501
Seighford Staffs 38 SJ8825
Seion Gwynd 44 SH5466
Seisdon Staffs 38 SO8495
Selattyn Shrops 36 SJ2633
Selborne Hants 11 SU7433
Selby N York 56 SE6132
Selham W Susx 12 SU9320
Selhurst Gt Lon 23 TQ3267
Selkirk Border 76 NT4728
Sellack Herefs 27 SO5627
Sellafield Station Cumb 58 NY0103
Sellafirth Shet 100 HU5198
Sellindge Kent 15 TR0938
Selling Kent 15 TR0456
Sells Green Wilts 20 ST9462
Selly Oak Birm 38 SP0482
Selmeston E Susx 13 TQ5007
Selsdon Gt Lon 23 TQ3562
Selsey W Susx 11 SZ8593
Selside N York 60 SD7875
Selsley Gloucs 28 SO8303
Selsted Kent 15 TR2144
Selston Notts 49 SK4553
Selworthy Somset 18 SS9246
Semer Suffk 32 TL9946
Semington Wilts 20 ST8960
Semley Wilts 9 ST8926
Send Surrey 22 TQ0155
Senghenydd Caerph 18 ST1190
Sennen Cnwll 2 SW3525
Sennen Cove Cnwll 2 SW3526
Sennybridge Powys 26 SN9228
Sessay N York 62 SE4575
Setchey Norfk 41 TF6313
Settle N York 54 SD8163
Settrington N York 56 SE8370
Sevenhampton Gloucs 28 SP0321
Sevenhampton Swindn 21 SU2090
Seven Kings Gt Lon 23 TQ4587
Sevenoaks Kent 23 TQ5255
Sevenoaks Weald Kent 13 TQ5250
Seven Sisters Neath 26 SN8208
Seven Star Green Essex 25 TL9325
Severn Beach S Glos 19 ST5484
Severn Bridge S Glos 19 ST5590
Severn Stoke Worcs 28 SO8644
Severn View Services S Glos 19 ST5789
Sevington Kent 15 TR0340
Sewards End Essex 24 TL5738
Sewell C Beds 30 SP9922
Sewerby E R Yk 57 TA1968
Seworgan Cnwll 2 SW7030
Sewstern Leics 40 SK8821
Shabbington Bucks 22 SP6606
Shackerstone Leics 39 SK3706
Shackleford Surrey 12 SU9345
Shader W Isls 90 NB3854
Shadforth Dur 62 NZ3440
Shadingfield Suffk 33 TM4384
Shadoxhurst Kent 15 TQ9737
Shadwell Leeds 55 SE3439
Shadwell Norfk 32 TL9383
Shaftenhoe End Herts 31 TL4037
Shaftesbury Dorset 9 ST8623
Shafton Barns 55 SE3911
Shakerley Wigan 47 SD6902
Shalbourne Wilts 21 SU3163
Shalden Hants 11 SU6941
Shaldon Devon 5 SX9372
Shalfleet IoW 10 SZ4189
Shalford Essex 24 TL7229
Shalford Surrey 12 TQ0047
Shalford Green Essex 24 TL7127
Shalmsford Street Kent 15 TR0954
Shalstone Bucks 29 SP6436
Shamley Green Surrey 12 TQ0343
Shandon Ag & B 80 NS2586
Shangton Leics 40 SP7196
Shanklin IoW 11 SZ5881
Shap Cumb 59 NY5615
Shapwick Dorset 9 ST9301
Shapwick Somset 19 ST4138
Shard End Birm 38 SP1588
Shardlow Derbys 39 SK4330
Shareshill Staffs 38 SJ9406
Sharlston Wakefd 55 SE3918
Sharman's Cross Solhll 38 SP1279
Sharnbrook Bed 30 SP9959
Sharnford Leics 39 SP4891
Sharoe Green Lancs 53 SD5333
Sharow N York 55 SE3371
Sharpenhoe C Beds 30 TL0630
Sharperton Nthumb 68 NT9503
Sharpness Gloucs 20 SO6702
Sharrington Norfk 42 TG0337
Shatterford Worcs 37 SO7981
Shaugh Prior Devon 5 SX5463
Shavington Ches E 47 SJ6951
Shaw Oldham 54 SD9308
Shaw Swindn 20 SU1185
Shaw W Berk 21 SU4768
Shaw Wilts 20 ST8965
Shawbirch Wrekin 37 SJ6413
Shawbost W Isls 90 NB2646
Shawbury Shrops 37 SJ5521
Shawell Leics 39 SP5480
Shawford Hants 11 SU4625
Shawhead D & G 66 NX8675
Shaw Mills N York 55 SE2562
Shearsby Leics 39 SP6290
Shearston Somset 8 ST2830
Shebbear Devon 6 SS4409
Shebdon Staffs 37 SJ7625
Shedfield Hants 11 SU5613
Sheen Staffs 48 SK1161
Sheepridge Kirk 55 SE1519
Sheepscar Leeds 55 SE3134
Sheepscombe Gloucs 28 SO8910
Sheepstor Devon 5 SX5667
Sheepwash Devon 6 SS4806
Sheepy Magna Leics 39 SK3201
Sheepy Parva Leics 39 SK3301
Sheering Essex 31 TL5014
Sheerness Kent 14 TQ9174
Sheerwater Surrey 22 TQ0360
Sheet Hants 11 SU7524
Sheffield Sheff 49 SK3587
Shefford C Beds 30 TL1439
Sheinton Shrops 37 SJ6003
Shelderton Shrops 36 SO4077
Sheldon Birm 38 SP1484
Sheldon Derbys 48 SK1768
Sheldon Devon 8 ST1208
Sheldwich Kent 15 TR0156
Shelfanger Norfk 33 TM1083
Shelford Notts 49 SK6642
Shelley Kirk 55 SE2011
Shelley Suffk 25 TM0238
Shellingford Oxon 21 SU3193
Shellow Bowells Essex 24 TL6007
Shelsley Beauchamp Worcs 28 SO7363
Shelsley Walsh Worcs 28 SO7263
Shelton Bed 30 TL0368
Shelton Norfk 33 TM2291
Shelton Notts 50 SK7844
Shelton Lock C Derb 39 SK3730
Shelton Under Harley Staffs 37 SJ8139
Shelve Shrops 36 SO3399
Shelwick Herefs 27 SO5242
Shenfield Essex 24 TQ6095
Shenington Oxon 29 SP3742
Shenley Herts 23 TL1800
Shenley Brook End M Keyn 30 SP8335
Shenley Church End M Keyn 30 SP8336
Shenmore Herefs 27 SO3937
Shenstone Staffs 38 SK1004
Shenstone Worcs 38 SO8673
Shenton Leics 39 SK3800
Shephall Herts 31 TL2623
Shepherd's Bush Gt Lon 23 TQ2380
Shepherdswell Kent 15 TR2647
Shepley Kirk 55 SE1909
Shepperton Surrey 22 TQ0867
Shepreth Cambs 31 TL3947
Shepshed Leics 39 SK4819
Shepton Beauchamp Somset 8 ST4017
Shepton Mallet Somset 19 ST6143
Shepton Montague Somset 9 ST6831
Shepway Kent 14 TQ7753
Sheraton Dur 62 NZ4435
Sherborne Dorset 9 ST6316
Sherborne Gloucs 29 SP1614
Sherborne Somset 19 ST5855
Sherborne St John Hants 21 SU6255
Sherbourne Warwks 29 SP2661
Sherburn Dur 62 NZ3142
Sherburn N York 63 SE9576
Sherburn Hill Dur 62 NZ3342
Sherburn in Elmet N York 55 SE4933
Shere Surrey 12 TQ0747
Shereford Norfk 42 TF8829
Sherfield English Hants 10 SU2922
Sherfield on Loddon Hants 22 SU6858
Sherford Devon 5 SX7844
Sheriffhales Shrops 37 SJ7512
Sheriff Hutton N York 56 SE6566
Sheringham Norfk 43 TG1543
Sherington M Keyn 30 SP8846
Shernborne Norfk 42 TF7132
Sherrington Wilts 20 ST9639
Sherston Wilts 20 ST8586
Sherwood C Nott 49 SK5643
Shettleston C Glas 74 NS6464
Shevington Wigan 53 SD5408
Sheviock Cnwll 4 SX3755
Shibden Head C Brad 55 SE0928
Shide IoW 11 SZ5088
Shidlaw Nthumb 76 NT8037
Shiel Bridge Highld 85 NG9318
Shieldaig Highld 91 NG8154
Shieldhill Falk 74 NS8976
Shifnal Shrops 37 SJ7407
Shilbottle Nthumb 69 NU1908
Shildon Dur 61 NZ2226
Shillingford Devon 7 SS9824
Shillingford Oxon 21 SU5992
Shillingford Abbot Devon 5 SX9088
Shillingford St George Devon 5 SX9087
Shillingstone Dorset 9 ST8211
Shillington C Beds 30 TL1234
Shilton Oxon 29 SP2608
Shilton Warwks 39 SP4084
Shimpling Norfk 33 TM1583
Shimpling Suffk 32 TL8651
Shimpling Street Suffk 32 TL8753
Shincliffe Dur 61 NZ2940
Shiney Row Sundld 69 NZ3252
Shinfield Wokham 22 SU7368
Shinness Highld 96 NC5314
Shipbourne Kent 13 TQ5952
Shipdham Norfk 42 TF9507
Shipham Somset 19 ST4457
Shiphay Torbay 5 SX8965
Shiplake Oxon 22 SU7678
Shipley C Brad 55 SE1537
Shipley W Susx 12 TQ1421
Shipley Bridge Surrey 12 TQ3040
Shipmeadow Suffk 33 TM3790
Shippon Oxon 21 SU4898
Shipston-on-Stour Warwks 29 SP2540
Shipton Gloucs 28 SP0318
Shipton N York 56 SE5558
Shipton Shrops 37 SO5692
Shipton Bellinger Hants 21 SU2345
Shipton Gorge Dorset 8 SY4991
Shipton Green W Susx 11 SZ8099
Shipton Moyne Gloucs 20 ST8989
Shipton-on-Cherwell Oxon 29 SP4716
Shiptonthorpe E R Yk 56 SE8543

Shipton-under-Wychwood – Stratton St Michael 135

Shipton-under-Wychwood Oxon 29 SP2817
Shirburn Oxon 22 SU6995
Shirdley Hill Lancs 53 SD3612
Shirebrook Derbys 49 SK5267
Shiregreen Sheff 49 SK3691
Shirehampton Bristl 19 ST5376
Shiremoor N Tyne 69 NZ3171
Shirenewton Mons 19 ST4793
Shireoaks Notts 49 SK5580
Shirland Derbys 49 SK4058
Shirley C Sotn 10 SU4014
Shirley Derbys 48 SK2141
Shirley Gt Lon 23 TQ3565
Shirley Solhll 38 SP1278
Shirrell Heath Hants 11 SU5714
Shirwell Devon 7 SS6037
Shiskine N Ayrs 72 NR9129
Shobdon Herefs 27 SO4062
Shobrooke Devon 7 SS8601
Shoby Leics 39 SK6820
Shocklach Ches W 46 SJ4349
Shoeburyness Sthend 25 TQ9385
Sholden Kent 15 TR3552
Sholing C Sotn 10 SU4511
Shop Cnwll 6 SS2214
Shoreditch Gt Lon 23 TQ3382
Shoreditch Somset 8 ST2422
Shoreham Kent 23 TQ5161
Shoreham-by-Sea W Susx 12 TQ2105
Shorley Hants 11 SU5726
Shorne Kent 14 TQ6970
Shortgate E Susx 13 TQ4915
Short Heath Birm 38 SP0992
Short Heath Wsall 38 SJ9700
Shortlanesend Cnwll 2 SW8047
Shortlees E Ayrs 73 NS4235
Shorwell IoW 10 SZ4583
Shoscombe BaNES 20 ST7156
Shotesham Norfk 43 TM2499
Shotgate Essex 24 TQ7592
Shotley Suffk 25 TM2335
Shotley Bridge Dur 68 NZ0953
Shotley Gate Suffk 25 TM2433
Shotley Street Suffk 25 TM2335
Shottenden Kent 15 TR0454
Shottery Warwks 29 SP1854
Shotteswell Warwks 29 SP4245
Shottisham Suffk 33 TM3244
Shottlegate Derbys 49 SK3147
Shotton Dur 62 NZ4139
Shotton Flints 46 SJ3168
Shotton Colliery Dur 62 NZ3941
Shotts N Lans 74 NS8759
Shotwick Ches W 46 SJ3371
Shouldham Norfk 42 TF6709
Shouldham Thorpe Norfk 42 TF6607
Shoulton Worcs 28 SO8159
Shrawardine Shrops 36 SJ3915
Shrawley Worcs 28 SO8065
Shrewley Warwks 29 SP2167
Shrewsbury Shrops 37 SJ4912
Shrewton Wilts 20 SU0643
Shripney W Susx 12 SU9302
Shrivenham Oxon 21 SU2389
Shropham Norfk 42 TL9893
Shroton Dorset 9 ST8512
Shucknall Herefs 27 SO5842
Shudy Camps Cambs 32 TL6244
Shurdington Gloucs 28 SO9218
Shurlock Row W & M 22 SU8374
Shurton Somset 19 ST2044
Shustoke Warwks 39 SP2290
Shute Devon 7 SS8900
Shute Devon 8 SY2597
Shutford Oxon 29 SP3840
Shut Heath Staffs 38 SJ8621
Shuthonger Gloucs 28 SO8935
Shutlanger Nhants 30 SP7249
Shuttington Warwks 39 SK2505
Shuttlewood Derbys 49 SK4673
Shuttleworth Bury 54 SD8017
Siabost W Isls 90 NB2646
Siadar W Isls 90 NB3854
Sibbertoft Nhants 39 SP6882
Sibford Ferris Oxon 29 SP3537
Sibford Gower Oxon 29 SP3537
Sible Hedingham Essex 24 TL7734
Sibley's Green Essex 24 TL6128
Sibsey Lincs 51 TF3550
Sibson Cambs 40 TL0997
Sibson Leics 39 SK3500
Sibthorpe Notts 49 SK7273
Sibthorpe Notts 50 SK7645
Sibton Suffk 33 TM3669
Sicklesmere Suffk 32 TL8760
Sicklinghall N York 55 SE3648
Sidbury Devon 8 SY1391
Sidbury Shrops 37 SO6885
Sidcot N Som 19 ST4257
Sidcup Gt Lon 23 TQ4672
Siddington Ches E 47 SJ8470
Siddington Gloucs 20 SU0399
Sidestrand Norfk 43 TG2539
Sidford Devon 8 SY1390
Sidlesham W Susx 11 SZ8599
Sidley E Susx 14 TQ7408
Sidmouth Devon 8 SY1287
Sigglesthorne E R Yk 57 TA1545
Sigingstone V Glam 18 SS9771
Silchester Hants 21 SU6261
Sileby Leics 39 SK6015
Silecroft Cumb 58 SD1381
Silfield Norfk 43 TM1299
Silkstone Barns 55 SE2805
Silkstone Common Barns 55 SE2904
Silk Willoughby Lincs 50 TF0542
Silloth Cumb 67 NY1153
Silpho N York 63 SE9692
Silsden C Brad 55 SE0446
Silsoe C Beds 30 TL0835
Silton Dorset 9 ST7829
Silverburn Mdloth 75 NT2060
Silverdale Lancs 59 SD4674
Silverdale Staffs 47 SJ8146
Silver End Essex 24 TL8119
Silverstone Nhants 30 SP6743
Silverton Devon 7 SS9502
Silvington Shrops 37 SO6279
Simonburn Nthumb 68 NY8773
Simonsbath Somset 7 SS7739
Simonstone Lancs 54 SD7734
Simpson M Keyn 30 SP8836
Simpson Cross Pembks 16 SM8919
Sinclairston E Ayrs 73 NS4716
Sinderby N York 62 SE3482
Sinderland Green Traffd 47 SJ7389
Sindlesham Wokham 22 SU7769
Sinfin C Derb 39 SK3431
Singleton Kent 15 TR0041
Singleton Lancs 53 SD3838
Singleton W Susx 11 SU8713
Singlewell Kent 14 TQ6570
Sinnington N York 63 SE7485
Sinton Worcs 28 SO8160
Sinton Worcs 28 SO8463
Sinton Green Worcs 28 SO8160
Sissinghurst Kent 14 TQ7937
Siston S Glos 20 ST6875
Sithney Cnwll 2 SW6328
Sittingbourne Kent 14 TQ9063
Six Ashes Shrops 37 SO7988
Sixhills Lincs 50 TF1787
Six Mile Bottom Cambs 31 TL5756
Sixpenny Handley Dorset 9 ST9917
Skares E Ayrs 74 NS5317
Skateraw Abers 89 NO9193
Skeeby N York 61 NZ1902
Skeffington Leics 40 SK7402
Skeffling E R Yk 57 TA3719
Skegby Notts 49 SK4961
Skegby Notts 50 SK7869
Skegness Lincs 51 TF5663
Skelbrooke Donc 55 SE5012
Skeldyke Lincs 41 TF3337
Skellingthorpe Lincs 50 SK9272
Skellow Donc 56 SE5310
Skelmanthorpe Kirk 55 SE2310
Skelmersdale Lancs 46 SD4606
Skelmorlie N Ayrs 73 NS1967
Skelton C York 56 SE5756
Skelton Cumb 59 NY4335
Skelton E R Yk 56 SE7625
Skelton R & Cl 62 NZ6618
Skelton on Ure N York 55 SE3668
Skelwith Bridge Cumb 59 NY3403
Skendleby Lincs 51 TF4369
Skenfrith Mons 27 SO4520
Skerne E R Yk 57 TA0455
Skerray Highld 99 NC6563
Skerton Lancs 53 SD4763
Sketchley Leics 39 SP4292
Sketty Swans 17 SS6292
Skewsby N York 56 SE6270
Skidby E R Yk 56 TA0133
Skilgate Somset 7 SS9827
Skillington Lincs 40 SK8925
Skinburness Cumb 67 NY1256
Skinflats Falk 82 NS9082
Skipness Ag & B 71 NR9057
Skipsea E R Yk 57 TA1654
Skipton N York 54 SD9851
Skipton-on-Swale N York 62 SE3679
Skipwith N York 56 SE6638
Skirlaugh E R Yk 57 TA1439
Skirling Border 75 NT0739
Skirmett Bucks 22 SU7790
Skirpenbeck E R Yk 56 SE7456
Skirwith Cumb 59 NY6132
Skye Green Essex 24 TL8722
Slack Calder 54 SD9728
Slad Gloucs 28 SO8707
Slade Devon 6 SS5046
Slade Green Gt Lon 23 TQ5276
Slade Hooton Rothm 49 SK5288
Slaggyford Nthumb 68 NY6752
Slaidburn Lancs 54 SD7152
Slaithwaite Kirk 55 SE0813
Slaley Nthumb 68 NY9657
Slamannan Falk 74 NS8572
Slapton Bucks 30 SP9320
Slapton Devon 5 SX8245
Slapton Nhants 29 SP6446
Slaugham W Susx 12 TQ2528
Slaughterford Wilts 20 ST8473
Slawston Leics 40 SP7894
Sleaford Hants 11 SU8038
Sleaford Lincs 50 TF0645
Sleagill Cumb 59 NY5919
Sleapford Wrekin 37 SJ6315
Sledmere E R Yk 56 SE9364
Sleetbeck Cumb 67 NY5076
Sleights N York 63 NZ8607
Sligachan Highld 84 NG4829
Slimbridge Gloucs 28 SO7303
Slindon Staffs 38 SJ8232
Slindon W Susx 12 SU9608
Slinfold W Susx 12 TQ1131
Slingsby N York 62 SE6974
Slip End C Beds 30 TL0718
Slip End Herts 31 TL2837
Slipton Nhants 40 SP9579
Slitting Mill Staffs 38 SK0217
Sloncombe Devon 5 SX7386
Sloothby Lincs 51 TF4970
Slough Slough 22 SU9879
Slough Green Somset 8 ST2719
Slyne Lancs 53 SD4765
Smailholm Border 76 NT6436
Smallburgh Norfk 43 TG3324
Small Dole W Susx 12 TQ2112
Smalley Derbys 49 SK4044
Smallfield Surrey 12 TQ3143
Small Heath Birm 38 SP1085
Small Hythe Kent 14 TQ8930
Smallridge Devon 8 ST3001
Smallthorne C Stke 47 SJ8850
Smallworth Norfk 32 TM0080
Smannell Hants 21 SU3749
Smarden Kent 14 TQ8742
Smarden Bell Kent 14 TQ8742
Smart's Hill Kent 13 TQ5242
Smeatharpe Devon 8 ST1910
Smeeth Kent 15 TR0739
Smeeton Westerby Leics 39 SP6892
Smestow Staffs 38 SO8591
Smethwick Sandw 38 SP0287
Smisby Derbys 39 SK3418
Smithfield Cumb 67 NY4465
Smith's Green Essex 32 TL6640
Smithstown Highld 91 NG7977
Smithton Highld 93 NH7145
Smythe's Green Essex 24 TL9218
Snailbeach Shrops 36 SJ3702
Snailwell Cambs 32 TL6467
Snainton N York 63 SE9282
Snaith E R Yk 56 SE6422
Snape N York 61 SE2684
Snape Suffk 33 TM3959
Snape Street Suffk 33 TM3958
Snaresbrook Gt Lon 23 TQ4089
Snarestone Leics 39 SK3409
Snarford Lincs 50 TF0482
Snargate Kent 15 TQ9928
Snave Kent 15 TR0129
Sneaton N York 63 NZ8907
Snelland Lincs 50 TF0780
Snelston Derbys 48 SK1543
Snetterton Norfk 32 TL9991
Snettisham Norfk 42 TF6834
Snitter Nthumb 68 NU0203
Snitterby Lincs 50 SK9894
Snitterfield Warwks 29 SP2159
Snitton Shrops 37 SO5575
Snodland Kent 14 TQ7061
Snow End Herts 31 TL4032
Snowshill Gloucs 28 SP0933
Soake Hants 11 SU6611
Soberton Hants 11 SU6116
Soberton Heath Hants 11 SU6014
Sockburn Darltn 62 NZ3406
Soham Cambs 31 TL5973
Solas W Isls 90 NF8074
Soldridge Hants 11 SU6535
Sole Street Kent 14 TQ6567
Sole Street Kent 15 TR0949
Solihull Solhll 38 SP1679
Sollers Dilwyn Herefs 27 SO4255
Sollers Hope Herefs 27 SO6132
Solva Pembks 16 SM8024
Somerby Leics 40 SK7710
Somerby Lincs 57 TA0606
Somercotes Derbys 49 SK4253
Somerford BCP 10 SZ1793
Somerford Keynes Gloucs 20 SU0195
Somerley W Susx 11 SZ8198
Somerleyton Suffk 43 TM4897
Somersal Herbert Derbys 38 SK1335
Somersby Lincs 51 TF3472
Somersham Cambs 31 TL3678
Somersham Suffk 33 TM0848
Somerton Oxon 29 SP4928
Somerton Somset 8 ST4928
Somerton Suffk 32 TL8153
Sompting W Susx 12 TQ1505
Sonning Wokham 22 SU7575
Sonning Common Oxon 22 SU7180
Sopley Hants 10 SZ1596
Sopwell Herts 23 TL1505
Sopworth Wilts 20 ST8286
Sorbie D & G 64 NX4346
Sorn E Ayrs 74 NS5526
Sotby Lincs 51 TF2078
Sotterley Suffk 33 TM4484
Soughton Flints 46 SJ2466
Soulbury Bucks 30 SP8826
Soulby Cumb 60 NY7411
Souldern Oxon 29 SP5231
Souldrop Bed 30 SP9861
Sound Ches E 47 SJ6247
Soundwell S Glos 19 ST6575
Sourton Devon 4 SX5390
Southgate Cumb 58 SD2281
South Acre Norfk 42 TF8114
South Alkham Kent 15 TR2441
Southall Gt Lon 22 TQ1279
South Allington Devon 5 SX7938
Southam Gloucs 28 SO9725
Southam Warwks 29 SP4161
South Ambersham W Susx 12 SU9120
Southampton C Sotn 10 SU4112
Southampton Airport Hants 10 SU4516
South Anston Rothm 49 SK5183
South Ashford Kent 15 TR0041
South Baddesley Hants 10 SZ3596
South Bank C York 56 SE5950
South Barrow Somset 9 ST6028
South Beddington Gt Lon 23 TQ2863
South Benfleet Essex 24 TQ7787
Southborough Gt Lon 23 TQ4267
Southborough Kent 13 TQ5842
Southbourne BCP 10 SZ1491
Southbourne W Susx 11 SU7705
South Bramwith Donc 56 SE6211
South Brent Devon 5 SX6960
South Brewham Somset 20 ST7236
South Broomhill Nthumb 69 NZ2499
Southburgh Norfk 42 TG0005
South Burlingham Norfk 43 TG3807
Southburn E R Yk 56 SE9854
South Cadbury Somset 9 ST6325
South Carlton Lincs 50 SK9476
South Carlton Notts 49 SK5883
South Cave E R Yk 56 SE9230
South Cerney Gloucs 20 SU0497
South Chailey E Susx 13 TQ3918
South Charlton Nthumb 77 NU1620
South Cheriton Somset 9 ST6924
South Church Dur 61 NZ2128
Southchurch Sthend 24 TQ9086
South Cliffe E R Yk 56 SE8735
South Clifton Notts 50 SK8270
South Cockerington Lincs 51 TF3788
South Cornelly Brdgnd 18 SS8280
Southcott Cnwll 6 SX1995
Southcott Devon 5 SX7580
Southcourt Bucks 30 SP8112
South Cove Suffk 33 TM4981
South Creake Norfk 42 TF8536
South Croxton Leics 40 SK6810
South Dalton E R Yk 56 SE9645
South Darenth Kent 14 TQ5669
South Duffield N York 56 SE6833
South Earlswood Surrey 12 TQ2747
Southease E Susx 13 TQ4205
South Elkington Lincs 51 TF2988
South Elmsall Wakefd 55 SE4711
Southend Ag & B 72 NR6908
Southend Airport Essex 24 TQ8789
Southend-on-Sea Sthend 24 TQ8885
Southerndown V Glam 18 SS8873
Southerness D & G 66 NX9754
Southerton Devon 8 SY0790
Southery Norfk 41 TL6194
South Fambridge Essex 24 TQ8694
South Ferriby N Linc 56 SE9820
South Field E R Yk 56 TA0225
Southfleet Kent 14 TQ6171
Southgate Gt Lon 23 TQ2994
Southgate Swans 17 SS5587
South Gorley Hants 10 SU1610
South Gosforth N u Ty 69 NZ2467
South Green Essex 24 TQ6893
South Green Kent 14 TQ8560
South Green Norfk 42 TG0510
South Gyle C Edin 75 NT1871
South Hanningfield Essex 24 TQ7497
South Harting W Susx 11 SU7819
South Hayling Hants 11 SZ7299
South Heath Bucks 22 SP9101
South Heighton E Susx 13 TQ4402
South Hetton Dur 69 NZ3845
South Hiendley Wakefd 55 SE3912
South Hill Cnwll 4 SX3272
South Hinksey Oxon 29 SP5104
South Holmwood Surrey 12 TQ1744
South Hornchurch Gt Lon 23 TQ5183
South Huish Devon 5 SX6941
South Hykeham Lincs 50 SK9364
South Hylton Sundld 69 NZ3556
Southill C Beds 31 TL1542
Southington Hants 21 SU5049
South Kelsey Lincs 50 TF0498
South Kessock Highld 93 NH6547
South Killingholme N Linc 57 TA1416
South Kilvington N York 62 SE4284
South Kilworth Leics 39 SP6081
South Kirkby Wakefd 55 SE4410
South Kyme Lincs 50 TF1749
Southleigh Devon 8 SY2093
South Leigh Oxon 29 SP3908
South Leverton Notts 50 SK7881
South Littleton Worcs 28 SP0746
South Lopham Norfk 32 TM0481
South Luffenham Rutlnd 40 SK9301
South Lynn Norfk 41 TF6119
South Malling E Susx 13 TQ4210
South Marston Swindn 21 SU1987
South Merstham Surrey 12 TQ2952
South Milford N York 55 SE4931
South Milton Devon 5 SX7042
South Mimms Herts 23 TL2201
South Mimms Services Herts 23 TL2200
Southminster Essex 25 TQ9599
South Molton Devon 7 SS7125
South Moor Dur 69 NZ1951
Southmoor Oxon 21 SU3998
South Moreton Oxon 21 SU5688
South Mundham W Susx 11 SU8700
South Newbald E R Yk 56 SE9035
South Newington Oxon 29 SP4033
South Newton Wilts 10 SU0834
South Normanton Derbys 49 SK4456
South Norwood Gt Lon 23 TQ3368
South Ockendon Thurr 24 TQ5983
Southoe Cambs 31 TL1864
Southolt Suffk 33 TM1968
South Ormsby Lincs 51 TF3675
Southorpe C Pete 40 TF0803
South Otterington N York 62 SE3787
Southover Dorset 9 SY6294
South Owersby Lincs 50 TF0693
Southowram Calder 55 SE1123
South Park Surrey 12 TQ2448
South Perrott Dorset 8 ST4706
South Petherton Somset 8 ST4316
South Petherwin Cnwll 4 SX3181
South Pickenham Norfk 42 TF8504
South Pill Cnwll 4 SX4259
South Pool Devon 5 SX7740
South Poorton Dorset 8 SY5297
Southport Sefton 53 SD3317
South Queensferry C Edin 82 NT1378
South Rauceby Lincs 50 TF0245
South Raynham Norfk 42 TF8723
South Reddish Stockp 48 SJ8991
Southrepps Norfk 43 TG2536
South Reston Lincs 51 TF4083
Southrey Lincs 50 TF1366
Southrop Gloucs 21 SP1903
Southrope Hants 22 SU6644
South Runcton Norfk 41 TF6308
South Scarle Notts 50 SK8464
Southsea C Port 11 SZ6599
South Shields S Tyne 69 NZ3666
South Shore Bpool 53 SD3033
Southside Dur 61 NZ1026
South Stainley N York 55 SE3063
South Stifford Thurr 24 TQ5977
South Stoke BaNES 20 ST7461
South Stoke Oxon 21 SU5983
South Stoke W Susx 12 TQ0209
South Street Kent 15 TR0557
South Street Kent 15 TR1265
South Tawton Devon 7 SX6594
South Tehidy Cnwll 2 SW6542
South Thoresby Lincs 51 TF4076
Southtown Norfk 43 TG5106
Southwaite Cumb 67 NY4445
Southwaite Services Cumb 67 NY4445
South Walsham Norfk 43 TG3613
Southwark Gt Lon 23 TQ3279
South Warnborough Hants 22 SU7247
Southwater W Susx 12 TQ1526
Southway C Plym 4 SX4860
South Weald Essex 24 TQ5694
Southwell Notts 49 SK6953
South Weston Oxon 22 SU7098
South Wheatley Notts 50 SK7685
Southwick Hants 11 SU6208
Southwick Nhants 40 TL0292
Southwick Sundld 69 NZ3758
Southwick W Susx 12 TQ2405
Southwick Wilts 20 ST8355
South Widcombe BaNES 19 ST5856
South Wigston Leics 39 SP5897
South Willesborough Kent 15 TR0240
South Willingham Lincs 50 TF1983
South Wingfield Derbys 49 SK3755
South Witham Lincs 40 SK9219
Southwold Suffk 33 TM5076
South Woodham Ferrers Essex 24 TQ8097
South Wootton Norfk 42 TF6422
South Wraxall Wilts 20 ST8364
South Zeal Devon 5 SX6593
Sovereign Harbour E Susx 13 TQ6302
Sowerby Calder 55 SE0423
Sowerby N York 62 SE4380
Sowerby Bridge Calder 55 SE0523
Sowood Calder 55 SE0818
Sowton Devon 4 SX5065
Sowton Devon 5 SX9792
Soyland Town Calder 55 SE0320
Spain's End Essex 24 TL6637
Spalding Lincs 41 TF2422
Spaldington E R Yk 56 SE7633
Spaldwick Cambs 30 TL1372
Spalford Notts 50 SK8369
Spanby Lincs 40 TF0938
Sparham Norfk 42 TG0719
Spark Bridge Cumb 58 SD3084
Sparkford Somset 9 ST6025
Sparkhill Birm 38 SP1083
Sparkwell Devon 5 SX5857
Sparrowpit Derbys 48 SK0880
Sparrows Green E Susx 13 TQ6332
Sparsholt Hants 10 SU4331
Sparsholt Oxon 21 SU3487
Spaunton N York 63 SE7289
Spaxton Somset 19 ST2237
Spean Bridge Highld 86 NN2281
Spearywell Hants 10 SU3127
Speen Bucks 22 SU8499
Speen W Berk 21 SU4567
Speeton N York 63 TA1574
Speke Lpool 46 SJ4383
Speldhurst Kent 13 TQ5541
Spellbrook Herts 31 TL4817
Spencers Wood Wokham 22 SU7166
Spen Green Ches E 47 SJ8160
Spennithorne N York 61 SE1388
Spennymoor Dur 61 NZ2533
Spetchley Worcs 28 SO8953
Spetisbury Dorset 9 ST9102
Spexhall Suffk 33 TM3780
Spey Bay Moray 94 NJ3565
Spilsby Lincs 51 TF4066
Spinkhill Derbys 49 SK4578
Spinningdale Highld 97 NH6789
Spital Wirral 46 SJ3482
Spital Hill Donc 49 SK6193
Spittal Highld 100 ND1654
Spittal Nthumb 77 NU0051
Spittal Pembks 16 SM9723
Spittalfield P & K 82 NO1040
Spittal of Glenshee P & K 88 NO1070
Spixworth Norfk 43 TG2415
Splatt Devon 7 SS6005
Splayne's Green E Susx 13 TQ4224
Splott Cardif 19 ST2076
Spofforth N York 55 SE3651
Spondon C Derb 39 SK4036
Spooner Row Norfk 43 TM0997
Sporle Norfk 42 TF8411
Spott E Loth 76 NT6775
Spratton Nhants 30 SP7169
Spreakley Surrey 11 SU8341
Spreyton Devon 7 SX6996
Spriddlestone Devon 4 SX5351
Spridlington Lincs 50 TF0084
Springburn C Glas 74 NS6068
Springfield D & G 67 NY3268
Springfield Essex 24 TL7208
Springfield Fife 83 NO3411
Springholm D & G 66 NX8070
Springside N Ayrs 73 NS3638
Springthorpe Lincs 50 SK8789
Springwell Sundld 69 NZ2858
Sproatley E R Yk 57 TA1934
Sproston Green Ches W 47 SJ7366
Sprotbrough Donc 49 SE5301
Sproughton Suffk 33 TM1244
Sprouston Border 76 NT7535
Sprowston Norfk 43 TG2512
Sproxton Leics 40 SK8524
Sproxton N York 62 SE6181
Spurstow Ches E 47 SJ5556
Spyway Dorset 8 SY5293
Stableford Shrops 37 SO7598
Stacey Bank Sheff 49 SK2890
Stackhouse N York 54 SD8165
Stackpole Pembks 16 SR9896
Stackpole Elidor Pembks 16 SR9897
Staddiscombe C Plym 4 SX5151
Stadhampton Oxon 21 SU6098
Stadhlaigearraidh W Isls 90 NF7638
Staffield Cumb 59 NY5442
Staffin Highld 90 NG4967
Stafford Staffs 38 SJ9223
Stafford Services (northbound) Staffs 38 SJ8831
Stafford Services (southbound) Staffs 38 SJ8930
Stagsden Bed 30 SP9848
Stainburn Cumb 58 NY0129
Stainby Lincs 40 SK9022
Staincross Barns 55 SE3210
Staindrop Dur 61 NZ1220
Staines-upon-Thames Surrey 22 TQ0371
Stainforth Donc 56 SE6411
Stainforth N York 54 SD8267
Staining Lancs 53 SD3436
Stainland Calder 55 SE0719
Stainsacre N York 63 NZ9108
Stainton Cumb 59 NY4828
Stainton Cumb 59 SD5285
Stainton Donc 49 SK5593
Stainton Dur 61 NZ0718
Stainton Middsb 62 NZ4714
Stainton by Langworth Lincs 50 TF0677
Staintondale N York 63 SE9998
Stainton le Vale Lincs 50 TF1794
Stainton with Adgarley Cumb 53 SD2472
Stair E Ayrs 73 NS4423
Stairhaven D & G 64 NX2153
Staithes N York 63 NZ7818
Stakes Hants 11 SU6808
Stalbridge Dorset 9 ST7317
Stalbridge Weston Dorset 9 ST7116
Stalham Norfk 43 TG3725
Stalisfield Green Kent 14 TQ9552
Stallen Dorset 9 ST6016
Stallingborough NE Lin 57 TA1911
Stalmine Lancs 53 SD3745
Stalybridge Tamesd 48 SJ9698
Stambourne Essex 32 TL7238
Stambourne Green Essex 24 TL6938
Stamford Lincs 40 TF0307
Stamford Nthumb 77 NU2219
Stamford Bridge Ches W 46 SJ4667
Stamford Bridge E R Yk 56 SE7155
Stamfordham Nthumb 68 NZ0771
Stamford Hill Gt Lon 23 TQ3387
Stanbridge C Beds 30 SP9624
Stanbury C Brad 54 SE0137
Standburn Falk 75 NS9274
Standeford Staffs 38 SJ9107
Standen Kent 14 TQ8540
Standerwick Somset 20 ST8150
Standford Hants 11 SU8134
Standingstone Cumb 58 NY0533
Standish Wigan 53 SD5610
Standlake Oxon 21 SP3903
Standon Hants 10 SU4226
Standon Herts 31 TL3922
Standon Staffs 37 SJ8135
Stane N Lans 74 NS8859
Stanfield Norfk 42 TF9320
Stanford C Beds 31 TL1640
Stanford Kent 15 TR1238
Stanford Bishop Herefs 28 SO6851
Stanford Bridge Worcs 28 SO7265
Stanford Dingley W Berk 21 SU5771
Stanford in the Vale Oxon 21 SU3493
Stanford le Hope Thurr 24 TQ6882
Stanford on Avon Nhants 39 SP5978
Stanford on Soar Notts 39 SK5421
Stanford on Teme Worcs 28 SO7065
Stanfree Derbys 49 SK4773
Stanghow R & Cl 62 NZ6715
Stanground C Pete 41 TL2097
Stanhoe Norfk 42 TF8036
Stanhope Dur 61 NY9939
Stanhope Kent 15 TR0040
Stanion Nhants 40 SP9186
Stanley Derbys 49 SK4140
Stanley Dur 69 NZ1953
Stanley P & K 82 NO1032
Stanley Staffs 48 SJ9352
Stanley Crook Dur 61 NZ1637
Stanley Pontlarge Gloucs 28 SP0030
Stanmer Br & H 12 TQ3309
Stanmore Gt Lon 23 TQ1692
Stanmore Hants 11 SU4628
Stannersburn Nthumb 68 NY7286
Stanningfield Suffk 32 TL8756
Stannington Nthumb 69 NZ2179
Stannington Sheff 49 SK2987
Stannington Station Nthumb 69 NZ2181
Stansbatch Herefs 27 SO3461
Stansfield Suffk 32 TL7852
Stanstead Suffk 32 TL8448
Stanstead Abbotts Herts 23 TL3811
Stansted Kent 14 TQ6062
Stansted Airport Essex 24 TL5523
Stansted Mountfitchet Essex 31 TL5125
Stanton Gloucs 28 SP0634
Stanton Nthumb 69 NZ1390
Stanton Staffs 48 SK1245
Stanton Suffk 32 TL9673
Stanton by Bridge Derbys 39 SK3726
Stanton by Dale Derbys 49 SK4637
Stanton Drew BaNES 19 ST5963
Stanton Fitzwarren Swindn 21 SU1790
Stanton Harcourt Oxon 29 SP4105
Stanton in Peak Derbys 48 SK2364
Stanton Lacy Shrops 37 SO4978
Stanton Lees Derbys 49 SK2562
Stanton Long Shrops 37 SO5791
Stanton-on-the-Wolds Notts 39 SK6330
Stanton Prior BaNES 20 ST6762
Stanton St Bernard Wilts 20 SU0961
Stanton St John Oxon 29 SP5709
Stanton St Quintin Wilts 20 ST9079
Stanton Street Suffk 32 TL9566
Stanton under Bardon Leics 39 SK4610
Stanton upon Hine Heath Shrops 37 SJ5624
Stanton Wick BaNES 19 ST6162
Stanway Essex 25 TL9424
Stanway Gloucs 28 SP0632
Stanwell Surrey 22 TQ0574
Stanwick Nhants 30 SP9771
Stanwix Cumb 67 NY3957
Staoinebrig W Isls 90 NF7532
Stape N York 63 SE7994
Stapeley Ches E 47 SJ6749
Stapenhill Staffs 39 SK2521
Staple Kent 15 TR2756
Staple Cross Devon 7 ST0320
Staplecross E Susx 14 TQ7822
Staplefield W Susx 12 TQ2728
Staple Fitzpaine Somset 8 ST2618
Stapleford Cambs 31 TL4751
Stapleford Herts 31 TL3117
Stapleford Leics 40 SK8018
Stapleford Lincs 50 SK8857
Stapleford Notts 49 SK4837
Stapleford Wilts 10 SU0737
Stapleford Abbotts Essex 23 TQ5194
Staplegrove Somset 8 ST2126
Staplehay Somset 8 ST2121
Staplehurst Kent 14 TQ7843
Staplers IoW 11 SZ5189
Staplestreet Kent 15 TR0660
Stapleton Herefs 27 SO3265
Stapleton Leics 39 SP4398
Stapleton N York 61 NZ2612
Stapleton Shrops 37 SJ4704
Stapleton Somset 8 ST4621
Stapley Somset 8 ST1913
Staploe Bed 31 TL1560
Staplow Herefs 28 SO6941
Star Fife 83 NO3103
Star Pembks 17 SN2434
Star Somset 19 ST4358
Starbeck N York 55 SE3255
Starbotton N York 61 SD9574
Starcross Devon 5 SX9781
Stareton Warwks 39 SP3371
Starlings Green Essex 31 TL4631
Starston Norfk 33 TM2384
Startforth Dur 61 NZ0415
Startley Wilts 20 ST9482
Statenborough Kent 15 TR3155
Statham Warrtn 47 SJ6787
Stathe Somset 8 ST3728
Stathern Leics 40 SK7731
Staughton Green Cambs 30 TL1365
Staunton Gloucs 27 SO5512
Staunton Gloucs 28 SO7829
Staunton on Arrow Herefs 27 SO3660
Staunton on Wye Herefs 27 SO3644
Staveley Cumb 59 SD4698
Staveley Derbys 49 SK4374
Staveley N York 55 SE3662
Staveley-in-Cartmel Cumb 59 SD3786
Staverton Devon 5 SX7964
Staverton Gloucs 28 SO8923
Staverton Nhants 29 SP5361
Staverton Wilts 20 ST8560
Stawell Somset 19 ST3738
Stawley Somset 7 ST0622
Staxigoe Highld 100 ND3852
Staxton N York 63 TA0179
Staynall Lancs 53 SD3643
Stean N York 61 SE0973
Stearsby N York 56 SE6071
Steart Somset 19 ST2745
Stebbing Essex 24 TL6624
Stechford Birm 38 SP1287
Stedham W Susx 11 SU8622
Steen's Bridge Herefs 27 SO5357
Steep Hants 11 SU7425
Steep Lane Calder 55 SE0223
Steeple Essex 25 TL9303
Steeple Ashton Wilts 20 ST9056
Steeple Aston Oxon 29 SP4725
Steeple Bumpstead Essex 32 TL6841
Steeple Claydon Bucks 30 SP7026
Steeple Gidding Cambs 40 TL1381
Steeple Langford Wilts 10 SU0337
Steeple Morden Cambs 31 TL2842
Steeton C Brad 55 SE0344
Stein Highld 90 NG2656
Stelling Minnis Kent 15 TR1447
Stembridge Somset 8 ST4220
Stenalees Cnwll 3 SX0156
Stenhousemuir Falk 82 NS8782
Stenson Fields Derbys 39 SK3331
Stenton E Loth 76 NT6274
Steornabhagh W Isls 90 NB4232
Stepaside Pembks 16 SN1407
Stepney Gt Lon 23 TQ3681
Steppingley C Beds 30 TL0035
Stepps N Lans 74 NS6568
Sternfield Suffk 33 TM3961
Stert Wilts 20 SU0259
Stetchworth Cambs 32 TL6459
Stevenage Herts 31 TL2325
Stevenston N Ayrs 73 NS2742
Steventon Hants 21 SU5447
Steventon Oxon 21 SU4691
Steventon End Essex 31 TL5942
Stevington Bed 30 SP9853
Stewartby Bed 30 TL0142
Stewartfield S Lans 74 NS6255
Stewarton E Ayrs 73 NS4245
Stewkley Bucks 30 SP8526
Stewley Somset 8 ST3118
Steyning W Susx 12 TQ1711
Steynton Pembks 16 SM9107
Stibb Cnwll 6 SS2210
Stibbard Norfk 42 TF9828
Stibb Cross Devon 6 SS4314
Stibb Green Wilts 21 SU2262
Stibbington Cambs 40 TL0898
Stichill Border 76 NT7138
Sticker Cnwll 3 SW9750
Stickford Lincs 51 TF3560
Sticklepath Devon 7 SX6494
Stickney Lincs 51 TF3457
Stiffkey Norfk 42 TF9742
Stifford Clays Thurr 24 TQ6280
Stilligarry W Isls 90 NF7638
Stillingfleet N York 56 SE5940
Stillington N York 56 SE5867
Stillington S on T 62 NZ3723
Stilton Cambs 40 TL1689
Stinchcombe Gloucs 20 ST7298
Stinsford Dorset 9 SY7091
Stiperstones Shrops 36 SJ3600
Stirchley Wrekin 37 SJ6907
Stirling Stirlg 81 NS7993
Stirling Services Stirlg 81 NS8088
Stirtloe Cambs 31 TL1966
Stirton N York 54 SD9752
Stisted Essex 24 TL8024
Stithians Cnwll 2 SW7336
Stivichall Covtry 39 SP3376
Stixwould Lincs 50 TF1765
Stoak Ches W 46 SJ4273
Stobo Border 75 NT1837
Stoborough Dorset 9 SY9286
Stobswood Nthumb 69 NZ2195
Stock Essex 24 TQ6998
Stock N Som 19 ST4561
Stockbridge Hants 10 SU3535
Stockbury Kent 14 TQ8461
Stockcross W Berk 21 SU4368
Stockerston Leics 40 SP8397
Stock Green Worcs 28 SO9859
Stocking Herefs 27 SO6230
Stockingford Warwks 39 SP3391
Stocking Pelham Herts 31 TL4529
Stockland Devon 8 ST2404
Stockland Bristol Somset 19 ST2443
Stockleigh English Devon 7 SS8506
Stockleigh Pomeroy Devon 7 SS8703
Stockley Wilts 20 ST9967
Stocklinch Somset 8 ST3817
Stockport Stockp 48 SJ8990
Stocksbridge Sheff 49 SK2698
Stocksfield Nthumb 68 NZ0561
Stockton Herefs 27 SO5261
Stockton Norfk 43 TM3894
Stockton Shrops 37 SO7299
Stockton Warwks 29 SP4363
Stockton Wilts 20 ST9838
Stockton Wrekin 37 SJ7716
Stockton Brook Staffs 48 SJ9152
Stockton Heath Warrtn 47 SJ6185
Stockton-on-Tees S on T 62 NZ4419
Stockton on Teme Worcs 28 SO7167
Stockton on the Forest C York 56 SE6556
Stockwell End Wolves 38 SJ8900
Stockwood Bristl 19 ST6268
Stockwood Dorset 9 ST5806
Stock Wood Worcs 28 SP0058
Stodmarsh Kent 15 TR2260
Stody Norfk 42 TG0535
Stoer Highld 98 NC0328
Stoford Somset 9 ST5613
Stoford Wilts 10 SU0835
Stogumber Somset 18 ST0937
Stogursey Somset 19 ST2042
Stoke Covtry 39 SP3778
Stoke Devon 6 SS2324
Stoke Hants 11 SU7202
Stoke Hants 21 SU4051
Stoke Medway 14 TQ8274
Stoke Abbott Dorset 8 ST4500
Stoke Albany Nhants 40 SP8088
Stoke Ash Suffk 33 TM1170
Stoke Bardolph Notts 49 SK6441
Stoke Bliss Worcs 27 SO6563
Stoke Bruerne Nhants 30 SP7449
Stoke-by-Clare Suffk 32 TL7443
Stoke-by-Nayland Suffk 25 TL9836
Stoke Canon Devon 7 SX9398
Stoke Charity Hants 11 SU4839
Stoke Climsland Cnwll 4 SX3674
Stoke Cross Herefs 27 SO6250
Stoke D'Abernon Surrey 22 TQ1258
Stoke Doyle Nhants 40 TL0286
Stoke Dry Rutlnd 40 SP8596
Stoke Edith Herefs 27 SO6040
Stoke Farthing Wilts 10 SU0525
Stoke Ferry Norfk 42 TF7000
Stoke Fleming Devon 5 SX8648
Stokeford Dorset 9 SY8687
Stoke Gabriel Devon 5 SX8557
Stoke Gifford S Glos 19 ST6279
Stoke Golding Leics 39 SP3997
Stoke Goldington M Keyn 30 SP8348
Stokeham Notts 50 SK7876
Stoke Hammond Bucks 30 SP8829
Stoke Holy Cross Norfk 43 TG2301
Stokeinteignhead Devon 5 SX9170
Stoke Lacy Herefs 27 SO6249
Stoke Lyne Oxon 29 SP5628
Stoke Mandeville Bucks 22 SP8310
Stokenchurch Bucks 22 SU7696
Stoke Newington Gt Lon 23 TQ3386
Stokenham Devon 5 SX8042
Stoke-on-Trent C Stke 47 SJ8847
Stoke Orchard Gloucs 28 SO9128
Stoke Poges Bucks 22 SU9783
Stoke Prior Herefs 27 SO5256
Stoke Prior Worcs 28 SO9467
Stoke Rivers Devon 7 SS6335
Stoke Rochford Lincs 40 SK9127
Stoke Row Oxon 22 SU6884
Stoke St Gregory Somset 8 ST3427
Stoke St Mary Somset 8 ST2622
Stoke St Michael Somset 20 ST6646
Stoke St Milborough Shrops 37 SO5682
Stokesby Norfk 43 TG4310
Stokesley N York 62 NZ5208
Stoke sub Hamdon Somset 8 ST4717
Stoke Talmage Oxon 22 SU6799
Stoke Trister Somset 9 ST7428
Stoke upon Tern Shrops 37 SJ6328
Stolford Somset 19 ST2345
Stondon Massey Essex 24 TL5800
Stone Bucks 30 SP7812
Stone Gloucs 20 ST6895
Stone Rothm 49 SK5589
Stone Staffs 38 SJ9034
Stone Worcs 38 SO8675
Stone Allerton Somset 19 ST3951
Ston Easton Somset 19 ST6253
Stonebridge N Som 19 ST3859
Stonebridge Warwks 39 SP2182
Stonebroom Derbys 49 SK4059
Stone Cross Kent 15 TR3257
Stonecrouch Kent 14 TQ7033
Stoneferry C KuH 57 TA1031
Stonegate E Susx 14 TQ6628
Stonegrave N York 62 SE6577
Stonehaven Abers 89 NO8786
Stonehouse C Plym 4 SX4654
Stonehouse Gloucs 28 SO8005
Stonehouse S Lans 74 NS7546
Stone in Oxney Kent 14 TQ9427
Stoneleigh Warwks 39 SP3372
Stonesby Leics 40 SK8224
Stonesfield Oxon 29 SP3917
Stones Green Essex 25 TM1626
Stone Street Kent 14 TQ5754
Stone Street Suffk 33 TM3882
Stoneybridge W Isls 90 NF7532
Stoneyburn W Loth 75 NS9862
Stoneygate C Leic 39 SK6002
Stoneykirk D & G 64 NX0853
Stoney Middleton Derbys 48 SK2275
Stoney Stanton Leics 39 SP4994
Stoney Stoke Somset 9 ST7032
Stoney Stratton Somset 20 ST6539
Stoneywood C Aber 95 NJ8811
Stonham Aspal Suffk 33 TM1359
Stonnall Staffs 38 SK0603
Stonor Oxon 22 SU7388
Stonton Wyville Leics 40 SP7395
Stony Houghton Derbys 49 SK4966
Stony Stratford M Keyn 30 SP7840
Stoodleigh Devon 7 SS6532
Stoodleigh Devon 7 SS9218
Stop 24 Services Kent 15 TR1337
Stopham W Susx 12 TQ0219
Stopsley Luton 30 TL1023
Stornoway W Isls 90 NB4232
Stornoway Airport W Isls 90 NB4632
Storrington W Susx 12 TQ0814
Storth Cumb 59 SD4779
Storwood E R Yk 56 SE7144
Stotfield Moray 94 NJ2270
Stotfold C Beds 31 TL2136
Stottesdon Shrops 37 SO6782
Stoughton Leics 39 SK6402
Stoughton Surrey 12 SU9851
Stoughton W Susx 11 SU8011
Stoulton Worcs 28 SO9049
Stourbridge Dudley 38 SO8983
Stourpaine Dorset 9 ST8609
Stourport-on-Severn Worcs 37 SO8171
Stour Provost Dorset 9 ST7921
Stour Row Dorset 9 ST8221
Stourton Staffs 38 SO8684
Stourton Warwks 29 SP2936
Stourton Wilts 9 ST7734
Stourton Caundle Dorset 9 ST7115
Stoven Suffk 33 TM4481
Stow Border 76 NT4544
Stow Lincs 50 SK8882
Stow Bardolph Norfk 41 TF6206
Stow Bedon Norfk 42 TL9596
Stowbridge Norfk 41 TF6007
Stow-cum-Quy Cambs 31 TL5260
Stowe Shrops 36 SO3173
Stowe by Chartley Staffs 38 SK0026
Stowell Somset 9 ST6822
Stowey BaNES 19 ST5959
Stowford Devon 4 SX4387
Stowlangtoft Suffk 32 TL9568
Stow Longa Cambs 30 TL1070
Stow Maries Essex 24 TQ8399
Stowmarket Suffk 32 TM0458
Stow-on-the-Wold Gloucs 29 SP1925
Stowting Kent 15 TR1242
Stowupland Suffk 32 TM0760
Strachan Abers 89 NO6792
Strachur Ag & B 80 NN0901
Stradbroke Suffk 33 TM2373
Stradishall Suffk 32 TL7452
Stradsett Norfk 42 TF6605
Stragglethorpe Lincs 50 SK9152
Straiton S Ayrs 73 NS3804
Straloch P & K 88 NO0463
Stramshall Staffs 38 SK0735
Strang IoM 52 SC3578
Strangeways Salfd 47 SJ8399
Strangford Herefs 27 SO5827
Stranraer D & G 64 NX0560
Stratfield Mortimer W Berk 22 SU6664
Stratfield Saye Hants 22 SU6861
Stratfield Turgis Hants 22 SU6959
Stratford Gt Lon 23 TQ3884
Stratford St Andrew Suffk 33 TM3560
Stratford St Mary Suffk 25 TM0434
Stratford sub Castle Wilts 10 SU1332
Stratford Tony Wilts 10 SU0926
Stratford-upon-Avon Warwks 29 SP2055
Strath Highld 91 NG7978
Strathaven S Lans 74 NS7044
Strathblane Stirlg 81 NS5679
Strathcanaird Highld 96 NC1501
Strathdon Abers 94 NJ3512
Strathkinness Fife 83 NO4516
Strathmiglo Fife 82 NO2109
Strathpeffer Highld 92 NH4858
Strathtay P & K 87 NN9153
Strathwhillan N Ayrs 72 NS0235
Strathy Highld 99 NC8464
Strathyre Stirlg 81 NN5617
Stratton Cnwll 6 SS2306
Stratton Dorset 9 SY6593
Stratton Gloucs 28 SP0103
Stratton Audley Oxon 29 SP6025
Stratton-on-the-Fosse Somset 20 ST6650
Stratton St Margaret Swindn 21 SU1786
Stratton St Michael Norfk 43 TM2093

136 Stratton Strawless – Trotton

Stratton Strawless Norfk 43 TG2220
Streat E Susx 12 TQ3515
Streatham Gt Lon 23 TQ3071
Streatley C Beds 30 TL0728
Streatley W Berk 21 SU5980
Street Devon 8 SY1888
Street Somset 19 ST4836
Street Ashton Warwks 39 SP4582
Street Dinas Shrops 36 SJ3338
Street End Kent 15 TR1453
Street End W Susx 11 SZ8599
Streethay Staffs 38 SK1410
Streetlam N York 61 SE3098
Streetly End Cambs 32 TL6148
Street on the Fosse Somset 19 ST6239
Strelley Notts 49 SK5141
Strensall C York 56 SE6360
Strensham Services (northbound) Worcs 28 SO8940
Strensham Services (southbound) Worcs 28 SO9040
Stretcholt Somset 19 ST2943
Strete Devon 5 SX8446
Stretford Traffd 47 SJ7994
Strethall Essex 31 TL4839
Stretham Cambs 31 TL5174
Strettington W Susx 11 SU8907
Stretton Derbys 49 SK3961
Stretton Rutlnd 40 SK9415
Stretton Staffs 38 SJ8811
Stretton Staffs 39 SK2526
Stretton Warrtn 47 SJ6282
Stretton Grandison Herefs 27 SO6344
Stretton-on-Dunsmore Warwks 39 SP4072
Stretton on Fosse Warwks 29 SP2238
Stretton Sugwas Herefs 27 SO4642
Stretton under Fosse Warwks 39 SP4581
Stretton Westwood Shrops 37 SO5998
Strichen Abers 95 NJ9455
Stringston Somset 19 ST1742
Strixton Nhants 30 SP9061
Stroat Gloucs 19 ST5797
Stromeferry Highld 85 NG8634
Stromness Ork 100 HY2508
Stronachlachar Stirlg 81 NN4010
Strone Ag & B 80 NS1980
Stronmilchan Ag & B 80 NN1528
Stronsay Airport Ork 100 HY6329
Strontian Highld 79 NM8161
Strood Medway 14 TQ7268
Stroud Gloucs 28 SO8505
Stroud Hants 11 SU7223
Stroud Green Gloucs 28 SO8007
Stroxton Lincs 40 SK9030
Struan Highld 84 NG3438
Strumpshaw Norfk 43 TG3407
Struy Highld 92 NH4040
Stuartfield Abers 95 NJ9745
Stubbington Hants 11 SU5503
Stubbins Lancs 54 SD7918
Stubton Lincs 50 SK8748
Stuckton Hants 10 SU1613
Studham C Beds 30 TL0215
Studland Dorset 10 SZ0382
Studley Warwks 28 SP0764
Studley Wilts 20 ST9671
Studley Roger N York 55 SE2970
Studley Royal N York 55 SE2770
Stuntney Cambs 31 TL5578
Sturmer Essex 32 TL6943
Sturminster Common Dorset 9 ST7812
Sturminster Marshall Dorset 9 ST9500
Sturminster Newton Dorset 9 ST7814
Sturry Kent 15 TR1760
Sturton N Linc 56 SE9604
Sturton by Stow Lincs 50 SK8980
Sturton le Steeple Notts 50 SK7883
Stuston Suffk 33 TM1377
Stutton N York 55 SE4841
Stutton Suffk 25 TM1534
Styal Ches E 47 SJ8383
Styrrup Notts 49 SK6090
Suckley Worcs 28 SO7251
Sudborough Nhants 40 SP9682
Sudbourne Suffk 33 TM4153
Sudbrook Lincs 50 SK9744
Sudbrook Mons 19 ST5087
Sudbrooke Lincs 50 TF0376
Sudbury Derbys 38 SK1631
Sudbury Gt Lon 23 TQ1685
Sudbury Suffk 32 TL8741
Suffield N York 63 SE9890
Suffield Norfk 43 TG2232
Sugnall Staffs 37 SJ7931
Sugwas Pool Herefs 27 SO4541
Sulby IoM 52 SC3894
Sulgrave Nhants 29 SP5544
Sulham W Berk 21 SU6474
Sulhamstead W Berk 21 SU6368
Sullom Shet 100 HU3573
Sully V Glam 19 ST1568
Sumburgh Airport Shet 100 HU3910
Summerbridge N York 55 SE2062
Summercourt Cnwll 3 SW8856
Summerfield Norfk 42 TF7538
Summerhill Pembks 17 SN1507
Summerhouse Darltn 61 NZ2019
Summersdale W Susx 11 SU8606
Summerseat Bury 54 SD7914
Summertown Oxon 29 SP5009
Sunbury-on-Thames Surrey 22 TQ1168
Sunderland Cumb 58 NY1735
Sunderland Lancs 53 SD4255
Sunderland Sundld 69 NZ3957
Sunderland Bridge Dur 61 NZ2637
Sundon Park Luton 30 TL0525
Sundridge Kent 23 TQ4855
Sunningdale W & M 22 SU9567
Sunninghill W & M 22 SU9367
Sunningwell Oxon 21 SP4900
Sunniside Dur 61 NZ1438
Sunniside Gatesd 69 NZ2059
Sunnyhill C Derb 39 SK3432
Sunnyhurst Bl w D 54 SD6722
Sunnymead Oxon 29 SP5009
Surbiton Gt Lon 23 TQ1867
Surfleet Lincs 41 TF2528
Surlingham Norfk 43 TG3106
Surrex Essex 24 TL8722
Sustead Norfk 43 TG1837
Susworth Lincs 50 SE8302
Sutcombe Devon 6 SS3411
Sutcombemill Devon 6 SS3411
Sutterby Lincs 51 TF3872
Sutterton Lincs 41 TF2835
Sutton C Beds 31 TL2247
Sutton C Pete 40 TL0998
Sutton Cambs 41 TL4479
Sutton Devon 5 SX7042
Sutton E Susx 13 TV4999
Sutton Gt Lon 23 TQ2564
Sutton Kent 15 TR3349
Sutton N York 55 SE4925
Sutton Norfk 43 TG3823
Sutton Notts 40 SK7637
Sutton Oxon 29 SP4106
Sutton Shrops 37 SJ5010
Sutton Shrops 37 SO7386
Sutton Staffs 37 SJ7622
Sutton Suffk 33 TM3046
Sutton W Susx 12 SU9715
Sutton-at-Hone Kent 14 TQ5569
Sutton Bassett Nhants 40 SP7790
Sutton Benger Wilts 20 ST9478
Sutton Bonington Notts 39 SK5024
Sutton Bridge Lincs 41 TF4721
Sutton Cheney Leics 39 SK4100
Sutton Coldfield Birm 38 SP1295
Sutton Courtenay Oxon 21 SU5094
Sutton cum Lound Notts 49 SK6784
Sutton Green Surrey 22 TQ0054
Sutton Howgrave N York 62 SE3179
Sutton-in-Ashfield Notts 49 SK4959
Sutton-in-Craven N York 54 SE0043
Sutton Maddock Shrops 37 SJ7201
Sutton Mallet Somset 19 ST3736
Sutton Mandeville Wilts 9 ST9828
Sutton Montis Somset 9 ST6224
Sutton-on-Hull C KuH 57 TA1232
Sutton on Sea Lincs 51 TF5281
Sutton-on-the-Forest N York 56 SE5864
Sutton on the Hill Derbys 39 SK2333
Sutton on Trent Notts 50 SK7965
Sutton St Edmund Lincs 41 TF3613
Sutton St James Lincs 41 TF3918
Sutton St Nicholas Herefs 27 SO5245
Sutton Scotney Hants 11 SU4639
Sutton-under-Brailes Warwks 29 SP3037
Sutton-under-Whitestonecliffe N York 62 SE4882
Sutton upon Derwent E R Yk 56 SE7047
Sutton Valence Kent 14 TQ8149
Sutton Veny Wilts 20 ST9041
Sutton Waldron Dorset 9 ST8615
Sutton Weaver Ches W 47 SJ5479
Sutton Wick BaNES 19 ST5759
Sutton Wick Oxon 21 SU4894
Swaby Lincs 51 TF3877
Swadlincote Derbys 39 SK2919
Swaffham Norfk 42 TF8108
Swaffham Bulbeck Cambs 31 TL5562
Swaffham Prior Cambs 31 TL5764
Swafield Norfk 43 TG2832
Swainby N York 62 NZ4701
Swainsthorpe Norfk 43 TG2101
Swainswick BaNES 20 ST7668
Swalcliffe Oxon 29 SP3737
Swalecliffe Kent 15 TR1367
Swallow Lincs 57 TA1703
Swallow Beck Lincs 50 SK9467
Swallowcliffe Wilts 9 ST9627
Swallowfield Wokham 22 SU7264
Swanage Dorset 10 SZ0378
Swanbourne Bucks 30 SP8026
Swan Green Ches W 47 SJ7373
Swanland E R Yk 56 SE9928
Swanley Kent 23 TQ5168
Swanley Village Kent 23 TQ5369
Swanmore Hants 11 SU5716
Swannington Leics 39 SK4116
Swannington Norfk 43 TG1319
Swanpool Lincs 50 SK9569
Swanscombe Kent 14 TQ6074
Swansea Swans 18 SS6592
Swansea Airport Swans 17 SS5691
Swansea West Services Swans 17 SS6299
Swanton Abbot Norfk 43 TG2625
Swanton Morley Norfk 42 TG0117
Swanton Novers Norfk 42 TG0231
Swan Village Sandw 38 SO9892
Swanwick Derbys 49 SK4053
Swanwick Hants 11 SU5109
Swarby Lincs 50 TF0440
Swardeston Norfk 43 TG2002
Swarkestone Derbys 39 SK3728
Swarland Nthumb 69 NU1603
Swarraton Hants 11 SU5636
Swarthmoor Cumb 58 SD2777
Swaton Lincs 40 TF1337
Swavesey Cambs 31 TL3668
Sway Hants 10 SZ2798
Swayfield Lincs 40 SK9922
Swaythling C Sotn 10 SU4416
Sweetham Devon 7 SX8899
Sweethaws E Susx 13 TQ5028
Sweets Cnwll 6 SX1595
Sweetshouse Cnwll 3 SX0861
Swefling Suffk 33 TM3463
Swepstone Leics 39 SK3610
Swerford Oxon 29 SP3731
Swettenham Ches E 47 SJ8067
Swilland Suffk 33 TM1852
Swillington Leeds 55 SE3830
Swimbridge Devon 7 SS6230
Swimbridge Newland Devon 7 SS6030
Swinbrook Oxon 29 SP2812
Swincliffe N York 55 SE2458
Swinderby Lincs 50 SK8663
Swindon Gloucs 28 SO9325
Swindon Staffs 38 SO8690
Swindon Swindn 20 SU1484
Swine E R Yk 57 TA1335
Swinefleet E R Yk 56 SE7621
Swineshead Bed 30 TL0565
Swineshead Lincs 51 TF2340
Swinford Leics 39 SP5679
Swingfield Minnis Kent 15 TR2142
Swingfield Street Kent 15 TR2343
Swingleton Green Suffk 32 TL9647
Swinhoe Nthumb 77 NU2128
Swinithwaite N York 61 SE0489
Swinside Cumb 58 NY2421
Swinstead Lincs 40 TF0122
Swinton Border 77 NT8347
Swinton N York 61 SE2179
Swinton N York 63 SE7573
Swinton Rothm 49 SK4599
Swinton Salfd 47 SD7701
Swithland Leics 39 SK5512
Swynnerton Staffs 38 SJ8535
Swyre Dorset 8 SY5288
Sychtyn Powys 35 SH9907
Syde Gloucs 28 SO9511
Sydenham Gt Lon 23 TQ3671
Sydenham Oxon 22 SP7301
Sydenham Damerel Devon 4 SX4176
Syderstone Norfk 42 TF8332
Sydling St Nicholas Dorset 9 SY6399
Sydmonton Hants 21 SU4857
Syerston Notts 50 SK7447
Sykehouse Donc 56 SE6316
Symbister Shet 100 HU5462
Symington S Ayrs 73 NS3831
Symington S Lans 75 NS9935
Symondsbury Dorset 8 SY4493
Symonds Yat (West) Herefs 27 SO5515
Syreford Gloucs 28 SP0220
Syresham Nhants 29 SP6241
Syston Leics 39 SK6211
Syston Lincs 50 SK9240
Sytchampton Worcs 28 SO8466
Sywell Nhants 30 SP8267

T

Tackley Oxon 29 SP4719
Tacolneston Norfk 43 TM1495
Tadcaster N York 55 SE4843
Taddington Derbys 48 SK1471
Tadley Hants 21 SU6061
Tadlow Cambs 31 TL2847
Tadmarton Oxon 29 SP3937
Tadworth Surrey 23 TQ2257
Taff's Well Rhondd 18 ST1283
Taibach Neath 18 SS7788
Tain Highld 97 NH7781
Tairbeart W Isls 90 NB1500
Takeley Essex 24 TL5621
Takeley Street Essex 24 TL5421
Talaton Devon 7 SY0699
Talbenny Pembks 16 SM8411
Talbot Village BCP 10 SZ0793
Taleford Devon 8 SY0997
Talerddig Powys 35 SH9300
Talgarreg Cerdgn 17 SN4251
Talgarth Powys 27 SO1533
Talke Staffs 47 SJ8253
Talke Pits Staffs 47 SJ8352
Talkin Cumb 67 NY5557
Talladale Highld 91 NG9170
Tallarn Green Wrexhm 46 SJ4444
Tallentire Cumb 58 NY1035
Talley Carmth 17 SN6332
Tallington Lincs 40 TF0908
Talmine Highld 99 NC5863
Talog Carmth 17 SN3325
Talsarn Cerdgn 34 SN5456
Talsarnau Gwynd 45 SH6135
Talskiddy Cnwll 3 SW9165
Talwrn IoA 44 SH4877
Tal-y-bont Cerdgn 35 SN6589
Tal-y-Bont Conwy 45 SH7668
Tal-y-bont Gwynd 34 SH5921
Tal-y-bont Gwynd 45 SH6070
Talybont-on-Usk Powys 26 SO1122
Tal-y-Cafn Conwy 45 SH7871
Tal-y-coed Mons 27 SO4115
Talysarn Gwynd 44 SH4952
Tamerton Foliot C Plym 4 SX4761
Tamworth Staffs 39 SK2003
Tamworth Services Warwks 39 SK2400
Tandridge Surrey 13 TQ3750
Tanfield Dur 69 NZ1855
Tanfield Lea Dur 69 NZ1854
Tangley Hants 21 SU3252
Tangmere W Susx 11 SU9006
Tankerness Ork 100 HY5109
Tankersley Barns 49 SK3499
Tankerton Kent 15 TR1166
Tannadice Angus 89 NO4758
Tanner's Green Worcs 38 SP0874
Tannington Suffk 33 TM2467
Tannochside N Lans 74 NS7061
Tansley Derbys 49 SK3259
Tansor Nhants 40 TL0590
Tantobie Dur 69 NZ1754
Tanworth in Arden Warwks 28 SP1170
Tan-y-groes Cerdgn 17 SN2849
Taplow Bucks 22 SU9182
Tarbert Ag & B 71 NR6551
Tarbert Ag & B 71 NR8668
Tarbert W Isls 90 NB1500
Tarbet Ag & B 80 NN3104
Tarbolton S Ayrs 73 NS4327
Tardebigge Worcs 28 SO9969
Tarfside Angus 89 NO4879
Tarland Abers 89 NJ4804
Tarleton Lancs 53 SD4520
Tarlton Gloucs 20 ST9599
Tarnock Somset 19 ST3752
Tarporley Ches W 47 SJ5562
Tarrant Crawford Dorset 9 ST9203
Tarrant Gunville Dorset 9 ST9213
Tarrant Hinton Dorset 9 ST9311
Tarrant Keyneston Dorset 9 ST9204
Tarrant Launceston Dorset 9 ST9409
Tarrant Monkton Dorset 9 ST9408
Tarrant Rawston Dorset 9 ST9306
Tarrant Rushton Dorset 9 ST9305
Tarring Neville E Susx 13 TQ4403
Tarrington Herefs 27 SO6140
Tarskavaig Highld 84 NG5810
Tarves Abers 95 NJ8631
Tarvin Ches W 46 SJ4966
Tasburgh Norfk 43 TM2095
Tatenhill Staffs 39 SK2021
Tathwell Lincs 51 TF3182
Tatsfield Surrey 23 TQ4156
Tattenhall Ches W 46 SJ4858
Tatterford Norfk 42 TF8628
Tattersett Norfk 42 TF8429
Tattershall Lincs 51 TF2157
Tattershall Thorpe Lincs 51 TF2159
Tattingstone Suffk 25 TM1337
Tattingstone White Horse Suffk 25 TM1338
Tatworth Somset 8 ST3205
Taunton Somset 8 ST2224
Taunton Deane Services Somset 8 ST1920
Taverham Norfk 43 TG1613
Tavernspite Pembks 17 SN1812
Tavistock Devon 4 SX4874
Taw Green Devon 7 SX6597
Tawstock Devon 6 SS5529
Taxal Derbys 48 SK0079
Tayinloan Ag & B 72 NR6946
Taynton Gloucs 28 SO7222
Taynton Oxon 29 SP2313
Taynuilt Ag & B 80 NN0031
Tayport Fife 83 NO4628
Tayvallich Ag & B 71 NR7487
Tealby Lincs 50 TF1590
Tealing Angus 83 NO4038
Team Valley Gatesd 69 NZ2459
Teangue Highld 85 NG6609
Tebay Cumb 59 NY6104
Tebay Services Cumb 59 NY6006
Tebworth C Beds 30 SP9926
Tedburn St Mary Devon 7 SX8194
Teddington Gloucs 28 SO9633
Teddington Gt Lon 23 TQ1670
Tedstone Delamere Herefs 28 SO6958
Tedstone Wafer Herefs 28 SO6759
Teeton Nhants 30 SP6970
Teffont Evias Wilts 9 ST9931
Teffont Magna Wilts 9 ST9932
Tegryn Pembks 17 SN2233
Teigh Rutlnd 40 SK8615
Teigngrace Devon 5 SX8574
Teignmouth Devon 5 SX9473
Telford Wrekin 37 SJ6908
Telford Services Shrops 37 SJ7308
Tellisford Somset 20 ST8055
Telscombe E Susx 13 TQ4003
Templand D & G 66 NY0886
Temple Cnwll 3 SX1473
Temple Mdloth 75 NT3158
Temple Bar Cerdgn 34 SN5354
Temple Cloud BaNES 19 ST6257
Templecombe Somset 9 ST7022
Temple Grafton Warwks 28 SP1255
Temple Guiting Gloucs 28 SP0928
Temple Hirst N York 56 SE6024
Temple Normanton Derbys 49 SK4167
Temple Sowerby Cumb 59 NY6127
Templeton Devon 7 SS8813
Templeton Pembks 16 SN1111
Templetown Dur 69 NZ1050
Tempsford C Beds 31 TL1753
Tenbury Wells Worcs 27 SO5968
Tenby Pembks 16 SN1300
Tendring Essex 25 TM1424
Tendring Green Essex 25 TM1325
Tendring Heath Essex 25 TM1326
Ten Mile Bank Norfk 41 TL5996
Tenterden Kent 14 TQ8833
Terling Essex 24 TL7715
Ternhill Shrops 37 SJ6332
Terrington N York 56 SE6770
Terrington St Clement Norfk 41 TF5520
Terrington St John Norfk 41 TF5314
Teston Kent 14 TQ7053
Testwood Hants 10 SU3514
Tetbury Gloucs 20 ST8993
Tetchill Shrops 36 SJ3832
Tetcott Devon 6 SX3396
Tetford Lincs 51 TF3374
Tetney Lincs 51 TA3100
Tetsworth Oxon 22 SP6801
Tettenhall Wolves 38 SJ8800
Tettenhall Wood Wolves 38 SO8899
Teversal Notts 49 SK4861
Teversham Cambs 31 TL4958
Teviothead Border 67 NT4005
Tewin Herts 31 TL2714
Tewkesbury Gloucs 28 SO8932
Teynham Kent 14 TQ9562
Thackley C Brad 55 SE1738
Thakeham W Susx 12 TQ1017
Thame Oxon 22 SP7005
Thames Ditton Surrey 23 TQ1567
Thamesmead Gt Lon 23 TQ4780
Thamesport Medway 14 TQ8774
Thanington Kent 15 TR1356
Thankerton S Lans 75 NS9737
Tharston Norfk 43 TM1894
Thatcham W Berk 21 SU5167
Thaxted Essex 24 TL6131
Theakston N York 61 SE3085
Thealby N Linc 56 SE8917
Theale Somset 19 ST4646
Theale W Berk 21 SU6471
Thearne E R Yk 57 TA0736
The Beeches Gloucs 20 SP0302
Theberton Suffk 33 TM4365
The Braes Highld 84 NG5234
The Bungalow IoM 52 SC3986
The Burf Worcs 28 SO8167
The City Bucks 22 SU7896
The Common Wilts 10 SU2432
Theddingworth Leics 39 SP6685
Theddlethorpe All Saints Lincs 51 TF4688
Theddlethorpe St Helen Lincs 51 TF4788
The Den N Ayrs 73 NS3251
The Forstal Kent 15 TR0438
The Green Cumb 58 SD1884
The Green Essex 24 TL7719
The Green N York 63 NZ7705
The Green Wilts 9 ST8731
The Headland Hartpl 62 NZ5234
The Hill Cumb 58 SD1783
The Lee Bucks 22 SP9004
The Lhen IoM 52 NX3801
Thelnetham Suffk 32 TM0178
Thelveton Norfk 33 TM1681
Thelwall Warrtn 47 SJ6587
Themelthorpe Norfk 42 TG0524
The Middles Dur 69 NZ2051
The Moor Kent 14 TQ7529
The Mumbles Swans 17 SS6187
The Murray S Lans 74 NS6353
Thenford Nhants 29 SP5241
The Reddings Gloucs 28 SO9121
Therfield Herts 31 TL3337
The Ross P & K 81 NN7621
The Spring Warwks 39 SP2873
The Stocks Kent 14 TQ9127
The Strand Wilts 20 ST9259
Thetford Norfk 32 TL8783
Theydon Bois Essex 23 TQ4499
Thickwood Wilts 20 ST8272
Thimbleby Lincs 51 TF2470
Thimbleby N York 62 SE4495
Thingwall Wirral 46 SJ2784
Thirkleby N York 62 SE4778
Thirlby N York 62 SE4883
Thirn N York 61 SE2185
Thirsk N York 62 SE4281
Thistleton Lancs 53 SD4037
Thistleton Rutlnd 40 SK9118
Thistley Green Suffk 32 TL6676
Thixendale N York 56 SE8460
Thockrington Nthumb 68 NY9578
Tholomas Drove Cambs 41 TF4006
Tholthorpe N York 55 SE4766
Thompson Norfk 42 TL9296
Thongsbridge Kirk 55 SE1509
Thoralby N York 61 SE0086
Thoresway Lincs 50 TF1696
Thorganby Lincs 51 TF2097
Thorganby N York 56 SE6841
Thorgill N York 63 SE7096
Thorington Suffk 33 TM4174
Thorington Street Suffk 25 TM0035
Thorlby N York 54 SD9653
Thorley Herts 31 TL4718
Thorley Street IoW 10 SZ3788
Thormanby N York 62 SE4974
Thornaby-on-Tees S on T 62 NZ4518
Thornage Norfk 42 TG0536
Thornborough Bucks 30 SP7433
Thornborough N York 61 SE2979
Thornbury C Brad 55 SE1933
Thornbury Devon 6 SS4008
Thornbury Herefs 27 SO6259
Thornbury S Glos 19 ST6390
Thornby Nhants 39 SP6775
Thorncliff Staffs 48 SK0158
Thorncombe Dorset 8 ST3703
Thorndon Suffk 33 TM1469
Thorndon Cross Devon 6 SX5394
Thorne Donc 56 SE6812
Thorner Leeds 55 SE3740
Thorne St Margaret Somset 8 ST1020
Thorney C Pete 41 TF2804
Thorney Notts 50 SK8572
Thorney Somset 8 ST4223
Thorney Hill Hants 10 SZ2099
Thornfalcon Somset 8 ST2823
Thornford Dorset 9 ST6012
Thorngrafton Nthumb 68 NY7865
Thorngumbald E R Yk 57 TA2026
Thornham Norfk 42 TF7343
Thornham Magna Suffk 33 TM1070
Thornham Parva Suffk 33 TM1072
Thornhaugh C Pete 40 TF0600
Thornhill C Sotn 11 SU4612
Thornhill Cumb 58 NY0108
Thornhill D & G 66 NX8795
Thornhill Derbys 48 SK1983
Thornhill Kirk 55 SE2518
Thornhill Stirlg 81 NN6600
Thornholme E R Yk 57 TA1164
Thornicombe Dorset 9 ST8703
Thornington Nthumb 77 NT8833
Thornley Dur 61 NZ1137
Thornley Dur 62 NZ3639
Thornliebank E Rens 74 NS5559
Thorns Suffk 32 TL7455
Thornsett Derbys 48 SK0086
Thornthwaite Cumb 58 NY2225
Thornthwaite N York 55 SE1758
Thornton Angus 88 NO3946
Thornton Bucks 30 SP7435
Thornton C Brad 55 SE0932
Thornton E R Yk 56 SE7645
Thornton Fife 83 NT2897
Thornton Lancs 53 SD3342
Thornton Leics 39 SK4607
Thornton Middsb 62 NZ4713
Thornton Nthumb 77 NT9547
Thornton Curtis N Linc 57 TA0817
Thorntonhall S Lans 74 NS5855
Thornton Heath Gt Lon 23 TQ3168
Thornton Hough Wirral 46 SJ3080
Thornton-in-Craven N York 54 SD9048
Thornton in Lonsdale N York 60 SD6873
Thornton-le-Beans N York 62 SE3990
Thornton-le-Clay N York 56 SE6865
Thornton-le-Dale N York 63 SE8383
Thornton le Moor Lincs 50 TF0496
Thornton-le-Moor N York 62 SE3988
Thornton-le-Moors Ches W 46 SJ4474
Thornton-le-Street N York 62 SE4186
Thornton Rust N York 61 SD9689
Thornton Steward N York 61 SE1787
Thornton Watlass N York 61 SE2385
Thornythwaite Cumb 59 NY3922
Thoroton Notts 50 SK7642
Thorp Arch Leeds 55 SE4345
Thorpe Derbys 48 SK1550
Thorpe E R Yk 56 SE9946
Thorpe N York 54 SE0161
Thorpe Notts 50 SK7649
Thorpe Surrey 22 TQ0168
Thorpe Abbotts Norfk 33 TM1979
Thorpe Arnold Leics 40 SK7720
Thorpe Audlin Wakefd 55 SE4715
Thorpe Bassett N York 63 SE8673
Thorpe Bay Sthend 24 TQ9185
Thorpe by Water Rutlnd 40 SP8996
Thorpe Constantine Staffs 39 SK2508
Thorpe End Norfk 43 TG2710
Thorpe Green Essex 25 TM1623
Thorpe Green Suffk 32 TL9354
Thorpe Hesley Rothm 49 SK3796
Thorpe in Balne Donc 56 SE5910
Thorpe Langton Leics 40 SP7492
Thorpe Lea Surrey 22 TQ0170
Thorpe-le-Soken Essex 25 TM1722
Thorpe le Street E R Yk 56 SE8343
Thorpe Malsor Nhants 40 SP8378
Thorpe Mandeville Nhants 29 SP5244
Thorpe Market Norfk 43 TG2436
Thorpe Marriot Norfk 43 TG1715
Thorpe Morieux Suffk 32 TL9453
Thorpeness Suffk 33 TM4759
Thorpe on the Hill Lincs 50 SK9065
Thorpe St Andrew Norfk 43 TG2709
Thorpe St Peter Lincs 51 TF4860
Thorpe Salvin Rothm 49 SK5181
Thorpe Satchville Leics 40 SK7311
Thorpe Thewles S on T 62 NZ3923
Thorpe Tilney Lincs 50 TF1257
Thorpe Underwood N York 55 SE4659
Thorpe Waterville Nhants 40 TL0281
Thorpe Willoughby N York 56 SE5731
Thorrington Essex 25 TM0919
Thorverton Devon 7 SS9202
Thrandeston Suffk 33 TM1176
Thrapston Nhants 30 SP9978
Threapwood Ches W 46 SJ4444
Threapwood Staffs 48 SK0342
Three Bridges W Susx 12 TQ2837
Three Chimneys Kent 14 TQ8238
Three Cocks Powys 27 SO1737
Three Crosses Swans 17 SS5794
Three Cups Corner E Susx 13 TQ6320
Threekingham Lincs 40 TF0836
Three Leg Cross E Susx 14 TQ6831
Three Legged Cross Dorset 10 SU0805
Three Mile Cross Wokham 22 SU7167
Threemilestone Cnwll 2 SW7745
Three Oaks E Susx 14 TQ8314
Threlkeld Cumb 58 NY3125
Threshers Bush Essex 23 TL4909
Threshfield N York 54 SD9863
Thrigby Norfk 43 TG4612
Thrintoft N York 62 SE3192
Thriplow Cambs 31 TL4346
Throcking Herts 31 TL3330
Throckley N u Ty 69 NZ1566
Throckmorton Worcs 28 SO9850
Throop BCP 10 SZ1195
Thropton Nthumb 68 NU0202
Throwleigh Devon 5 SX6690
Throwley Forstal Kent 15 TQ9854
Thrumpton Notts 39 SK5031
Thrumster Highld 100 ND3345
Thrunscoe NE Lin 57 TA3107
Thrupp Gloucs 28 SO8603
Thrussington Leics 39 SK6515
Thruxton Hants 21 SU2945
Thruxton Herefs 27 SO4334
Thrybergh Rothm 49 SK4695
Thulston Derbys 39 SK4031
Thundersley Essex 24 TQ7988
Thurcaston Leics 39 SK5610
Thurcroft Rothm 49 SK4988
Thurgarton Norfk 43 TG1834
Thurgarton Notts 49 SK6949
Thurgoland Barns 49 SE2901
Thurlaston Leics 39 SP5099
Thurlaston Warwks 29 SP4670
Thurlbear Somset 8 ST2621
Thurlby Lincs 40 TF0916
Thurlby Lincs 50 SK9061
Thurlby Lincs 51 TF4875
Thurleigh Bed 30 TL0558
Thurlestone Devon 5 SX6742
Thurloxton Somset 8 ST2730
Thurlstone Barns 55 SE2303
Thurlton Norfk 43 TM4198
Thurmaston Leics 39 SK6109
Thurnby Leics 39 SK6403
Thurne Norfk 43 TG4015
Thurnham Kent 14 TQ8057
Thurning Nhants 40 TL0882
Thurning Norfk 42 TG0729
Thurnscoe Barns 55 SE4505
Thurrock Services Thurr 24 TQ5778
Thursby Cumb 67 NY3250
Thursford Norfk 42 TF9833
Thursley Surrey 11 SU9039
Thurso Highld 100 ND1168
Thurstaston Wirral 46 SJ2484
Thurston Suffk 32 TL9165
Thurstonfield Cumb 67 NY3156
Thurstonland Kirk 55 SE1610
Thurton Norfk 43 TG3200
Thurvaston Derbys 48 SK2437
Thuxton Norfk 42 TG0307
Thwaite N York 60 SD8998
Thwaite Suffk 33 TM1168
Thwaite Head Cumb 59 SD3490
Thwaite St Mary Norfk 43 TM3395
Thwing E R Yk 57 TA0470
Tibbermore P & K 82 NO0423
Tibberton Gloucs 28 SO7521
Tibberton Worcs 28 SO9057
Tibberton Wrekin 37 SJ6820
Tibenham Norfk 33 TM1389
Tibshelf Derbys 49 SK4461
Tibshelf Services Derbys 49 SK4460
Tibthorpe E R Yk 56 SE9555
Ticehurst E Susx 14 TQ6830
Tichborne Hants 11 SU5730
Tickencote Rutlnd 40 SK9809
Tickenham N Som 19 ST4571
Tickhill Donc 49 SK5993
Ticklerton Shrops 37 SO4890
Ticknall Derbys 39 SK3523
Tickton E R Yk 57 TA0541
Tidcombe Wilts 21 SU2858
Tiddington Oxon 29 SP6404
Tiddington Warwks 29 SP2255
Tidebrook E Susx 13 TQ6130
Tideford Cnwll 4 SX3559
Tidenham Gloucs 19 ST5595
Tideswell Derbys 48 SK1575
Tidmarsh W Berk 21 SU6374
Tidmington Warwks 29 SP2538
Tidworth Wilts 21 SU2348
Tiers Cross Pembks 16 SM9010
Tiffield Nhants 30 SP7051
Tigh a' Ghearraidh W Isls 90 NF7171
Tigharry W Isls 90 NF7171
Tighnabruaich Ag & B 71 NR9873
Tigley Devon 5 SX7660
Tilbrook Cambs 30 TL0869
Tilbury Thurr 24 TQ6476
Tile Cross Birm 38 SP1687
Tile Hill Covtry 39 SP2777
Tilehurst Readg 22 SU6673
Tilford Surrey 11 SU8743
Tilgate W Susx 12 TQ2734
Tilham Street Somset 9 ST5535
Tillicoultry Clacks 82 NS9197
Tillingham Essex 25 TL9904
Tillington Herefs 27 SO4644
Tillington W Susx 12 SU9621
Tillington Common Herefs 27 SO4545
Tillyfourie Abers 94 NJ6412
Tilmanstone Kent 15 TR3051
Tilney All Saints Norfk 41 TF5618
Tilney High End Norfk 41 TF5617
Tilney St Lawrence Norfk 41 TF5414
Tilshead Wilts 20 SU0347
Tilstock Shrops 37 SJ5437
Tilston Ches W 46 SJ4650
Tilstone Fearnall Ches W 47 SJ5660
Tilsworth C Beds 30 SP9824
Tilton on the Hill Leics 40 SK7405
Tiltups End Gloucs 20 ST8497
Timberland Lincs 50 TF1258
Timbersbrook Ches E 48 SJ8962
Timberscombe Somset 7 SS9542
Timble N York 55 SE1853
Timperley Traffd 47 SJ7888
Timsbury BaNES 20 ST6758
Timsbury Hants 10 SU3424
Timworth Suffk 32 TL8669
Timworth Green Suffk 32 TL8669
Tincleton Dorset 9 SY7692
Tindale Cumb 68 NY6159
Tingewick Bucks 29 SP6532
Tingrith C Beds 30 TL0032
Tingwall Airport Shet 100 HU4145
Tinhay Devon 4 SX3985
Tinsley Sheff 49 SK4090
Tinsley Green W Susx 12 TQ2839
Tintagel Cnwll 4 SX0588
Tintern Mons 19 SO5200
Tintinhull Somset 8 ST4919
Tintwistle Derbys 48 SK0197
Tinwell Rutlnd 40 TF0006
Tipton Sandw 38 SO9693
Tipton Green Sandw 38 SO9592
Tipton St John Devon 8 SY0991
Tiptree Essex 24 TL8916
Tiptree Heath Essex 24 TL8815
Tirabad Powys 26 SN8741
Tiree Airport Ag & B 78 NM0044
Tirley Gloucs 28 SO8328
Tirphil Caerph 18 SO1303
Tirril Cumb 59 NY5026
Tisbury Wilts 9 ST9429
Tissington Derbys 48 SK1752
Titchberry Devon 6 SS2427
Titchfield Hants 11 SU5405
Titchmarsh Nhants 40 TL0279
Titchwell Norfk 42 TF7643
Tithby Notts 40 SK6937
Titley Herefs 27 SO3360
Titsey Surrey 23 TQ4054
Titson Cnwll 6 SS2401
Tittensor Staffs 38 SJ8738
Tittleshall Norfk 42 TF8921
Titton Worcs 28 SO8370
Tiverton Ches W 47 SJ5560
Tiverton Devon 7 SS9512
Tivetshall St Margaret Norfk 33 TM1787
Tivetshall St Mary Norfk 33 TM1686
Tixall Staffs 38 SJ9722
Tixover Rutlnd 40 SK9700
Tobermory Ag & B 79 NM5055
Toberonochy Ag & B 79 NM7408
Tobha Mòr W Isls 90 NF7536
Tockenham Wilts 20 SU0379
Tockholes Bl w D 54 SD6623
Tockington S Glos 19 ST6086
Tockwith N York 55 SE4652
Todber Dorset 9 ST7919
Toddington C Beds 30 TL0128
Toddington Gloucs 28 SP0332
Toddington Services C Beds 30 TL0228
Todenham Gloucs 29 SP2335
Todhills Rest Area Cumb 67 NY3762
Todmorden Calder 54 SD9324
Todwick Rothm 49 SK4984
Toft Cambs 31 TL3656
Toft Lincs 40 TF0717
Toft Shet 100 HU4376
Toft Hill Dur 61 NZ1528
Toft Monks Norfk 43 TM4294
Toft next Newton Lincs 50 TF0388
Toftrees Norfk 42 TF8927
Togston Nthumb 69 NU2401
Tokers Green Oxon 22 SU7077
Tolastadh bho Thuath W Isls 90 NB5347
Tolland Somset 8 ST1032
Tollard Royal Wilts 9 ST9417
Toll Bar Donc 56 SE5507
Toller Fratrum Dorset 9 SY5797
Toller Porcorum Dorset 9 SY5698
Tollerton N York 55 SE5164
Tollerton Notts 39 SK6134
Tollesbury Essex 25 TL9510
Tolleshunt D'Arcy Essex 25 TL9211
Tolleshunt Knights Essex 24 TL9114
Tolleshunt Major Essex 24 TL9011
Tolpuddle Dorset 9 SY7994
Tolworth Gt Lon 23 TQ1966
Tomatin Highld 93 NH8028
Tomintoul Moray 94 NJ1619
Tomnavoulin Moray 94 NJ2126
Tonbridge Kent 13 TQ5846
Tondu Brdgnd 18 SS8984
Tonedale Somset 8 ST1321
Tong C Brad 55 SE2230
Tong Kent 15 TQ9556
Tong Shrops 37 SJ7907
Tonge Leics 39 SK4123
Tongham Surrey 22 SU8848
Tongland D & G 65 NX6954
Tong Norton Shrops 37 SJ7908
Tongue Highld 99 NC5956
Tongwynlais Cardif 18 ST1382
Tonmawr Neath 18 SS8096
Tonna Neath 18 SS7798
Tonwell Herts 31 TL3316
Tonypandy Rhondd 18 SS9991
Tonyrefail Rhondd 18 ST0188
Toot Baldon Oxon 21 SP5600
Toot Hill Essex 23 TL5102
Toothill Swindn 20 SU1183
Tooting Gt Lon 23 TQ2771
Tooting Bec Gt Lon 23 TQ2872
Topcliffe N York 62 SE3976
Topcroft Norfk 43 TM2693
Topcroft Street Norfk 33 TM2691
Toppesfield Essex 24 TL7437
Toprow Norfk 43 TM1698
Topsham Devon 5 SX9688
Torbeg N Ayrs 72 NR8929
Torbryan Devon 5 SX8266
Torcross Devon 5 SX8241
Tore Highld 92 NH6052
Torksey Lincs 50 SK8378
Tormarton S Glos 20 ST7678
Toronto Dur 61 NZ1930
Torpenhow Cumb 58 NY2039
Torphichen W Loth 75 NS9672
Torphins Abers 89 NJ6202
Torpoint Cnwll 4 SX4355
Torquay Torbay 5 SX9164
Torrance E Duns 74 NS6173
Torridon Highld 91 NG9055
Torrin Highld 84 NG5721
Torrisholme Lancs 53 SD4563
Torry C Aber 89 NJ9405
Torryburn Fife 82 NT0286
Torthorwald D & G 66 NY0378
Tortington W Susx 12 TQ0004
Torton Worcs 38 SO8472
Tortworth S Glos 20 ST7093
Torver Cumb 58 SD2894
Torworth Notts 49 SK6586
Toseland Cambs 31 TL2462
Tosside Lancs 54 SD7656
Tostock Suffk 32 TL9563
Totaig Highld 90 NG2050
Tote Highld 90 NG4149
Totland IoW 10 SZ3287
Totley Sheff 49 SK3079
Totley Brook Sheff 49 SK3180
Totnes Devon 5 SX8060
Toton Notts 39 SK5034
Tottenham Gt Lon 23 TQ3390
Tottenhill Norfk 42 TF6411
Totteridge Gt Lon 23 TQ2494
Totternhoe C Beds 30 SP9821
Tottington Bury 54 SD7712
Totton Hants 10 SU3613
Toulton Somset 8 ST1931
Tovil Kent 14 TQ7554
Towcester Nhants 30 SP6948
Towednack Cnwll 2 SW4838
Towersey Oxon 22 SP7305
Tow Law Dur 61 NZ1138
Town End Cambs 41 TL4195
Townend W Duns 80 NS3976
Townhead Barns 55 SE1602
Town Littleworth E Susx 13 TQ4117
Townshend Cnwll 2 SW5932
Town Street Suffk 32 TL7785
Town Yetholm Border 77 NT8128
Towthorpe C York 56 SE6258
Towton N York 55 SE4839
Towyn Conwy 45 SH9779
Toxteth Lpool 46 SJ3588
Toynton All Saints Lincs 51 TF3963
Toy's Hill Kent 13 TQ4651
Trafford Park Traffd 47 SJ7996
Trallong Powys 26 SN9629
Tranent E Loth 76 NT4072
Tranmere Wirral 46 SJ3187
Trap Carmth 26 SN6518
Traquair Border 75 NT3334
Trawden Lancs 54 SD9138
Trawsfynydd Gwynd 45 SH7035
Trealaw Rhondd 18 ST0092
Treales Lancs 53 SD4332
Trearddur Bay IoA 44 SH2579
Trebetherick Cnwll 3 SW9378
Treborough Somset 7 ST0136
Trebullett Cnwll 4 SX3278
Treburley Cnwll 4 SX3577
Trecastle Powys 26 SN8829
Trecwn Pembks 16 SM9632
Trecynon Rhondd 18 SN9903
Tredegar Blae G 26 SO1408
Tredington Gloucs 28 SO9029
Tredington Warwks 29 SP2543
Tredunnock Mons 19 ST3794
Treen Cnwll 2 SW3923
Treeton Rothm 49 SK4387
Trefasser Pembks 16 SM8938
Trefecca Powys 26 SO1431
Trefeglwys Powys 35 SN9690
Treffgarne Pembks 16 SM9523
Treffgarne Owen Pembks 16 SM8625
Trefilan Cerdgn 34 SN5456
Trefin Pembks 16 SM8432
Trefnant Denbgs 45 SJ0570
Trefonen Shrops 36 SJ2526
Trefor Gwynd 44 SH3746
Treforest Rhondd 18 ST0888
Trefriw Conwy 45 SH7863
Tregadillett Cnwll 4 SX2983
Tregare Mons 27 SO4110
Tregaron Cerdgn 26 SN6759
Tregarth Gwynd 45 SH6067
Tregeare Cnwll 4 SX2486
Tregeiriog Wrexhm 36 SJ1733
Tregele IoA 44 SH3592
Treglemais Pembks 16 SM8229
Tregonetha Cnwll 3 SW9563
Tregony Cnwll 3 SW9244
Tregorrick Cnwll 3 SX0151
Tregoyd Powys 27 SO1937
Tre-groes Cerdgn 17 SN4044
Tregynon Powys 36 SO0998
Tre-gynwr Carmth 17 SN4219
Trehafod Rhondd 18 ST0490
Trehan Cnwll 4 SX4058
Treharris Myr Td 18 ST0996
Treherbert Rhondd 18 SS9498
Trekenner Cnwll 4 SX3478
Treknow Cnwll 4 SX0586
Trelawnyd Flints 46 SJ0979
Trelech Carmth 17 SN2830
Treleddyd-fawr Pembks 16 SM7528
Trelewis Myr Td 18 ST1096
Trelights Cnwll 3 SW9979
Trelill Cnwll 3 SX0478
Trellech Mons 27 SO5005
Trelogan Flints 46 SJ1180
Tremadog Gwynd 44 SH5640
Tremail Cnwll 4 SX1686
Tremain Cerdgn 17 SN2348
Tremaine Cnwll 4 SX2389
Tremar Cnwll 4 SX2568
Trematon Cnwll 4 SX3959
Tremeirchion Denbgs 46 SJ0873
Trenance Cnwll 3 SW8568
Trenance Cnwll 3 SW9270
Trench Wrekin 37 SJ6912
Trenear Cnwll 2 SW6731
Treneglos Cnwll 4 SX2088
Trent Dorset 9 ST5918
Trentham C Stke 38 SJ8740
Trentishoe Devon 18 SS6448
Trent Vale C Stke 47 SJ8643
Treoes V Glam 18 SS9478
Treorchy Rhondd 18 SS9597
Trequite Cnwll 3 SX0377
Trerhyngyll V Glam 18 ST0077
Trerulefoot Cnwll 4 SX3358
Tresaith Cerdgn 17 SN2851
Trescowe Cnwll 2 SW5731
Tresean Cnwll 2 SW7858
Tresham Gloucs 20 ST7991
Tresillian Cnwll 3 SW8646
Treskinnick Cross Cnwll 6 SX2098
Tresmeer Cnwll 4 SX2387
Tresparrett Cnwll 4 SX1491
Tresta Shet 100 HU3650
Tresta Shet 100 HU6090
Treswell Notts 50 SK7879
Tre Taliesin Cerdgn 35 SN6591
Trethevey Cnwll 4 SX0789
Trethewey Cnwll 2 SW3823
Trethurgy Cnwll 3 SX0355
Tretire Herefs 27 SO5123
Tretower Powys 27 SO1821
Treuddyn Flints 46 SJ2557
Trevalga Cnwll 4 SX0890
Trevalyn Wrexhm 46 SJ3856
Trevarrian Cnwll 3 SW8566
Treveal Cnwll 2 SW7858
Treveighan Cnwll 3 SX0779
Trevellas Downs Cnwll 2 SW7452
Trevelmond Cnwll 4 SX2063
Treverva Cnwll 2 SW7531
Trevescan Cnwll 2 SW3524
Treviscoe Cnwll 3 SW9455
Trevone Cnwll 3 SW8975
Trevor Wrexhm 46 SJ2742
Trewalder Cnwll 3 SX0782
Trewarmett Cnwll 4 SX0686
Trewen Cnwll 4 SX2583
Trewint Cnwll 4 SX2180
Trewithian Cnwll 3 SW8737
Trewoon Cnwll 3 SW9952
Treyford W Susx 11 SU8218
Trimdon Dur 62 NZ3634
Trimdon Colliery Dur 62 NZ3735
Trimdon Grange Dur 62 NZ3635
Trimingham Norfk 43 TG2838
Trimley St Martin Suffk 25 TM2737
Trimley St Mary Suffk 25 TM2836
Trimsaran Carmth 17 SN4504
Trimstone Devon 6 SS5043
Tring Herts 22 SP9211
Trinity Angus 89 NO6061
Triscombe Somset 8 ST1535
Trispen Cnwll 3 SW8450
Tritlington Nthumb 69 NZ2092
Trochry P & K 82 NN9740
Troedyraur Cerdgn 17 SN3245
Troedyrhiw Myr Td 18 SO0702
Troon Cnwll 2 SW6638
Troon S Ayrs 73 NS3230
Troston Suffk 32 TL8972
Trotshill Worcs 28 SO8855
Trottiscliffe Kent 14 TQ6460
Trotton W Susx 11 SU8322

West Stour Dorset 9 ST7822
West Stourmouth Kent 15 TR2562
West Stow Suffk 32 TL8171
West Stowell Wilts 20 SU1361
West Stowell Suffk 32 TL9871
West Tanfield N York 61 SE2678
West Taphouse Cnwll 3 SX1463
West Tarring W Susx 12 TQ1103
West Thirston Nthumb 69 NZ1999
West Thorney W Susx 11 SU7602
West Thorpe Notts 36 SK6225
West Thurrock Thurr 24 TQ5877
West Tilbury Thurr 24 TQ6678
West Tisted Hants 11 SU6529
West Torrington Lincs 50 TF1381
West Town Hants 11 SZ7199
West Town N Som 34 ST4868
West Tytherley Hants 10 SU2729
West Walton Norfk 41 TF4613
Westward Cumb 67 NY2744
Westward Ho! Devon 6 SS4329
Westwell Kent 15 TQ9947
Westwell Oxon 29 SP2209
Westwell Leacon Kent 15 TQ9647
West Wellow Hants 10 SU2819
West Wembury Devon 5 SX5249
West Wemyss Fife 83 NT3294
Westwick Cambs 31 TL4265
West Wickham Cambs 32 TL6149
West Wickham Gt Lon 23 TQ3766
West Williamston Pembks 16 SN0305
West Winch Norfk 41 TF6316
West Winterslow Wilts 10 SU2331
West Wittering W Susx 11 SZ7898
West Witton N York 61 SE0588
Westwood Devon 7 SY0199
Westwood Kent 15 TR3667
Westwood Wilts 20 ST8059
West Woodburn Nthumb 68 NY8987
West Woodhay W Berk 21 SU3963
Westwoodside N Linc 50 SE7400
West Worldham Hants 11 SU7436
West Worthing W Susx 12 TQ1302
West Wratting Cambs 31 TL6052
West Wylam Nthumb 69 NZ1063
Wetheral Cumb 67 NY4654
Wetherby Leeds 55 SE4048
Wetherby Services N York 55 SE4150
Wetherden Suffk 32 TM0062
Wetheringsett Suffk 33 TM1266
Wethersfield Essex 24 TL7131
Wetherup Street Suffk 33 TM1464
Wetley Rocks Staffs 48 SJ9649
Wettenhall Ches E 47 SJ6261
Wetton Staffs 48 SK1055
Wetwang E R Yk 56 SE9359
Wetwood Staffs 37 SJ7733
Wexcombe Wilts 21 SU2758
Weybourne Norfk 43 TG1142
Weybourne Surrey 22 SU8549
Weybread Suffk 33 TM2480
Weybread Street Suffk 33 TM2479
Weybridge Surrey 22 TQ0764
Weycroft Devon 8 SY3099
Weyhill Hants 21 SU3146
Weymouth Dorset 9 SY6779
Whaddon Bucks 30 SP8034
Whaddon Cambs 31 TL3546
Whaddon Gloucs 28 SO8313
Whaddon Wilts 10 SU1926
Whaddon Wilts 20 ST8861
Whaley Derbys 49 SK5171
Whaley Bridge Derbys 48 SK0181
Whaley Thorns Derbys 49 SK5271
Whalley Lancs 54 SD7336
Whalton Nthumb 69 NZ1381
Whaplode Lincs 41 TF3224
Whaplode Drove Lincs 41 TF3213
Wharf Warwks 29 SP4352
Wharfe N York 54 SD7869
Wharles Lancs 53 SD4435
Wharley End C Beds 30 SP9443
Wharncliffe Side Sheff 49 SK2994
Wharram-le-Street N York 56 SE8665
Wharton Herefs 27 SO5055
Whashton N York 61 NZ1506
Whasset Cumb 59 SD5080
Whatcote Warwks 29 SP2944
Whateley Warwks 39 SP2299
Whatfield Suffk 32 TM0246
Whatley Somset 8 ST3607
Whatley Somset 20 ST7347
Whatlington E Susx 14 TQ7618
Whatton-in-the-Vale Notts 40 SK7439
Whauphill D & G 64 NX4049
Wheatacre Norfk 44 TM4694
Wheathampstead Herts 31 TL1714
Wheatley Hants 11 SU7840
Wheatley Oxon 29 SP5905
Wheatley Hill Dur 62 NZ3738
Wheatley Hills Donc 56 SE5904
Wheaton Aston Staffs 38 SJ8512
Wheddon Cross Somset 7 SS9228
Wheeler's Green Wokham 22 SU7672
Wheelock Ches E 47 SJ7559
Wheelton Lancs 54 SD6021
Wheldrake York 56 SE6844
Whelford Gloucs 20 SU1699
Whelpley Hill Bucks 22 SP9904
Whempstead Herts 31 TL3121
Whenby N York 56 SE6369
Whepstead Suffk 32 TL8358
Wherstead Suffk 33 TM1540
Wherwell Hants 21 SU3840
Wheston Derbys 48 SK1376
Whetsted Kent 14 TQ6646
Whetstone Leics 39 SP5597
Whicham Cumb 58 SD1382
Whichford Warwks 29 SP3134
Whickham Gatesd 69 NZ2061
Whiddon Down Devon 5 SX6992
Whigstreet Angus 93 NO4844
Whilton Nhants 29 SP6364
Whimple Devon 7 SY0497
Whimpwell Green Norfk 43 TG3829
Whinburgh Norfk 42 TG0009
Whinnyfold Abers 95 NK0733
Whippingham IoW 11 SZ5193
Whipsnade C Beds 30 TL0117
Whipton Devon 5 SX9493
Whisby Lincs 50 SK9067
Whissendine Rutlnd 40 SK8214
Whissonsett Norfk 42 TF9123
Whistley Green Wokham 22 SU7974
Whiston Knows 46 SJ4791
Whiston Nhants 30 SP8460
Whiston Rothm 49 SK4489
Whiston Staffs 38 SJ8914
Whiston Staffs 38 SK0347
Whitbeck Cumb 58 SD1184
Whitbourne Herefs 28 SO7257
Whitburn S Tyne 69 NZ4062
Whitburn W Loth 75 NS9464
Whitby N York 63 NZ8910
Whitchurch BaNES 17 ST6167
Whitchurch Bucks 30 SP8020

Whitchurch Cardif 19 ST1579
Whitchurch Devon 4 SX4972
Whitchurch Hants 21 SU4648
Whitchurch Herefs 27 SO5517
Whitchurch Oxon 21 SU6377
Whitchurch Pembks 16 SM8025
Whitchurch Shrops 37 SJ5341
Whitchurch Canonicorum Dorset 8 SY3995
Whitchurch Hill Oxon 21 SU6378
Whitcombe Dorset 9 SY7188
Whitcot Shrops 36 SO3791
Whitcott Keysett Shrops 36 SO2782
Whiteacre Heath Warwks 39 SP2192
White Ball Somset 8 ST1019
Whitebridge Highld 92 NH4815
Whitebrook Mons 27 SO5306
Whitebushes Surrey 12 TQ2847
Whitechapel Gt Lon 23 TQ3381
White Chapel Lancs 53 SD5541
White Colne Essex 24 TL8729
Whitecraig E Loth 75 NT3470
White Cross Cnwll 2 SW6821
Whitefaulds S Ayrs 73 NS2509
Whitefield Bury 47 SD8006
Whitefield Somset 8 ST0729
Whiteford Abers 95 NJ7126
Whitegate Ches W 47 SJ6269
Whitehall Ork 100 HY6528
Whitehaven Cumb 58 NX9718
Whitehill and Bordon Hants 11 SU7834
Whitehills Abers 94 NJ6565
Whitehouse Abers 94 NJ6114
Whitehouse Ag & B 71 NR8161
Whitehouse Common Birm 38 SP1397
Whitekirk E Loth 83 NT5981
White Lackington Dorset 9 SY7198
Whitelackington Somset 8 ST3815
White Ladies Aston Worcs 28 SO9252
Whiteleaf Bucks 22 SP8204
Whiteley Hants 11 SU5209
Whiteley Bank IoW 11 SZ5581
Whitemoor C Nott 49 SK5441
Whitemoor Cnwll 3 SW9757
White Notley Essex 24 TL7818
Whiteparish Wilts 10 SU2423
White Pit Lincs 51 TF3777
Whiterashes Abers 95 NJ8523
White Roding Essex 24 TL5613
Whiteshill Gloucs 28 SO8406
Whitesmith E Susx 13 TQ5213
Whitestaunton Somset 8 ST2810
Whitestone Cross Devon 5 SX8993
White Waltham W & M 22 SU8477
Whitewell Lancs 54 SD6446
Whitfield C Dund 93 NO4333
Whitfield Kent 15 TR3045
Whitfield Nhants 29 SP6039
Whitfield Nthumb 68 NY7857
Whitfield S Gloucs 28 ST6791
Whitford Devon 8 SY2595
Whitford Flints 46 SJ1478
Whitgift E R Yk 56 SE8122
Whitgreave Staffs 38 SJ9028
Whithorn D & G 64 NX4440
Whiting Bay N Ayrs 72 NS0425
Whitkirk Leeds 55 SE3633
Whitland Carmth 17 SN1916
Whitletts S Ayrs 73 NS3623
Whitley N York 56 SE5620
Whitley Readg 22 SU7270
Whitley Sheff 49 SK3494
Whitley Wilts 20 ST8866
Whitley Bay N Tyne 69 NZ3571
Whitley Chapel Nthumb 68 NY9257
Whitley Lower Kirk 55 SE2217
Whitminster Gloucs 28 SO7708
Whitmore Staffs 37 SJ8140
Whitnage Devon 7 ST0215
Whitnash Warwks 29 SP3263
Whitney-on-Wye Herefs 27 SO2747
Whitsbury Hants 10 SU1219
Whitsome Border 77 NT8650
Whitson Newpt 19 ST3883
Whitstable Kent 15 TR1066
Whitstone Cnwll 6 SX2698
Whittingham Nthumb 68 NU0611
Whittingslow Shrops 36 SO4288
Whittington Derbys 49 SK3875
Whittington Gloucs 28 SP0120
Whittington Lancs 60 SD6075
Whittington Norfk 42 TL7199
Whittington Shrops 37 SJ3231
Whittington Staffs 38 SK1508
Whittington Staffs 38 SO8682
Whittington Warwks 39 SP2999
Whittington Worcs 28 SO8753
Whittlebury Nhants 30 SP4943
Whittle-le-Woods Lancs 54 SD5721
Whittlesey Cambs 41 TL2697
Whittlesford Cambs 31 TL4748
Whitton N Linc 56 SE9024
Whitton Nthumb 68 NU0501
Whitton Powys 27 SO2767
Whitton S on T 62 NZ3822
Whitton Shrops 27 SO5772
Whittonstall Nthumb 69 NZ0757
Whitway Hants 21 SU4559
Whitwell Derbys 49 SK5276
Whitwell Herts 31 TL1820
Whitwell IoW 11 SZ5277
Whitwell N York 61 SE2899
Whitwell Rutlnd 40 SK9208
Whitwell-on-the-Hill N York 56 SE7265
Whitwell Street Norfk 43 TG1022
Whitwick Leics 39 SK4315
Whitworth Lancs 54 SD8918
Whixall Shrops 37 SJ5134
Whixley N York 55 SE4458
Whorlton Dur 61 NZ1014
Why Herefs 27 SO5561
Whyteleafe Surrey 13 TQ3358
Wibsey C Brad 55 SE1430
Wibtoft Warwks 39 SP4787
Wichenford Worcs 28 SO7860
Wichling Kent 14 TQ9256
Wick BCP 10 SZ1591
Wick Highld 100 ND3650
Wick S Glos 20 ST7072
Wick V Glam 18 SS9271
Wick W Susx 12 TQ0203
Wicken Cambs 31 TL5670
Wicken Nhants 30 SP7439
Wicken Bonhunt Essex 31 TL4933
Wicken Green Village Norfk 42 TF8732
Wickersley Rothm 49 SK4791
Wicker Street Green Suffk 32 TL9742
Wickford Essex 24 TQ7493
Wickham W Berk 21 SU3971

Wickham Bishops Essex 24 TL8412
Wickhambreaux Kent 15 TR2158
Wickhambrook Suffk 32 TL7554
Wickhamford Worcs 28 SP0641
Wickham Green Suffk 33 TM0969
Wickham Market Suffk 33 TM3055
Wickhampton Norfk 43 TG4205
Wickham St Paul Essex 24 TL8336
Wickham Skeith Suffk 33 TM0969
Wickham Street Suffk 33 TM0869
Wicklewood Norfk 42 TG0702
Wickmere Norfk 43 TG1733
Wick St Lawrence N Som 19 ST3665
Wickwar S Glos 20 ST7288
Widdington Essex 24 TL5331
Widdrington Nthumb 69 NZ2595
Widdrington Station Nthumb 69 NZ2493
Widecombe in the Moor Devon 5 SX7176
Widegates Cnwll 4 SX2858
Widemouth Bay Cnwll 6 SS2002
Wide Open N Tyne 69 NZ2472
Widford Essex 24 TL6904
Widford Herts 31 TL4216
Widmer End Bucks 22 SU8896
Widmerpool Notts 39 SK6327
Widmore Gt Lon 23 TQ4268
Widnes Halton 46 SJ5185
Widworthy Devon 8 SY2199
Wigan Wigan 47 SD5805
Wigborough Somset 8 ST4415
Wiggaton Devon 8 SY1092
Wiggenhall St Germans Norfk 41 TF5914
Wiggenhall St Mary Magdalen Norfk 41 TF5911
Wiggenhall St Mary the Virgin Norfk 41 TF5813
Wigginton C York 56 SE5998
Wigginton Herts 22 SP9310
Wigginton Oxon 29 SP3813
Wigginton Staffs 39 SK2006
Wigglesworth N York 54 SD8156
Wiggonby Cumb 67 NY2952
Wighill N York 55 SE4746
Wighton Norfk 42 TF9439
Wightwick Wolves 38 SO8698
Wigley Hants 10 SU3217
Wigmore Herefs 27 SO4169
Wigmore Medway 14 TQ7964
Wigsley Notts 50 SK8570
Wigsthorpe Nhants 40 TL0482
Wigston Leics 39 SP6198
Wigston Fields Leics 39 SK6000
Wigston Parva Leics 39 SP4689
Wigthorpe Notts 49 SK5983
Wigtoft Lincs 41 TF2636
Wigton Cumb 67 NY2548
Wigtown D & G 64 NX4355
Wike Leeds 55 SE3342
Wilbarston Nhants 40 SP8188
Wilberfoss E R Yk 56 SE7350
Wilburton Cambs 31 TL4775
Wilby Nhants 30 SP8666
Wilby Norfk 32 TM0389
Wilby Suffk 33 TM2472
Wilcot Wilts 20 SU1360
Wilcott Shrops 36 SJ3718
Wildboarclough Ches E 48 SJ9868
Wilden Bed 30 TL0955
Wilden Worcs 38 SO8272
Wildmill Brdgnd 18 SS9081
Wildmoor Worcs 38 SO9575
Wildsworth Lincs 50 SK8097
Wilford C Nott 49 SK5637
Wilkesley Ches E 37 SJ6241
Wilkieston W Loth 75 NT1268
Willand Devon 7 ST0310
Willaston Ches E 47 SJ6852
Willaston Ches W 47 SJ3377
Willen M Keyn 30 SP8741
Willenhall Covtry 39 SP3676
Willenhall Wsall 38 SO9798
Willerby E R Yk 56 TA0230
Willerby N York 63 TA0079
Willersey Gloucs 28 SP1039
Willersley Herefs 27 SO3147
Willesborough Kent 15 TR0441
Willesborough Lees Kent 15 TR0342
Willesden Gt Lon 23 TQ2284
Willesley Wilts 20 ST8588
Willett Somset 8 ST1033
Willey Shrops 37 SO6799
Willey Warwks 39 SP4984
Willey Green Surrey 12 SU9351
Williamscot Oxon 29 SP4845
Willian Herts 31 TL2230
Willingale Essex 24 TL5907
Willingdon E Susx 13 TQ5802
Willingham Cambs 31 TL4070
Willingham by Stow Lincs 50 SK8784
Willingham St Mary Suffk 33 TM4384
Willington Bed 30 TL1150
Willington Derbys 39 SK2928
Willington Dur 69 NZ1935
Willington Kent 14 TQ7953
Willington N Tyne 69 NZ3267
Willington Warwks 29 SP2639
Willitoft E R Yk 56 SE7434
Williton Somset 18 ST0741
Willoughby Lincs 51 TF4771
Willoughby Warwks 29 SP5167
Willoughby-on-the-Wolds Notts 36 SK6325
Willoughby Waterleys Leics 39 SP5792
Willoughton Lincs 50 SK9293
Willows Green Essex 24 TL7219
Willtown Somset 8 ST3924
Wilmcote Warwks 29 SP1658
Wilmington Devon 8 SY2199
Wilmington E Susx 13 TQ5404
Wilmington Kent 14 TQ5372
Wilmslow Ches E 47 SJ8481
Wilpshire Lancs 54 SD6832
Wilsden C Brad 55 SE0936
Wilsford Lincs 40 TF0042
Wilsford Wilts 10 SU1057
Wilsford Wilts 20 SU1339
Wilshaw Kirk 55 SE1109
Wilsill N York 55 SE1864
Wilson Leics 39 SK4024
Wilsontown S Lans 75 NS9455
Wilstead Bed 30 TL0643
Wilsthorpe Lincs 40 TF0913
Wilstone Herts 30 SP9014
Wilton Herefs 27 SO5824
Wilton N York 63 SE8582
Wilton R & C 62 NZ5819
Wilton Wilts 10 SU0931
Wilton Wilts 21 SU2661
Wimbish Essex 24 TL6035
Wimbish Green Essex 24 TL6035
Wimbledon Gt Lon 23 TQ2570
Wimblington Cambs 41 TL4192
Wimboldsley Ches W 47 SJ6962

Wimborne Minster Dorset 10 SZ0199
Wimborne St Giles Dorset 10 SU0311
Wimbotsham Norfk 41 TF6205
Wimpole Cambs 31 TL3549
Wimpstone Warwks 29 SP2148
Wincanton Somset 20 ST7128
Winchburgh W Loth 75 NT0974
Winchcombe Gloucs 28 SP0228
Winchelsea E Susx 14 TQ9017
Winchelsea Beach E Susx 14 TQ9017
Winchester Hants 11 SU4829
Winchester Services Hants 11 SU5235
Winchet Hill Kent 14 TQ7340
Winchfield Hants 22 SU7654
Winchmore Hill Bucks 22 SU9395
Winchmore Hill Gt Lon 23 TQ3194
Wincle Ches E 48 SJ9566
Wincobank Sheff 49 SK3891
Windermere Cumb 60 SD4098
Winderton Warwks 29 SP3240
Windlesham Surrey 22 SU9363
Windmill Cnwll 3 SW8974
Windmill Hill E Susx 13 TQ6412
Windmill Hill Somset 8 ST3116
Windrush Gloucs 29 SP1913
Windsor W & M 22 SU9576
Windsoredge Gloucs 20 SO8400
Windsor Green Suffk 32 TL8954
Windygates Fife 93 NO3400
Wineham W Susx 12 TQ2320
Winestead E R Yk 57 TA2924
Winfarthing Norfk 33 TM1085
Winford IoW 11 SZ5584
Winford N Som 19 ST5464
Winforton Herefs 27 SO2946
Winfrith Newburgh Dorset 9 SY8084
Wing Bucks 30 SP8822
Wing Rutlnd 40 SK8903
Wingate Dur 62 NZ4036
Wingates Bolton 47 SD6507
Wingates Nthumb 69 NZ0995
Wingerworth Derbys 49 SK3867
Wingfield C Beds 30 TL0026
Wingfield Suffk 33 TM2277
Wingfield Wilts 20 ST8256
Wingham Kent 15 TR2457
Wingrave Bucks 30 SP8719
Winkburn Notts 49 SK7058
Winkfield Br For 22 SU9072
Winkfield Row Br For 22 SU8971
Winkhill Staffs 48 SK0651
Winkleigh Devon 6 SS6308
Winksley N York 55 SE2571
Winlaton Gatesd 69 NZ1762
Winmarleigh Lancs 53 SD4647
Winnall Hants 11 SU4829
Winnersh Wokham 22 SU7870
Winnington Ches W 47 SJ6474
Winscombe N Som 19 ST4257
Winsford Ches W 47 SJ6566
Winsford Somset 7 SS9034
Winsham Somset 8 ST3706
Winshill Staffs 39 SK2623
Winshwen Swans 18 SS6896
Winskill Cumb 67 NY5834
Winsley Wilts 20 ST7960
Winslow Bucks 30 SP7727
Winson Gloucs 28 SP0908
Winsor Hants 10 SU3114
Winster Cumb 59 SD4193
Winster Derbys 48 SK2460
Winston Dur 61 NZ1416
Winston Suffk 33 TM1861
Winstone Gloucs 28 SO9509
Winswell Devon 6 SS4913
Winterborne Came Dorset 9 SY7088
Winterborne Clenston Dorset 9 ST8303
Winterborne Houghton Dorset 9 ST8204
Winterborne Kingston Dorset 9 SY8697
Winterborne Monkton Dorset 9 SY6787
Winterborne Stickland Dorset 9 ST8304
Winterborne Whitechurch Dorset 9 ST8300
Winterborne Zelston Dorset 9 SY8997
Winterbourne S Gloucs 19 ST6480
Winterbourne W Berk 21 SU4572
Winterbourne Abbas Dorset 9 SY6190
Winterbourne Bassett Wilts 20 SU0974
Winterbourne Dauntsey Wilts 10 SU1734
Winterbourne Earls Wilts 10 SU1734
Winterbourne Gunner Wilts 10 SU1735
Winterbourne Monkton Wilts 20 SU0971
Winterbourne Steepleton Dorset 9 SY6289
Winterbourne Stoke Wilts 20 SU0741
Winterburn N York 54 SD9358
Winteringham N Linc 56 SE9221
Winterley Ches E 47 SJ7457
Winterslow Wilts 10 SU2332
Winterton N Linc 56 SE9218
Winterton-on-Sea Norfk 43 TG4919
Winthorpe Lincs 51 TF5665
Winthorpe Notts 50 SK8156
Winton BCP 10 SZ0893
Winton Cumb 60 NY7810
Wintringham N York 63 SE8873
Winwick Cambs 40 TL1080
Winwick Nhants 40 SP6273
Winwick Warrtn 47 SJ6092
Wirksworth Derbys 48 SK2854
Wirswall Ches E 37 SJ5444
Wisbech Cambs 41 TF4609
Wisbech St Mary Cambs 41 TF4208
Wisborough Green W Susx 12 TQ0525
Wiseman's Bridge Pembks 16 SN1406
Wiseton Notts 49 SK7189
Wishaw N Lans 75 NS7955
Wishaw Warwks 38 SP1794
Wispington Lincs 51 TF2071
Wissett Suffk 33 TM3679
Wissington Suffk 25 TL9533
Wistanstow Shrops 36 SO4385
Wistanswick Shrops 37 SJ6629
Wistaston Ches E 47 SJ6853
Wistaston Green Ches E 47 SJ6854
Wiston Pembks 16 SN0218
Wiston S Lans 75 NS9532
Wiston W Susx 12 TQ1512
Wistow Cambs 41 TL2781
Wistow Leics 39 SP6495
Wistow N York 56 SE5935
Wiswell Lancs 54 SD7437
Witcham Cambs 41 TL4680
Witchampton Dorset 9 ST9806
Witchford Cambs 41 TL5078
Witcombe Somset 8 ST4721
Witham Essex 24 TL8214

Witham Friary Somset 20 ST7441
Witham on the Hill Lincs 40 TF0516
Witham St Hughs Lincs 50 SK8964
Withcall Lincs 51 TF2883
Withdean Br & H 12 TQ3007
Witherenden Hill E Susx 13 TQ6426
Witheridge Devon 7 SS8014
Witherley Leics 39 SP3297
Withern Lincs 51 TF4282
Withernsea E R Yk 57 TA3427
Withernwick E R Yk 57 TA1940
Withersdale Street Suffk 33 TM2680
Withersfield Suffk 32 TL6547
Witherslack Cumb 59 SD4384
Withiel Cnwll 3 SW9965
Withiel Florey Somset 7 SS9833
Withington Gloucs 28 SP0315
Withington Herefs 27 SO5643
Withington Manch 47 SJ8492
Withington Shrops 37 SJ5713
Withington Staffs 38 SK0335
Withleigh Devon 7 SS9012
Withnell Lancs 54 SD6322
Withybed Green Worcs 38 SP0172
Withybrook Warwks 39 SP4383
Withycombe Somset 7 ST0141
Withyham E Susx 13 TQ4935
Withypool Somset 7 SS8435
Withywood Bristl 19 ST5667
Witley Surrey 12 SU9439
Witnesham Suffk 33 TM1751
Witney Oxon 29 SP3510
Wittering C Pete 40 TF0602
Wittersham Kent 14 TQ9027
Witton Birm 38 SP0790
Witton Norfk 43 TG3109
Witton Norfk 43 TG3331
Witton Gilbert Dur 69 NZ2345
Witton le Wear Dur 61 NZ1431
Witton Park Dur 61 NZ1730
Wiveliscombe Somset 8 ST0827
Wivelrod Hants 11 SU6738
Wivelsfield E Susx 12 TQ3420
Wivelsfield Green E Susx 12 TQ3519
Wivenhoe Essex 25 TM0321
Wiveton Norfk 42 TG0442
Wix Essex 25 TM1628
Wixams Bed 30 TL0544
Wixford Warwks 28 SP0854
Wixoe Suffk 32 TL7143
Woburn C Beds 30 SP9433
Woburn Sands M Keyn 30 SP9235
Woking Surrey 22 TQ0058
Wokingham Wokham 22 SU8168
Wolborough Devon 5 SX8570
Woldingham Surrey 23 TQ3755
Wold Newton E R Yk 63 TA0473
Wold Newton NE Lin 51 TF2496
Wolferton Norfk 42 TF6528
Wolfhampcote Warwks 29 SP5265
Wolf's Castle Pembks 16 SM9526
Wolfsdale Pembks 16 SM9321
Wollaston Dudley 38 SO8884
Wollaston Nhants 30 SP9062
Wollaston Shrops 36 SJ3212
Wollaton C Nott 49 SK5239
Wollerton Shrops 37 SJ6130
Wollescote Dudley 38 SO9283
Wolseley Bridge Staffs 38 SK0220
Wolsingham Dur 61 NZ0737
Wolstanton Staffs 47 SJ8548
Wolston Warwks 39 SP4175
Wolvercote Oxon 29 SP4910
Wolverhampton Wolves 38 SO9198
Wolverhampton Halfpenny Green Airport Staffs 38 SO8291
Wolverley Shrops 37 SJ4731
Wolverley Worcs 38 SO8279
Wolverton Hants 21 SU5558
Wolverton M Keyn 30 SP8141
Wolverton Warwks 29 SP2062
Wolverton Wilts 20 ST7831
Wolvesnewton Mons 19 ST4599
Wolvey Warwks 39 SP4387
Wolvey Heath Warwks 39 SP4388
Wolviston S on T 62 NZ4525
Wombleton N York 62 SE6683
Wombourne Staffs 38 SO8793
Wombwell Barns 55 SE4002
Womenswold Kent 15 TR2250
Womersley N York 56 SE5319
Wonersh Surrey 12 TQ0145
Wonford Devon 5 SX9491
Wonston Dorset 9 ST7408
Wonston Hants 11 SU4739
Wooburn Bucks 22 SU9087
Wooburn Green Bucks 22 SU9188
Woodacott Devon 6 SS3807
Woodall Rothm 49 SK4880
Woodbastwick Norfk 43 TG3315
Wood Bevington Warwks 28 SP0553
Woodborough Notts 49 SK6347
Woodborough Wilts 20 SU1159
Woodbridge Suffk 33 TM2649
Woodbury Salterton Devon 5 SY0087
Woodchester Gloucs 20 SO8302
Woodchurch Kent 14 TQ9434
Woodcombe Somset 18 SS9546
Woodcote Oxon 21 SU6481
Woodcote Wrekin 37 SJ7615
Woodcott Hants 21 SU4354
Woodcroft Gloucs 19 ST5495
Wood Dalling Norfk 43 TG0827
Woodditton Cambs 32 TL6559
Woodeaton Oxon 29 SP5312
Wood End Gt Lon 23 TQ1081
Wood End Herts 31 TL3225
Wood End W Susx 11 SU8108
Woodend Nhants 29 SP6149
Woodend Staffs 38 SK1426
Wood End Warwks 38 SP2498
Wood End Wolves 38 SJ9400
Wood Enderby Lincs 51 TF2764
Woodfalls Wilts 10 SU1920
Woodford Cnwll 6 SS2113
Woodford Gloucs 20 ST6995
Woodford Gt Lon 23 TQ4191
Woodford Nhants 40 SP9676
Woodford Stockp 47 SJ8882
Woodford Bridge Gt Lon 23 TQ4191
Woodford Green Gt Lon 23 TQ4191
Woodford Halse Nhants 29 SP5452
Woodford Wells Gt Lon 23 TQ4093
Wood Green Gt Lon 23 TQ3191
Woodgate Birm 38 SO9982
Woodgate Devon 7 ST1016
Woodgate Norfk 42 TG0015
Woodgate W Susx 12 SU9304
Woodgreen Hants 10 SU1717
Woodhall N York 60 SD9790
Woodhall Spa Lincs 51 TF1963
Woodham Bucks 29 SP7018
Woodham Surrey 22 TQ0462

Woodham Ferrers Essex 24 TQ7999
Woodham Mortimer Essex 24 TL8104
Woodham Walter Essex 24 TL8007
Wood Hayes Wolves 38 SJ9401
Woodhead Abers 95 NJ7838
Woodhill Shrops 37 SO7884
Woodhill Somset 8 ST3527
Woodhorn Nthumb 69 NZ2988
Woodhouse Leeds 55 SE2935
Woodhouse Leics 39 SK5314
Woodhouse Sheff 49 SK4284
Woodhouse Wakefd 55 SE3821
Woodhouse Eaves Leics 39 SK5214
Woodhouses Oldham 48 SD9100
Woodhouses Staffs 38 SK1518
Woodhurst Cambs 31 TL3176
Woodkirk Leeds 55 SE2725
Woodland Devon 5 SX6256
Woodland Devon 5 SX7968
Woodland Dur 61 NZ0726
Woodlands Donc 56 SE5308
Woodlands Dorset 10 SU0509
Woodlands Hants 10 SU3211
Woodlands N York 55 SE3253
Woodlands Somset 18 ST1141
Woodlands Park W & M 22 SU8678
Woodleigh Devon 5 SX7349
Woodley Stockp 48 SJ9392
Woodley Wokham 22 SU7673
Woodmancote Gloucs 20 ST7597
Woodmancote Gloucs 28 SO9727
Woodmancote Gloucs 28 SP0008
Woodmancote W Susx 11 SU7707
Woodmancote W Susx 12 TQ2314
Woodmancott Hants 21 SU5642
Woodmansey E R Yk 57 TA0538
Woodmansgreen W Susx 11 SU8627
Woodmansterne Surrey 23 TQ2759
Woodmanton Devon 9 SY0186
Woodnesborough Kent 15 TR3157
Woodnewton Nhants 40 TL0394
Wood Norton Norfk 42 TG0127
Woodplumpton Lancs 53 SD4934
Woodrising Norfk 42 TF9803
Wood's Corner E Susx 14 TQ6619
Woodseaves Staffs 37 SJ7925
Woodsetts Rothm 49 SK5483
Woodsford Dorset 9 SY7590
Wood's Green E Susx 13 TQ6333
Woodside Br For 22 SU9371
Woodside Fife 83 NO4207
Woodside Hants 10 SZ3196
Wood Street Norfk 43 TG3722
Wood Street Village Surrey 22 SU9550
Woodstock Oxon 29 SP4416
Woodston C Pete 40 TL1897
Wood Walton Cambs 41 TL2180
Woofferton Shrops 27 SO5268
Wookey Somset 19 ST5145
Wookey Hole Somset 19 ST5347
Wool Dorset 9 SY8486
Woolacombe Devon 6 SS4543
Woolage Green Kent 15 TR2349
Woolaston Gloucs 19 ST5899
Woolaston Common Gloucs 19 ST5801
Woolavington Somset 19 ST3441
Woolbeding W Susx 11 SU8722
Woolbrook Devon 8 SY1289
Wooler Nthumb 77 NT9927
Woolfardisworthy Devon 7 SS8208
Woolfardisworthy Devon 6 SS3321
Woolfords S Lans 75 NT0256
Woolhampton W Berk 21 SU5766
Woolhope Herefs 27 SO6135
Woolland Dorset 9 ST7707
Woolley BaNES 20 ST7468
Woolley Cambs 31 TL1574
Woolley Wakefd 55 SE3212
Woolley Edge Services Wakefd 55 SE3014
Woolmere Green Worcs 28 SO9663
Woolmer Green Herts 31 TL2518
Woolminstone Somset 8 ST4108
Woolpit Suffk 32 TL9762
Woolstaston Shrops 36 SO4598
Woolsthorpe by Belvoir Lincs 40 SK8333
Woolsthorpe-by-Colsterworth Lincs 40 SK9224
Woolston C Sotn 10 SU4310
Woolston Shrops 36 SJ3224
Woolston Shrops 36 SO4287
Woolston Somset 18 ST0939
Woolston Somset 20 ST6527
Woolston Warrtn 47 SJ6489
Woolstone Gloucs 28 SO9630
Woolstone M Keyn 30 SP8738
Woolstone Oxon 20 SU2987
Woolton Lpool 46 SJ4286
Woolton Hill Hants 21 SU4261
Woolverstone Suffk 25 TM1738
Woolverton Somset 20 ST7953
Woolwich Gt Lon 23 TQ4478
Woonton Herefs 27 SO3552
Woore Shrops 37 SJ7342
Wootten Green Suffk 33 TM2372
Wootton Bed 30 TL0044
Wootton Kent 15 TR2246
Wootton N Linc 57 TA0815
Wootton Nhants 30 SP7656
Wootton Oxon 29 SP4319
Wootton Oxon 29 SP4701
Wootton Shrops 36 SO3278
Wootton Staffs 38 SK1044
Wootton Bassett Wilts 20 SU0682
Wootton Bridge IoW 11 SZ5492
Wootton Courtenay Somset 7 SS9343
Wootton Fitzpaine Dorset 8 SY3695
Wootton Rivers Wilts 21 SU1962
Wootton St Lawrence Hants 21 SU5953
Wootton Wawen Warwks 28 SP1563
Worcester Worcs 28 SO8554
Worcester Park Gt Lon 23 TQ2265
Wordsley Dudley 38 SO8987
Worfield Shrops 38 SO7595
Worgret Dorset 9 SY9086
Workington Cumb 58 NY0028
Worksop Notts 49 SK5879
Worlaby Lincs 51 TA0113
Worlaby N Linc 56 TA0113

Wormelow Tump Herefs 27 SO4930
Wormhill Derbys 48 SK1274
Worminghall Bucks 29 SP6408
Wormingford Essex 25 TL9332
Wormington Gloucs 28 SP0336
Wormit Fife 83 NO4026
Wormleighton Warwks 29 SP4553
Wormley Herts 31 TL3605
Wormley Surrey 12 SU9438
Wormshill Kent 14 TQ8857
Wormsley Herefs 27 SO4247
Worplesdon Surrey 22 SU9753
Worrall Sheff 49 SK3092
Worsbrough Barns 49 SE3502
Worsbrough Bridge Barns 55 SE3503
Worsbrough Dale Barns 55 SE3604
Worsley Salfd 47 SD7500
Worstead Norfk 43 TG3026
Worsthorne Lancs 54 SD8732
Worston Devon 5 SX5953
Worston Lancs 54 SD7742
Worth Kent 15 TR3355
Wortham Suffk 32 TM0877
Worthen Shrops 36 SJ3204
Worthenbury Wrexhm 46 SJ4146
Worthing Norfk 42 TF9919
Worthing W Susx 12 TQ1403
Worthington Leics 39 SK4020
Worth Matravers Dorset 9 SY9777
Wortley Barns 49 SK3099
Wortley Leeds 55 SE2732
Worton N York 61 SD9589
Worton Wilts 20 ST9757
Wortwell Norfk 33 TM2784
Wotton-under-Edge Gloucs 20 ST7593
Wotton Underwood Bucks 30 SP6815
Woughton on the Green M Keyn 30 SP8737
Wouldham Kent 14 TQ7164
Wrabness Essex 25 TM1731
Wrafton Devon 6 SS4935
Wragby Lincs 50 TF1378
Wragby Wakefd 55 SE4116
Wrangaton Devon 5 SX6758
Wrangle Lincs 51 TF4250
Wrangway Somset 8 ST1218
Wrantage Somset 8 ST3022
Wrawby N Linc 56 TA0108
Wraxall N Som 19 ST4971
Wraxall Somset 20 ST6036
Wray Lancs 54 SD6067
Wraysbury W & M 22 TQ0074
Wrayton Lancs 60 SD6172
Wrea Green Lancs 53 SD3931
Wreay Cumb 67 NY4348
Wrecclesham Surrey 22 SU8244
Wrekenton Gatesd 69 NZ2759
Wrelton N York 62 SE7686
Wrenbury Ches E 47 SJ5947
Wreningham Norfk 43 TM1698
Wrentham Suffk 33 TM4982
Wrentnall Shrops 36 SJ4203
Wressle E R Yk 56 SE7131
Wressle N Linc 56 SE9709
Wrestlingworth C Beds 31 TL2547
Wretton Norfk 42 TF6900
Wrexham Wrexhm 46 SJ3350
Wrexham Industrial Estate Wrexhm 46 SJ3850
Wribbenhall Worcs 37 SO7975
Wrinehill Staffs 37 SJ7547
Wrington N Som 19 ST4762
Writhlington BaNES 20 ST7054
Writtle Essex 24 TL6706
Wrockwardine Wrekin 37 SJ6212
Wroot N Linc 56 SE7103
Wrose C Brad 55 SE1636
Wrotham Kent 14 TQ6158
Wrotham Heath Kent 14 TQ6359
Wroughton Swindn 20 SU1480
Wroxall IoW 11 SZ5579
Wroxall Warwks 39 SP2271
Wroxeter Shrops 37 SJ5608
Wroxham Norfk 43 TG3017
Wroxton Oxon 29 SP4141
Wyaston Derbys 48 SK1842
Wyberton Lincs 51 TF3240
Wyboston Bed 31 TL1656
Wybunbury Ches E 47 SJ6949
Wychbold Worcs 28 SO9265
Wychnor Staffs 38 SK1715
Wyck Rissington Gloucs 29 SP1821
Wycliffe Dur 61 NZ1114
Wycoller Lancs 54 SD9339
Wycomb Leics 40 SK7724
Wycombe Marsh Bucks 22 SU8892
Wyddial Herts 31 TL3731
Wye Kent 15 TR0546
Wyke C Brad 55 SE1526
Wyke Dorset 20 ST7926
Wyke Champflower Somset 20 ST6634
Wykeham N York 63 SE9683
Wyken Covtry 39 SP3780
Wyken Shrops 37 SO7695
Wyke Regis Dorset 9 SY6677
Wykey Shrops 36 SJ3824
Wylam Nthumb 69 NZ1164
Wylde Green Birm 38 SP1294
Wylye Wilts 10 SU0037
Wymeswold Leics 36 SK6023
Wymington Bed 30 SP9564
Wymondham Leics 40 SK8518
Wymondham Norfk 43 TG1101
Wynford Eagle Dorset 9 SY5896
Wyre Piddle Worcs 28 SO9647
Wysall Notts 39 SK6027
Wythall Worcs 38 SP0875
Wytham Oxon 29 SP4708
Wythenshawe Manch 47 SJ8386
Wyton Cambs 31 TL2772
Wyton E R Yk 57 TA1733
Wyverstone Suffk 32 TM0367
Wyverstone Street Suffk 32 TM0367

Yarm S on T 62 NZ4112
Yarmouth IoW 10 SZ3589
Yarnbrook Wilts 20 ST8654
Yarnfield Staffs 38 SJ8632
Yarnscombe Devon 6 SS5623
Yarnton Oxon 29 SP4711
Yarpole Herefs 27 SO4764
Yarrowford Border 76 NT4030
Yarwell Nhants 40 TL0697
Yate S Glos 20 ST7081
Yateley Hants 22 SU8161
Yatesbury Wilts 20 SU0671
Yattendon W Berk 21 SU5574
Yatton Herefs 27 SO4366
Yatton N Som 19 ST4365
Yatton Keynell Wilts 20 ST8676
Yaverland IoW 11 SZ6185
Yaxham Norfk 42 TG0010
Yaxley Cambs 40 TL1891
Yaxley Suffk 33 TM1274
Yazor Herefs 27 SO4046
Yeading Gt Lon 22 TQ1182
Yeadon Leeds 55 SE2041
Yealand Conyers Lancs 59 SD5074
Yealand Redmayne Lancs 59 SD5057
Yealmpton Devon 5 SX5851
Yearsley N York 56 SE5974
Yeaton Shrops 36 SJ4319
Yeaveley Derbys 48 SK1840
Yeavering Nthumb 77 NT9330
Yedingham N York 63 SE8979
Yelford Oxon 29 SP3604
Yelling Cambs 31 TL2562
Yelvertoft Nhants 39 SP5975
Yelverton Devon 5 SX5267
Yelverton Norfk 43 TG2902
Yenston Somset 9 ST7121
Yeoford Devon 7 SX7898
Yeolmbridge Cnwll 4 SX3187
Yeovil Somset 9 ST5515
Yeovil Marsh Somset 9 ST5418
Yeovilton Somset 8 ST5423
Yesnaby Ork 100 HY2215
Yetminster Dorset 9 ST5910
Yettington Devon 8 SY0585
Yetts o'Muckhart Clacks 82 NO0001
Yew Tree Sandw 38 SO0295
Y Felinheli Gwynd 44 SH5265
Y Ferwig Cerdgn 17 SN1849
Y Ffôr Gwynd 44 SH3939
Yielden Bed 30 TL0167
Yiewsley Gt Lon 22 TQ0680
Ynysddu Caerph 19 ST1792
Ynyshir Rhondd 18 ST0292
Ynystawe Swans 18 SN6800
Ynysybwl Rhondd 18 ST0594
Yockleton Shrops 36 SJ3910
Yokefleet E R Yk 56 SE8124
York C York 56 SE6051
Yorkletts Kent 15 TR0963
Yorkley Gloucs 27 SO6307
York Town Surrey 22 SU8660
Youlgreave Derbys 48 SK2164
Youlthorpe E R Yk 56 SE7655
Youlton N York 55 SE4963
Yoxall Staffs 38 SK1418
Yoxford Suffk 33 TM3968
Y Rhiw Gwynd 44 SH2228
Ysbyty Ifan Conwy 45 SH8448
Ysbyty Ystwyth Cerdgn 35 SN7371
Ysceifiog Flints 46 SJ1571
Ystalyfera Neath 26 SN7608
Ystrad Rhondd 18 SS9895
Ystrad Aeron Cerdgn 34 SN5256
Ystradfellte Powys 26 SN9313
Ystradgynlais Powys 26 SN7810
Ystrad Meurig Cerdgn 35 SN7067
Ystrad Mynach Caerph 19 ST1494
Ystradowen V Glam 18 ST0177
Ythanwells Abers 94 NJ6338

Z

Zeal Monachorum Devon 7 SS7204
Zeals Wilts 9 ST7831
Zelah Cnwll 2 SW8151
Zennor Cnwll 2 SW4538
Zouch Notts 39 SK5023